HEALING SPACES, MODERN ARCHITECTURE, AND THE BODY

Healing Spaces, Modern Architecture, and the Body brings together cutting-edge scholarship examining the myriad ways that architects, urban planners, medical practitioners, and everyday people have applied modern ideas about health and the body to the spaces in which they live, work, and heal. The book's contributors explore North American and European understandings of the relationship between physical movement, bodily health, technological innovation, medical concepts, natural environments, and architectural settings from the nineteenth century through the heyday of modernist architectural experimentation in the 1920s and 1930s and onward into the 1970s. Not only does the book focus on how professionals have engaged with the architecture of healing and the body, it also explores how urban dwellers have strategized and modified their living environments themselves to create a kind of vernacular modernist architecture of health in their homes, gardens, and backyards. This new work builds upon a growing interdisciplinary field incorporating the urban humanities, geography, architectural history, the history of medicine, and critical visual studies that reflects our current preoccupation with the body and its corresponding therapeutic culture.

Sarah Schrank is Professor of History at California State University, Long Beach where she teaches graduate and undergraduate courses in United States women's history, urban history, body theory, popular environmentalism, and critical visual studies. She received her PhD in United States history from the University of California, San Diego and has held research fellowships from the Haynes Foundation, The Huntington Library, the Shelby Cullom Davis Center at Princeton University, and The Wolfsonian-Florida International University. She is the author of *Art and the City: Civic Imagination and Cultural Authority in Los Angeles* (University of Pennsylvania Press, 2009) as well as numerous essays and articles on public art, urbanism, vernacular architecture, and American body culture. She is currently completing two new books: *Naked: Natural Living and the American Cult of the Body* for the University of Pennsylvania Press's *Nature and Culture* series, and *Urban History Goes to the Movies: The City in the American Popular Imagination* for Routledge.

Didem Ekici is Assistant Professor in the Department of Architecture and Built Environment at the University of Nottingham. She is the author of several articles and chapters that explore the relationship between modern architecture, health, body culture, and asceticism as well as the city and memory. Her current research focuses on the transformation of architecture regarding concepts of the body in the German-speaking world of the nineteenth and early twentieth centuries. It is supported by grants from the Wellcome Trust in Medical History and Humanities and the German Academic Exchange.

Ashgate Studies in Architecture Series

SERIES EDITOR: EAMONN CANNIFFE, MANCHESTER SCHOOL OF ARCHITECTURE,
MANCHESTER METROPOLITAN UNIVERSITY, UK

The discipline of Architecture is undergoing subtle transformation as design awareness permeates our visually dominated culture. Technological change, the search for sustainability and debates around the value of place and meaning of the architectural gesture are aspects which will affect the cities we inhabit. This series seeks to address such topics, both theoretically and in practice, through the publication of high quality original research, written and visual.

Other titles in this series

The City Crown by Bruno Taut
Edited by Matthew Mindrup and Ulrike Altenmuller-Lewis
ISBN 978 1 4724 2199 9

In-Between: Architectural Drawing and Imaginative Knowledge in Islamic and Western Traditions
Hooman Koliji
ISBN 978 1 4724 3868 3

Architectural Projects of Marco Frascari: The Pleasure of a Demonstration
Sam Ridgway
ISBN 978 1 4724 4174 4

Phenomenologies of the City Studies in the History and Philosophy of Architecture
Edited by Henriette Steiner and Maximilian Sternberg
ISBN 978 1 4094 5479 3

From Formalism to Weak Form: The Architecture and Philosophy of Peter Eisenman
Stefano Corbo
ISBN 978 1 4724 4314 4

Forthcoming titles in this series

The Practice Turn in Architecture: Brussels after 1968
Isabelle Doucet
ISBN 978 1 4724 3735 8

Global Perspectives on Critical Architecture Praxis Reloaded
Edited by Gevork Hartoonian
ISBN 978 1 4724 3813 3

Healing Spaces, Modern Architecture, and the Body

Edited by

Sarah Schrank and Didem Ekici

LONDON AND NEW YORK

First published 2017
by Routledge
2 Park Square, Milton Park, Abingdon, Oxon OX14 4RN

and by Routledge
711 Third Avenue, New York, NY 10017

First issued in paperback 2018

Routledge is an imprint of the Taylor & Francis Group, an informa business

British Library Cataloguing in Publication Data
A catalogue record for this book is available from the British Library

Library of Congress Cataloging in Publication Data
Names: Schrank, Sarah, author. | Ekici, Didem, author.
Title: Healing spaces, modern architecture, and the body / Sarah Schrank and Didem Ekici.
Description: New York : Routledge, 2016. | Series: Ashgate studies in architecture series | Includes bibliographical references and index.
Identifiers: LCCN 2016003281| ISBN 9781472470836 (hb : alk. paper)
Subjects: LCSH: Architecture—Health aspects. | Architecture, Modern—Themes, motives.
Classification: LCC RA566.6 .S37 2016 | DDC 725/.51--dc23LC record available at https://lccn.loc.gov/2016003281

ISBN 13: 978-1-138-58869-1 (pbk)
ISBN 13: 978-1-4724-7083-6 (hbk)

Typeset in Myriad Pro
by Swales & Willis Ltd, Exeter, Devon, UK

Contents

Figures

Contributors

Annmarie Adams is William C. Macdonald Professor and former Director at the School of Architecture, McGill University, Montreal. She is the author of *Architecture in the Family Way: Doctors, Houses, and Women, 1870–1900* (McGill-Queens University Press, 1996), *Medicine by Design: The Architect and the Modern Hospital, 1893–1943* (University of Minnesota Press, 2008), and co-author of *Designing Women: Gender and the Architectural Profession* (University of Toronto Press, 2000). Her research has garnered numerous awards, including the Jason Hannah Medal from the Royal Society of Canada, a CIHR Health Career Award, a YWCA Woman of Distinction prize, and Fellowship in the Royal Architectural Institute of Canada.

Didem Ekici is Assistant Professor in the Department of Architecture and Built Environment at the University of Nottingham. She holds a PhD in Architectural History and Theory from the University of Michigan, Ann Arbor. She is the author of several articles and chapters that explore the relationship between modern architecture, health, body culture, and asceticism as well as the city and memory. Her current research focuses on the transformation of architecture regarding concepts of the body in the German-speaking world of the nineteenth and early twentieth centuries. She has held research grants from the Wellcome Trust in Medical History and Humanities, the German Academic Exchange, The Wolfsonian-Florida International University, and the University of Michigan Institute for the Humanities.

Stephanie Pilat is a designer and architectural historian whose work and practice examines points of intersection between aesthetics, politics, and architecture. She holds a professional degree in Architecture from the University of Cincinnati and a Master's and PhD from the University of Michigan. She is Assistant Professor at the University of Oklahoma. She is the author of *Reconstructing Italy: The Ina-Casa Neighborhoods of the Postwar Era* (Ashgate, 2014). Her research has been supported by a Fulbright Fellowship, a Rome Prize from the American Academy, a Wolfsonian-FIU Fellowship and the American Association of University Women.

Sabrina Gabrielle Richard is trained as an architect and currently pursuing a doctoral degree at the University of California, Berkeley. She is the recipient of the Spiro

Kostof Fellowship in Architectural History, as well as a Power Corporation of Canada Award from the Canadian Centre for Architecture in Montreal. Her research focuses on the transformative events of the 1960s and their influence on urban design, visual culture, and architectural history. Sabrina is a founding partner in the cultural consultancy Bespoke, based in Toronto.

John Stanislav Sadar is Adjunct Senior Research Fellow in Architecture at Monash University in Melbourne, Australia, and a partner of Little Wonder design studio. Having studied architecture at McGill University, Aalto University, and the University of Pennsylvania, he is interested in the way our technological artifacts mediate the relationship between our bodies and the environment. His book, *Through the Healing Glass: Shaping the Modern Body through Glass Architecture, 1925–35*, was published by Routledge in 2016.

Sarah Schrank is Professor of History at California State University, Long Beach where she teaches graduate and undergraduate courses in United States women's history, urban history, body theory, popular environmentalism, and critical visual studies. She received her PhD in United States History from the University of California, San Diego and has held research fellowships from the Haynes Foundation, The Huntington Library, the Shelby Cullom Davis Center at Princeton University, and The Wolfsonian-Florida International University. She is the author of *Art and the City: Civic Imagination and Cultural Authority in Los Angeles* (University of Pennsylvania Press, 2009) as well as numerous essays and articles on public art, urbanism, vernacular architecture, and American body culture. She is currently completing two new books, *Naked: Natural Living and the American Cult of the Body* for the University of Pennsylvania Press's *Nature and Culture* series and *Urban History Goes to the Movies: The City in the American Popular Imagination* for Routledge.

Camille Shamble is a doctoral candidate in the History of Art and Architecture at the University of Virginia and a licensed architect who has worked on projects in health care and education sectors. Her work focuses on twentieth-century American architecture and landscape, with a specific interest in education environments, constructions of childhood and child wellness, and their intersections with racial, gender, and class inequality. Support for her work has come from Dumbarton Oaks Research Library and Collection, The Huntington Library, and the Institute of Humanities and Global Cultures at the University of Virginia. She holds a Master of Architecture degree from the University of Oregon.

Thomas Strickland is Assistant Professor in the School of Architecture at Laurentian University. His PhD in Architectural History at McGill University was funded by Max Binz and J.W. McConnell Fellowships. He was a fellow at the Canadian Centre for Architecture in 2009, and is an alumnus of the Health Care, Technology and Place, CIHR Strategic Research Initiative, University of Toronto. His current research focuses on health and the built environment, subaltern place-making, and the post-industrial city. He is interested in the capacity for the built environment to be sustenance for human rights and a resource, spatial and otherwise, for social and cultural innovation.

David Theodore holds a PhD in the History of Architecture, Medicine, and Science from Harvard University and is currently Assistant Professor in the School of Architecture, McGill University. His recent scholarship focuses on early uses of computers in design and medicine. His research has received support from SSHRC, CIHR, The Graham Foundation, and the Pierre Elliott Trudeau Foundation. He has co-published on the history of healthcare architecture in the journals *Social Science and Medicine*, *Technology and Culture*, and the *Canadian Bulletin of Medical History*. An active design journalist and critic, he is a regional correspondent for *Canadian Architect*, a contributing editor at *Azure*, and a contributor to *The Phaidon Atlas of Twenty-First-Century World Architecture*.

Jennifer L. Thomas is a PhD candidate (history/theory track) in the Department of Landscape Architecture at the University of Illinois at Urbana-Champaign. She was a 2013–14 graduate fellow at the Illinois Program for Research in the Humanities and has a Bachelor of Arts in Art History from the University of Oregon and a Master of Landscape Architecture with a certificate in Historic Preservation from the University of Colorado Denver. Her dissertation—"Madness, Landscape, and State: The Nineteenth-Century Insane Asylum System of New York State"—focuses on nineteenth-century insane asylum landscapes of New York State as spatial, verbal and visual expressions of social ideologies and an apparatus reflecting an emergent state-wide mental illness/health treatment system.

Leslie Topp is Senior Lecturer in History of Architecture in the Department of History of Art at Birkbeck, University of London. She is the author of *Architecture and Truth in Fin-de-Siècle Vienna* (Cambridge University Press, 2004), co-editor of *Madness, Architecture and the Built Environment* (Routledge, 2007), and co-curator of the exhibition "Madness and Modernity" (Wellcome Collection, London, and Wien Museum, Vienna, 2009–10.) Her book *Freedom and the Cage: Modern Architecture and Psychiatry in Central Europe, 1890–1914* will be published by Penn State University Press in the *Buildings, Landscapes and Societies* series in 2017.

Robin Veder is Associate Professor of Humanities and Art History/Visual Culture at Penn State University, Harrisburg. Her book *The Living Line: Modern Art and the Economy of Energy* was published in the Dartmouth College Press/University Press of New England's visual culture series in 2015, and her articles have appeared in *Journal of the Society of Architectural Historians*, *Modernism/Modernity*, *Journal of Victorian Culture*, *International Journal of the History of Sport*, and *American Art*.

Introduction

Sarah Schrank and Didem Ekici

Health was one of modernism's central motifs, from the improvement of the built environment and the formulation of aesthetic theory, to the institution of social reform. The origins of modernism's health consciousness can be found in the nineteenth-century public health movement, which brought cities under scrutiny as pollution and squalid urban industrial living conditions caused mass epidemics of contagious disease. Modernist architecture in the early twentieth century thus focused on medical and structural efforts to banish the crowded, disease-ridden quarters of the nineteenth century and usher in an era of sanitary transparency that kept surfaces clean and spaces open to sun, air, and light. Although the concern for the impact of the built environment on health goes back to classical antiquity, no previous architectural movement was as preoccupied with health.[1] The modernist ideal was health-giving nature but, if urban life was the lived reality for most people, then it was to be clinical, orderly, and scrubbed free of disease.

At the center of each sanitarium, private residence, or urban park, however, remained the human body, which carried the promise of physical vitality and longevity and yet remained vulnerable to the elements, whether organic and climatic, or those produced by social inequality and the horrors of modern urban industrial life. As architectural historian Beatriz Colomina puts it, beautifully,

> *Modernity is driven by illness. The engine of modern architecture is not a heroic, shiny functional machine marching across the globe but a languid fragile body suspended outside daily life in a cocoon of new technologies and geometries. It is the difficulty of each breath and therefore the treasure of each breath. The melancholy of modernity.*[2]

The body as the locus of both rejuvenation and anxiety also acted as a metaphor for the body politic. In order to strengthen humanity for an unknowable future, modernism called for corporeal as well as social and national regeneration. Modern architecture responded with plans for not only improved living and working spaces, but a wholesome social body.

How the built environment in North America and Europe reflected and contributed to this idea of the body as both harbinger of a healthful, even utopian, modernity and as a vector of disease and social degeneration is the theme of our volume, *Healing Spaces, Modern Architecture, and the Body*. Here, we bring together current, innovative scholarship examining myriad ways that architects, urban planners, medical practitioners, and everyday people applied modern ideas about health and the body to the spaces in which they lived, worked, and healed. We are interested in how professionals have engaged with the architecture of healing and the body but also how urban dwellers have strategized and modified their living environments themselves to create a kind of vernacular modernist architecture of health in their homes, gardens, and backyards. The contributions compiled here explore modern understandings of the relationship between physical movement, bodily health, technological innovation, medical concepts, natural environments, and architectural settings from the nineteenth century through the heyday of modernist architectural experimentation in the 1920s and 1930s and onward into the 1970s. This new work builds upon a growing interdisciplinary field incorporating the urban humanities, geography, architectural history, the history of medicine, and critical visual studies that reflects our current preoccupation with the body and its corresponding therapeutic culture.

The last few decades have witnessed an enormous rise of popular interest in matters of health. Newspapers, magazines, television, and internet are replete with features on healthy living and the body beautiful promoting how to eat well, keep fit, and stay young. Within our globalized consumer culture, the weight loss, fitness, cosmetic, and pharmaceutical industries promise improved health and longevity by reducing anxiety-producing bodily imperfections. As today's understanding of "health" moves well beyond narrow concepts of the medical treatment of illness to a political economy of "wellness," which, in turn, is harnessed to the entitlements of wealth, social status, and racial privilege, it has become increasingly pressing to study how this shift has played out historically. Understanding how health itself is an arbitrary construction has profound, global implications for public policy, healthcare access, and the stemming of a consumer-based "healthy lifestyle" that promises to further segregate the wealthy and healthy from the poor and sick while scrutinizing, judging, and punishing those whose bodies fail to meet the criteria of social acceptability. The economic inequalities, cultural presumptions, and social hierarchies that are reinforced and reproduced in the name of health are driving critical concern about the political implications of defining corporeal imperfections and shaping new interest in medicine and architecture from a historical perspective.

Recent exhibitions and academic publications in the humanities have explored the multifaceted relationship between the built environment and the body in the modern era. *Harvard Design Magazine*'s special issue, *Well, Well, Well* (Spring–Summer 2015), brings together a range of panaceas, from the ancients to the present, suggesting that the tension between "clean" medicine and the messiness of the human body can be found built into the very infrastructure of Western health paradigms.[3] Barbara Lamprecht's new work on Richard Neutra's furniture design focuses on the architect's concern for how the body, both physically and emotionally, navigated modern living space.[4] In *Light, Air and Openness: Modern Architecture between the Wars* (2007), Paul Overy traces modern architecture's preoccupation with health and hygiene in the 1920s and 1930s while the Canadian Centre for Architecture's 2011–12 exhibition and accompanying essay collection, *Imperfect Health: The Medicalization of Architecture*, makes a strong case for the paradox of new emphases on urban "public architectures of health" to improve the greater good through medical science while we increasingly fear the harmful effects of technology and industrial production on the body. We want natural health and freedom from contamination and disease and yet we expect the modern built environment to deliver it. As the curators, Giovanna Borasi and Mirko Zardini, write:

> *[The] ambition for total well-being is fragmented and parceled out in a series of policies and disconnected actions. The means to overcome old and new illnesses, the production of a new, healthier body to withstand (inevitable) deterioration is today achieved through voluntary biomedical technology and individual efforts ("staying in shape"), supported by new environmental urban planning policies.*[5]

Davina Cooper's *Everyday Utopias: The Conceptual Life of Promising Spaces* (2014); Esther M. Sternberg's *Healing Spaces: The Science of Place and Well-Being* (2009); and Clare Cooper Marcus's *Therapeutic Landscapes: An Evidence-Based Approach to Designing Healing Gardens and Restorative Outdoor Spaces* (2013) approach the topic of space, healing, and the body differently but together apply scholarly and working methodologies to the question of how to build health into the modern environments in which we live.

Healing Spaces, Modern Architecture, and the Body is divided into three parts. The first, "Interior Spaces and Everyday Therapeutic Architecture," emphasizes private spaces, examining how architects, scientists, doctors, and suburbanites used new technologies and innovative concepts of personal space to create indoor environments of health and healing; "Healing Landscapes and the Body Out-of-Doors" focuses on the body's physical placement in exterior spaces as a vessel for play and movement but also as literal exercises in control and surveillance; and "Public Health and Modern Medical Institutions," which challenges common and academic assumptions about the role of hospitals in the modern healing process while analyzing the role of architecture in medical education. This last group of chapters examines the aesthetics, geography, and politics of the modern hospital, focusing attention on the unintended consequences of public medical policy, administrative emphases on speed and efficiency in treating patients, and constantly shifting meanings of bodily health.

NOTES

1 See, for example, Roman architect Vitruvius's *Ten Books on Architecture*, which offered advice on how to make buildings and cities healthy by taking into account climate, location, orientation, etc. Vitruvius, *The Ten Books on Architecture* (New York: Dover, 1960).

2 Beatriz Colomina, "X-Ray Architecture: The Tuberculosis Effect," *Harvard Design Magazine* 40, *Well, Well, Well* (Spring–Summer 2015): 73.

3 Jennifer Sigler, "Checkup," *Harvard Design Magazine* 40, *Well, Well, Well* (Spring–Summer 2015): 3.

4 Barbara Lamprecht, *Richard Neutra, Furniture: The Body and the Senses* (New York: Wasmuth, 2015).

5 Giovanna Borasi and Mirko Zardini, *Imperfect Health: The Medicalization of Architecture* (Montreal: Canadian Centre for Architecture and Lars Müller Publishers, 2012), 15.

PART 1

Interior Spaces and Everyday Therapeutic Architecture

1

Naked Houses: The Architecture of Nudism and the Rethinking of the American Suburbs

Sarah Schrank

In 1960, the flagship journal of the American naturist movement, *Sunshine and Health*, published a series of articles outlining the architectural challenges of designing houses for nudists.[1] For the previous twenty years, featured architect Kenn Trumble had built a career designing modest suburban homes that accommodated "the recent trend toward outdoor living."[2] Traditional clients generally requested that some sort of patio, lanai, or other backyard living space be added to their home with the expressed concern that it still resemble other houses in their subdivision. The desire of the suburban dweller for both outdoor living *and* a nudist practice, however, created additional architectural problems. Common zoning restrictions against high fences made it impossible to add an open yet private patio to the outside of standard suburban homes and the glass doors that made the outside visible to the inside exposed naked residents to their neighbors' gaze, potentially an unpleasant source of personal humiliation or legal action.

When an unsatisfied client sold his Trumble-designed home, the architect learned that suntanning was a crucial element of the nudist lifestyle and that for this particular demographic, the benefit of suburban living meant the ability to lie naked in the sun as much as it meant a seamless flow of movement from indoors out. This inspired him to incorporate small, fully enclosed screened patios into the homes' basic design:

> *By keeping the privacy problem of the nudist in mind I . . . incorporated the outdoor living aspects of a home right into the basic concept of the house rather than trying to attach a chunk of outdoor living to the rear wall of a conventional house.*[3]

The drawings for Trumble's standard 1950s one-story ranch house show enclosed patio rooms with open roofs above to allow for private nude sunbathing. Because there were no extensions attached to the house, from the outside at least, the nudist home looked like any other postwar suburban dwelling (Figure 1.1).

1.1 Kenn Trumble's designs for the "Sun-Fan House," "Alternates #1 and #2." Source: *Sunshine and Health* 29, no. 4 (April 1960). The Wolfsonian-Florida International University, Miami Beach, Florida, Gift of Robert J. Young, XC2000.81.33.159. Photo: Silvia Ros.

Privacy from nosey neighbors and accessible sun exposure were not the only problems, however, that a savvy architect would need to address in order to satisfy the mid-range suburban nudist customer. It was also important to allow visitors entry to the home without forcing everyone inside to frantically pull on their clothes every time the doorbell rang. To this end, Trumble designed a floor plan that included a reception room off the main entry and a conveniently placed planter-and-screen combination that blocked views of the rest of the house without obviously hiding the other rooms. As with the patio additions, clients worried that their house not look too radically different from others on the block and that their nudism remain unknown to the neighborhood. Even if this was the era of backyard bomb shelters, no one wanted their home to look like a bunker. Trumble addressed this aesthetic concern by setting a large picture window into the front street-facing wall, thus emulating an archetypical 1950s suburban architectural feature while still camouflaging the house's nudist function[4] (Figure 1.2).

The fact that suburban nudists converted typical, mass-produced ranch houses into postwar homes for naked living represents an unusual, if logical, cumulative response to the historical relationship of the American body to the city and the desire to transfer the experience of natural living to urban environments. At the turn of the twentieth century, middle-class Americans became increasingly concerned about their bodies, both their appearance and their performance. Purposive exercise, body-building, dieting, and cosmetic use became both therapeutic and consumer habits of a social class in search of self-identity and status in the midst of modern industrial urbanization and as part of an economy of leisure. As Jackson Lears, John Kasson, and others have argued, concern with personal physical appearance was intertwined with the anonymity, physical mobility, increased visuality, and consumer practices that characterized daily life in cities.[5] How one looked and how one was perceived from the outside became critical factors in the successful navigation of urban capitalism. The bicycle, the electric exercise machine, and body-building itself were in large part about maintaining healthful bodies in the city. A well-formed body became a highly desired quality in a modern urban culture that increasingly fetishized fitness while the industrial economy increasingly relied less upon human strength. As Carolyn Thomas de la Peña points out in *The Body Electric*, the machine, and the electricity that powered it, was incorporated into urban health and exercise practices as part of the modern industrial era's concerns about male impotence and effeminacy in the face of the corporate restructuring of labor into white-collar classes and grey flannel suits.[6]

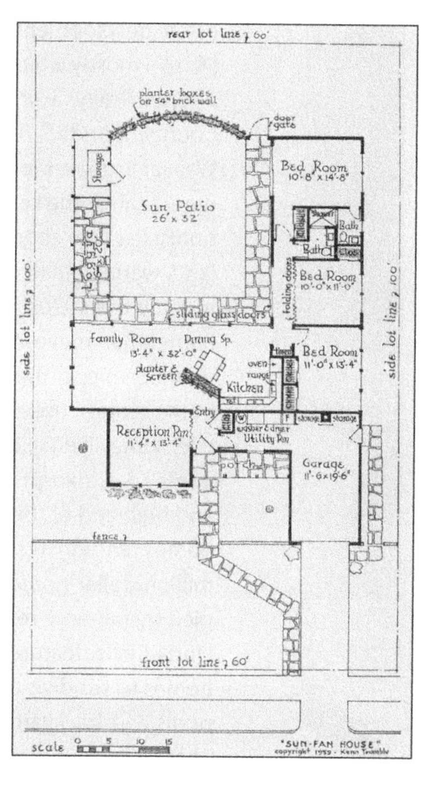

1.2 "The basic floor plan for the Sun-Fan House." Source: *Sunshine and Health* 29, no. 4 (April 1960). The Wolfsonian-Florida International University, Miami Beach, Florida, Gift of Robert J. Young, XC2000.81.33.159. Photo: Silvia Ros.

At the same time, middle-class Americans considered physical culture practiced *outside* the city as a sought-after ideal that included visits to health sanitaria, "tenting" (camping), and out-of-doors adventures permitting exposure to the sun and fresh air.[7] Once rejuvenated, modern Americans, and especially men, could return to their city life taking some of their "natural" experience back with them. Early twentieth-century celebrities such as Pierre Bernard, the "Mighty Oom," who popularized the physical practice of yoga in the United States, and body-builder Bernarr Macfadden, publisher of *Physical Culture* magazine, sold urban dwellers weekend retreats for physical and spiritual nourishment as part of a general regimen of rigorous dieting and exercise.[8] If nature was the place where the body could rejuvenate, it was the city where the body would be displayed. Suburban nudism offered an ideal compromise, combining the outdoor experience of the backyard or open-air patio with the security and status of home ownership. Even if nude bodies were not openly displayed in the suburbs, bodies bearing (baring) the supposed enviable benefits of nudism—suntans, glowing skin, vitality, confidence—could be shown off to friends and neighbors. Suburbia, with the appropriate architecture and careful planning, could allow the central tenet of nudist practice, the embrace of the natural body, to flourish at home, creating an innovative space between city and country that incorporated a concept of the natural into a postwar consumer economy.

Trumble's entrepreneurial goal was to sell his "Sun-Fan" house to a broad United States public but the market was in the new Sunbelt suburbs that sprang up in the late 1950s and 1960s and ran from Florida through the southwest and into southern California. Sunbelt suburbs typically housed white middle-class families and retired couples seeking a leisurely lifestyle at a cut-rate price.[9] With an easily exploitable immigrant labor force, expanded service-sector economy, powerful anti-union lobbies, and minimal taxation combined with federally subsidized business and real estate development, the Sunbelt offered cheap housing and a convenient suburban life to a mostly white, and conservative, middle-class clientele.

Specifically, Trumble focused on Land O'Lakes, a suburban region of Pasco County, Florida, whose nudist history began in 1949 when Dorothy and Avery Weaver Brubaker founded the Florida Athletic and Health Association and opened a nudist camp, the Lake Como Club, on their 210-acre property.[10] Subsequently, other nudists set up shop in the area, taking advantage of west central Florida's cheap land, warm climate, and natural environment conducive to nudists' outdoor activities. By the 1970s, suburban Tampa began to surround the quiet, semi-rural area. Rather than move, the nudist community of Pasco County grew, with a surge of new membership in the 1980s and 1990s. The camps, which generally offered mobile home rentals, trailer lots, and tent sites, became more sophisticated and competitive; some, like Caliente, have developed into clothing-optional tourist resorts with pools, spas, luxury hotel accommodations, and condos for sale at both the mid-range and high end of the market.[11] Paradise Lakes became a nudist subdivision with 700 homes ranging in size from tiny 400-square-foot studios priced under $100,000 to million-dollar homes. Realtors estimate that 60 percent of Paradise Lakes is occupied by full-time residents. Others, like Oasis, The Woods, Riverboat Club, and Lake Linda Circle, feature mixed developments with anywhere from twenty-five mobile homes to subdivisions featuring hundreds of moderately priced, small houses with pools and backyard sunbathing decks, with most built in the past twenty years.[12] These communities are marketed as clothing-optional nudist environments, but realtors describe residents as living a "hybrid" experience: clothed in the front yard but nude in the fenced backyard.[13] In an effort to branch out, in 2004, Quaker Bill Martin opened a 240-acre Christian nudist resort in Hudson, in the far northwestern corner of Pasco County with 500 homes for sale.[14] Concentrated along a six-mile (11km) stretch of US Highway 41 in suburban Pasco County, Land O'Lakes remains the epicenter of American nudism, hosting six nudist resorts and hundreds of acres of gated, privately held land with several thousand residences.[15]

When Trumble met with nudist families in the midst of constructing homes in a Land O'Lakes subdivision in 1960, it was already an area known for its nudist camps, but it is highly unlikely that the subdivision itself was built with nudists in mind; hence the market for a nudist-friendly architect who could shield them from potentially unfriendly surveillance. While socializing naked by the pool, architect and clients discussed floor plans for prefab designs like the Sun-Fan "Islander," which featured "South Sea flavor that is compatible with casual living and yet is sufficiently 'conventional' to be built in any area," while the Sun-Fan "Tropical" offered a more modern exterior for the client with a taste for the avant-garde.[16] Individual nudist families could buy plans for their own Sun-Fan house for a mere twenty-five dollars but the more lucrative customer Trumble wanted to attract was the developer of moderately priced subdivisions. If the nudist-designed suburban tract home proved successful, Trumble envisioned applying his techniques for sun-drenched outdoor privacy to multiple-unit garden apartments that suggested that 1960s nudist living could go fashionably urban and, perhaps, encourage neighborly nudism.

While it is unclear if Trumble himself designed more than a few houses in the Land O'Lakes area, his plan for mid-range naked houses was not unprecedented in the history of Sunbelt architecture. Much as famed ranch house architect Cliff May reconfigured designs for resort hotels into prefab suburban homes, Trumble's designs adapted high-end naked homes for a mass market. As Lawrence Culver notes in his study of the postwar appetite for southern California leisure culture, Sunbelt suburban developments often appropriated the indoor-outdoor modernist southwestern designs of elite private commissions and repackaged them as affordable middle-class homes.[17] Part of the appeal of these cheaper homes was that they permitted sun exposure and encouraged the embrace of a body-centered lifestyle made popular in exotic tourist locales like Palm Springs, St. Barthes, and Monaco. Even if ritualized nudist practice was not intentionally part of the design (although many of the early twentieth-century modernist homes built for the Hollywood jet set incorporated screened patios and sun porches for nude sunbathing[18]), desert homes built by E. Stewart Williams, Albert Frey, and Richard Neutra were awash in natural light, featured a seamless indoor-outdoor living experience, employed sensual materials that drew the eye, and innovated heating and cooling systems to ensure the body, clothed or unclothed, the utmost comfort.[19]

Aware that many could not afford professional architects, mid-range or not, *Sunshine and Health* magazine suggested DIY alternatives such as fiberglass paneling, which could vertically extend a backyard fence, at least as far as building codes allowed. Ideally, however, one's backyard retreat would also include a swimming pool, a covered patio with awnings, and a recreation area allowing for a barbeque and dart game, all of which would require the hiring of contractors. But, as millions of suburbanites were encouraged by banks and the federal government in the 1950s and 1960s, credit and installment plans would make the American dream of private home ownership possible for the nude as well as the clothed:

1.3 "Building a backyard retreat." Source: *Sunshine and Health* 29, no. 12 (December 1960). The Wolfsonian-Florida International University, Miami Beach, Florida, Gift of Robert J. Young, XC2000.81.33.167. Photo: Silvia Ros.

> *The backyard retreat for nudist use does represent a substantial amount of money, however, in essence it is an investment which will pay rich dividends in health and happiness for the whole family. When and if the home with the backyard retreat such as is shown here is sold, the investment will pay off handsomely in hard cash. Spreading the payments over a several year period make it possible for people of modest income to enjoy these modern luxuries.*[20] *[Figure 1.3]*

Ritualized suburban naked living represented a significant shift in the meaning of nudism, at least in how it developed in the United States. Nudism, and the outdoor experience it encouraged, grew out of *Lebensreform* (or "life reform"), a mid-nineteenth-century German health movement that encouraged urban dwellers to address the ills of industrial society by living more naturally, a philosophy that included vegetarianism, exposure to fresh air, water, and sunlight, abstinence from tobacco and alcohol, and back-to-nature activities like gardening, hiking, and camping.[21] By the 1860s and 1870s, health seeking became an important pastime for the American middle and upper classes, with southern California emerging as a national center for tuberculosis sanitaria, health colonies, and the pursuit of optimal well-being through a wide range of practices including outdoor sleeping, massage, hydrotherapy, sweat baths, raw foods, fasting, and sun exposure.[22] Indeed, organized nudism in the United States might have been a relatively marginal practice but it was certainly in line with other health and body practices attracting impressive numbers of followers. Vegetable-rich, if not outright vegetarian, diets and purposive exercise were centerpieces of organized nudism in the United States with suntanning the practice perhaps most shared by nudists with other body cultists. Promoted in the early twentieth century by the American medical establishment as an important source of Vitamin D and a cure for a host of ailments, by the 1920s and 1930s suntanning was increasingly seen as a marker of leisure time and social status.[23] For nudists, suntanning was first and foremost a health measure but one that fell nicely in line with contemporary fashion.

With the 1929 formation of the American League for Physical Culture in New York, several hundred Americans began traveling to rural nudist camps where clothing was eschewed in favor of what was considered a free and uninhibited experience that encouraged sex-positive attitudes, physical health, and liberation from hypocritical social mores. Families were encouraged to attend and stay as long as possible. Nudists placed great emphasis on outdoor activities but these were no resort spas; it involved enormous collective labor to build and maintain the camps' infrastructure. The collectivity of social nudism provided one of the most enduring bonds between practitioners, as many would regularly reconvene at the same colonies and camps, working together to install an in-ground swimming pool or build new cabins. Though the culture of collectivity would imply a progressive social vision, the political leanings of nudists covered a wide spectrum, from socialism to right-of-center and the camps, through the 1950s, were usually racially exclusive, if more by custom than by camp policy or local law, and prohibited any homosexual coupling.

In addition to the pursuit of health, suntans, and social activities, a key element of nudist culture was viewing and photographing the nude body, a feature noted by historian Marguerite S. Shaffer in her work on the environmental nude. Nudist magazines proliferated in the United States from the 1930s through the 1960s with pages primarily dedicated to outdoor nudes, along with text celebrating the naturist lifestyle. Shaffer argues that the photographs were essential to nudist practice because they highlighted the natural state of the naked human body by positioning it in the environmental context of nature.[24] For urban dwellers, photographs emphasizing the placement of their bodies in natural, outdoor settings served as tools for the successful straddling of city and rural experiences, confirming the authenticity of their natural, nudist practice (Figure 1.4). As such, the publication of nudist magazines was instrumental in creating and shaping a subculture in which alternative home design and DIY architectural innovations could be shared and celebrated. Since so much of suburban nudist culture emphasized *not* being exposed to non-nudists, the magazines served as a critical space in which suburban nudism could actually be seen. Not only did they provide the visual interface for nudists to see their own subculture in practice, nudist magazines allowed invited readers to learn how nudists imagined and promoted their world. As it is impossible to know with any precision what anyone does in the privacy of their own home, nudist magazines served as the main source of insight into how nudists adapted their suburban surroundings to accommodate their body practice and, in turn, how they envisioned their impact on their suburban surroundings.

1.4 "Mother and child gather stores of knowledge." Source: *The Nudist* 2, no. 5 (July 1933). The Wolfsonian-Florida International University, Miami Beach, Florida, Gift of Robert J. Young, XC2000.81.33.1. Photo: Silvia Ros.

While other magazines such as *Sol*, *Sun Tan*, *Modern Sunbathing*, and *Sun Lore* entered the market in the 1950s and 1960s, the most widely read in the United States was *Sunshine and Health*. Originally titled *The Nudist*, the magazine was first published in 1933 by Reverend Ilsley Boone, a Baptist minister and one of the driving forces behind organized nudism in the United States. Boone established the magazine in order to communicate the mission of his organization, the International Nudist Conference (INC). The organization's mission statement, which appeared unchanged for the better part of thirty years, included the claim that "we believe in the essential wholesomeness of the human body and all its functions. We therefore regard the body neither as an object of shame nor as a subject for levity or erotic exploitations."[25] Thought prurient interests and legal censure would contribute to the undoing of nudist magazines in the United States, Boone and his editors tried to make it clear that nudism, while a practice of the flesh, was family-oriented and not an erotic enterprise.

Sensitivity to accusations of sexual impropriety or a political agenda was made clear in the mid-1930s when the INC changed its name to the American Sunbathing Association (a change that accompanied the renaming of the magazine *The Nudist* with the less suggestive title *Sunshine and Health*). Presumably the change occurred to distance the organization from the word "nudist," which had increasingly taken on eroticized connotations in American popular culture. As the magazine's editorial board framed it: "in the interest of dissociation of the nudist movement from the morbid and burlesque forms of nakedness, these terms shall hereafter be left almost exclusively to the theatrical, the night club, and the pornographic fields."[26] It also seems plausible that the terms *international* and *conference* evoked too strongly political organizations subject to Congressional scrutiny as subversive as well as evoking German *Nacktkultur*, which, by the mid-1930s, was entirely, and inaccurately, associated with the Third Reich. By 1936, the INC was taking great pains to separate itself from German nudism as Hitler had decimated that country's nudist groups because of their leftist working-class egalitarian politics, replacing the physical culture of socialist nudism with the body cultism of fascist Aryanism.[27] This sharp political distinction was not lost on the INC but its members ultimately had enough concerns about obscenity charges, police harassment, and Comstock laws that they sought to fly below the national political radar as much as possible.[28] As such, names evoking the sun carried the far more neutral connotation of health and fitness than any nudist nomenclature could offer.

However innocuous a name *Sunshine and Health* may have been, it nevertheless attracted a large audience, both nudist and not. In 1933, *Time* magazine reported that the original publication, *The Nudist*, had 2,000 subscribers with a monthly newsstand circulation of 110,000.[29] In his excellent history of nudist magazines, imagery, and obscenity law, Brian Hoffman reports that over the next few years, sales of the magazines varied from 40,000 to 100,000 a month with 6,000 to 8,000 mailed to subscribers and newsstand sales accounting for the remaining issues.[30] By the mid-1950s, similar circulation numbers were cited in court transcripts related to obscenity hearings, with 40,000 issues of *Sunshine and Health* printed in February 1955, 10,000 of which were mailed to subscribers.[31] Hoffman suggests that part of *Sunshine and Health*'s postwar appeal was an increased emphasis on homoerotic male nude imagery that, sandwiched between photos of naked women, slipped by the censors.[32] The fact that newsstand sales far outnumbered subscriber sales implies a pornographic appeal, but one may also reasonably assume that several thousand monthly readers were, in fact, practicing nudists: by 1958, the American Sunbathing Association alone claimed almost 7,800 members.[33] While never a mainstream cultural activity, nudism was a widely practiced and well-organized American subculture that occasionally attracted media attention, frequently encountered legal challenges, and was already well established by the time it surfaced as a notorious feature of the 1960s counterculture.

1.5 "Entertaining at home while a domestic nudist." Source: *Sunshine and Health* 25, no. 6 (June 1956). The Wolfsonian-Florida International University, Miami Beach, Florida, Gift of Robert J. Young, XC2000.81.33.115. Photo: Silvia Ros.

With the outbreak of World War II and the ensuing cultural conservatism of the postwar period, social nudism as it existed in the 1930s and 1940s became more difficult to practice in the United States. Fearing the loss of a community and a culture that had taken decades to build, advocates like the editors of *Sunshine and Health* recommended that members of local clubs and colonies take their practice home with them. Though much of the ideology behind nudism was tightly linked to a natural outdoor life, American nudists began to experiment with a private indoor nudist practice they called domestic nudism (Figure 1.5).

Domestic nudism meant converting what was essentially a communal outdoor social display into a hidden indoor private activity. It also meant either rethinking the health ideologies behind nudist practice, as sun and open air would be less accessible, or redesigning one's home to accommodate the nudist family's desire for healthful, natural living while in the city. Domestic nudism, or the practice of everyday naked living in one's private home, was not meant to supplant the organized activity and social life of summer nudist camps or year-long communes but practicing nudism at home was considered a way to allow continuity in one's life and to promote natural living and self-acceptance among one's family. Indeed, in the first broad sociological study of nudism in the United States, published by William Hartman, Marilyn Fithian, and Donald Johnson in 1970, the authors concluded that, of their sample, close to 90 percent of those who visited nudist camps also practiced "home nudism."[34]

Domestic nudism as an architectural project was first introduced in the United States when Philip Lovell (born Morris Saperstein), a Jewish leftist from New York City, reinvented himself in 1920s Los Angeles as a "Drugless Practitioner" and health guru proselytizing the benefits of a wide variety of alternative healing practices.[35] Alongside vegetarianism, fasting, and tanning, Lovell believed that building healthful homes was an important strategy for natural living in a modern urban environment and that to reach optimum health, one ought to place nudism at the center of one's living space.

Beyond the hundreds of columns of health advice he penned over thirty years for the *Los Angeles Times*, his most important legacy were the buildings he and his wife, Leah, commissioned from R.M. Schindler (Lovell Beach House) and Richard Neutra (Lovell Health House), which featured International Style design that merged technology and nature into a hypermodern structure built into a tree-covered hillside.[36] For the 1929 Health House, Lovell asked Neutra to build a home that fused architectural modernism with the alternative health practices that he disseminated each week in his *Los Angeles Times* column, "Care of the Body," specifying that the house permit indoor nude sunbathing.[37] With the Lovell commission, Neutra explored his theories of the interrelationship between health and architecture which, as historian Merry Ovnick has pointed out, articulated his belief that domestic architecture's goal should be "to bring modern man back into a symbiotic harmony with nature."[38] Grace Lewis Miller, a teacher of the Mensendieck exercise system, also commissioned Neutra to build her a home in Palm Springs in 1937 that would allow the body access to sun and air.[39] While combining concepts of the natural environment with health practices, these were, of course, elite projects available only to the wealthiest city dwellers who could afford private architectural commissions. Even so, the Health House was a sensation with the larger Los Angeles public, attracting thousands of visitors during two weekends of tours of the innovative home.[40] Perhaps only the rich could afford such a place but clearly thousands of others were intrigued by the new living possibilities offered by modern design's incorporation of health, nature, and the body. Later in life, Neutra would appear in *Nude Living* magazine, discussing with editors Ed and June Lange the importance of nudism to healthy sexuality and human expression, suggesting that architects consider the symbiotic relationship between the nude body and the home.[41]

Lovell was acutely aware of his audience and he directed his columns toward the middle-class suburban population that boomed exponentially in 1920s Los Angeles. Lovell identified the design restrictions of both budget and form, which were circumscribed by modern sanitation and building codes and often formalized by suburban developers. Within the narrow parameters allowed, he encouraged his readers, to construct their homes to better their health by balancing natural living with modern convenience. In ways reminiscent of today's green home movement that encourages the use of long-use light bulbs, solar power, and water reclamation, among other contemporary innovations in environmental technology and policy, Lovell too voiced concerns about the chemical make-up of the home. He suggested wood-burning over oil, avoiding white walls and fierce artificial light that strained the eyes, and forgoing cheap wallpaper that emitted a sharp chemical odor Lovell considered poisonous. He also advocated for the open-air sleeping porch rather than the bedroom, arguing that Americans over-insulated their sleeping quarters, trapping germs and preventing the circulation of fresh air. He considered the shower more hygienic to the bathtub and most emphatically encouraged the construction of outdoor spaces, including flat roofs that permitted naked sunbathing:

> *Besides the value of the outdoor sleeping room as a children's playground, a flat, open roof can be of immense value as a sun parlor. The value of sun bathing for anemia, tuberculosis, and practically all of the wasting diseases has been shown repeatedly. An open roof with a view-tight fence solves this problem without offense to the neighbors. There, for several hours per day, the children may play nude in the healthful sunshine. There the sick and the suffering may get the benefit of the life-giving rays of the sun without the expense of a sanatorium. There man may get in touch with the cosmic forces of nature far better than in closed rooms and confined spaces.*[42]

Lovell was so keen to spread word of healthful homes that in 1926 he invited Schindler, at the peak of his career, to write a series of six articles for "Care of the Body." Subject matter ranged from decoration and furnishing to structural concerns and plumbing. In his final installment as guest writer, Schindler contemplated the obsolescence of dark, over-decorated rooms that plagued historic American homes and were cheaply imitated in contemporary suburban houses as owners sought status-enhancing styles. He suggested that instead of revisiting these flawed decors that rendered one's home both lifeless and tacky, homeowners ought to think more carefully about the direct relationship between the body and its environment. Rather than fearing nature, and building houses that served as protective fortresses to keep nature at bay, healthful homes should let nature in and allow the nude body out:

> *The house and the dress of the future will give us control of our environment, without interfering with our mental and physical nakedness. Our rooms will descend close to the ground and the garden will become an integral part of the house. The distinction between the indoors and the out-of-doors will disappear. The walls will be few, thin, and removable. All rooms will become part of an organic unit, instead of being small separate boxes with peep-holes.*[43]

Schindler and Lovell's views on architecture's relationship to the nude body were not without critics. In 1937, Leicester B. Holland, FAIA, one of the country's leading architects and historical preservation specialists, argued in a tongue-in-cheek piece in *The Architect and Engineer* that if modern architecture was to continue in the United States, its designers needed appropriate scale figures. In a contemptuous tone obviously directed at his modernist contemporaries, Holland suggested that nudists would fit the bill as

> *the Nudist costume has much in common with modern architecture; it is functional, it eschews all ornament, it revels in sunlight . . . All things considered, I am convinced that Nudist and modern architecture do or should go hand in hand . . . Nudism in its philosophy is the negation of ornament, the negation of artificiality, and therefore, I believe, the negation of man's pride in his humanity as distinguished from simple animal nature. It is the negation of civilization.*[44]

Though Holland intended his commentary as a critique of the bare modernist design trend he viewed as a harbinger of Western civilization's decline, the connection he drew between architecture and nudism highlighted a set of very real relationships between home design and the body cultivated by Americans pursuing natural living in suburban environments.

However traditional architects might have sneered, the idea of the home as a seamless interface between human civilization and the outdoors was theorized as a suburban experience by Maurice Parmelee, a sociologist, political theorist, and liberal social critic (and founder of criminology in the United States). In his landmark work, the 1931 *Nudism in Modern Life*, Parmelee integrated a concept of biotechnics, Lewis Mumford's theory of the potentially sympathetic relationship of nature and technology, into gymnosophy, a school of thought that argued for a more natural and culturally uplifted human experience channeled through the naked human body. Parmelee's philosophy rejected nudism's traditional antiurban ethos, feeling strongly that the city and the natural body could organically coexist.[45] For Parmelee, nudism did not necessitate the rejection of the city; rather, it could "aid materially in bringing mankind closer to nature, in promoting more genuine and sincere relations between the sexes, and in rearing the young. It is symbolic of a life healthier and saner than our present hectic existence."[46]

Parmelee understood that as idyllic as rural life was for nudists, the fact that the body practice was accompanied by a progressive ideology of social equality and sexual health meant that the countryside was not the place where nudism would materialize as a social movement. In fact, he concluded that rural areas in the United States were too conservative to accommodate a progressive nudist practice beyond basic trade; i.e., exchanging tolerance for cash when nudist camps rented space or purchased food and sundries at local country stores. While organized nudism might take place in rural areas, it would be in cities where it would flourish as both a philosophy and a physical practice.[47] And Parmelee was not alone in considering the social conservatism of the United States as a problematic limitation on the progressive possibilities of organized nudism. Frances and Mason Merrill, two of his contemporaries and outspoken proponents of nudist culture feared that no such organized social movement could ever take root in the United States. In their 1931 treatise, *Among the Nudists*, the Merrills argued that there would always be strong social, economic, and political pressures opposing progressive body politics, ranging from the Protestant prudery of American social reform movements to the Ku Klux Klan's xenophobia. Not only were naturists inherently indecent but their cultural practice had foreign origins.[48] Trying to take a more optimistic tone, the Merrills also noted that despite Americans' inherent social conservatism, there were

> *certain factors in American life that might favor the progress of the [naturist] movement. The most obvious is the popularity of sunbathing in recent years. During the past few summers, whether seeking health or merely a fashionable "sun tan," countless Americans have been toasting themselves.*[49]

But the widespread popularity of suntans in the 1920s and 1930s was not symptomatic of a broader utopian social movement; rather, the suntan's popularity was tightly connected to a consumer economy directed toward a new youth market with money to spend on outdoor activities and ready-made clothing like the swimsuit and the backless sundress. Suntans signified leisure and wealth, not socialism or social experimentation. Mulling over the naturist legacies of Whitman and Thoreau, the Merrills concluded that the only future a nudist movement could have in America is one of individual rather than social conviction, practiced in small, intimate associations. Even at the height of the 1930s progressive nudist movement, its most outspoken advocates envisioned a type of social practice that, with its individual ethos and smaller, atomized groupings, would be well suited to suburban environments.

Thereby sharing the Merrills' concerns about the countryside's shortcomings, Parmelee's vision of nudism was not rural escapism but a suburban experience that blended modern conveniences with natural space, indoors and out. Suburbia, however, would need to undergo some changes before it would prove an appropriate landscape for a nudist experiment. The mass consumption undergirding suburban growth was antithetical to the simpler way of life nudism advocated and thus "unnecessary and unhealthy clothing, useless structures built largely for show, ugly and uncomfortable furniture, much trumpery bric-a-brac intended for decoration, and many superfluous and injurious kinds of food and drink," much of it part of middle-class domestic life in the 1930s, would have to go.[50] Meanwhile, architects and designers would have to accommodate suburban living with furniture that was comfortable against bare skin, and

> *dwelling-houses, offices, factories, public-meeting places, etc., will be so constructed as to be well ventilated at all times, comfortably warm in cold weather, and airy and relatively cool in hot weather. They will have extensive window space to admit as much sunlight as possible, sleeping porches, swimming pools and gymnasiums in the basements, and solaria upon the roofs to use in winter.*[51]

Ideally, nudism would reshape the American city, as much as it would transform the modern human relationship with the body. Parmelee was not suggesting that a return to a rural pre-modern life was the solution to the ills of modern industrial urban society; rather, he suggested that people cut back on the consumer durables and forge an environment that coupled sprawl and nature, individual fulfillment and collective living, technology and the body which would assuage society's malaise and build a stronger society by building better, more beautiful bodies. While this might queasily remind one of fascist body cultism, Ruth Barcan reminds us that Parmelee pointedly warned of the troubling "potential for the aesthetic discourse within nudism to be co-opted into militaristic nationalism" and envisioned instead a utopian suburbia where flesh met sun and adults shared property and experience, accepting the imperfect body as part of the experiment.[52]

Parmelee's designs for suburban nudism adapted elements of turn-of-the-century British planner Ebenezer Howard's Garden City, which integrated nature and industry, agriculture and affordable housing. Much like German *Lebensreform*, which in fact adopted Garden City plans in the early twentieth century, the Garden City movement in Britain strove to produce a healthier and more equitable living environment amid the overcrowded and unsanitary conditions of urban industrialized Europe.[53] Parmelee appropriated the famous "wheel and spokes" design, replacing Howard's plan for industrial sites and health sanitaria with nudist amenities such as fields for sun exposure and exercise:

> *In the first stage enclosed recreation centers can be established in vacant spaces in cities or on their outskirts. The next stage will be in the development of garden cities on the outskirts or just outside of cities. Here each gymnosophist can have a small plot of ground to till, and can build a shelter, cabin, cottage or house for temporary use or permanent occupancy. In the middle of the garden city should be a large open space for the use of the inhabitants where they can play games and enjoy the sunlight.*[54]

1.6 "Woman in a suburban backyard 'Sun Tub.'" Source: *The Nudist: Sunshine and Health* 7, no. 6 (June 1938). The Wolfsonian-Florida International University, Miami Beach, Florida, Gift of Robert J. Young, XC2000.81.33.34. Photo: Silvia Ros.

Whatever Parmelee's protests to the contrary, the movement of nudism from a collective outdoor rural pursuit into an indoor suburban activity was actively tied to consumerism by the 1930s, primarily through the magazines that highlighted the practice and sold advertising space. As early as 1937, advertisements for home sunlamps appeared in nudist magazines, promising Palm Beach color in the privacy of one's own room.[55] What was on offer was less nudist practice per se than the *look* of the nudist. In 1938, *The Nudist* featured a review of the Florida-invented "sun tub," a pre-fabricated, enclosed mobile unit that allowed nudists to follow the sun's rays around their private backyard. In a perfect homage to Mumford and Parmelee's merging of modern technology with the organic, the sun tub allowed a nudist to fully enjoy the natural rays of the sun and all she "has to do to keep her body fully exposed to sunshine during her bath is to reach out with one hand and turn the steering wheel, much like that of a modern motor car"[56] (Figure 1.6). It is important to note that the urbanist philosophies of Mumford and Parmelee were known to practicing nudists who frequently cited them in treatises on the health benefits of their body practice. While Parmelee was, of course, a famous nudist, it might come as a surprise that Mumford was celebrated as a proponent of nude beaches and claimed by nudists in the 1930s as one of their own.[57]

The 1930s enthusiasm for social nudism waned during World War II but Americans returned to colonies and resorts in the late 1950s as part of a resurgence nostalgically remembered now as the "golden age" of American nudism.

1.7 American Sunbathing Association Headquarters at Sunshine Park near May's Landing, New Jersey. Source: *Sunshine and Health* 15, no. 12 (December 1946). The Wolfsonian-Florida International University, Miami Beach, Florida, Gift of Robert J. Young, XC2000.81.33.72. Photo: Silvia Ros.

In 1958, in a nationally significant anticensorship case, *Sunshine Book Co. v. Summerfield*, the United States Supreme Court ruled that *Sunshine and Health* was not obscene, thereby lifting restrictions on sending nudist magazines through the mail, a case carefully followed by the Mattachine Society as it also lifted bans on specifically gay magazines.[58] Then, in 1959, in another precedent-setting case, the Michigan State Supreme Court ruled that nudists had the right to practice in privately owned resorts.[59] This was a significant legal victory given that many nudist colonies functioned under threat of police raids and permit revocation. Southern California, for example, home to several well-known colonies in the 1930s including Elysia and Olympic Fields, suffered a setback at the end of the decade when the Los Angeles County Board of Supervisors passed ordinance No. 3428 which banned social nudism, defined by the ordinance as anyone "within the unincorporated county of Los Angeles [who] willfully exposes his or her private parts in the presence and view of two or more persons of the opposite sex whose private parts are similarly exposed," a rather narrow view of nudist practice but devastating in its legal implications. A similar ordinance was passed in the city of Los Angeles that allowed nudist colonies but prevented men and women from being naked in front of one another. The municipal ordinance defined a nudist colony as "any place where three persons or more, not members of the same family, gather in the nude."[60] With local police historically mandated to raid colonies for spurious reasons, having state and federal courts supporting nudists inspired American practitioners in the 1950s to form hundreds of affiliate colonies, some year-round, with thousands of members.

With all the renewed interest in camps and colonies in the 1950s, *Sunshine and Health* nevertheless continued to publish articles addressing the benefits of domestic nudism, along with "how-to" guides to redesigning one's backyard, fence, deck, and pool and helpful suggestions like installing an intercom system to warn nude family members of non-nudist visitors.[61] The Sunshine Park national nudist headquarters building in New Jersey, for example, appears on the cover of *Sunshine and Health* as a middle-class suburban nudist fantasy[62] (Figure 1.7). Clearly, domestic nudism had, by the late 1940s, merged with the postwar suburban landscape, one that an architect like Kenn Trumble could capitalize upon in his efforts to expand the commercial appeal of the indoor-outdoor ranch home. Most striking is how evocative the published images are of standard 1950s suburban fare, with attractive, white nuclear families engaged in gender-normative activities in their commodity-filled homes. On the surface it appears that nudism, for all its original countercultural appeal, fit seamlessly into postwar consumer culture and its concomitant social conservatism grounded in traditional gender roles and private home ownership. In some ways suburban nudism did not contradict or challenge the broadest parameters of American cold war culture. Instead, it could be nestled quite nicely next to advertisements for barbeques, automobiles, clothing, and suburban homes (Figure 1.8).

1.8 "Stay at home and like it," a nudist suburbia pictorial. Source: *Sunshine and Health* 29, no. 9 (September 1960). The Wolfsonian-Florida International University, Miami Beach, Florida, Gift of Robert J. Young, XC2000.81.33.164. Photo: Silvia Ros.

But to argue suburban nudism was simply an offshoot of conservative social mores and Cold War domestic ideologies of consumer-based patriotism would be a mistake. The lifestyle promoted by magazines like *Sunshine and Health* represented a heterosexuality that fell within the social restrictions of the 1950s but relaxed the strict gender norms demanded by the feminine mystique. And, as Brian Hoffman and Whitney Strub remind us in their work on Cold War era obscenity cases, a queer interpretative gaze was also possible. Freudian psychotherapy seems to have had little place in the world of organized nudism as healthy body practices eased the perceived social challenges of sexual frigidity on the one hand and nymphomania on the other. That there existed the possibility for a commercial market for nudist homes in the American Sunbelt certainly sheds new light on the commonly held assumption that the postwar suburbs were a staid barbiturate-laced dystopia of frustrated housewives and unhappy commuter husbands.

Twenty-five years of critical scholarship have irrefutably demonstrated how the combination of Federal Housing Authority mortgage policies, the interstate highway system, federal urban policy, and the baby boom created new suburban regions that promoted conspicuous consumerism, reified suffocating gender norms, and privileged white middle-class prosperity at the expense of racial and ethnic minorities left behind in deteriorating urban centers.[63] While critics of the suburbs in recent years have rightfully focused on the racial segregation that accompanied suburbanization, as well as the alienating experience it created for women, it is important to remember that in the 1950s and 1960s, popular and academic criticism of suburbia smacked of an ugly misogyny. Contemporary observers applauded the racial exclusivity suburbia encouraged while fearing the feminization of living space that accompanied it. In September 1955, the National Institute of Mental Health presented a report to the American Society of Planning Officials and the Community Planning Association of Canada that was deeply critical of the "matriarchal society" that suburbia had birthed.[64] According to Dr. Leonard J. Duhl,

> *the suburbs are dominated by mothers and children know fathers as only night-time residents and week-end guests. This is responsible for maladjusted children . . . as youngsters have become oriented toward their mothers only, rather than toward both sexes, which they need for normal development.*[65]

Meanwhile, *Playboy* magazine, playing to every insecurity a suburban male might have had, suggested that the domesticity of the postwar tract home infantilized and feminized their readers with its family rooms and open-plan layout that minimized male privacy (and the ability to enjoy *Playboy* in peace, one might gather).

In her wonderful article, "The Answer to Suburbia: *Playboy*'s Urban Lifestyle," Elizabeth Fraterrigo argues that "the magazine mapped out space in the penthouse and the city to counter both the apparent encroachment of women into the public sphere and the 'feminized' spaces of suburbia."[66] Whatever Hugh Heffner's contributions to the sexual revolution, his magazine's antisuburban marketing strategy fell neatly in line with the unapologetically sexist view that male desires for entertainment and sexual fulfillment were to be found only in urban venues rather than suburban homes. Suburbia, by virtue of its married female inhabitants, was a frigid, emasculating force. This created a troubling cultural paradox as suburbia, with its presumed family-making role in American society, was upheld in the postwar era as a sexualized key to national economic prosperity, political and social stability and, as Elaine Tyler May has argued, an ideology of American domestic capitalism that could fend off the Cold War's communist threat.[67] Suburbia, like many gendered features of the American Cold War cultural landscape, was fraught with anxious ambiguity as it was presumed to harbor social ills such as emasculated sexual inadequacy while it simultaneously cradled good, healthy, patriotic American families.

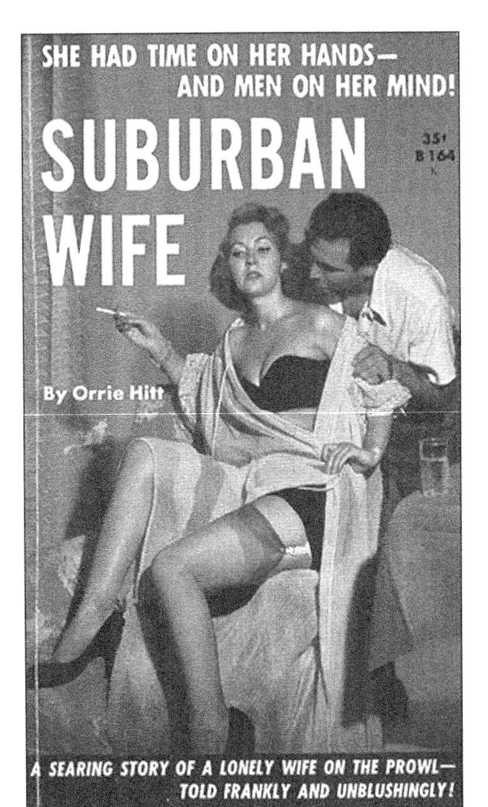

1.9 Pulp fiction eroticizes suburbia in the late 1950s and early 1960s, challenging the wholesome family image promoted by suburban nudists. Collection of the author.

Suburban nudism, with its ideological focus on both sexual health and family togetherness would seem well placed to absorb some of these contradictions and offer a drug-free antidote to so much cultural anxiety. As the 1950s wore on, however, both nudism and suburbia became increasingly eroticized in the popular imagination of pulp fiction and the visual landscape of pornography. Social nudity lost its family-based origins and suburbia lost some of its notorious conservatism as both were absorbed into the new cultural practices and erotic fantasies of the 1960s and 1970s. Indeed, it was in the suburbs that swinging took hold as a middle-class married variant of the sexual revolution and it was in a suburban setting that the dalliances of the nymphomaniac housewife played out in seedy pulp fiction.[68] Pulpy novels, with racy plots, pervaded 1950s popular culture. Titles like *Suburban Wife* (1958), *Suburban Sin Club* (1959), *The Big Bedroom* (1959), *Bachelor in Suburbia* (1962), and *Shopping Center Sex* (1964) (Figure 1.9) captured the prurient fantasy of suburban orgies and key parties. In the wake of the Kinsey reports, cheesy pornography could masquerade as scientific study, and American suburbia provided a rich research lab indeed. Thus Irving Wallace's *The Chapman Report*, a 1960 fictional account of Kinsey's *Sexual Behavior in the Human Female*, explored the sensual exploits and sexual pathologies of women in a wealthy Los Angeles suburb.[69] Uncovering the people behind a sexologist's dry statistics may have been the stated goal of *The Chapman Report* but any progressive meaning was lost, according to a scathing *New York Times* review, "in a swamp of hectic erotica."[70] The eroticism of the suburbs was of course also encouraged by *Playboy*, which for all of its marketing to the inhabitant of the urban bachelor pad pandered to a suburban audience. The proverbial "girls next door" were just as likely to be in a suburban ranch house as they were to be in your busy apartment building.

Eroticized suburbia encountered nudism in *Jaybird*, a glossy hippie magazine that was published in southern California from 1965 until the early 1970s and which celebrated the sexuality of the nudist suburbs through its bohemian mix of porno and performance art (Figure 1.10). The magazine emerged from a collaboration by longtime nudists Ed Lange and friend Stan Sohler (who had reported on Kenn Trumble's Sun-Fan houses for *Sunshine and Health*) to market a racier nudist culture more in line with the adult activities of the sexual revolution. Together with pornographer Milton Luros, they began publishing much sexier nudist magazines with professional models and film sets, with *Jaybird* the best known and most popular, selling about 20,000 copies per issue by 1968. The team split early, with Lange maintaining his allegiance to family-friendly nudism with the publication of *Nude Living*, but the short-lived collaboration had long-term results by essentially killing off the nudist magazine, which is where the world of suburban nudism ultimately lived and breathed.[71]

1.10 Nudism meets erotic suburbia in *Jaybird*, a late 1960s hippie nudist magazine. Collection of the author.

As pornography magazines moved toward hard-core imagery, the courts became less lenient, culminating in the 1973 *Miller v. California* US Supreme Court case that confirmed obscenity was not protected by the First Amendment and defined obscenity more broadly than in the past. This case fueled new laws, mostly enacted on the local level, that ordered magazines with explicit sexual imagery, and especially the blatant display of pubic hair, to be sold in isolated venues, thus giving rise to the adult bookstore.[72] In a reversal of the 1958 law that permitted nudist magazines to be sent through the mail, thereby lifting their obscenity status, the new legislation judged nudist magazines erotic and thereby relegated to the triple-X store, a move that effectively ended the era of the nudist print magazine in the United States. Since nudist magazines no longer offered titillation that could not be found in standard porn (nor could they compete with the ultra-raunchy magazines), while nudists distanced themselves from the newly explicit publications, nudist magazines simply grew obsolete. By 1985, a sociological study of adult bookstores in New York found that only 1 percent of magazines sold featured nudism.[73] Today, there are only two published in this country.

While nudism itself continues as both a suburban and an outdoor retreat culture, when featured in twenty-first-century advertisements for tourist resorts, it is highly sexualized in ways never seen in the suburban nudist pictorials of the postwar period. In an article highly critical of contemporary nudist culture, Ellen E. Woodall contrasts early nudist practice (collective, inexpensive) with today's version, which she argues is brashly commercial, sexist in its promotion of mainstream representations of women (young, white, thin), and ultimately just another part of the corporate hotel and entertainment industry.[74] A marked transition in the sexualized nature of modern nudism can also found outside the commercial resort industry, on the nude beach. A continual site for public controversy, nude beaches emerged as highly public forms of nudism in the 1960s and, unlike the camps and colonies, were often places for queer and straight cruising. Nude beaches have thus been more obviously part of an American sexual geography than other nudist sites. Not all people who visit nude beaches, of course, seek a sexual encounter but the public nature of beaches changes the interpretative signification of nudist display.[75]

As nudism has grown increasingly eroticized, so too has the representation of suburbia. For all the accounts of the emotional trauma wrought by suburbia's pathological conformity and hyperfemininity, it was a sexy place in the 1950s and 1960s American popular imagination and has, in fact, remained as such. Not only do suburban sexual fantasies like *Desperate Housewives* offer a counterweight to self-consciously urban soaps like *Sex in the City*, but in Los Angeles' San Fernando Valley the "sexy suburbs" fantasy has produced a global multi-billion dollar pornography industry. Housed temporarily inside ordinary tract homes or, sometimes, posh gated communities, pornographers and their stars and staff stage erotic dramas in mundane settings. Alongside breakfast nooks, kiddy pools, and two-car garages the majority of all American triple-X films are shot for an enormous international audience. But as Laura Kipnis argues in her work on pornography and the politics of fantasy, what these suburban film sets promise, ultimately, is the eroticism of the banal.[76] It becomes less a convenience that pornography is made in the suburbs and more a necessity of the sought-for aesthetic in which the everyday, even as quotidian as a suburban backyard, promises unfettered experiential sexuality. The location of the world's pornography industry in the middle of that quintessential trope of white middle-class suburbia, the "Valley," suggests the impossible task confronting mid-century nudists who promoted a body culture enmeshed in wholesome postwar domesticity. Given the historical trajectory from pulp fiction's sexualization of suburbia to nudism's appropriation by the 1960s sexual revolution to the contemporary production of suburban pornography, it seems unlikely that suburban nudism could have ever retained its modesty. Today, as in the early decades of the American nudist movement, activist groups like the Naturist Society and the Naturist Action Committee campaign vigorously to fight anti-nudity laws and restore nudism as a natural body practice performed in natural environments with an open, collective sense of inclusion that is separate and distinct from the sexualized and commercial nudist resort culture.[77]

In an era when suburban Americans were known for building backyard bomb shelters and creating an atomized, closed-in, and presumably repressive domestic culture, it is important to contemplate another suburban experience in which families adopted a body practice with roots in the collective social experiments of the 1930s. Whether or not we can consider this a progressive body culture is unclear, the waters muddied by the ease of immersion in consumerism and its hidden, if not surreptitious, nature. Organized nudism was at moments marked by racial segregation and homophobia and thus prohibits a simple celebratory reclamation.

What suburban nudism does for urban history, however, is excavate a moment when, despite pronounced social opposition and an especially inhospitable political climate, Americans forged a space for themselves using their bodies as a platform for imagining an alternative future where nature, however conceptualized, would be integrated into the everyday experience of modern living. Challenged by censors on the one hand and prurient interests on the other, nudists did not have an easy time of it. People could go to jail or be placed under an unpleasant scrutiny for participating in this culture and it took planning, a personal philosophy, and a committed belief in something beyond the mainstream to make it work. The existence of suburban nudism as both a cultural idea and a practice forces a reevaluation of postwar domestic culture and insists on the need to think critically about the relationships between city and country, living space, sexuality, and shifting understandings of the natural body within the parameters of American consumerism.

NOTES

1 This chapter was originally published in the *Journal of Urban History* 38, no. 4: 635–661, ©2012 Sage Publications. It is reprinted here with the full permission of the press. DOI: 10.1177/0096144211434988 http://juh.sagepub.com. The research for this chapter was funded by a Wolfsonian-Florida International University Residential Fellowship.

2 Kenn Trumble, as told to Stan Sohler, "Sun-Fan House," *Sunshine and Health* 29, no. 4 (April 1960): 4. Robert J. Young Collection, The Wolfsonian-Florida International University Rare Book and Special Collections Library, Miami Beach, Florida.

3 Ibid., 6.

4 Ibid., 8. I would like to thank Ron Rarick PhD, of the School of Art, Ball State University, for correcting my previous interpretation of this architectural feature.

5 There is a large literature on the transformation of American culture in the late nineteenth and early twentieth centuries and its role in reshaping of body norms and rituals. See, for example, Jackson Lears, *No Place of Grace: Antimodernism and the Transformation of American Culture, 1880–1920* (Chicago, IL: University of Chicago Press, 1994 [1981]); John Kasson, *Houdini, Tarzan, and the Perfect Man: The White Male Body and the Challenge of Modernity in America* (New York: Hill & Wang, 2002); Heather Addison, *Hollywood and the Rise of Physical Culture* (New York: Routledge, 2003); Joan Jacobs Brumberg, *Fasting Girls: The Emergence of Anorexia Nervosa as a Modern Disease* (Cambridge, MA: Harvard University Press, 1988); Anthony Giddens, *Modernity and Self-Identity: Self and Society in the Late Modern Age* (Stanford, CA: Stanford University Press, 1991); Harvey Green, *Fit For America: Health, Fitness, Sport and American Society* (New York: Pantheon, 1986); Margaret A. Lowe, *Looking Good: College Women and Body Image, 1875–1930* (Baltimore, MD and London: Johns Hopkins University Press, 2003); Hillel Schwarz, *Never Satisfied: A Cultural History of Diets, Fantasies, and Fat* (New York: Free Press, 1986); and Peter Stearns, *Fat History: Bodies and Beauty in the Modern West* (New York: New York University Press, 2002 [1997]).

6 Carolyn Thomas De La Peña, *The Body Electric: How Strange Machines Built the Modern American* (New York: New York University Press, 2003).

7 For more on turn-of-the-century middle-class camping practices, and the relationship between outdoor experience and class reification, see Phoebe Kropp, "Wilderness Wives and Dishwashing Husbands: Comfort and the Domestic Arts of Camping in America, 1880–1910," *Journal of Social History* 43, no. 1 (Fall 2009): 5–30.

8 See Robert Love, *The Great Oom: The Improbably Birth of Yoga in America* (New York: Viking, 2010); and Mark Adams, *Mr. America: How Muscular Millionaire Bernarr Macfadden Transformed the Nation Through Sex, Salad, and the Ultimate Starvation Diet* (New York: Harper, 2009).

9 See Carl Abbott, *New Urban History: Growth and Politics in Sunbelt Cities* (Chapel Hill, NC: University of North Carolina Press, 1981) and *How Cities Won the West: Four Centuries of Urban Change in Western North America* (Albuquerque, NM: University of New Mexico Press, 2008); Raymond Mohl, ed., *Searching for the Sunbelt: Historical Perspectives on a Region* (Knoxville, TN: University of Tennessee Press, 1990); Gary Mormino, *Land of Sunshine, State of Dreams: A Social History of Modern Florida* (Gainesville, FA: University Press of Florida, 2008); and Michelle Nickerson and Darren Dochuk, eds., *Sunbelt Rising: The Politics of Place, Space, and Region* (Philadelphia, PA: University of Pennsylvania Press, 2011).

10 Trumble, "Sun-Fan House," 8; Angie de Angeles, "The Naked Truth," *Orange and Blue Magazine* (College of Journalism and Communications, University of Florida) (Spring 2007), http://www.jou.ufl.edu/pubs/onb/s07/index.php?id+67, accessed June 25, 2011.

11 Phillip Edward Buchy, "A Nudist Resort," Master of Architecture thesis, Miami University, 2005. Perusing the real estate listings for Pasco County and especially the broader Tampa area reveals hundreds of clothing-optional condominiums for sale in the Caliente and Paradise Lakes developments. For examples, see http://www.tampa-mls.com/communities/caliente.html, accessed June 26, 2011; and *Pasco Naturally Magazine* (January 2011): 20–21.

12 De Angeles, "The Naked Truth"; "Modern Naturism," November 7, 2009, at http://amazingdata.com/modern-naturism/, accessed June 26, 2011.

13 Ibid.

14 Sean Mussenden, "Man Envisions Christian Nudist Colony for Families," *Orlando Sentinel*, January 6, 2004; Lisa San Pascual, "Bare Naked Christians," *Religion in the News* 7 (Spring 2004), at http://www.trincoll.edu/depts/csrpl/rinvol17no1/Bare%20Naked%20Christians.htm, accessed June 26, 2011; David Usborne, "Call to Bare at Nudist Camp for Christians," *The Independent*, January 8, 2004, at http://independent.co.uk/news/world/americas/call-to-bare-at-nudist-camp-for-christians-578483.html, accessed June 25, 2011.

15 Phil Davis, Associated Press, "Florida County is Nudist Mecca," June 12, 2006, at http://news.yahoo.com/s/ap_travel/20060612/ap_tr_ge/travel_trip_nude_tourism_1, accessed June 26, 2011.

16 Trumble, "Sun-Fan House," 8, 28.

17 See ch. 7, "From Resorts to the Ranch House," in Lawrence Culver's *The Frontier of Leisure: Southern California and the Shaping of Modern America* (Oxford and New York: Oxford University Press, 2010).

18 Culver, *The Frontier of Leisure*, 160.

19 See Adele Cygelman, David Glomb, and Joseph Rosa, *Palm Springs Modern: Houses in the California Desert* (New York: Rizzoli, 1999); and Alan Hess and Andrew Danish, *Palm Springs Weekend: The Architecture and Design of a Midcentury Oasis* (San Francisco, CA: Chronicle Books, 2001).

20 Lee Edmunds, "Build a Backyard Retreat," *Sunshine and Health* 29 (December 1960): 25. Robert J. Young Collection, The Wolfsonian's Rare Book and Special Collections Library, Miami Beach, Florida.

21 John Alexander Williams, *Turning to Nature in Germany: Hiking, Nudism, and Conservation, 1900–1940* (Stanford, CA: Stanford University Press), 11–12. There is a growing literature on the origins of nudist practice, particularly outside the United States. In addition to Williams, also see Evert Peeters, "Authenticity and Asceticism: Discourse and Performance in Nude Culture and Health Reform in Belgium, 1920–1940," *Journal of the History of Sexuality* 15 (September 2006): 432–461; Nina J. Morris, "Naked in Nature: Naturism, Nature, and the Senses in Early Twentieth Century Britain," *Cultural Geographies* 16 (2009): 283–308; and Caroline Daley, *Leisure and Pleasure: Reshaping and Revealing the New Zealand Body 1900–1960* (Auckland: Auckland University Press, 2003).

22 For more on California's place in the health movements of the nineteenth century, see John Baur's classic *The Health Seekers of Southern California, 1870–1900* (San Marino, CA: Huntington Library, 1959). For a brilliant study of the relationship of California's nineteenth-century health-seekers and the political economy of the environment, see Linda Nash, *Inescapable Ecologies: A History of Environment, Disease, and Knowledge* (Berkeley and Los Angeles, CA: University of California Press, 2006).

23 Catherine Cocks, "The Pleasures of Degeneration: Climate, Race, and the Origins of the Global Tourist South in the Americas, Discourse 29 (Spring and Fall 2007): 228; Kerry Segrave, *Suntanning in Twentieth Century America* (Jefferson, NC and London: McFarland, 2005).

24 Marguerite S. Shaffer, "On the Environmental Nude," *Environmental History* 13 (January 2008): 127.

25 *The Nudist. Official Publication of the International Nudist Conference* 1 (July 1933): 5. Robert J. Young Collection, The Wolfsonian's Rare Book and Special Collections Library, Miami Beach, Florida.

26 *The Nudist: Sunshine and Health* 5 (November 1936): 9. Robert J. Young Collection, The Wolfsonian-Florida International University Rare Book and Special Collections Library, Miami Beach, Florida.

27 See Chad Ross, *Naked Germany: Health, Race, and the Nation* (Oxford and New York: Berg, 2005); and Williams, *Turning to Nature*.

28 For references to German nudism, as well as discussions as to the fate of naturism in Europe, see *The Nudist* 1 (July 1933): 5, 26; "The Restoration of German Nudism," *The Nudist: Sunshine and Health* 5 (August 1936): 7. Robert J. Young Collection, The Wolfsonian-Florida International University Rare Book and Special Collections Library, Miami Beach, Florida.

29 "The Press: Sunshine," *Time*, Monday, November 27, 1933.

30 Brian Hoffman, "'A Certain Amount of Prudishness': Nudist Magazines and the Liberalization of American Obscenity Law, 1947–58," *Gender and History* 22 (November 2010): 711.

31 Sunshine Book Company and Solair Union Naturisme, Inc., Appellants, v. Arthur E. Summerfield, Individually and as Postmaster General of the United States, Appellee. No. 12622. United States Court of Appeals, District of Columbia Circuit. Reargued September 25, 1956. Decided October 3, 1957. Cited in Edward De Grazia, *Censorship Landmarks* (New York and London: R.R. Bowker, 1969), 248. The 1956 circulation figures of 40,000 (10,000 to subscribers) were cited in conservative columnist James Jackson Kilpatrick's 1960 anti-obscenity treatise, *The Smut Peddlers*, as greater than the circulation of either *The Reporter, New Republic, The Nation,* or *National Review*. James Jackson Kilpatrick, *The Smut Peddlers* (Garden City, NJ: Doubleday, 1960), 15.

32 Hoffman, "A Certain Amount of Prudishness," 714–716.

33 Fred Ilfeld, Jr. and Roger Lauer, *Social Nudism in America* (New Haven, CT: College and University Press, 1964), 143.

34 William E. Hartman, Marilyn Fithian, and Donald Johnson, *Nudist Society: The Controversial Study of the Clothes-Free Naturist Movement in America* (Los Angeles, CA: Elysium Press, 1970; rev. 1991), 187, 428.

35 Gary Marmorstein, "Steel and Slurry: Dr. Philip M. Lovell, Architectural Patron," *Southern California Quarterly* 84 (Fall 2002): 241–244.

36 Thomas S. Hines, *Richard Neutra and the Search for Modern Architecture* (New York and Oxford: University of Oxford Press, 1982).

37 Philip M. Lovell, "The Home Built for Health," *Los Angeles Times*, December 15, 1929.

38 Merry Ovnick, *Los Angeles: The End of the Rainbow* (Los Angeles, CA: Balcony Press, 1994), 219.

39 Hines, *Richard Neutra*, 121.

40 Marmorstein, "Steel and Slurry," 255.

41 Richard J. Neutra, "Some Notes on the Complex of Nudism," *Nude Living* 1 (April 1962): 7–10. Richard and Dion Neutra Papers, Collection 1179. Box 1476, folder 14. Department of Special Collections, Charles E. Young Research Library, University of California, Los Angeles.

42 Philip M. Lovell, N.D., "Care of the Body," *Los Angeles Times*, June 29, 1924: J24. Lovell's desire for a flat roof as a health cure was inspired by the tuberculosis architecture of the late nineteenth century. See Margaret Campbell, "What Tuberculosis Did for Modernism: The Influence of a Curative Environment on Modernist Design and Architecture," *Medical History* 49 (2005): 463–488.

43 R.M. Schindler, "Care of the Body," *Los Angeles Times*, May 2, 1926: K28.

44 Leicester B. Holland, FAIA, "Nudism and Modern Architecture," *The Architect and Engineer*, March 1937: 41–42. California Historical Society Collection, San Francisco, California.

45 Maurice Farr Parmelee, *Nudism in Modern Life* (New York: Garden City, 1931), 258.

46 Ibid., 6.

47 Ibid., 220–221.

48 Frances and Mason Merrill, *Among the Nudists* (New York: Garden City, 1933); 234–235.

49 Ibid., 241.

50 Parmelee, *Nudism in Modern Life*, 213.

51 Ibid., 216.

52 Ruth Barcan, "'The Moral Bath of Bodily Unconsciousness': Female Nudism, Bodily Exposure, and the Gaze," *Continuum: Journal of Media and Cultural Studies* 15 (November 2001): 309.

53 Ebenezer Howard, *Garden Cities of To-Morrow* (London, 1902). Reprinted, edited with a preface by F.J. Osborn and an introductory essay by Lewis Mumford (London: Faber & Faber, 1946); Williams, *Turning to Nature*, 12.

54 Parmelee, *Nudism in Modern Life*, 222–223.

55 *The Nudist: Sunshine and Health* 6 (January 1937): 22. Robert J. Young Collection, The Wolfsonian-Florida International University Rare Book and Special Collections Library, Miami Beach, Florida.

56 *The Nudist: Sunshine and Health* 7 (June 1938): 12. Robert J. Young Collection, The Wolfsonian-Florida International University Rare Book and Special Collections Library, Miami Beach, Florida.

The innovators of the sun tub may have been inspired by the revolving summerhouses constructed in the United Kingdom in the early twentieth century. See Campbell, "What Tuberculosis Did," 478–482.

57 "Beaches for Nude Bathing," *The Nudist: Sunshine and Health* 8, no. 4 (April 1939): 3. Robert J. Young Collection, The Wolfsonian-Florida International University Rare Book and Special Collections Library, Miami Beach, Florida. Lewis Mumford's suggestion for nude beaches, or at least segregated areas that permitted the practice, appeared in his report, *Whither Honolulu? A Memorandum on Park and City Planning* (Honolulu: Honolulu City and County Board, 1938) republished in Lewis Mumford, *City Development: Studies in Disintegration and Renewal* (New York: Harcourt, Brace, 1945), 124–125.

58 Hoffman, "A Certain Amount of Prudishness," 728; Whitney Strub, "The Clearly Obscene and the Queerly Obscene: Heternormativity and Obscenity in Cold War Los Angeles," *American Quarterly* 60, no. 2 (2008): 380–381; and Strub, "Perversion for Profit: Citizens for Decent Literature and the Arousal of an Antiporn Public in the 1960s," *Journal of the History of Sexuality* 15, no. 2 (May 2006): 258–291.

59 Southern California Naturist Association, "A Brief History of Naturism," Calabasas, CA: Southern California Naturist Association, 4; John Logan, "Victory for *One*," *Mattachine Review*, February 1958: 4.

60 John H. Burnett, "The Fallen Fathers of the Angel City," *Sunshine and Health* 9 (February 1940): 20–21. Robert J. Young Collection, The Wolfsonian-Florida International University Rare Book and Special Collections Library, Miami Beach, Florida.

61 Ken Price, "Let's Visit the Smiths," *Sunshine and Health* 25 (June 1956): 6–11. Robert J. Young Collection, The Wolfsonian-Florida International University Rare Book and Special Collections Library, Miami Beach, Florida.

62 *Sunshine and Health* 25 (December 1946), cover. Robert J. Young Collection, The Wolfsonian-Florida International University Rare Book and Special Collections Library, Miami Beach, Florida.

63 For effects of suburbia on gender relations and norms see Betty Friedan, *The Feminine Mystique* (New York: Norton, 1963); Daniel Horowitz, *Betty Friedan and the Making of "The Feminine Mystique": The American Left, the Cold War, and Modern Feminism* (Amherst, MA: University of Massachusetts Press, 2000); Elaine Tyler May, *Homeward Bound: American Families in the Cold War Era* (New York: Basic Books, 2008 [1988]). Dolores Hayden, *Redesigning the American Dream: Gender, Housing, and Family Life* (New York: Norton, 2002). For suburbia and consumer culture see Karal Ann Marling, *As Seen on TV: The Visual Culture of Everyday Life in the 1950s* (Cambridge, MA: Harvard University Press, 1996); Lynn Spigel, *Make Room for TV: Television and the Family Ideal in Postwar America* (Chicago, IL: University of Chicago Press, 1992); Lizabeth Cohen, *A Consumer's Republic: The Politics of Mass Consumption in Postwar America* (New York: Vintage, 2003). For political economy of race and identity see Thomas Sugrue, *The Origins of the Urban Crisis: Race and Inequality in Postwar Detroit* (Princeton, NJ: Princeton University Press, 2005, rev. edn); Lisa McGirr, *Suburban Warriors: The Origins of the New American Right* (Princeton, NJ: Princeton University Press, 2002); Kevin Kruse, *White Flight: Atlanta and the Making of Modern Conservatism* (Princeton, NJ: Princeton University Press, 2007); and Eric Avila, *Popular Culture in the Age of White Flight: Fear and Fantasy in Suburban Los Angeles* (Berkeley and Los Angeles, CA: University of California Press, 2004).

64 Joseph C. Ingraham, "Housing Delays Laid to Politics," *New York Times*, September 29, 1955: 55.

65 Ibid.

66 Elizabeth Fraterrigo, "The Answer to Suburbia: *Playboy*'s Urban Lifestyle," *Journal of Urban History* 34 (July 2008): 751.

67 May, *Homeward Bound*.

68 For more on swinging in the suburbs see David Allyn, *Make Love, Not War: A History of the Sexual Revolution* (New York: Routledge, 2001), 206–227.

69 Irving Wallace, *The Chapman Report* (New York: Simon & Schuster, 1960).

70 Daniel Talbot, "In a Swamp of Erotica," *New York Times*, May 29, 1960: BR 18.

71 Dian Hanson, *Naked as a Jaybird and Loving It* (Los Angeles, CA: Taschen, 2003), 24–29.

72 See Eric Schaefer and Eithne Johnson, "Quarantined! A Case Study of Boston's Combat Zone," in Henry Jenkins, Tara McPherson, and Jane Shattuc, eds., *Hop on Pop: The Politics and Pleasures of Popular Culture* (Durham, NC: Duke University Press, 2002), 430–453; Whitney Strub, *Perversion for Profit: The Politics of Pornography and the Rise of the New Right* (New York: Columbia University Press, 2011), 170–172; and Hanson, *Naked as a Jaybird*.

73 Charles Winick, "A Content Analysis of Sexually Explicit Magazines Sold in an Adult Bookstore," *The Journal of Sex Research* 21 (May 1985): 208.

74 Ellen E. Woodall, "The American Nudist Movement: From Cooperative to Capital, the Song Remains the Same," *Journal of Popular Culture* 36 (November 2002): 264–284.

75 Much of the interest in nude beaches, and their sexual significance, was recorded in the 1970s. See Jack D. Douglas, Paul K. Rasmussen, and Carol Ann Flanagan, *The Nude Beach* (Beverly Hills, CA and London: Sage, 1977); and Hartman et al., *Nudist Society*.

76 See Laura Kipnis, *Bound and Gagged: Pornography and the Politics of Fantasy in America* (Durham, NC: Duke University Press, 1998).

77 The Naturist Society grew out of the Free Beach Movement of the 1970s while the Naturist Action Committee (NAC) was formed in 1993 as the political organ of the Naturist Society. Both are dedicated to protecting the legality of nude beaches and permitting nudism in natural environments. Members are not opposed to nudist camps and resorts but are more interested in facilitating free and natural nudism rather than promoting the private, gated experience of most contemporary nudist culture. See *The Newsletter* published by the Naturist Action Committee, The Naturist Society, and the Naturist Education Foundation.

2

Inputs, Outputs, Flows: The Bio-Architecture of Whole Systems Design, the Energy Pavilion, and the Integral Urban House

Sabrina Gabrielle Richard

The social and cultural revolutions of the 1960s produced a host of architectural icons that represented an effort to redefine the future of human habitation. Buckminster Fuller's geodesic domes, Ant Farm's ephemeral architecture, and experiments in communal living, such as "Drop City" and "Arcosanti," vilified the urban environment, rejected social conventions, and revealed an interest in childhood and creative experimentation that would eventually define the American counterculture. Yet these familiar examples represent only a small portion of the diverse spatial experimentation of the period and the complex reimagining of nature, technology, and the body that occurred in the field of architecture. In the wake of the 1960s environmental movement, a little-known architectural proposition emerged in the California Bay Area called "Whole Systems Design." Attributed to architect Sim Van der Ryn, Whole Systems Design theorized an urban ecology movement of self-contained ecological residences designed to harness the energy circulating between the environment, technology, and bodies, both human and animal. The resulting architecture was "physiological," positioning housing as integral to a synthetic metabolic cycle, with the human body at the center receiving heat, nutrients, and calories from surrounding technological sources. Van der Ryn represented his proposal through a series of publications, architectural diagrams, and subsequently realized two physical models of the system—the Energy Pavilion (1973), a temporary architectural installation built on the campus of the University of California, Berkeley, and the "Integral Urban House" (1974), a laboratory and full-scale demonstration project in West Berkeley. Whole Systems Design, and its architectural manifestations, is representative of a larger epistemic movement that would come to define ecological architecture of the period. Through the adoption of "appropriate technology," systems thinking, and a new model of human physiology filtered through contemporary developments in ecology, cybernetics, and the aerospace industry, ecological design in the 1970s positioned man and machines as networked organisms in artificially constructed ecologies. The following analysis will trace the cultural and intellectual history of Whole Systems Design as a form of "biotechnology," operating on, protecting, and extending the notion of the human body in a post-industrial urban environment perceived as "toxic" and "hostile to life." The Energy Pavilion and the Integral Urban House will be positioned as sites of confluence for the ideas of several influential proponents for the reconceptualization of technology and ecology, including Ian McHarg, Norbert Wiener, E.F. Schumacher, and Steward Brand. This intellectual trajectory will also be contrasted with a contemporaneous cultural critique of the relationship between technology and the human body. The central argument of this chapter is the paradox of Whole System Design's adoption of a cybernetic notion of ecology. This technocratic approach to the environment, characterized by optimal calibrations of resources, organisms, and technological systems, rather than allowing for social and individual autonomy as suggested, required strict regulation and control of the body, from daily habits and labor practices to bodily inputs and outputs.

In his first State of the Union address given on January 22, 1970, United States President Richard Nixon, stated: "The great question of the seventies is, shall we surrender to our surroundings, or shall we make our peace with nature."[1] Nixon's sentiments reflected the increasingly adversarial relationship between humanity and the environment felt at the beginning of the 1970s. While social and cultural revolutions had dominated the 1960s, it was not until late in the decade, when revolutionary sentiments were waning and once-radical causes became increasingly mainstream, that activists would turn towards environmentalism, or "ecology," as it was called at the time.[2] In Berkeley, California, regarded by many as the epicenter of the nationwide social and cultural uprisings, it would take tragic events to mobilize local activists and members of the counterculture around the perceived "ecological crisis."

On April 20, 1969, more than one hundred local residents, activists, and members of the counterculture would assemble on a vacant lot owned by the University of California. The site had sat derelict since the university razed the area of housing a year earlier, and the public gathering was part of an initiative to rehabilitate the land by planting trees, grass, flowers, and vegetables. Adopting the name "People's Park," the location quickly became a rallying place for reimagining property ownership, urban land use, and the relationship between the human and non-human world. To the university administration, however, the construction of the park was a blatant form of trespassing and illegal occupation. During these events Sim Van der Ryn was a professor of architecture at the University of California, as well as chair of the Berkeley Campus Life Committee. Van der Ryn attempted, unsuccessfully, to negotiate a compromise between the park occupiers, the Office of the Governor of California, and the university. Very quickly the conflict escalated and Governor Ronald Reagan enlisted the National Guard to forcibly clear the land on May 15, 1969. This state action was met with violent protest, the occupation of Berkeley by state and federal troops, and the shooting death of student James Rector. Seventeen days after the violent escalation the state withdrew their forces and ceded the area. While the university ultimately refused to turn the land over to the city, People's Park remains a community space, albeit a contested site, to this day.[3]

Referred to as "Bloody Thursday," the battle over People's Park was a critical event in the American 1960s.[4] For the first time the state had attacked its own citizens for attempting to improve the urban environment and the incident would spark widespread discussions of "ecology" alongside humanistic and revolutionary goals among activists and members of the counterculture. While warnings of the "ecological crisis" had appeared in mainstream culture throughout the decade they had largely failed to rally the kinds of participatory democracy associated with the social and cultural movements of the era.[5] The creation of People's Park, however, had successfully aligned the fight for the environment with struggles for peace, social justice, and personal freedom, and ushered in a new preoccupation with environmental "survival." In Berkeley, local activists and members of the counterculture began to organize ecological sit-ins, happenings, and other forms of environmental activism just days after the battle for the park.[6] According to the *Berkeley Tribe* newspaper, "People's Park is the beginning of the Revolutionary Ecology Movement. It is the model of the struggle we are going to have to wage in the future if life is going to survive at all on this planet."[7]

The traumatic founding of People's Park, as well as increasing national discourse around ecology, would prove vital to Van der Ryn's evolving design ethos and the conception of Whole Systems Design. Prior to the events of People's Park, Van der Ryn's teaching and architectural research focused primarily on social justice issues and studies of institutions.[8] The driving ideology of his practice had been the integration of architectural design with social science, scientific methodologies, and rational planning principles.[9] After People's Park, Van der Ryn would relocate his family from Berkeley to Inverness, a rural community in Marin County, California, and begin conducting practicum on "self-sufficient" living in ecological architecture.[10] Van der Ryn's shift in focus away from social justice towards environmentalism reflected a broader cultural turn in the late 1960s.[11]

To underscore the point, on November 11, 1969, the *New York Times* ran a front-page story stating the environment would soon eclipse the Vietnam War as the number one issue on college campuses.[12] *Newsweek* would make a similar prediction one month later.[13] By the end of the decade, the environmental cause had attracted millions of Americans, especially those in their teens and twenties, making environmentalism yet another mass youth movement. A number of scholars have convincingly argued that this widespread sensitivity towards the environment was influenced by the architecture of the postwar economic boom, especially suburban development.[14] One of the many goals of the suburbs was the creation of residential settings designed to bring people into close contact with "nature" and the "countryside." In these new developments families would often be in immediate proximity with nearby forests and fields and as a result many outdoor leisure activities, such as fishing, hiking, and camping, became increasingly popular. To many suburbanites the environment came to symbolize a source of American moral and ethical values, such as "freedom," "authenticity," "shared inheritance," and "physical vitality."[15] By the 1970s, many suburban youth would bring their environmental sensitivity to the student movement's overall social critique.

The ethos of how to integrate the growing concern over the environment within architecture, landscape architecture, and regional planning was pioneered by the work of Ian L. McHarg. A landscape architecture professor at the University of Pennsylvania, McHarg taught an influential design studio titled "Man and the

Environment," focused on studying the ethics and ideology of the environment in design. In 1969, he would publish the seminal text *Design with Nature*, which called on designers to address the "ecological crisis" through a holistic approach to the economy, design, and planning. *Design with Nature* functioned as a set of step-by-step instructions for designers to analyze and integrate soil conditions, climate, hydrology and other "natural systems" within the design process.[16] McHarg's work was widely followed within architectural circles where he lectured extensively on the importance of ecology. Sim Van der Ryn was especially familiar with McHarg's work, having taught with him at University of Pennsylvania as a visiting professor in 1967.[17]

WHOLE SYSTEMS DESIGN: PEDAGOGY TO PRAXIS

In 1972 Van der Ryn would return to the University of California, Berkeley to teach an architectural design studio titled "Natural Energy Design." While influenced by McHarg's methodologies, the course also drew on the College of Environmental Design's interest in architectural research, discussions of systems thinking by faculty such as Christopher Alexander, and the controversial "social factors" curriculum, which emphasized economics, planning, and sociology alongside design education.[18] Premised on both the science and philosophy of ecology, students in the Natural Energy Design course looked to environmental research, sustainable building systems, and technological systems as generators of architectural design. It was during this course that Van der Ryn first articulated his vision for Whole Systems Design and produced its first iteration, a diagram titled "Energy Flows in Closed System Habitat"[19] (Figure 2.1). Comprised of three nested circles, the Whole Systems Design diagram represented energy flowing between the environment and the human body by way of technological machines. It is a diagram of the natural world abstracted into inorganic resources—wind, sun, soil, and water, which are then ascribed to specific devices, such as solar energy collectors and wind energy generators. These technologies were assigned the purpose of transmitting energy to the "shelter functions" inscribed within the diagram's inner circle. The list of "shelter functions" indicates activities intended to take place *within* a dwelling, yet they conflate bodily functions, such as "shitting," "eating," and "drinking," with domestic activities, such as "cooking" and "washing," and technologies such as "lighting" and "space heating." The Whole Systems Design diagram represented the first design challenge of Van der Ryn's proposal—the need to present information in a theoretically significant configuration in order to legitimize his conception of ecology.[20] A close reading of the diagram therefore reveals that several new ideologies had entered into the discourse of architecture, namely the notion of energy-based, cybernetic "eco-systems" and a new appreciation for technology in ecological thought.

Ecology has always had architectural implications. As Richard Ingersoll has pointed out, "the appearance of ecology within the discourse of architecture hinges on a historic paradox: every act of building betrays the environment, as it requires the displacement of 'natural' relationships."[21] Initially the study of organisms and their "home," the fundamental insight of ecology is the realization that all forms of

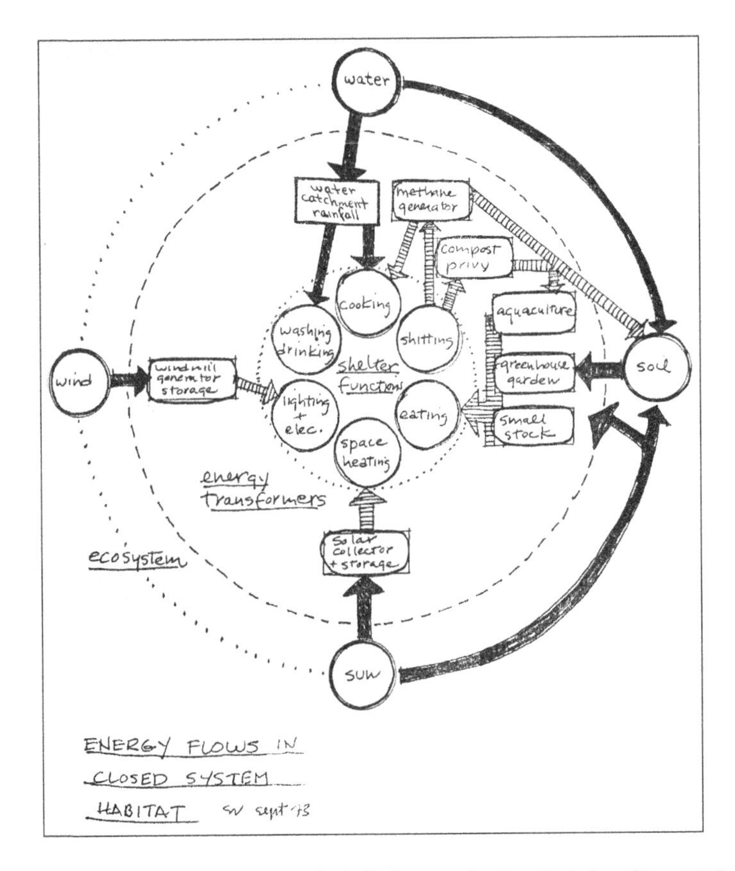

2.1 Sim Van der Ryn, diagram of Whole Systems Design. Berkeley, CA, c. 1973. Courtesy of Sim Van der Ryn.

matter are connected to one another.[22] While the science of ecology initially functioned as a system of classification, owing in part to the dominance of biology in the nineteenth century, after the Second World War, ecologists would turn to the discourse of systems theory and the physics of energy fields to create new models for causality and equilibrium in the environment. The implications were transformative; suddenly "energy" became the common substance between all matter, recasting common phenomena as the result of energy flows within a balanced ecosystem.[23] The entry of energy systems into ecological thought would resonate in the epistemology of Whole Systems Design. Reflecting on his design ethos, Van der Ryn would state, "most people think buildings are sculptural objects or works of art, but my view has always been that buildings are organisms and ecosystems, and humans make up an important part of these systems."[24]

While the physics of energy flows transformed the environment into a series of ecosystems, it was cybernetic theory that would provide the means to influence and ultimately control those systems. A derivative of systems thinking, cybernetics emerged in the late 1940s to explain the regulation and transmission of information.[25] Based on the notion that human thought and computerized information systems operate according to the same rules and processes, cybernetics implied that biological life and technology are equally engaged in the drive to maintain and circulate energy in a balanced system.[26] The result was the provision of a powerful epistemology for ecological thought, offering a means to organize the energy flows between various interrelated components with the use of technology. Whole Systems Design's adoption of cybernetic theory would result in a flattening of the environment, machines, architecture, and the body into equivalent technologies for regulating energy flows in a closed ecosystem.

THE ENERGY PAVILION

After the completion of the Natural Energy Design course, Van der Ryn and a number of students would set out to test the ability of environmental technologies to enable an autonomous ecosystem. Funds were raised to build a physical model of Whole Systems Design in the form of a full-scale architectural installation they titled the "Energy Pavilion" (Figure 2.2). Located on the grounds of the University of California, Berkeley campus, the Energy Pavilion stood two stories high, fabricated out of wood frames, timber beams, and tension cables. The unusual structure included three platforms, connected by a series of staircases, which housed energy collection and recycling technologies fabricated by the students. While the Energy Pavilion made literal the Whole Systems Design diagram, in this iteration the architecture was a substantial element—forming the physical scaffold of the system, networking the energy-collecting instruments, and materializing their interactions. Rainwater collectors made of salvaged plastic drums on the top platform were connected though pipes to a sink outfitted with a water-preserving faucet on the lowest platform. Primitive

2.2 The Energy Pavilion, Berkeley, California, c. 1973.
Courtesy of Jim Campe.

solar collectors used electromagnetic energy to heat water for cooking and washing. The pavilion included a small greenhouse made of plastic and PVC pipe, in which peas and lettuce grew in beds of compost. A small windmill generated energy to run a food mill that ground grains into flour. Human and plant solid waste were collected in a compost privy and the pavilion featured a urine collection system. While only superficially inhabitable, the Energy Pavilion was essentially the freestanding service core of an ecologically sustainable and autonomous home. The assemblage of technological machines performed as building systems that mediated between natural resources and the fundamental processes of the human body—temperature regulation, nutrient input, and waste matter output. The realization of the Energy Pavilion, even more so than the Whole Systems Design diagram, made explicit the increasingly dominant role of technology in contemporary ecological thought.

Throughout the twentieth century, political and intellectual tension between the modernist faith in technology, and the anti-modernist idealization of a utopian wilderness, had created a divide in American environmentalism. By the 1970s, however, a number of environmentalists were determined to move beyond the long-standing dualism between nature and technology, and in doing so embraced a seemingly contradictory notion—that the desire to return to a simpler, prelapsarian time could be achieved through technological progress. This sentiment found expression in "appropriate technology." The Appropriate Technology Movement emerged in the early 1970s from critiques of large-scale industrial technology. Influenced by New Left thinkers, such as Herbert Marcuse and Murray Bookchin, and associated with E.F. Schumacher's 1973 book *Small is Beautiful*, the Appropriate Technology Movement reevaluated the relationship between nature and technology with an ecological sensibility that embraced alternative technologies.[27] The use of "appropriate" energy-saving technologies became a driving force in environmental advocacy and a foundational concept for architecture based on ecological design. Sim Van der Ryn would emerge as a key proponent of appropriate technology, eventually establishing an "Office of Appropriate Technology" in the State Architects Office of Governor Jerry Brown. According to Van der Ryn, writing in the *Natural Energy Design Handbook*:

> *There are technologies available to us other than the energy-intensive ones we are familiar with that can offer us different opportunities for personal and cultural growth. There are ways of living that can avoid the alienation and separation resultant from our own, while generating more positive work and learning. Happiness comes from generating energy rather than consuming it.*[28]

Van der Ryn's technological rhetoric, as well as the Whole System Design diagram and the Energy Pavilion, reveals that ecological design had fundamentally recast technology as *the* means through which the human body would interact with the environment in the future. Whole Systems Design had effectively positioned technology in the role previously occupied by architecture—the mediator between the body and the external environment.

It is worth noting that this epistemic shift in the conception of technology was at once rapid, profound, and wide-sweeping across many facets of American culture. In the decades following the Second World War, attitudes towards technology had been ambivalent. Despite the technology boom of the Cold War, the notion of a technological future had become indivisible from the horrors of the War and the rapid transformations of the post-industrial economy. The devastation caused by the use of the atomic bomb had inspired a growing segment of American society to recognize and question the environmental implications of modern technology and a number of influential and widely read books appeared warning of an apocalyptic future if the course of human technology remained unaltered. One of the most influential criticisms came in the form of Rachel Carson's *Silent Spring* (1962), which relayed in vivid detail the ecological consequences of humanity's attempt to control and regulate the environment through the use of pesticides. Carson's book became an international bestseller and is often credited with both launching the modern environmental era and establishing the use of scientific evidence to link human technologies with environmental destruction. The public intellectual and architectural critic Lewis Mumford would also take a stance on the "megamachine" of technology and later published his critiques in the two-part volume *The Myth of the Machine* (1970). A year after Mumford's publication, biologist Barry Commoner would publish the best-selling book *The Closing Circle* (1971), which detailed a series of historical case studies of how the technological choices made since the 1940s were largely responsible for the severity of the country's pollution problems. These, as well as several other examples, reflect the burgeoning literature on the future of industrial societies that emerged in the mid-century. The controversy surrounding publications such as *Silent Spring, The Myth of the Machine*, and *The Closing Circle*, as well as the extensive press coverage of ecological disasters such as the 1969 Santa Barbara oil spill and the 1971 Birmingham smog episode, drew public attention to the harm that technology was inflicting upon both "nature" and "humanity." The effect was not only the distrust of modern technology but also the perception of the modern environment as fragile, depleted, toxic, and therefore no longer able to sustain life. Rather than integrate with the current state of the environment, ecologists and architects increasingly believed that human beings should build their own autonomous ecosystems, away from the damaged environment. According to Van der Ryn,

> *All the evidence indicates that within the next generation we must design and live more in harmony with the earth's finite resources, or an exhausted, ravished and depleted earth will no longer support human life [. . .] we do not propose the autonomous dwelling unit as* the *solution for* the *future, but rather as a unique laboratory to study and become aware of the pattern of energy use, its inputs and outputs.*[29]

THE INTEGRAL URBAN HOUSE

In October of 1974, Sim Van der Ryn, architect Jim Campe, and biologists Bill and Helga Olkowski launched the "Integral Urban House" project. Collectively, under the umbrella of the newly formed Farallones Institute, they purchased a dilapidated Victorian home in the economically depressed neighborhood of West Berkeley. Intended as both a "laboratory for sustainable living" and a "demonstration house," the original dwelling and surrounding site was redesigned to encompass food production, waste recycling, and independent energy generation (Figures 2.3 and 2.4). Surprisingly, the majority of

2.3 The Integral Urban House, Berkeley, California, c. 1974–84. Courtesy of Jim Campe.

the "new technologies" were found outside, rather than within, the house. Instead of using the front lawn of the house as an ornamental green surface, it was planted with fruit trees and edible plants to feed inhabitants. Rather than lay a conventional asphalt driveway, woodchips collected and processed from trees on the site created an innocuous ground surface. Methods for integrating energy-producing technologies within the home were demonstrated, such as solar collectors on south-facing external walls and windows adapted to absorb solar heat during the day and radiate it back into the house at night. Based on the exposure to sunlight, the backyard of the house was planted with an extensive garden, populated with cages for rabbits and chickens, beehives, as well as a pond stocked with fish—all of which transformed sunlight, rain, insects and garden waste into nutrients that the occupants could consume. Within the home a gray-water recycling system was installed, and composting toilets performed human waste recycling in order to create a closed feedback loop. The Integral Urban House re-conceived the architecture and building systems of the home based on its ability to hybridize with environmental technology and transform ecological resources into energy for the purpose of its human residents. The project was in many ways indebted to the previous era of space travel, both in ideology and material resources.

A number of scholars have drawn explicit connections between the architecture of the US aerospace program, in particular the design of the spacesuit and space capsule, and ecological architecture of the 1970s.[30] According to historian Peder Anker,

2.4 The Integral Urban House. Berkeley, California, c. 1974–84. Courtesy of Jim Campe.

"[l]iving in harmony with Earth's ecosystem became, for the majority of ecological designers, a question of adopting space technologies, analytical tools, and ways of living."[31] Van der Ryn would further make explicit the ideological connections between Whole Systems Design and the aerospace industry in the following statement drawn from his book *Design for Life*:

> *Whole Systems Design [. . .] calls for not just designing buildings but designing the essential life support components that go with them: energy, food production and nutrient recycling, water supply and reuse, and human waste disposal and recycling. The US space program was involved in a similar endeavor [. . .] The scientists and designers were figuring out how to design and integrate systems providing breathable air, energy, food, water, and human waste disposal for astronauts.*[32]

In addition to supplying the model for the autonomous ecosystem, many of the technological innovations that enabled this closed system were repurposed from the declining aerospace industry. By the late 1960s, many corporations that supplied aerospace technology to NASA began to diversify and adapt their products for a civilian consumer market. As a result, a number of module housing units, energy recirculation technology, and waste disposal units were repurposed from aerospace equipment to ecological domestic technology.[33] One such company, Grumman Corporation, who manufactured these domestic technologies under the label "Grumman's Integrated Household System," supplied many of the components for the Integral Urban House's "life-support" technologies. Despite their reverence for "nature" and the earth's environment, ecological designers imagined the future of human settlement in "bounded" or closed ecosystems, not dependent on the earth's fragile environment, but an autonomous, engineered ecology in which scientists would reproduce food systems, complete with plants and animals, capable of supplying humanity with all the necessary resources for survival. They would evoke the image and technology of life in outer space as a model for this new ecology on Earth, suggesting, "We can use the astronaut as our instructor: he too is pursuing the same quest. His aspiration is survival."[34]

In addition to its role as a laboratory, the Integral Urban House also fulfilled an important didactic function as a demonstration project. The house included an exhibition space complete with displays and educational material intended to instruct visitors on the science and design of ecological housing. It offered public classes on topics such as solar energy systems, habitat design, urban food stock raising, aquaculture, and beekeeping. Teacher training programs, environmental education seminars, and professional consultation were also offered to people seeking guidance on how to modify their own homes in the logic of Whole Systems Design (Figure 2.5). In spreading the gospel of ecological design the Integral Urban House contributed to the redirection of collective action for social justice towards individual choices to further the environmental cause.

In 1971, Keep America Beautiful would launch the iconic "Crying Indian" campaign featuring the slogan, "People start pollution. People can stop it." The 1970s marked the beginning of a new focus on the impact of the individual and his/her actions on the environment. While the social movements of the 1960s had proclaimed that

2.5 The Integral Urban House. Berkeley, California, c. 1974–84. Courtesy of Jim Campe.

individual freedom, above all else, was necessary to achieve a better world, the new environmentalism was fundamentally at odds with this form of liberalism. The environmental movement maintained that, in addition to mass technology and centralized bureaucracies, individual freedom and choices were the cause of much environmental harm. Therefore, individuals, as well as institutions, needed to restrict their activities and "police" their daily lives to ensure a sustainable world. The perception of environmentalism as a type of "lifestyle critique" influenced many people to modify their homes and the manner in which they lived, the sources of their food, their mode of transportation, and their approach to personal health. Communal living, the "Back-to-the Land" movement, vegetarianism, organic gardening, recycling, and alternative medicines, as a means of environmentalism, integrated seamlessly with the themes of autonomy and "Do-It-Yourself" that the Integral Urban House promoted.[35] The message immediately found a devoted audience in the same "techno-ecological" individuals that looked to the influential *Whole Earth Catalog* for guides to "self-sufficient" living and "everyday environmentalism."[36] The notion of the "whole" which appears in the title of both Whole Systems Design and *Whole Earth Catalog*, presupposed not only a privileged point of view and expansive global perspective, but also an enclosed, autonomous, and self-sufficient system that reflected the ideology of both endeavors.

The Integral Urban House experiment lasted ten years. Thousands of interested and curious visitors toured the site and partook in workshops and demonstrations on sustainable urban living. A series of University of California, Berkeley students lived in the house as interns and residents, both operating the "system," observing how it worked, and evaluating its successes and failures. Much of the information they collected was published in the 1975 book *The City People's Book of Raising*

Food and the 1979 work, *The Integral Urban House: Self-Reliant Living in the City*. The project was also featured in numerous publications, including newspapers around the country. While the ultimate goal of the Farallones Institute was to expand the Integral Urban House and eventually create the "Integral Urban Neighborhood," the project remained a unique demonstration home and the notion of Whole System Design was never widely adopted.

Like the cybernetic metaphor of the closed system, able to be abstracted and reduced to measurable elements, the epistemology of Whole Systems Design was predicated on an artificial exclusion of social conditions and political economy. As the downturn in land prices reversed in the early 1980s, the once-derelict and marginalized neighborhood around the Integral Urban House began to rapidly gentrify, attracting new homeowners, many of whom strongly objected to the project. The smell from human waste composting, and the numerous animals housed on the site, as well as the many flies the system attracted, caused frequent problems with these new neighbors. In addition, Whole Systems Design had failed to account for the many hours of human labor, in this case supplied by unpaid Berkeley architecture students, needed to construct and run the system. As Van der Ryn left Berkeley for other endeavors, such as a position in Governor Jerry Brown's office, he was no longer able to attract students willing to volunteer at the House and maintain the "self-regulating" system. These dynamic contingencies, unaccounted for in the closed-loop ecology system, ultimately destabilized and disrupted the home's predicted performance as an ecosystem in equilibrium. While the building that encapsulated the Integral Urban House experiment still stands on its original site, it no longer functions as a model for ecological urban living, and has since been converted back to a conventional residential home.

In the decades since the 1970s, ecological design has resulted in predominantly conventional architecture, built in ways that better conserve energy, but still within existing social and cultural conventions. As a whole, contemporary sustainable architecture is a significant departure from the ambitions of Whole System Design, which attempted to fundamentally alter the relationship between nature, technology, and the body by employing a cybernetic view of ecology. Underlying Whole Systems Design's systemization of architecture with environmental technologies was the idea that we are profoundly not "at home" in our environment. In response, the architectural impulse to fashion space and create shelter was redirected toward the creation of mediated, bounded, and technologically engineered zones, designed to intervene between the body and the "hostile" world—be that world toxic, authoritarian, violent, or comprised of unusable forms of energy and abundant waste. The resulting "bio-architecture" relied on technological objects, the networking of organic and inorganic bodies, and a complex systems-based notion of ecology. While relegated to the fringes of architectural culture, Whole Systems Design marks a time when the relationship between environmental ecology and biological human survival enlivened the notion of architecture as a potential "life-support system," inspiring many architects to suggest new ways of inhabiting the planet. And yet, the "closed" ecology of Whole Systems Design failed to account for the social, cultural, and material contexts within which these systems were embedded. Ironically, while the rhetoric and epistemology of Whole Systems Design promoted individualism, self-reliance, and autonomy, it required the regulation and control of daily habits, personal routines, and ultimately one's relationship to society at large, in order to maintain its bounded ecosystem.

NOTES

1 Richard Nixon: "Annual Message to the Congress on the State of the Union," January 22, 1970. Online by Gerhard Peters and John T. Woolley, *The American Presidency Project*, at http://www.presidency.ucsb.edu/ws/?pid=2921.

2 When viewed in detail the shift in focus from social justice to environmentalism was due to a myriad of causes, including the assassination of political leaders, the military failures of the Vietnam War, the rise of a conservative backlash against the advances of civil rights, social justice, and feminism, the influx of hard drugs and violence into the counterculture, and the alienation of young Americans from the political process. Two of the best syntheses of the rise of the environmental movement in relation to the history of the decade are Adam Rome, "Give Earth A Chance: The Environmental Movement and the Sixties," *Journal of American History* 90, no. 2 (September 2003): 525–554; and Terry Anderson's *The Movement and the Sixties: Protest in America from Greensboro to Wounded Knee* (New York: Oxford University Press, 1995).

3 This account of People's Park is largely based on W.J. Rorabaugh, *Berkeley At War* (New York: Oxford University Press, 1989), Ch. 4.

4 According to historian Keith M. Woodhouse, "The event that, more than any other, sparked widespread discussion of ecology on the left was the fight for a small plot of dirt in Berkeley, California." Keith M. Woodhouse, "Environmentalism and Liberalism," *Journal for the Study of Radicalism* 2, no. 2 (2009): 70.

5 See ibid., 71.

6 In the days following the events of People's Park, over 2,000 people gathered on the campus of the University of California, Berkeley for an "Ecology and Politics in America" teach-in; the activist group "Ecology Action" held an ecology workshop and an "extinction fair" over the summer; the Eco-Liberation Front temporarily hijacked a meeting of the Bay Area Pollution Control District; and a coalition of "eco-minded" groups launched a campaign to grow trees on unused Bay Area Rapid Transit land. For more examples of the various environmental post-People's Park actions and events, see "Earth Read-Out," *The Fifth Estate* (June 12–25,1969): 10; "Eco-Tripping," *Berkeley Tribe* (1:9, September 5–12,1969): 7; "Extinction Fair—Dig?" *Berkeley Barb* (8:23, June 6–12,1969): 13; "Ecolibrium," *Berkeley Tribe* (2:5, February 6–13,1970): 13; and "Tree Conspiracy Spreads," *Berkeley Tribe* (2:2, January 16–23,1970): 7.

7 ". . . and but for the sky there are no fences facing . . .," *Berkeley Tribe* (2:10, March 13–20,1970): 13–16.

8 For example, during the 1966/67 semesters, Van der Ryn was the design studio leader for "Three Proposals for Innovative Correctional Facilities," under the newly created "Social and Cultural Factors" study area in architecture at the University of California, Berkeley.

9 See Sim Van der Ryn, *Architecture, Institutions, and Social Change* (Berkeley, CA: Library of Environmental Design, unpublished manuscript, 1968): 15; and Sim Van der Ryn, *Dorms*

at Berkeley: An Environmental Analysis (New York: Educational Facilities Laboratories, 1967).

10 In the summer of 1971, Sim Van der Ryn and Jim Campe led a studio course titled "Making a Place in the Country." Set in Marin County, California, the course attempted the construction of a commune premised upon ecological design principles.

11 Interestingly, many critics believe that the Environmental Movement derailed the radical revolutionary and cultural movements of the 1960s, shifting attention, manpower, and resources away from potential social reform. For example, see Woodhouse, "Environmentalism and Liberalism," 72.

12 *New York Times* (November 30, 1969): 1, 57.

13 "New Bag on Campus," *Newsweek* (December 22, 1969): 72.

14 The relationship between the growth of the modern environmental movement and suburban development, as early as the nineteenth century, has been analyzed by numerous scholars, in particular Adam Rome in *Bulldozer in the Countryside: Suburban Sprawl and the Rise of American Environmentalism* (New York: Cambridge University Press, 2001); and "Give Earth a Chance: The Environmental Movement and the Sixties," *The Journal of American History* (September 2003): 541; Dolores Hayden, *Building Suburbia: Green Fields and Urban Growth, 1820–2000* (New York: Pantheon, 2003); and more recently Christopher C. Sellers' *Crabgrass Crucible: Suburban Nature and the Rise of Environmentalism in Twentieth-Century America* (Chapel Hill, NC: University of North Carolina Press, 2012). Sellers' text is an important contribution to this discussion, arguing that the origin of the modern ecological movements lies in the "urban edge" nature found in the America suburbs.

15 For a discussion of the sentiment created in the suburbs towards the environment see Sellers' *Crabgrass Crucible*, 22, 27.

16 See Ian McHarg, *Design with Nature* (Garden City, NY: Doubleday,1969).

17 See Sim Van der Ryn interview with Jeffrey Inaban, "Convergence," *Volume Magazine 24: Counterculture* (2010): 31.

18 For more on the history of "social factors" and "human-centered design" curriculum at the University of California, Berkeley, see Clare Cooper Marcus, "Social Factors in Architecture, 1960–2004," in Waverly Lowell, Elizabeth Byrne, and Betsy Frederick-Rothwell, eds., *Design on the Edge: A Century of Teaching Architecture at the University of California, Berkeley, 1903–2003* (Berkeley, CA: University of California, Berkeley College of Environmental Design, 2009), 141–145.

19 Carl Anthony, Jim Campe, and Sim Van der Ryn, *The Natural Energy Design Handbook* (Berkeley, CA: University of California, Berkeley College of Environmental Design,1973), 17.

20 According to historian Simon Sadler, "Diagrams aren't simply supplementary evidence for the study of countercultural architecture; the buildings of counterculture, extant, extinct and un-built, were supplements to the diagrams." See Simon Sadler, "Diagrams of Countercultural Architecture," *Design and Culture* 4, no. 3 (2012): 347.

21 Richard Ingersoll, "The Ecology Questions and Architecture," in C. Greig Crysler, Stephen Cairns, and Hilde Heynen, eds., *The SAGE Handbook of Architectural Theory* (London: Sage, 2012): 573–590.

22 German natural Ernst Haeckel coined the word *Oekology* in the late nineteenth century by combining the Greek roots *oikos*, meaning household, and *logos*, meaning knowledge.

23 For a greater discussion of the impact of "energy" on ecology, also referred to as "bioenergetics," see Gregory Bateson, "Form, Substance, and Difference (1970)," in *Steps to an Ecology of Mind* (New York: Ballantine, 1972).

24 Jeffrey Inaban and Sim Van der Ryn, "Convergence," *Volume Magazine 24: Counterculture* (2010): 31.

25 Cybernetic theory is largely attributed to the work of Norbert Wiener and his book *Cybernetics or Control and Communication in the Animal and Machine* (New York: John Wiley, 1948).

26 According to Norbert Wiener, "the physical functioning of the living organism and the operation of some of the newer communications machines are precisely parallel in their analogous attempts to control entropy through feedback." See Norbert Weiner, *The Human Use of Human Beings: Cybernetics and Society* (Boston, MA: Houghton Mifflin, 1950), 26.

27 See Herbert Marcuse, "Some Social Implications of Modern Technology," in Douglas Kellner, ed., *Technology, War and Fascism* (London and New York: Routledge, 1998); and Murray Bookchin, *Post Scarcity Anarchism* (Berkeley, CA: Rampart, 1971).

28 Anthony et al., *The Natural Energy Design Handbook*, 62.

29 Ibid., 9.

30 For example, see Peder Anker, "The Closed World of Ecological Architecture," *The Journal of Architecture* 10, no. 5 (2005): 527–552; and Lydia Kallipoliti, "Feedback Man," in *Log*, no. 13/14 (Fall 2008): 115–118.

31 Anker, "The Closed World," 529.

32 Sim Van der Ryn, *Design for Life: The Architecture of Sim van der Ryn* (Layton, UT: Gibbs Smith, 2005), 44.

33 Lydia Kallipoliti, "Return to Earth: Feedback Houses," *Cornell Journal of Architecture* 8 (2011): 28.

34 McHarg, *Design with Nature*, 95.

35 This is not a new phenomenon; in the American 1930s, for example, there were numerous proposals for a decentralized society, a technology of smaller scale, organic gardening and farming, and personal health care that emphasized preventive medicine. See Ralph Boorsodi. *Flight from the City* (New York: Harper Brothers, 1933).

36 Developed in 1968 by Stewart Brand and founded in the San Francisco Bay Area, the *Whole Earth Catalog* promoted ecological consciousness and pragmatic, self-sufficient lifestyles. It also provided accessible articles on systems thinking, cybernetics, and appropriate technology by proponents such as Buckminster Fuller, Heinz von Foerster, Ludwig von Bertalanffy, and Norbert Wiener. See Andrew G. Kirk. *Counterculture Green: The Whole Earth Catalog and American Environmentalism* (Lawrence, KA: University of Kansas Press, 2007).

3

The Physiology of the House: Modern Architecture and the Science of Hygiene

Didem Ekici

Physician Max von Pettenkofer (1818–1901) designed a sprawling mechanism in 1862, which he named a "respiratory apparatus." Despite the implication of its name, this unique device was not a medical ventilator. It was composed of mainly two parts: a sheet iron chamber in the form of a cube with sides eight feet (2.40m) in length and a complex piping mechanism attached to the chamber (Figure 3.1). The chamber was austere, with a door and a window outside and a single bed, table, and chair inside. According to Pettenkofer, it provided the smallest space to comfortably house a human subject for a 24-hour period. By analyzing the contents of the air entering and exiting the chamber, Pettenkofer measured the exact amount of carbon dioxide and water vapor discharged by the subject while engaged in daily

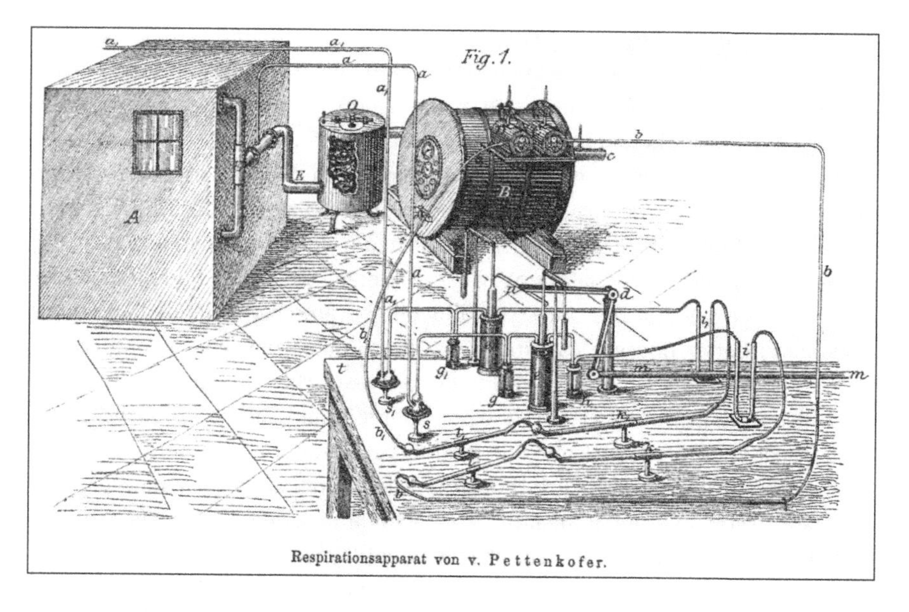

Respirationsapparat von v. Pettenkofer.

3.1 Respiratory apparatus by Max von Pettenkofer. Source: Theodor Weyl, ed., *Handbuch der Hygiene*, vol. 3 (Jena: Gustav Fischer, 1895).

activities.[1] His ultimate goal was to calculate the optimal air exchange required in a room for a person to remain healthy and comfortable.

Such experiments brought Pettenkofer international recognition and earned him a place in history as the founder of the science of hygiene. Pettenkofer and his followers proved that all the vague qualities of space could be substantiated by explicit data obtained via experimentation. His scientific method of mapping everyday environments formed the basis of modern hygiene and changed the ways everyday spaces were conceived, designed, and occupied. It was not only everyday spaces that underwent change; hygiene also transformed the way in which bodies were figured in a wide range of social practices and domains of knowledge. Medicine had for a long time treated bodies as if they were detached from their environment. Hygiene introduced the idea that bodies were inextricably bound up with their environment. By monitoring the exchange between the human body and built space, experimental hygiene rendered the inhabitant's relationship to architecture solely in physiological terms. A number of instruments externalized and expanded the physiological functions of the body in an effort to detail and regulate the body's exchange with its immediate environment whether it was in the form of air, water, or food intake or the disposal of carbon dioxide, sweat, urine, and feces. The young science of hygiene focused on the human dwelling in an effort to improve the sanitary conditions of everyday spaces. This study analyzes the transformation of the dwelling through the science of hygiene in the second half of the nineteenth century.

The emergence of hygiene as an international concern should be understood in relation to the public health movement in Germany. Starting in the 1830s and 1840s, a growing number of middle-class reformers in Germany, as well as in Britain, France, and the United States, raised public awareness of various health crises. Reformers were driven by a desire to eliminate not only recurring epidemics such as cholera but also any working-class political threat by improving living standards and work efficiency.[2] As the bourgeoisie gained authority and wealth, they employed more and more medical strategies to eliminate threats to their own safety and status, such as crime and social unrest. The health of the nation gradually became a national ideology as the state began to intervene in the issues of hygiene.

Doctors were prominent members of the educated middle classes due to the growing influence of medicine as a scientifically based profession. Together with other scientifically educated experts, they gained a significant role in prescribing social policies and individual lifestyles. Pettenkofer along with Rudolf Virschow, Professor of Hygiene at the University of Berlin, became highly influential figures demanding better housing conditions in cities. Doctors involved in the Lower-Rhenish Association for Public Health (Niederrheinischer Verein für öffentliche Gesundheitspflege, founded in Düsseldorf in 1869) and German Association for Public Health (Deutscher Verein für öffentliche Gesundheitspflege, founded in 1873 in Frankfurt) contributed to the large-scale sanitation and planning projects designed to improve public health.[3] Their agenda included all aspects of urban design, from sewers and water supplies to street layouts and the construction of healthy housing. Together with architects, engineers, and the members of municipal governments, doctors demanded stronger regulations for new urban development. Many doctors lectured and published books on the design of healthy houses and went even further by designing model houses.[4] Several societies involved in public health provided education through lectures, meetings, and journals.

Sanitary reform went hand-in-hand with the housing reform. The house was at the heart of the sanitation movement as hygienists declared "both the physical and moral health of a nation depended on its conditions of housing."[5] Housing reform efforts in Germany date back to 1840 report by Victor Aime Huber, Professor of Philology, on miserable living conditions among workers. By the early 1870s, a growing segment of the educated middle class believed in the need for reform.

Physicians involved in domestic sanitation reform established themselves as experts in sanitary design and regarded the architect's task to be confined to the aesthetic appearance of a building.[6] Munich-based physician Christian Ruepprecht opined, "If the architect is concerned about perfecting the external form of the building, the doctor specifies the health requirements for that building."[7] As the influence of physicians grew on urban policies and building regulations, architects likened themselves to physicians. In 1866, one observer claimed that the architect could rightfully be called the "dwelling doctor," because as the doctor healed the human body, the architect healed the sick dwelling.[8] In the following decades, the idea of the architect as the "dwelling doctor" became more widespread along with the belief that houses were sick; however, it was applied more generally to matters of taste. The architect was described in such terms in a 1921 article:

> *The true space and dwelling artist must be a physician in some respect. In artistic terms, there are technically and spatially diseased, infectious, toxic things, mentally infectious appliances and art objects that are likely to inhibit the healthy development of a generation. Warding off such pests from our homes, breaking their evil spell, that's the medical side of the high calling to* Wohnungs-Kunst *[the art of dwelling].*[9]

The architect would diagnose and treat the sick dwelling, much like a physician treating a patient. Not only architects, but other experts dealing with the housing question likened their methods to those of physicians reflecting the increasing medicalization of architecture. In his influential book *Handbuch des Wohnungswesens und der Wohnungsfrage* (Handbook of Housing and the Housing Question, 1909), economist Rudolf Eberstadt wrote that the science of the human body had its physiology and pathology and the physician should know about both the state of being healthy and sick. He continued, "The science of housing, just like medicine, had its physiology and pathology." For Eberstadt, the exploration of the normal state was the task of housing experts and the analysis of the sick state was the task of the experts dealing with the housing question.[10]

Mass printing allowed for the expansion of popular scientific literature and the inclusion of striking illustrations. Several books and manuals written by physicians aimed to educate building professionals, state and municipal officials, and the general public in the hygiene of the house.[11] Pettenkofer was arguably the most cited physician in such publications. He was born as the fifth child of a small farmer in Lichtenheim in 1818 and brought up in Munich by his childless uncle who was a court pharmacist. He acquired a degree in medicine in Munich in 1843 and served as a chemist at the Mint in 1845.[12] In 1848 when he was just twenty-nine years old, the King recommended him to be appointed Extraordinary Professor of Medical Chemistry at the University of Munich. He later shifted his interest from physiological chemistry to hygiene, then a new field. In 1865, three years after he designed his respiratory apparatus, Pettenkofer became the first university chair of hygiene to be appointed at a German university and, later in 1879, he established the first hygiene institute in Munich. Under his stimulus, the new science of hygiene developed rapidly as his students went on to teach at the newly founded institutes of hygiene at several European universities.

Epidemic diseases such as cholera and typhoid were causes of great concern at the time. In the 1860s and 1870s, Pettenkofer became the undisputed authority on epidemic prevention. He investigated the hygiene of the atmosphere, water, clothing, and housing in clinical studies. He quantified each aspect of everyday spaces via experiments. At which point does air in a room become vitiated? How much air volume does an individual require to maintain her health in a room? How much window surface is needed in proportion to the room size to receive enough natural light? Pettenkofer's clinical studies contributed to biostatistics, which became the prevalent means of analyzing the built environment in the hygiene movement.

In broader terms, the emergence of hygiene as a scientific discipline coincides with the rationalization of knowledge and its segmentation into disciplinary divisions from the late eighteenth century onwards. All sciences and arts were increasingly brought under numerological domination.[13] Statistics, which developed as a field of study in the second half of the eighteenth century, was increasingly used in the interpretation of demographic data as well as in medical sciences. Art historian Barbara Stafford has argued that the misuse of statistics in medical sciences fostered an oversimplification of such concepts as norm, type, ideal, and deviation while promoting a formulaic approach to the body, as if it were a quantifiable entity.[14] Similarly, Georges Teyssot has analyzed the reduction of the body to a measurable type in nineteenth-century criminology and ethnography. He has argued that such notions of type encouraged the statistical definition of the dwelling. In major cities like London and Paris, sanitation files of houses were created. The analysis of the house was reduced to "measurable data and to a diagrammatic scheme." This new scientific authority culminated in the idea of normalization and "a new semiotics of the house."[15] In broader terms, such views of the house were in line with the production of homogenous abstract space in modern industrial capitalism, which was defined by norms, productivity, and labor power.[16] Experimental hygiene's contribution to this new semiotics has been highly significant. While physicians meticulously measured bodies, hygienists measured dwellings to determine the optimal height and distance between each apartment, cubic air volume, window area, ceiling height in each room, and so on for the body to remain healthy. They converted their findings into statistical data to arrive at universal norms for the healthy house.

Hygiene's abstraction of the house is visible in the 1895 edition of the popular *Handbuch der Hygiene*, where the author explains that the analysis of the dwelling in hygiene is twofold: the first is the examination of the dwelling from an experimental, physiological, and pathological viewpoint to show how the poor state of building site and materials, dampness, the lack of light and air, and overcrowding are detrimental to health. The second is the mapping of the state of housing through mass surveillance; that is, through statistics.[17] Starting from 1861, regular surveys on housing conditions were undertaken in Berlin and other big German cities as part of the general population census. The inhabitants were asked various questions including whether they were owners or tenants, on which floor they lived, the total numbers of rooms, heated rooms, and rooms with windows, whether those faced the street or back, and whether there was a kitchen, water supply, bathroom, or toilet in their flats.[18] In more detailed surveys, physical descriptions of each dwelling were meticulously recorded. For example, an 1889 housing survey of Basel documented descriptions of each room in houses including function, location, width, height, window area, and the manner of ventilation and artificial lighting.[19] Medical archives of existing housing were formed through such ocular inspection and quantitative data. Using them as scientific evidence, hygienists pointed to an acute housing crisis in big cities caused by overcrowding and insanitary conditions. They demanded for more comprehensive sanitary and public health provisions to regulate new buildings.

Advice books and manuals on hygiene usually devoted a chapter to the dwelling.[20] In their analysis of the dwelling, physicians utilized data that ranged from statistical and empirical data to technical drawings and house diagrams. The house was systematically dissected, from its foundations to the roof. Starting with the building site, all elements of the house, including materials, walls, floors, individual rooms, and roof, were examined. Each spatial and structural component was discussed in terms of proper construction methods and materials.

When hygiene first emerged as a new science in the early nineteenth century, it was closely associated with physiology. Nineteenth-century scientific thought was dominated by physiology, which provided conceptual models for the laws of life and mind.[21] This pervasiveness of physiology originated in the Enlightenment, when, in Stafford's words, "the human body represented the ultimate visual compendium, the comprehensive method of methods, the organizing structure of structures."[22] Pettenkofer dubbed hygiene "applied physiology."[23] He wrote:

> *It is not only a matter of the physiology of the body; we now need—insofar as the extent of its health is influenced by it—a physiology of its environment. We need knowledge of the air, of the soil, of nourishment, of the house, of clothes, of the bed; we need a physiology which continues beyond the organism.*[24]

In other words, hygiene became the physiology of the everyday spaces the body occupied. Elsewhere, Pettenkofer described hygiene as a young science that emerged from physiology and pathology.[25] Physiology studied the reactions of the healthy organism to normal stimuli whereby the organism could adapt itself. When the stimuli exceeded the organism's adaptability, it displayed signs of disease, which then became the subject of pathology. Using the knowledge produced in both disciplines, the science of hygiene aimed to determine the optimal stimuli in an environment in exact figures for the organism to remain healthy. It quantified and rationalized the relationship between the body and everyday spaces according to health criteria.

It was not a coincidence then, at its inception in 1865, Pettenkofer's hygiene department was located in the Physiological Institute where he collaborated with a group of physiologists.[26] This close alliance between hygiene and physiology can also be seen in the journal Pettenkofer co-edited from 1865 to 1882, *Zeitschrift für Biologie*, which was partly devoted to hygiene and partly to physiology. By 1883, all German universities had hygiene departments. As hygiene gained more independent existence, Pettenkofer co-founded the *Archiv für Hygiene* in 1883 and co-edited it until 1894.[27]

As architectural historian Annmarie Adams has shown, the domestic sanitation movement regarded "the house as an extension of the body and the body as a reduction of the house."[28] Physicians applied the language and visual techniques of physiology to examine dwellings. Houses and bodies were represented in section diagrams in the popular press to show the overlapping circulatory systems.[29] Physiology succeeded in the division of the body into increasingly distinct and specific systems and networks. Similarly, house diagrams mimicking the body diagrams in physiology mapped the complex network of systems of ventilation, water circulation, heating, and drainage (Figure 3.2). The physiological systems of respiration, circulation, and digestion became models for the healthy circulation of air, water, heat, and expulsion of sewage in the dwelling. The house was increasingly mechanized as the circulation systems became more intricate. Jonathan Crary has observed that mechanical invention is not an independent dynamic that imposes itself onto a social field from the outside; on the contrary, it is always a subordinate part of other forces.[30] Many technological developments in the nineteenth century were modeled on the body.[31] By the end of the nineteenth century, scientific work attempted to increase the performance of the body by various mechanical devices. According to Tim Armstrong, modernity regards the body as lacking and offers technological compensation. Gradually, that compensation has been integrated into capitalism's fantasy of the complete body. Instruments of advertising, cosmetics, cosmetic surgery, and cinema are all prosthetic in the sense that they promise the perfection of the body.[32]

As early as 1877, German philosopher Ernst Kapp (1808–96) presented a philosophy of technology that examined a two-way analogous relationship between the body and mechanical instruments whereby tools became prosthetic mechanical extensions. Kapp remarked, "man unconsciously transfers the form, function, and normal proportions of his body to the works of his hands."[33] He dubbed this unconscious act as "organ-projection." While all technological artifacts imitated the form of human organs, Kapp claimed, at the same time the human body was increasingly understood in terms of mechanical instruments. To prove his point, he compared various inorganic artifacts with human parts and systems of the body. Tools such as the hook, bowl, plow, or shovel imitated the finger, hand, and arm, telegraph cables imitated the nervous system, and railroads imitated the vascular system.

Practitioners of the discipline of hygiene viewed the body and the house through such a two-way analogous relationship. Physicians came to understand the anatomical body as a mechanized house or a factory. They used the machine metaphor to describe the functioning of the body and purposeful interdependence of parts within the organism.[34] For example, in his 1887 book, *The Physiology and Hygiene of the House in Which We Live*, American physician Marcus Patten Hatfield likened the body's metabolism to the heating system, plumbing, water supply, and communication network in a house.[35] In Germany, such an analogy was still visible in the popular 1920s anatomy book *Das Leben der Menschen* (The Life of Humans, 1926–31). The author Fritz Kahn represented the functions of the human body as a factory. The mechanisms of breathing were illustrated in terms of a transport system in a modern factory composed of a complex network of pipes, with elevators carrying oxygen to the lungs, the blood, and organs.[36] Another illustration depicted the process of smelling as a mechanical process in a factory.

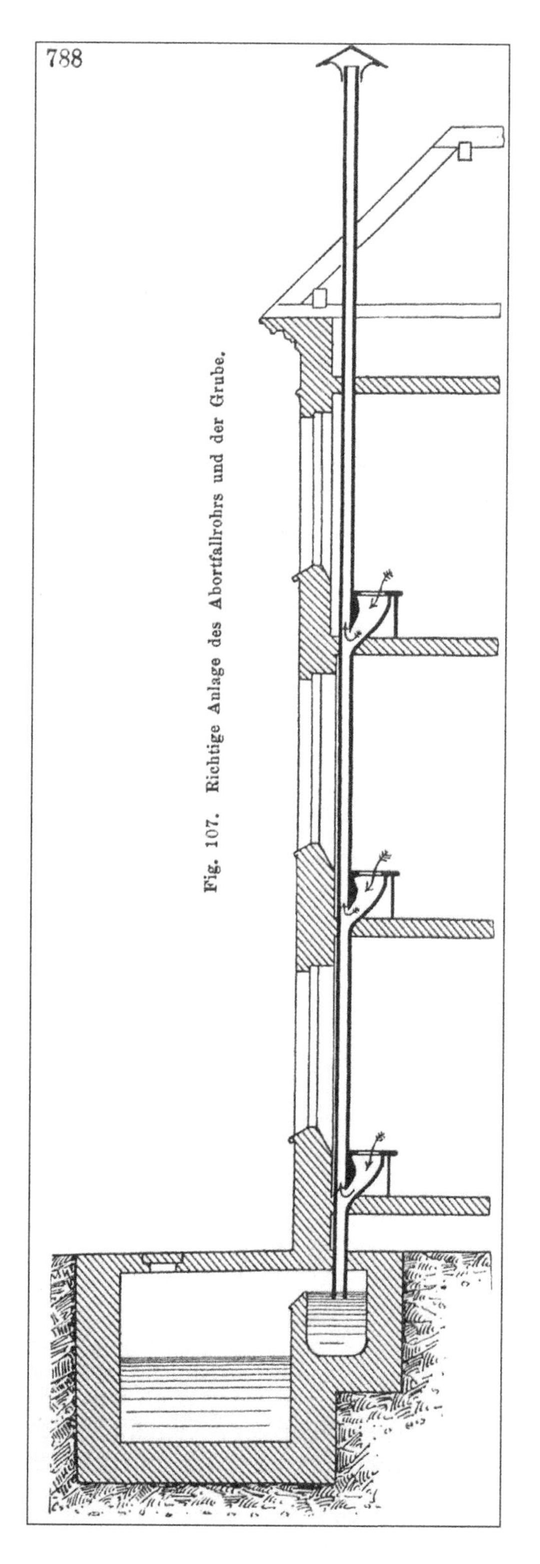

3.2 Drainage system in an apartment. Source: Christian Nussbaum, "Das Wohnhaus," in Theodor Weyl, ed., *Handbuch der Hygiene*, vol. 4 (Jena: Gustav Fischer, 1896).

Conversely, the more the house was mechanized to facilitate healthy circulation, the more it resembled the anatomical body. German architect Heinrich Muthesius depicted the modern house in 1904:

> *Houses now become veritable networks of pipes, supply-pipes and waste pipes, pipes of every kind, for hot water, heating, electric light, for the news service, so that they resemble complex organisms with arteries, veins and nerves like the human body.*[37]

The view of the building as a network of mechanical systems replaced the concept of architecture as an autonomous aesthetic practice with one that highlights infrastructure and performance.

Such a house taken over by mechanical equipment is visible in an advertisement titled "A Modern Country House" published in *Gartenstadt* in 1912 (Figure 3.3). A seemingly traditional rustic villa in a wooded area is sliced open in a detailed section perspective, allowing the reader to see how it is infiltrated by cables, pipes, ducts,

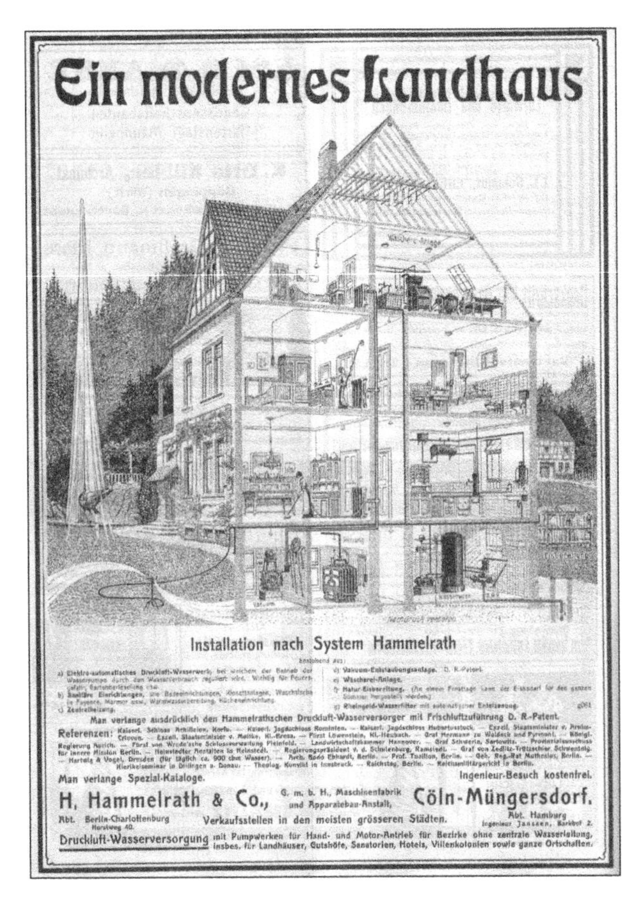

3.3 Advertisement titled "Modern Country House." Source: *Gartenstadt* (1912). Staatsbibliothek zu Berlin, Preußischer Kulturbesitz, shelf mark: 4" Fd 3494/26.

and various machines. The equipment advertised include electrical-automatic compressed-air waterworks, sanitary systems (bathroom, water closet, washstand, water heater, kitchen), central heating, central vacuum unit, laundry, natural ice maker, and water filter. The exposed cables, pipes, and machines dominate the house as the manifestations of the new domestic health regime.[38]

Physicians' perception of the dwelling highlighted its spatial envelope that facilitated exchange with its environment. The majority of the circulation that involved air, water, heat, and sewage was integrated into the envelope of the domestic spaces composed of foundations, floors, walls, ceilings, and roof. This concept of the house suggested the house was essentially a type of skin. The idea that the house was a form of skin in hygiene was first developed by Pettenkofer who viewed the functions of clothing and the house in a similar manner to the skin.[39] He argued that clothing and dwelling partially took over "the functions of the natural surface of the body." Hence their main purpose was physiological, "namely the regulation of heat flow from the body."[40]

The dwelling and clothing protected the body against atmospheric effects, including wind, rain, solar rays, and temperature changes. Heating and ventilation were regarded as the essential means of freeing the body from external environmental conditions.[41] They also regulated the indoor air quality, which emerged as an important health criterion in nineteenth-century theories of disease, such as the miasmatic theory.[42] Overcrowded rental blocks came under a sustained attack by hygienists and physicians.[43] They warned against breathing vitiated air in badly ventilated, overcrowded rooms as it caused drowsiness and headache. One of the earliest theories on the impact of indoor air quality on health was French chemist Antoine Lavoisier's 1777 study, which claimed that an excess of carbon dioxide from respiration in overcrowded rooms caused discomfort.[44] In the mid-1850s, Pettenkofer proposed a major shift in Lavoisier's theory. He argued:

> *What makes the air in a room filled with people unpleasant and oppressive, what affects our nerves and gives rise to symptoms such as fainting is not simply the heat or the humidity or the carbon dioxide or the depletion of oxygen . . . It seems to us obnoxious due to its having been breathed several times or as it has come into contact with the skin numerous times, as it is thus laden with organic exhalations, even in minute quantities.*[45]

While carbon dioxide did not directly cause specific diseases, it indicated other impurities that diminished the body's resistance against disease-producing agencies. Pettenkofer established the rule taught by physicians and hygienists till the turn of the twentieth century that the proportion of carbon dioxide in inhabited places affords a safe indication as to the amount of other impurities resulting from respiration and other exhalations from the bodies of the occupants.[46]

At the time, heat or cold could be reasonably measured with simple instruments, whereas the freshness or stuffiness of air could not be easily measured.[47] The challenge Pettenkofer faced was to assess the air quality in enclosed areas in numerical terms. His respiratory apparatus was an attempt to accurately measure the amount of carbon dioxide and water vapor discharged by a human being in the course of a day. Based on his study, Pettenkofer came up with a standard amount of ventilation required for an occupant to remain healthy in a room, which was sixty cubic meters in an hour.[48]

The requirement of consistent exchange with the atmosphere involved a rethinking of the spatial boundaries of the house. Hygiene manuals discussed natural and artificial methods of ventilation. Pettenkofer described natural ventilation as slow air exchange in an enclosed room without a draft. It occurred through walls, doors, and windows because of wind pressure and temperature difference between outside and inside. External walls presented a challenge in terms of natural ventilation; while they had to protect against heat and cold, they also had to provide constant access to fresh air. According to Pettenkofer, those two conflicting requirements were the greatest influence the house exerted on health.[49]

Pettenkofer advocated that external walls should be porous to facilitate fresh air access and to prevent humidity in the house. He did several experiments to test the porosity of various building materials. His ideas on porosity of walls were cited by many hygienists till they were scientifically discredited in the 1920s. Construction materials such as stone, brick, concrete, and granite were tested to compare their permeability rate.[50] Physicians argued that porous walls purified air to a certain degree by absorbing odors and humidity.[51] In the mid-1880s, the *Verein für öffentliche Gesundheitspflege* identified dampness in walls not only as an agent capable of fostering disease, but also as an impediment to ventilation by clogging the pores of brickwork or plaster with vapor.[52] Referring to a clothing metaphor, Pettenkofer warned that impermeable walls would create a climate in which one would experience discomfort similar to the experience of wearing a rubber suit all day long. Badly ventilated, overheated rooms caused the skin to be damp. Once outside the heated room, the skin immediately cooled down, preparing the bodily conditions for serious diseases.[53] In other words, the skin could breathe only if walls did.

Artificial methods of ventilation included ventilating fireplaces and diverse ventilation systems with ducts. One such system was the central heat-extraction system, which involved letting fresh air into each room through inlets and extracting foul air via ducts leading to a large central exhaust flue with a furnace at its base. Like ventilating fireplaces, it used suction fire to draw the foul interior air.[54] Other systems used extraction fans.

The spatial boundaries of the house remained under scrutiny in the 1880s and 1890s, as bacteriologist and physician Robert Koch's germ theory of disease came to dominate the sanitary discussion. Koch's theory regarded the presence of germs as a necessary condition for sickness.[55] With the new focus on germs, the germ-killing effects of sunlight came to the fore. "Light and air" became the motto of the sanitary reform. The house and its surroundings came to be seen as the locus of germs.[56] In an 1892 article titled "Breeding Places of Bacteria in Houses," the author views the house in this new light:

> *From the time man learnt that bacteria played an important role in nature and can turn into an endless, small but scary enemy of man, man has striven to trace the obscure life and activities of these uncanny, invisible guests. Until now, there is not much success in discovering the places germs live outside the human body. But we know that a contagion does not only occur from one person to another and that the germs survive outside the human body and sometimes breed. Where do they find haven from which they pose a constant threat to human beings? First, we must turn to the dwelling and its surroundings.*[57]

The surfaces of domestic spaces were brought under microscopic inspection to detect germs. House dust and infill materials found between floor slabs were seen as potential mediums where germs thrived. Bacteriologists analyzed samples of each to warn against the dangers lurking in them. Physicians claimed the infill materials could germinate pathogens leading to diseases as varied as typhus, cholera, and pneumonia. Purification processes and machines that sterilize the infill materials were developed (Figure 3.4). The standards of cleanliness in the house were altered to eliminate house dust. The vacuum cleaner emerged as an indispensable household item in the removal of dust (Figure 3.5).

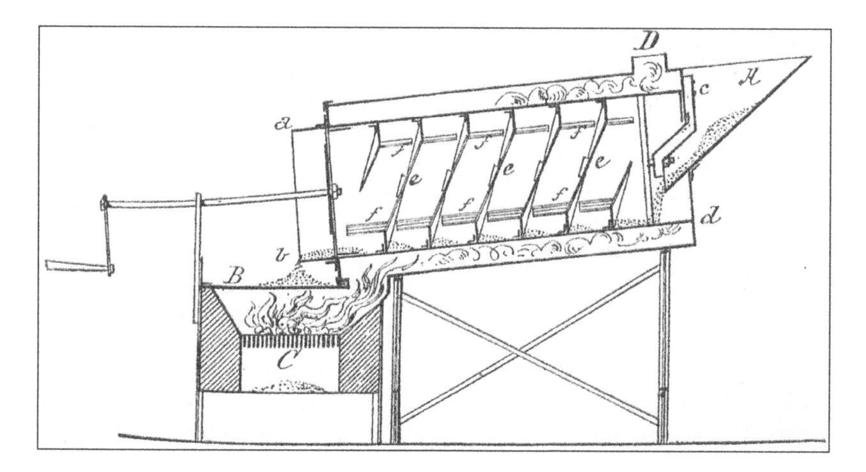

3.4 Oven for thermal disinfection of infill materials. Source: Rudolf Emmerich, "Die Wohnung," in *Handbuch der Hygiene und der Gewerbekrankheiten* (Leipzig: F.C.W. Vogel, 1894). Staatsbibliothek zu Berlin, Preußischer Kulturbesitz, shelf mark: 4" J 6347.

3.5 Advertisement for vacuum cleaner. Source: *Hygiene* 6, no. 3 (1913).

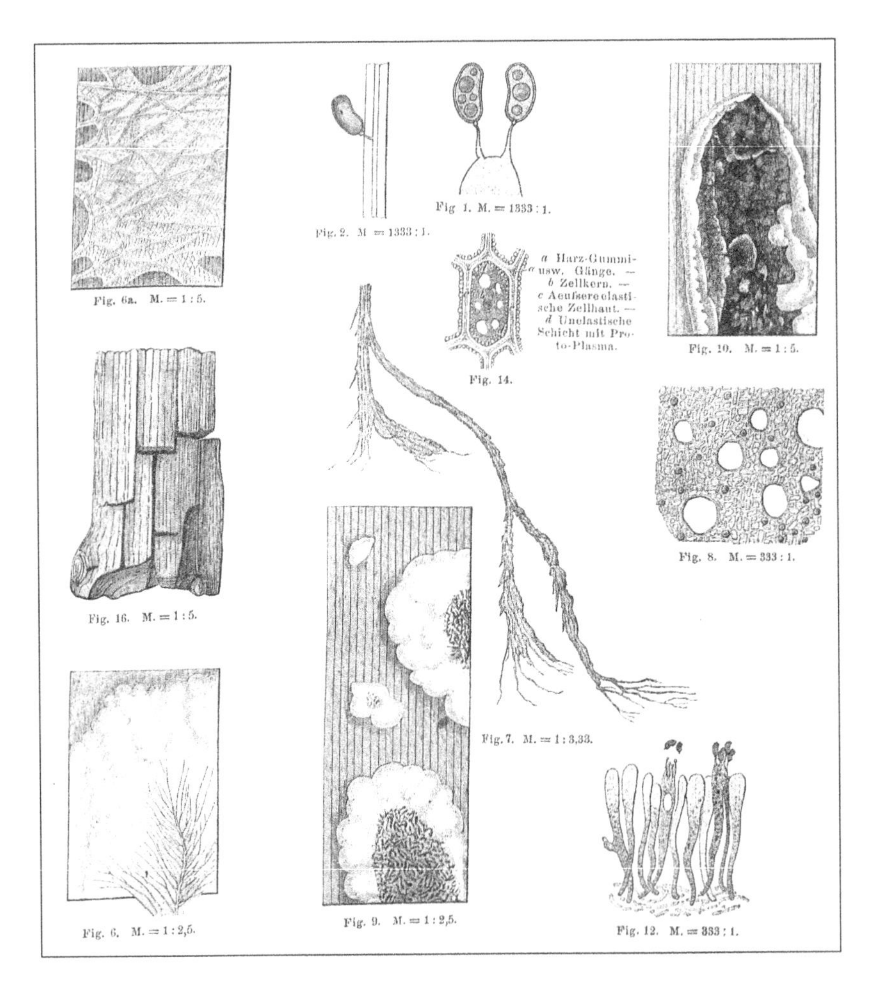

3.6 Microscopic images of dry rot. Source: Ueber den Hausschwamm (merulius lacrimans), *Deutsche Bauzeitung* 22, no. 14 (1888). Staatsbibliothek zu Berlin, Preußischer Kulturbesitz, shelf mark: 4" Ny 2724.

Bacteriologists inspecting spatial surfaces identified house diseases such as dry rot. They argued that dry rot was toxic and hence detrimental to health.[58] Wooden surfaces in humid houses were more susceptible to dry rot infection. Like contagious diseases, dry rot could spread either through workers moving from house to house or through reuse of infected wooden elements from older buildings.[59] Microscopic images of dry rot on domestic surfaces testified to the clinical inspection of the house (Figure 3.6). Although later experiments indicated that humans inhaling or consuming its spores were not infected, physicians continued to warn against it as a symptom of humidity in houses.[60]

Physicians stressed the importance of spatial segregation to prevent the spread of germs through air. Hence, they advocated ceilings and floors that did not transmit air and heat to abolish the danger of infection. "The worst evils of the floor decks in relation to the health of the house stem from their leakiness and the wrong selection of infill materials," wrote architect Hans Christian Nussbaum.[61] He had wooden floors in mind. In choosing infill materials, one had to take into account cleanliness, dryness, lightness, and fireproofing qualities. Washed and dried gravel and sand were regarded as good filling materials. The roof had to be insulated against rain and heat. An air gap between the roof and the attic apartment was recommended as a way of insulation. Similarly, foundations and basement floors had to be technically better insulated against water and air as they were the most exposed to miasmas in the ground soil.[62] Well-insulated materials such as asphalt and cement were recommended for the basement floor so that poisonous air could not infiltrate the house.

Porous walls presented a dilemma in terms of the requirement for spatial segregation. In the 1880s and 1890s, several physicians undertook tests on whether walls

Zimmer-Desinfektion mit dem Apparat nach Lingner.

Einleitung von Ammoniakdämpfen.

3.7 Room disinfection devices. Source: G. Sobernheim, ed., *Sonderkatalog der Gruppe Desinfektion der International Hygiene-Ausstellung* (Dresden, 1911). Staatsbibliothek zu Berlin, Preußischer Kulturbesitz, shelf mark: Kr 1960/104-2.

could be infected with bacteria present in the room dust. Some warned that porous walls were prone to infection with pathogen microorganisms. In suitable conditions, they could permeate deeper layers of walls and reach the air inside the room. Thus impermeable walls were recommended for hospital wards.[63] This argument was rejected in 1894 by bacteriologist Rudolf Emmerich who claimed that porous walls were less prone to infection than impermeable walls. He argued the latter was more likely to have water condensation, which resolved the nutrient in dust and made it easy for bacteria to grow.[64]

The idea that residential spaces could be infected culminated in the development of disinfection devices for residential use. At the 1911 International Hygiene Exhibition in Dresden, a special section was reserved to exhibit those new equipment. Such chemicals as ammoniac, formaldehyde, and steam were sprayed into the enclosed room. The spraying equipment could be deployed inside a room or through a keyhole from the outside (Figure 3.7). The air and surfaces of the room were purified.

In the upcoming decades, the obsession with light, air, and cleanliness became the defining features of modernist architecture. The science of hygiene played a significant role in the medicalization of architecture. Physicians blurred the boundaries between the body and dwelling, turning the latter into a corporeal extension that enhanced the physiological functions of the body. This reduction of architecture to the basic metabolic functions of the body persisted throughout the twentieth century. The twentieth-century avant-garde continued to pursue the concept of architecture as a permeable membrane and well-tempered space.[65] As the house became more open and more mechanized, architectural critic Reyner Banham declared in the title of his 1965 article "A Home is not a House," that it had become "little more than a service core set in infinite space."[66] Ultimately, the performance of the house in terms of physical comfort and health came to be its overriding function.

NOTES

This research has been funded by fellowships from the Wellcome Trust and DAAD (The German Academic Exchange).

1 Max von Pettenkofer, "Über einen neuen Respirations-Apparat," *Abhandlungen der Mathemat-Physikalischen Classe der Königlich Bayerischen Akdamie der Wissenschaften* 9, no. 2 (1862).

2 Eike Reichardt, *Health, "Race" and Empire: Popular-Scientific Spectacles and National Identity in Imperial Germany, 1871–1914* (lulu.com, 2008), 55.

3 Brian Ladd, *Urban Planning and Civic Order in Germany, 1860–1914* (Cambridge, MA: Harvard University Press, 1990), 38–76.

4 See, for example, David Sarason, *Das Freilufthaus: Ein neues Bausystem für Krankenanstaltenund Wohngebäude* (Munich: J.F. Lehmanns Verlag, 1913).

5 Prof. Dr. C. Franeken, "Vorwort," in *Weyl's Handbuch der Hygiene: Bau und Wohnungshygiene* (Leipzig: Verlag von Johann Ambrosius Barth, 1914), iii.

6 Annmarie Adams has examined the similar role Victorian physicians played in the domestic sanitation movement. As physicians gained authority during the final decades of the nineteenth century as designers of a healthy domestic environment, the public became increasingly wary of building professionals. Physicians promoted a systematic and scientific view of the house whereas the role of architects was perceived to be limited to form and decoration of houses. See Annmarie Adams, *Architecture in the Family Way: Doctors, Houses and Women, 1870–1900* (Montreal: McGill-Queens University Press, 1996), 36–72.

7 Dr. Christian Rueprecht, *Mensch und seine Wohnung in ihrer Wechselbeziehung* (Munich: Theodor Ackermann, 1885), 3–4.

8 A. v. Cohausen, "Kasernen-Abtritte," *Archiv für die Offiziere der Königlich Preußischen Artillerie und Ingenieur-Korps* 60 (1866): 245.

9 Kuno Graf von Hardenberg, "Wohnungs-und Raumkünstler," *Architektur und Wohnform* 32 (1921).

10 Rudolf Eberstadt, *Handbuch des Wohnungswesens und der Wohnungsfrage* (Jena: G. Fischer, 1910), 1.

11 Those include Jozsef von Fodor's *Das gesunde Haus und die gesunde Wohnung* (1878), relevant sections in Max von Pettenkofer and Hugo Wilhelm von Ziemssen's *Handbuch der Hygiene* (1882–1910), Carl Flügge's *Grundriss der* Hygiene (1889), Theodor Weyl's *Handbuch der Hygiene* (1882–1910), and later Rudolf Abel's *Handbuch der praktischen Hygiene* (1913).

12 During his time at the Mint, he came into the limelight through a series of discoveries. He developed a method to separate gold and silver, which was seen as an important discovery. King Ludwig I commissioned him to rediscover the production process of the mysterious haematinum of ancient times: Pettenkofer provided the experimental proof that it was in fact a copper-colored glass. On Pettenkofer's life, see Alfred Beyer, *Max von Pettenkofer* (Verlag Volk und Gesundheit, 1956); H. Breyer, *Max von Pettenkofer: Arzt im Vorfeld der Krankheit* (S. Hirzel, 1981); Martin Weyer-von Schoultz, *Max von Pettenkofer (1818–1901): die Entstehung der modernen Hygiene aus den empirischen Studien menschlicher Lebensgrundlagen* (Frankfurt am Main: Lang, 2006); Karl Wieninger, *Max von Pettenkofer: Das Leben eines Wohltäters* (Munich: Hugendubel, 1987).

13 Barbara M. Stafford, *Body Criticism: Imaging the Unseen in Enlightenment Art and Medicine* (Cambridge, MA: MIT Press, 1991), 107.

14 Ibid.

15 Georges Teyssot, "Norm and Type: Variations on a Theme," in Alessandra Ponte and Antoine Picon, eds., *Architecture and the Sciences: Exchanging Metaphors* (New York: Princeton Architectural Press, 2003), 156.

16 See "The Production of Abstract Space," in Mary Poovey, *Making a Social Body: British Cultural Formation, 1830–1864* (Chicago, IL and London: University of Chicago Press, 1995), 25–54.

17 A. Oldendorff, "Einfluss der Wohnung auf die Gesundheit," in Theodor Weyl , ed., *Handbuch der Hygiene* (Jena: Gustav Fischer, 1895).

18 H. Albrecht, "Wohnungsstatistik und Wohnungsenquete," in Theodor Weyl, ed., *Handbuch der Hygiene: Allgemeine Bau und Wohnungshygiene* (Jena: Gustav Fischer, 1895), 13–16.

19 Ibid., 17–19.

20 Carl Flügge's chapter on the dwelling in *Grundriss der Hygiene* (1889) is symptomatic of the physicians' approach to the topic. He was a German bacteriologist and hygienist who was a prolific contributor to publications on hygiene. The book's first section deals with urban design policy recommendations on reserving open spaces for each housing site, pulling buildings back from the street, regulating minimum distances between each building, limiting the height of buildings, and orientation of streets to allow balanced sun exposure for each side of a building. He then zooms in on the individual house.

21 Bruce Haley, *The Healthy Body and Victorian Culture* (Cambridge, MA and London: Harvard University Press, 1978), 69.

22 Stafford, *Body Criticism*, 12.

23 Pettenkofer, "Über die Mittel zur Förderung der Theorie und Praxis der öffentlichen Gesundheitspflege," *Zeitschrift für Biologie* 7 (1871): 503.

24 Pettenkofer cited in Klaus Bergdolt, *Wellbeing: A Cultural History of Healthy Living* (Cambridge: Polity Press, 2008), 280.

25 Pettenkofer, "Was ist und was will 'Gesundheitslehre?'" *Die Gartenlaube* 20 (1878): 328.

26 Pettenkofer had been working in the laboratories in the Physiological Institute since 1855, when he became a full professor. See Henry E. Sigerist, "Introduction to the Value of Health to a City," *Bulletin of the History of Medicine* 10 (1941): 478.

27 Ibid., 479.

28 Adams, *Architecture in the Family Way*, 3.

29 Victorian Thomas Teale's illustrated book, *Dangers to Public Health: A Pictorial Guide* (1879) is the most well-known example of this genre. Ibid., 64–65.

30 Jonathan Crary, *Techniques of the Observer: On Vision and Modernity in the Nineteenth Century* (Cambridge, MA and London: MIT Press, 1990).

31 For an excellent account of the body's relationship to technology, see Tim Armstrong, *Modernism, Technology, and the Body: A Cultural Study* (Cambridge and New York: Cambridge University Press, 1998), 81.

32 Ibid., 3.

33 Ernst Kapp, *Grundlinien einer Philosophie der Technik: zur Entstehungsgeschichte der Cultur aus neuen Gesichtspunkten* (Brunswick: George Westermann, 1877), v–vi.

34 At the first international hygiene exhibition in Dresden in 1911, the core of the exhibition was the popular division titled *Der Mensch* (The Human), which showed functions of human organs to foster an understanding of man as "both a work of art and a complex machine." See *Katalog der Internationalen Hygieneausstellung Dresden* (Berlin, 1911), 375–400. Quoted in Michael Hau, *The Cult of Health and Beauty in Germany* (Chicago, IL: Univeristy of Chicago Press), 108. In his study of the human sciences, *The Order of Things* (1970), Foucault argued that the body under the clinical gaze of doctors becomes an anatomical machine, an object of knowledge. See Michel Foucault, *The Order of Things: An Archaeology of the Human Sciences* (London: Tavistock, 1970).

35 Hatfield wrote: "The body in this book has been likened, in its various parts, to a house, and it may be truthfully claimed that no other of man's dwellings has as many 'modern conveniences' as his body. There is nothing that his ingenuity has yet devised for the safety and comfort of his home that he may not find foreshadowed, and usually bettered in the body. Where, for instance, can you find an automatic steam of hot-water heater that will perform its work as well as the thermogenetic system of the body?

Where can the block or building be found that is as well sewered and ventilated?" Furthermore, he finds in this house of ours elevators, telegraphs and telephones innumerable, also pictures, photographs, library and music-rooms, and a dining room from twenty to thirty feet long." See Marcus Patten Hatfield, *The Physiology and Hygiene of the House in Which We Live* (New York: Chautauqua Press, 1887), 3.

36 Fritz Kahn, *Das Leben des Menschen: eine volkstümliche Anatomie, Biologie, Physiologie und Entwicklungsgeschichte des Menschen*, vol. 3 (Stuttgart: Franckh'sche Verlagshandlung, 1927), plate 12.

37 Hermann Muthesius, *The English House*, ed. Dennis Sharp, trans. Janet Seligman (New York: Rizzoli, 1979), 163.

38 Didem Ekici, "From Rikli's Light-and-air Hut to Tessenow's Patenthaus: Körperkultur and the Modern Dwelling in Germany, 1890-1914," *Journal of Architecture* 13, no. 4 (2008): 388–90.

39 See Didem Ekici, "Skin, Clothing, and Dwelling: Max von Pettenkofer, the Science of Hygiene and Breathing Walls" in *Journal of the Society of Architectural Historians* 75, no.3 (September 2016).

40 Pettenkofer, "Über die Funktion der Kleider," *Zeitschrift für Biologie* 1 (1865): 180.

41 Hermann Fischer, "Heizung und Lüftung der Räume," in Josef Durm et al., eds., *Handbuch der Architektur* (Darmstadt: Arnold Bergstraesser, 1890), 91.

42 The miasmatic theory, which Pettenkofer called the ground-water theory, was the most dominant theory of disease at the time. He advocated that the germs of disease were spread through vapors in air coming out of contaminated soil. Depending on its moisture content, the contaminated soil could germinate epidemic diseases such as cholera and typhus. The disease, then, was transmitted through polluted air.

43 The common belief was that urban masses became uprooted in rental blocks, which led to their physical as well as moral degeneration. Building one's own house rather than living in rental apartments was promoted in popular literature in hygiene. For example, in 1903, under a heading "Is it advisable to build one's own house?" architect Georg Uster discussed the benefits of living in one's own house: "One builds for himself, for his family and frees himself from miseries and tutelage of others." See Louise Holle, ed., *Im deutschen Hause* (Hanau: Fr. Königs Verlagsbuchhandlung, 1903), 5.

44 On Lavoisier's theory, see David Hansen, *Indoor Air Quality Issues* (New York: Taylor & Francis, 1999), 4–5.

45 Pettenkofer, "Über einen neuen Respirations-Apparat," 234.

46 John S. Billings, David H. Bergey, and Silas W. Mitchell, *The Composition of Expired Air and Its Effects upon Animal Life* (Washington, DC: Smithsonian Institution, 1895), 3–4; Hermann Schülke, *Gesunde Wohnungen* (Berlin: J. Springer, 1880), 99.

47 Reyner Banham, *The Architecture of the Well-Tempered Environment* (Chicago, IL: University of Chicago Press, 1984), 40–41.

48 Pettenkofer, "Über einen neuen Respirations-Apparat," 236.

49 Pettenkofer, *Über den Werth der Gesundheit für eine Stadt* (Brunswick: Friedrich Vieweg und Sohn, 1973), 35.

50 See, for example, Adolf Wolpert, *Theorie und Praxis der Ventilation und Heizung* (Leipzig: Baumgaertners Buchhandlung, 1887), 331.

51 Rudolf Emmerich, "Die Wohnung," in Max von Pettenkofer and H. v. Ziemssen, eds., *Handbuch der Hygiene und der Gewerbekrankheiten* (Leipzig: F.C.W. Vogel, 1894), 127.

52 Nicholas Bullock and James Read, *The Movement for Housing Reform in Germany and France, 1840–1914* (Cambridge and New York: Cambridge University Press, 1985), 97.

53 Maximilian Bresgen, *Klima, Witterung und Wohnung, Kleidung und Körperpflege in ihren Beziehungen zu den Entzündungen der Luftwege* (Halle an der Saale: Carl Marhold, 1900), 25, 30.

54 August Gärtner, *Leitfaden der Hygiene* (Berlin: S. Karger, 1892), 162–167.

55 Koch built his work largely on research by Louis Pasteur. Koch's research on the bacterium that causes anthrax was very successful; he became one of the founding fathers of the new science of microbiology. On Koch and germ theory, see Thomas D. Brock, *Robert Koch: A Life in Medicine and Bacteriology* (New York: Springer, 1988); Ruth E. Simpson, "The Germ Culture: Metaphor, Modernity, and Epidemic," PhD thesis, State University of New Jersey, 2006.

56 The belief that the house was potentially dangerous was also shared by Victorians. Adams has shown that, contrary to the common belief that the home symbolized a safe haven to Victorians, middle-class houses were actually considered poisonous, hence in need of intense medical scrutiny. See Adams, *Architecture in the Family Way*, 36–72.

57 "Brutstättender Bakterien im Haus," in *Wiener Illustrierter Zeitung* 2564, August 20, 1892.

58 See, for example, Emmerich, "Die Wohnung," 122.

59 F. Hueppe, "Bakteriologie und Biologie der Wohnung," in Theodor Weyl, ed., *Handbuch der Hygiene: Allgemeine Bau- und Wohnungshygiene* (Jena: Gustav Fischer, 1895), 928.

60 Dr. Emil Gotschlich, "Die hygienische Bedeuting des Hausschwammes," *Zeitschrift fuer Hygiene und Infektionskrankheiten* 20 (1895): 509–511.

61 Hans Christian Nussbaum, "Hygienische Forderungen an die Zwischendecken der Wohnhauser," *Archiv für Hygiene* 5 (1886): 265.

62 Moritz Alsberg, *Die gesunde Wohnung* (Berlin: C. Habel, 1882), 9. The ideal building site should have soil that was porous, dry, and not polluted. Removing waste from urban areas by sewerage systems became a priority in sanitary reform.

63 Emmerich, "Die Wohnung," 122.

64 Ibid., 126.

65 Laurent Stalder, "Air, Light, and Air-Conditioning," *Grey Room*, no. 40 (2010).

66 Reyner Banham, "A Home is Not a House," *Architectural Design*, no. 1 (1969): 47.

4

Material Heliotechnics: A Tale of Two Bodies

John Stanislav Sadar

At the beginning of the twentieth century, disease was the primary fear in urban centers. Tuberculosis and rickets mysteriously savaged the populations of cities, particularly the young and the elderly. Disease enfeebled both the military and economic might of the British Empire. During the Boer War, 40 percent of British draftees were deemed unfit to serve. At the outbreak of the First World War, the situation was much the same with over a third deemed unfit to serve. Although the microbial agent responsible for tuberculosis had been known since the latter nineteenth century, little was available in the way of treatment, other than to prescribe bedrest and let nature take its course. The cause of rickets, on the other hand, remained a mystery until 1919, when Edward Mellanby identified it as a vitamin D deficiency. Casimir Funk had coined the term *vitamines*, or *vital amines*, in researching beri-beri in 1912. In 1927, Otto Rosenheim and Thomas Webster found that the body produced vitamin D when exposed to sunlight. In parallel, Nobel laureate Niels Finsen made the startling discovery that tuberculosis could be treated by nothing more than plentiful sunlight.

Sunlight, Finsen found, was a natural disinfectant, which could destroy disease-causing microbial agents and stimulate biological processes. The polluted atmospheres of industrial cities robbed citizens of healthy sunlight. Dark interiors were contradictory to a healthy and productive citizenry. Finsen's understanding of the sun as a force of vitality spread rapidly, and by the 1920s maximizing bodily exposure to the sun was seen as having medicinal and social value; the suntan became emblematic of a healthy life. An array of lobby groups coalesced around the joint cause of better health and greater access to sunlight in cities and buildings, and broadcast their calls for action widely.

Given the context of health and disease and the awareness of sunlight's remedial value, it is perhaps little surprise that attention turned to the window. The problem was that windows effectively blocked the very aspect of sunlight that was effective in curing disease: the ultraviolet spectrum. In the late nineteenth century, Erik Johan Widmark discovered that ultraviolet radiation caused the skin to redden. Building on that, Niels Finsen found that ultraviolet similarly destroyed microbes, and thus that ultraviolet was a crucial ally in the battle against disease. Yet, to ultraviolet light, glass was opaque. Just making windows larger would not suffice in bringing sunlight's health-bringing power indoors; the composition and quality of the window glass itself was now a health issue. By the 1920s, the link between health, sunlight, ultraviolet, and glass had become explicit.

Thus, in the mid-1920s, British glass giants Pilkington Bros. and Chance Bros. came to cooperate on a project which sought to instrumentalize sunlight to eradicate disease and bring health to indoor life. In 1914, while studying protective eyewear for glassworkers, William Crookes found iron impurities in glass effectively absorbed ultraviolet radiation. In response, glass chemist Francis Everard Lamplough, who had been head of glass technology at Chance Bros., developed a low-iron glass, which would transmit ultraviolet where ordinary glass did not. Anticipating a large demand for Lamplough's invention, in an unprecedented move, Chance and Pilkington both licensed the glass, and entered into an agreement to co-develop it. With the materials science of "Vita" Glass, Pilkington and Chance sought to compress a generation's hopes for a healthy future into a pane of window glass. Embedded in the heliotechnics of their "Vita" Glass, one finds two seemingly opposed understandings of the body: a passive body, in need of external management, and an active body, continually adjusting its relationship to the world.

HELIOTHERAPY AND THE BENEFICENT SUN

In the aftermath of the death and destruction wrought by the First World War and the Influenza Pandemic, and with tuberculosis and rickets mysteriously claiming and debilitating the youth of the day, concern about health reached a crescendo. In the wake of bacteriology, sunlight's ultraviolet spectrum became a genuine health tonic. Sunlight caused bacteria to die, bodies to tan, and biochemistry to produce vitamin D.

This was an about-face from the latter nineteenth century, when sunlight was viewed with suspicion. While the sun and air had been observed for their therapeutic properties in antiquity, as embodied in Greek and Roman asclepeia and sun baths, they had since been forgotten by medicine. Although health reformers sought a close connection to beneficial air, water, and light, even in the mid-nineteenth century sunlight was widely understood as harmful and damaging to the skin. Because sunlight caused moisture in marshlands to evaporate and miasmatists understood foul odors emanating from swamps as a source of disease, they surmised the sun to be harmful.[1] At the same time, Victorian health reformers like Florence Nightingale deemed naturism offensive to their values of social modesty and restraint.

At the turn of the century, however, bacteriology reignited a reverence for the natural world.[2] In the late nineteenth century, Robert Koch and Louis Pasteur had determined that disease was the result not of noxious odors, but of the actions of invisible, microbial organisms.[3] Their findings brought new hope that these newly identified microbes could be combatted, and disease could be eradicated with the right agents. One approach was to look for targeted chemical therapies. While these would eventually appear in the guides of sulfa drugs and antibiotics, their slow development opened the door for other treatments. For Niels Finsen, sunlight's ultraviolet spectrum was an active germicidal agent, which he sought to instrumentalize to cure illness and bring health. He standardized the application and dosage of ultraviolet light, and defined physiological units of solar exposure, so as to render the sun as a sophisticated and precise therapeutic tool.

Finsen and his followers, such as Axel Reyn and Ove Strandberg of the Finsen Institute, and Nobel Prize nominees Oskar Bernhard and Auguste Rollier, presented the natural world as actively curative.[4] Prior to their treatments, the dominant way of treating tuberculosis involved little more than the palliative therapy of bedrest whilst waiting to let nature take its course—or *therapeutic nihilism*. After Pasteur found that mountain air contained fewer microbes than urban air and Finsen found ultraviolet radiation to be germicidal, Rollier put these together into a notion that the environment itself could cure an ailing society. The medicalization of the environment by Finsen and Rollier transformed the stasis of bedrest into the activity of a body stimulated by a fluctuating environment. At his Swiss Alpine health resort, Rollier developed a heliotherapy regime combining physical exercise, dietary nutrition, fresh air, and ample sunlight, which proved remarkably successful in curing tuberculosis and rickets.[5] Rollier's heliotherapy influenced the tuberculosis sanatorium, which embraced his ethos of active, outdoor living in the sunlight and fresh air. The flat roof became a therapeutic provision for reclining in the germicidal sun. Together, the sunporch and flat roof became hallmarks of sanatoria. Word of Rollier's extraordinary success in treating disease with sunlight spread. As it did, he became an icon of health to those outside the profession. His proposition gained currency in the popular press, making his Alpine heliotherapy clinic an emblem of the scientific value of sunlight. Soon, patients flocked to his Leysin clinic, seeking to rid themselves of disease by harnessing the power of the sun. Rollier's notoriety catalyzed the development of sanatoria, open-air schools, and health resorts, shaped new values in city planning, and spurred the formation of lobby groups.

One such lobby group, the People's League of Health, founded by British actress Olga Nethersole in 1917, took a holistic approach to health, which encompassed environment, nutrition and heredity. To address the widespread health problems and poor living conditions among the working class, the League lobbied for improved living conditions, and emphasized the need for sanitation and housing reform, and improved nutrition. The League's environmental concerns attracted the attention of sunlight advocates like Caleb Saleeby, heliotherapist Henry Gauvain, and physiologist Leonard Hill, who gave many presentations to the League on the nutritional and germicidal benefits of sunshine.[6]

The New Health Society, founded by surgeon William Arbuthnot-Lane, succeeded the People's League of Health in 1925 to become the nexus of health and body issues. For the New Health Society disease was a preventable product of urban civilization and hence an unnecessary expense for the community to bear. Thus, its journal, *New Health*, focused on preventing disease through improved nutrition and hygiene, loose clothing, and fresh air and sunlight.[7] To find an escape from the filthy, dark and damp working conditions of the nineteenth century in favor of a more hygienic and humane society, the Society reached back to the late nineteenth century ideal of a *simple life*, to promote a *back-to-nature* regimen of open-air living, pure food, and outdoor activities, from hiking to suntanning to swimming as a modern way of life. At the same time, the Society championed those products of modern science and technology, which it saw as remedial, from breakfast cereal to artificial sun lamps.[8]

The Sunlight League was an offshoot of the New Health Society, founded by Caleb Saleeby in 1924. Given the state of interest in sunlight's role in promoting health, the Sunlight League advocated improving the quality of urban life by bringing sunlight into the city. The League promoted a renewed relationship to the outdoors, increased sunlight exposure in cities, changing social values to accept less restrictive clothing, and adopting new lighting technologies. Through the pages of its journal, *Sunlight*, the League lobbied the government on the hazards of the atmospheric pollution of coal-burning and the benefits of clean electricity, and campaigned for suntanning and open-air living and schooling.[9]

TRANSMITTING HEALTH THROUGH GLASS ARCHITECTURE

In the 1910s, architect Bruno Taut and writer Paul Scheerbart saw glass as a preventive measure, which held the potential to cure society of all its ills. In the early twentieth century, glass was becoming the ideal material for architects seeking to give expression to a new society. To overcome the pollution, darkness, poor living conditions, and disease of the nineteenth century, architects sought transparency, lightness, airiness, greenery, and hygiene by using new industrial materials. Metaphorically, glass conveyed the idea of banishing darkness and shadow in favor of rational illumination, shedding new light on old modes of thought. They sought to embody scientific rationality and the products of technology in projects and buildings at a variety of scales, from pavilions to entire cities. Joseph Paxton's Crystal Palace of 1851 emerged as a model for such a new approach to architecture.[10] Taking inspiration from the biology of the water lily, Paxton minimized the Crystal Palace's structure to enable a minimal buffer with the outdoors. The glass itself was of the thinnest possible sheets, and was oriented for maximum daylight penetration. This biological approach further influenced the relationship of parts to the whole, which systematically accounted for exhibitors, construction, material performance, and the Hyde Park locale. Together, for architects in the early twentieth century, these approaches enabled new opportunities for architectural expression.

By the mid-1920s, glass was firmly entrenched as a material of a new architecture, which would be remedial for mind and body and both house and enable a new society. In his writings, Paul Scheerbart saw the evanescent materiality of the Crystal Palace as not only a new opportunity for expression, but also a vehicle for social change, which would illuminate both body and spirit, and foster cultural enlightenment.[11] He imagined a crystalline architecture of double-skinned walls and multi-colored filters, which offered both physical comfort and mental stimulation to reset society on a new course. With its prismatic and multi-colored glass walls, Bruno Taut's Glass Pavilion for the 1914 Deutscher Werkbund exhibition was a direct manifestation of Scheerbart's ideas. In Taut's book, *Alpine Architecture* of 1919, he proposed crystalline shards of glass architecture rising from the Alps, which would transform thought and offer social redemption. After the First World War, glass sparked not only speculative and utopian projects for skyscrapers by Ludwig Mies van der Rohe and Le Corbusier, but also realized buildings by Walter Gropius; Johannes Duiker and Bernard Bijvoet; Johannes Brinkmann, Leendert Cornelis van der Vlugt and Mart Stam; Pierre Chareau; Owen Williams; and Berthold Lubetkin. The degree to which glass surface became central to the architectural efforts of the late 1920s and early 1930s was further reflected in the appearance of technical articles and books which attempted to offer technical explanations and showcase architectural examples, such as Arthur Korn's *Glas im Bau und als Gebrauchsgegenstand* in 1929 and Raymond McGrath's *Glass in Architecture and Decoration* in 1937.[12]

Yet, unfortunately—as Niels Finsen found—glass filtered sunlight of its health-giving, bactericidal properties. Thus, for those like physiologist Leonard Hill, indoor daylight and outdoor daylight were vastly different things from a physiological perspective. That Britons spent so much of their lives indoors directly contributed to the general malaise of the population. Thus, attention turned to the window, and the problem of remediating its ultraviolet opacity. In response, Hill encouraged glass technologist Francis Everard Lamplough to develop a glass that would enable ultraviolet-rich light to penetrate interiors and thereby transform buildings into therapeutic instruments.

Although manipulating the properties of glass to increase its brilliance or change its color was a practice dating back to antiquity, glass chemistry had only emerged as a subject of scientific study at the end of the nineteenth century. Germans Otto Schott and Ernst Abbe systematically studied the effects of adding different substances to ordinary soda-lime glass, and became so versed as to be able to develop glass with particular performance criteria, such as withstanding thermal shock or controlling its refraction.[13] They presented their results of their glass chemistry investigations in the Schott und Genossen glass catalog of 1886. Into the twentieth century, glass became an increasingly malleable material, and its field of use expanded to encompass the laboratory, the kitchen, automobiles, and airplanes.[14]

Lamplough's development of "Vita" Glass's particular chemistry was contingent upon three important observations. First was Niels Finsen's 1896 finding that the ultraviolet component of sunlight was germicidal and hence therapeutic.[15] Until that time, while there was speculation on the relationship between blue light and germs, the mechanics were unknown.[16] Finsen's work served to make this connection explicit.[17] Secondly, Finsen built on the experiments of Erik Johan Widmark in 1889, in which Widmark had found ultraviolet radiation to be the responsible agent for the reddening of the skin, or erythema.[18] In his own experiments, Finsen found that ordinary soda-lime window glass impeded the transmission of bactericidal ultraviolet radiation.[19] Third, while researching glass for protecting the eyes of glassworkers from infrared, physicist Sir William Crookes identified iron as the element responsible for the ultraviolet opacity of glass. Using a spectrograph, he found that ferric iron (Fe_2O_3) absorbed ultraviolet radiation (while transmitting visible light), and that ferrous iron (FeO) transmitted it (while absorbing infrared).[20]

Following this logic, at the urging of Leonard Hill and the London Zoo, Lamplough was able to develop a glass of extremely low iron content, which enabled increased ultraviolet transparency, and economically transmitted the health rays of the sun.[21] Basic window glass chemistry comprises a forming agent (silica sand), a flux (soda), and a stabilizer (lime). Although iron is not a necessary part of any of these components, trace amounts enter into the mix through the tooling and through impurities in the sand and other components. Because ferrous iron readily oxidizes into ferric iron, Lamplough focused on not only reducing iron impurities in the former, flux, stabilizer, and tooling, but also on ensuring a reducing (rather than oxidizing) atmosphere in the factory. This enabled him to develop a glass of very low ferric oxide content. The care needed in the selection and handling of materials meant that while the glass was of high quality, it was also costly to produce. Yet, with its reduced iron content, both in quantity and chemistry, Lamplough's glass transmitted Finsen's therapeutic ultraviolet rays, where regular soda-lime glass did not (Figure 4.1).[22]

"VITA" GLASS

Lets in the Health Rays of Light

"Vita" Glass gives health in the natural way, and gives it all the daylight hours. The principal benefits of outdoor life, that doctors recommend, are provided for all workers and dwellers in buildings where "Vita" Glass is fitted.

"Vita" Glass lets in the vitamin rays, those invisible, ultra-violet rays with which nature floods the daylight out-of-doors, but of which ordinary window glass says: "they shall not pass."

"Vita" Glass looks like ordinary window glass, but is as different from it as a diamond is different from sparkling paste.

"Vita" Glass does not need sunshine to render its contribution to health. The ultra-violet rays, which make outdoors the source of natural health, are present in all direct light.

"Vita" Glass allows the passage of these vitamin rays through north windows just as certainly as it does through east, west, and south windows.

"Vita" Glass in the windows of a building actively helps those who work or dwell within to keep well.

"Vita" Glass stimulates healthy growth, increases both red and white corpuscles, and makes the mind more active. It even gives the skin the tanned health of outdoor life.

Write to the "Vita" Glass Marketing Board about "Vita" Glass for a nursery window or an entire building.

"VITA" GLASS MARKETING BOARD,
5, Aldwych House, London, W.C.2.

health through your windows

"VITA" is the registered trade mark of Pilkington Brothers Ltd., St. Helens

4.1 "Vita" Glass advertisement. Source: *The Times*, April 16, 1928. Permissions courtesy Pilkington Group Ltd.

Lamplough's "Vita" Glass had the potential to transform windows at a time of grave concerns around the relationship between the body, buildings, and the sun. Sensing the potential of "Vita" Glass to saturate building interiors with ultraviolet light and infuse them with health, Lamplough approached his former employer, Chance Bros., to license his invention. After signing an agreement with Lamplough, Chance Bros. saw the potential for "Vita" Glass to claim the entire window glass market and saw their own limited manufacturing capacity as lacking in this regard. In turn, Chance Bros. took the unusual step of entering into an agreement with their much larger rival, Pilkington Bros., to jointly manufacture and market "Vita" Glass. By 1928, Pilkington had become the sole European producer of "Vita" Glass and was distributing it worldwide, from Britain to Canada to South Africa to Australia to Argentina.

ULTRAVIOLET HEALTH GLASS AND THE DREAM OF THE ARTIFICIAL CLIMATE

Taut and Scheerbart saw in glass the potential to transform society and cure it of its ailments, whether individual or social, physical or mental. In response, the ultraviolet transmission of low-iron "Vita" Glass embedded the strident medical heliotechnics of Rollier and Bernhard into material performance. In the place of Alpine resorts, "Vita" Glass would offer the promise of urban, interior spaces that freely admitted the health-giving rays of the sun. By crystallizing the Alpine atmosphere sought by Taut and Scheerbart in their materials science, Pilkington and Chance sought to create an interior atmosphere that was *nearer to nature*.

For those cases where the sun could not penetrate the urban atmosphere, Niels Finsen devised phototherapy—a means of reproducing the sun's curative power indoors with carbon arc lamps. Carbon arc lamps emitted ultraviolet-rich radiation that replicated—and even outperformed—the germicidal rays of open-air health clinics. Phototherapy became sought after, not only by clinics and hospitals but by homeowners seeking the best preventive and therapeutic health measures. Finsen's technology rendered the effects of the germicidal rays of Alpine and Mediterranean health clinics portable, making them attainable in polluted, sun-deprived, northerly cities.

Matthew Luckiesh was a leading authority and writer on the technics of electric lighting, visual perception, optics, and ultraviolet radiation. In his role as the director of General Electric's Lighting Research Laboratory from 1924 to 1949, he developed lamps, lighting specifications, and even tools for measuring ultraviolet radiation and the bacterial content of air. Following the connections made between light and health by Niels Finsen, Oskar Bernhard, Auguste Rollier, Edward Mellanby, Otto Rosenheim, and Thomas Webster, Luckiesh realized lighting could no longer merely overcome darkness, but needed to provide the biological impulse of sunlight. As Luckiesh noted, daylight was the ideal condition for engaging in all of life's activities, as its effects extended beyond mere illumination to encompass light's perceptual, physical, and biological effects. In his 1945 pamphlet, *The Meaning and Magic of Windows*, Luckiesh presented his understanding of the window as a mediator between the building interior and the natural world. He saw the window as bringing "indoors some of the beneficence of the outdoors," and even improving on the natural world by selectively admitting light while repelling other environmental forces.[23] The window enabled solar energy and diurnal and seasonal cycles of life to permeate the indoors, where it would aid vision, stimulate physical development, or invigorate the imagination. It made the interior practicable, endurable, and enjoyable, and enabled a "new era of luminosity."[24]

Daylight became the model for Luckiesh's ambition to develop "dual-purpose lighting" that would serve both vision and health. Luckiesh desired no less than *artificial sunlight*, artificial lighting that would meet or exceed the performance of the sun, bringing "the outdoors indoors," and "challenging the sun" in every respect.[25] While filament lamps had been used for illumination since the late nineteenth century, they did not produce therapeutic, ultraviolet wavelengths. Medical arc lamps, on the other hand, produced brilliant, ultraviolet-rich light to eradicate germs, but their color balance was nothing like the sun's. Thus, while arc lamps could disinfect a petri dish in one twentieth of the time that sunlight could, they were unsuited for illumination.[26] To achieve *artificial sunlight*, it was essential to replicate both sunlight's visual spectrum and its unseen "germicidal, biological, therapeutic, chemical and physical properties."[27] To that end, he designed lamps that hybridized the medical technology of arc lamps with typical, household tungsten filaments, which he housed in a "Vita" Glass bulb.[28]

With both lightbulbs and windows, glass was a paramount concern. If the ordinary glass used for their bulbs absorbed the germicidal and anti-rachitic rays, even the best sources for emitting ultraviolet radiation would be therapeutically useless. Medical phototherapy lamps used costly quartz in lieu of glass to transmit ultraviolet radiation. Yet quartz did not offer the visual performance or durability of glass. "Vita" Glass provided an option that offered the medical performance of quartz and the visual and economic performance of glass. The material qualities of "Vita" Glass enabled *artificial sunlight* apparatuses to enter the home. In Britain, Ajax Ltd produced *artificial sunlight* apparatuses for both clinical and home light therapy, which their advertising touted as offering an experience identical to the outdoors. In sun-starved British homes, Ajax imagined their light therapy devices would assume the role of the fireplace, with families gathering around them to absorb their healthy, ultraviolet light.

Efforts to replicate and domesticate natural phenomena by subjecting them to management and control were not limited to Luckiesh's *artificial sunlight*. In the United States, Willis Carrier sought to manufacture *artificial weather*. As with light, concerns about ventilation were motivated by concerns for disease: dark and poorly ventilated spaces brought tuberculosis. One solution was offered by the open-air living movement, which advocated outdoor hospitals and schools. At the beginning of the twentieth century, Carrier sought another approach. He combined the nineteenth-century inventions of the electric fan and mechanical refrigeration with air filtration and dehumidification to produce an air-conditioning system which promised a complete interior weather system distinct from the outdoors.[29] With *artificial weather*, Carrier sought to improve on the natural condition by producing air that technology had rendered clean, comfortable, and predictable—an idealized form of air.[30] The ideal interior climate became a set of attributes that could be scientifically measured, charted, and standardized, such as air freshness, in terms of carbon dioxide levels, relative humidity, temperature, and velocity. Indoors, measurements revealed that products of respiration (heat, carbon dioxide, and humidity) that would otherwise naturally dissipate into the atmosphere instead accumulated to concerning levels.[31] The technologies of Carrier's mechanical air-conditioning systems held the potential to restore the balance between the beneficial conditions provided by nature and the potentially dangerous byproducts of human habitation that afflicted indoor environments. By the 1920s, mechanical systems could cool and heat air, add or remove moisture content, and filter dust and bacteria, to provide interiors with air quality that was quantitatively better than the outdoors.[32] The adoption of such systems started with businesses, but by the 1930s, *artificial weather*, like *artificial sunlight*, was introducing full control of indoor heat and humidity levels to households in the United States.[33]

Together, Carrier's *artificial weather* and Luckiesh's *artificial sunlight* offered no less than a technological replication of environmental phenomena in the building interior, a complete *artificial climate*.[34] The technological management and climatic replication system of the artificial climate promised its occupants a building interior that was " nearer to nature," to use Luckiesh's words. For Luckiesh, such control over the forces of nature was central to making the technological world of the interior "possible, endurable, and enjoyable."[35] "Vita" Glass, like *artificial sunlight* and *artificial weather*, was part and parcel of this motivation to manage natural phenomena and direct them to magically act in our best interests.[36] It promised the possibility of transforming the built environment into one replete with germicidal and health-giving powers. It would offer the health advantages of the outdoors and the environmental control of the indoors; it would create an *artificial climate* that would surpass the climate outdoors.

PASSIVE BODIES

"Vita" Glass promised all the benefits of Rollier's heliotherapy with none of the inconvenience of living in a clinic. It offered the possibility of an ideal relationship with a beneficent sun in the less-than-ideal surroundings of northern, industrialized cities. It is little wonder that Hill, Peter Chalmers Mitchell of the London Zoo, Lamplough, Chance Bros., and Pilkington Bros. all envisioned the day when "Vita" Glass would be standard equipment in all homes, schools, clinics, and workplaces (Figure 4.2).

Yet, for all its promise, Chance Bros. and Pilkington Bros. faced a crucial problem when it came to actually selling "Vita" Glass: a market for it did not exist. This is a problem it shared with other technological innovations of the early twentieth century, such as vacuum cleaners and household antiseptics. Before "Vita" Glass could be sold, its market had to be created. Not only that but to the glass trade glass was *glass*, a commodity item that was simply used to make windows, rather than a proprietary, designed product which provided health benefits. To make these matters even worse, its materials science and biological effects were unseen. It could not rely on visibly spectacular effects, as with stained glass, to demonstrate its advantageous performance. It needed to find other ways, and to overcome its costliness.

To create the market, educate the trade, and evangelize the product, Chance Bros. and Pilkington Bros. took the unlikely step of forming a joint marketing agency. The

FACTORIES—OFFICES—SCHOOLS
HOTELS—HOSPITALS—CLUBS—HOMES

Wherever people are gathered indoors, there "VITA" Glass can deliver its vital health rays

The most modern building in the world shuts out the most important element to health—unless its windows are fitted with "Vita" Glass. The ultra-violet rays which flood the open air cannot penetrate ordinary window glass. Yet men must have ultra-violet rays if they are to be strong and healthy and do their work properly.

"Vita" Glass, the latest and one of the greatest triumphs of science, is so compounded as to allow the passage of the health, or ultra-violet, rays existent in the open air.

Until the production of "Vita" Glass, the only way that those who live and work indoors could obtain the vitamin essential to normal health and growth was through arduous diet and dosing with medicine. They obtained their vitamins, not as nature intended, but by indirect, artificial methods.

People have not so far realised that they sacrifice their health indoors needlessly. If they could *see* the health rays of light, they would realise how "black" or empty of health an ordinary building can be. No longer would they tolerate such an unnecessary state of affairs, and "Vita" Glass windows would bring new health and new happiness to those who live and toil indoors.

"Vita" Glass gives visible proof of its power by actually tanning the skin of those who live and work in buildings where it is installed.

Fix "Vita" Glass in your factory or office and increase the efficiency of your staff. "Vita" Glass in your home is health insurance.

Fullest information about "Vita" Glass for any purpose will be gladly and promptly supplied by the "VITA" GLASS MARKETING BOARD, 5 Aldwych House, London, W.C.2.

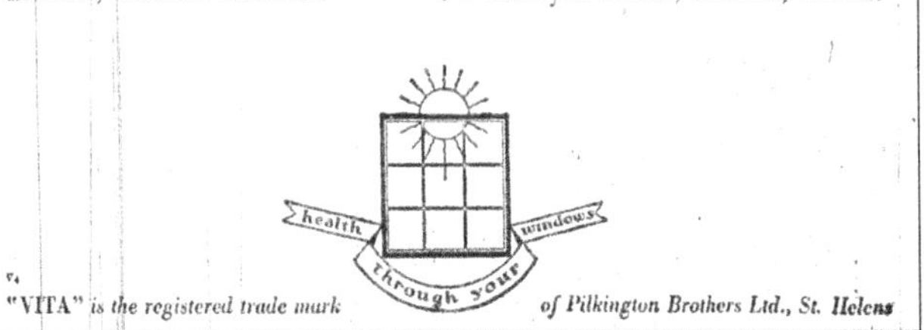

"VITA" *is the registered trade mark of Pilkington Brothers Ltd., St. Helens*

4.2 "Vita" Glass advertisement. Source: *The Times*, May 9, 1928. Permissions courtesy Pilkington Group Ltd.

independent "Vita" Glass Marketing Board was armed with a budget greater than the rest of the Pilkington Bros. marketing budget, and even larger than the Chance Bros. corporate office budget. The Board, in turn, enlisted the help of the innovative marketing firm Pritchard & Partners to help them sell the idea of health-giving glass to the profession, the trade, and the public. The Board was charged with the task of market creation, and to that end it liaised with Pritchard on market research and strategy, print advertising, and public demonstrations and exhibitions.[37] Together, Pritchard and the Board took the unlikely step of positioning "Vita" Glass not as *glass*, but as a means to health.

One approach taken by the "Vita" Glass Marketing Board was to make an appeal to the burgeoning interest and faith put in quantification, statistics, and efficiency.[38] The issue of efficiency was a matter of national concern across Europe and North America in the 1920s. On one hand, in the United States and the United Kingdom, the fall of domestic service marked the rise of the homemaking housewife. Rapidly developing medical science and the availability of labor-saving, domestic equipment (such as vacuum cleaners and dishwashers) for upper-class women engaging in housework provided one means of the ethos of efficiency to enter the mindset.[39] On the other hand, at a governmental level there was the issue of international competitiveness. In Britain, the government hoped that a program of National Efficiency would instill greater discipline and ingenuity, which would enable them to produce more with less effort and fewer materials.[40] This concern with greater efficiency would ultimately pervade all aspects of life in the 1920s and 1930s, from medical care to the management of people.

For the "Vita" Glass Marketing Board, statistics and quantification were key to the campaign to sell the idea of health-giving glass. To draw connections between glass and ultraviolet light, the Board's marketing materials used graphs which presented the ultraviolet transmission of "Vita" Glass in relation to ordinary glass, vision, and the biological effects of bactericide and skin erythema (Figure 4.3). The Board sponsored studies, such as the Smethwick tests in 1927 at the Crocketts Lane Council Schools. Placing one group of students in a classroom glazed with ordinary glass and another in a classroom glazed with "Vita" Glass windows revealed that the students in the "Vita" Glass-glazed classroom outperformed their counterparts in key indicators: they grew 50 percent more and gained more than double the weight while also increasing their blood hemoglobin and decreasing their absenteeism by equally radical amounts over the year-long experiment period.[41] Another year-long test at

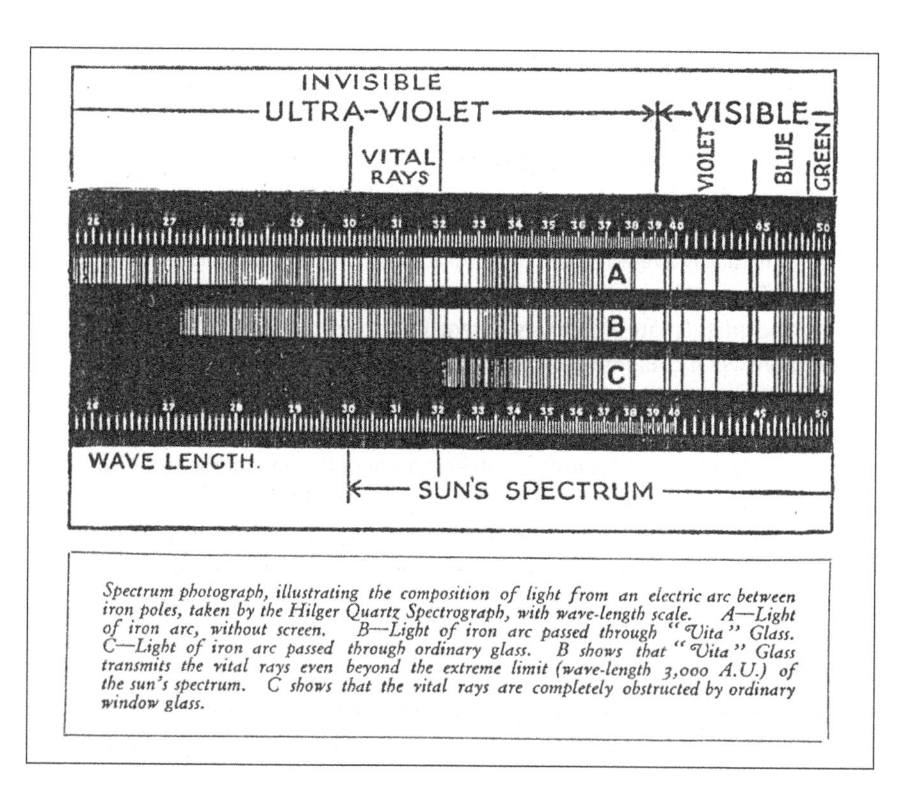

Spectrum photograph, illustrating the composition of light from an electric arc between iron poles, taken by the Hilger Quartz Spectrograph, with wave-length scale. A—Light of iron arc, without screen. B—Light of iron arc passed through "Vita" Glass. C—Light of iron arc passed through ordinary glass. B shows that "Vita" Glass transmits the vital rays even beyond the extreme limit (wave-length 3,000 A.U.) of the sun's spectrum. C shows that the vital rays are completely obstructed by ordinary window glass.

4.3 Comparisons of the spectrum transmitted by "Vita" Glass in relation to ordinary glass. Permissions courtesy Pilkington Group Ltd.

the Greet Green Infant School in West Bromwich found that the students in the "Vita" Glass-glazed classroom were not only taller and heavier, but also scored better on standardized intelligence tests than those in the classroom glazed with ordinary glass.[42] At still other installations, whether in New York or Northern Ireland, there were similar results, with students having fewer illnesses and less absenteeism.[43] This emphasis on quantitative indicators even extended to plants and animals, as zoologists and horticulturalists made similar claims of ideal coloration, size, and structure in the testimonials they wrote to the Board. The Sunlight League's Caleb Saleeby wrote of how produce in "Vita" Glass-clad glasshouses was a "deeper green," while the head keeper of monkeys at the London Zoo wrote of how disease amongst monkeys had decreased since moving into the new "Vita" Glass Experimental Monkey House.[44]

Whether in plants, animals, or children, the installation of "Vita" Glass brought more of the population into agreement with idealized hopes and expectations for them—with norms. The idea that there were normal values for physical traits like heights, weights, and blood counts had emerged over the course of the nineteenth century, starting with birth and death registration and infant mortality statistics, and continuing through the compiling of medical statistics—such as temperature, pulse, blood count, and blood sugar—into biochemical and anatomical norms.[45] French sociologist Émile Durkheim extended data collection and statistical analysis to the social realm by quantifying and developing norms for literacy, gender, crime, and schooling.[46] By the 1900s, even intelligence, behavior, and morality became quantifiable, measurable, and testable.[47] The nineteenth-century Belgian social physicist Adolphe Quetelet encapsulated this amassed data and statistics into the concept of an *average man*. This was a mathematical average of the collected data of social, moral, mental, and physical characteristics. So far as *normal* meant average, as it did to Durkheim, Quetelet's *average man* was the definition of normal. It was an index of society, but it also was an embodiment of the existing social order. Thus, to be normal became an aspirational ideal for all citizens.[48] By the 1920s, normal was the statistically average, or commonplace, and the commonplace was good.[49]

As sociologist Richard Stivers notes, the combination of measurement, data collection, and mathematical analysis meant that everything could be quantified.[50] Furthermore, what could be quantified could then be charted and rationalized. The statistical definition of normality also created its converse, abnormality, which might be either desirable or undesirable, and could be subject to control. Normality, in short, became a technical problem subject to scientific management by experts.[51] For builder Frank Gilbreth and engineer Frederick Winslow Taylor, the data-driven, scientific management of workers could lead to improved worker health and improved efficiency.[52] They dissected the actions of brick-laying into their components, seeking to economize the movements and time needed to complete a task. Taylor saw their approach as applicable to a wide variety of human affairs, and having the possibility of addressing the national efficiency problem in the United States. Taylor's scientific management became the foundation for theorist Thorstein Veblen's call for *technocrats*—engineers and scientists—to assume a leading role in governing in his 1921 text, *The Engineers and the Price System*.[53] Veblen's call was answered by the emergence of technocratic political groups in both the United States and the United

Kingdom.[54] The Technical Alliance and Technocracy, Inc. in the United States, and Political and Economic Planning (PEP) in the United Kingdom sought to subject the whole of government to "scientific national management," optimizing energy, labor, and time to improve efficiency to a predetermined goal.[55]

Far from having marginal appeal, the technocratic interests of deriving norms and managing deficiencies characterized the 1920s and 1930s. Scientific management and technocracy assumed a wide cultural presence, making conditions ripe for technical products that promised to remediate society of its ills, such as "Vita" Glass. That Fleetwood Pritchard, principal of Pritchard & Partners, was a founding member of PEP is equally telling of the degree to which the ideal of expert technocratic solutions was embedded in the "Vita" Glass project. Agriculture and child development shared fundamental concerns of normal health, growth, and development. Thus, educators, health professionals, horticulturalists, and zoologists all charted normal performance, whether in terms of the health of patients or animals, or the yield of produce. It was thus only natural that its marketing campaigns used data gleaned from scientific testing to appeal to experts (Figure 4.4). For Pritchard, the "Vita" Glass Marketing Board, Chance Bros., Pilkington Bros., and even Lamplough himself, the

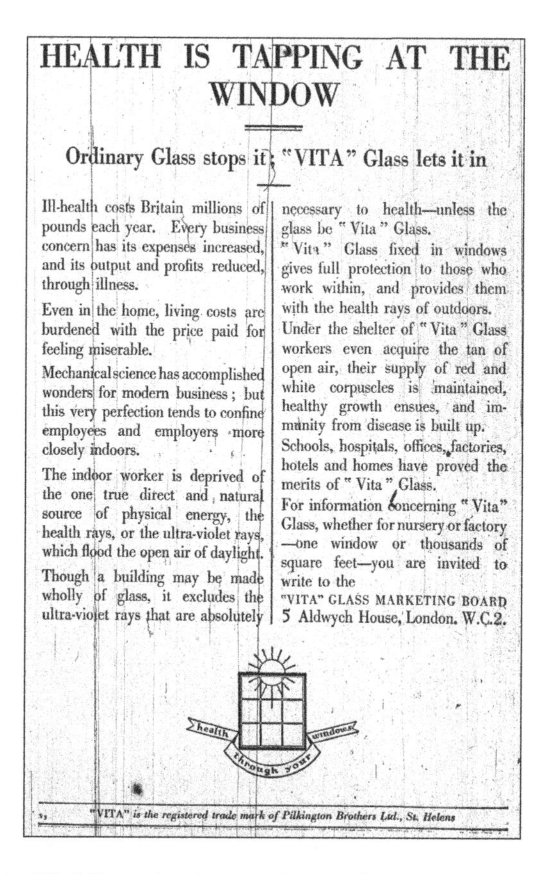

4.4 "Vita" Glass advertisement. Source: *The Times*, May 2, 1928. Permissions courtesy Pilkington Group Ltd.

sick body of the 1920s required bolstering. Not equipped to heal itself, it required expert intervention: to manage it, to make it grow taller and sturdier, to strengthen its biochemistry, to make it healthier for an optimal relationship with the world. Whereas the productive regime of heliotherapy required spending months in the clinics of Rollier and Bernhard, who offered recovery though a combination of fresh air, pure water, nutritious food, rigorous exercise, and plentiful bedrest, Pilkington and Chance offered a labor-free path to health that only required installing new windows. Like magic, the material did the work where the body did not.[56] In displacing the regime of heliotherapy and managing the body with a pane of glass, "Vita" Glass assumed a passive body, which required the work of outside agents to bring it health.

ACTIVE BODIES

Yet while the "Vita" Glass Marketing Board's marketing materials presented a passive body, in need of scientific management to bring it to health, at the same time it depicted the physically fit and suntanned, active body as a symbol of health. A series of advertisements for "Vita" Glass in *The Architectural Review* presented not data or statistics, nor even windows or glass, but rather photographs of active children, illuminated by the sun (Figure 4.5). In particular, in the photographic spread of a May 1934 advertisement, the iconic shadows of window muntins fall onto the youthful bodies of two vibrant children (Figure 4.6). One child is wide awake and about to arise from bed to face a new day, while the other is stretching in the sun. Underneath the images, a caption proclaims, "Health is let in through 'Vita' Glass windows permanently." As Fleetwood Pritchard and the "Vita" Glass Marketing Board sought to portray "Vita" Glass not as window glass, but as a health product, this approach was part of the effort to distance "Vita" Glass from the ordinary window glass market and to position it as a means to health. In Pritchard's mind, the presence of active, healthy children served to attract the eye of the reader, and to use the children as symbols of health. It also served to portray "Vita" Glass as part of an active lifestyle. As Pritchard himself wrote:

> *People now recognize vigorous and beautiful children and good-looking, energetic men and women as the symbols of good health. Happiness and an air of eager life should color every "Vita" Glass picture. A sense of movement should help to create the idea of good health, and at the same time win the attention of the casual reader.*[57]

For Neils Finsen and his followers, the natural world was actively curative, but also inherently variable. The body was equally dynamic in adapting to the shifting conditions posed by the natural world. The British heliotherapist Henry Gauvain wrote in *The Lancet* in 1927 of how the sun provided the body with energy, which the body then expended through its vigorous life. For Gauvain, the changing conditions of sunlight interacting with variable environmental conditions, such as humidity, dust, pollutants, and clouds, were precisely the key to heliotherapy's successes. Instead of offering a single, optimized ideal for germicidal effect, such as medical phototherapy, heliotherapy offered changing conditions for an adaptive body. Rather

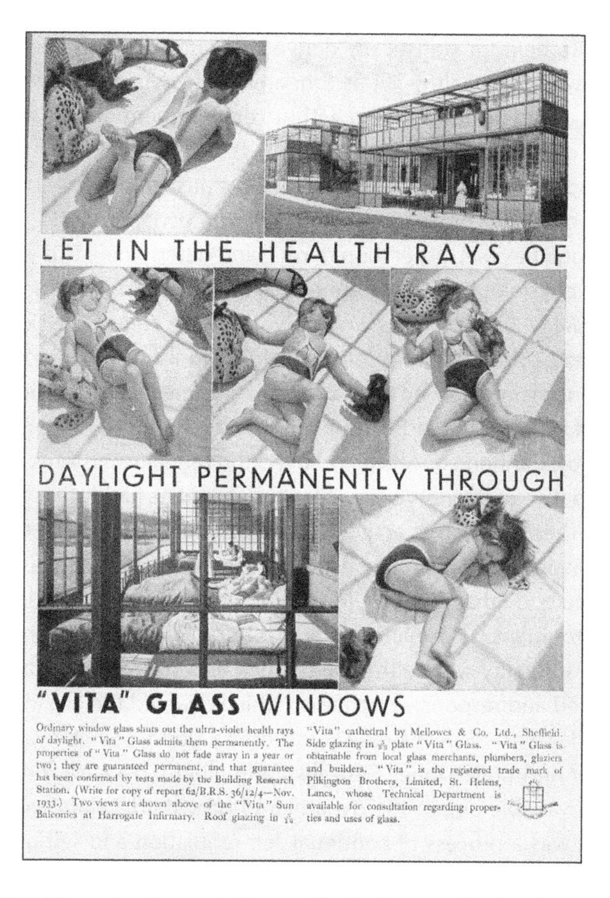

4.5 "Vita" Glass advertisement. Source: *The Architectural Review*, January 1935. Permissions courtesy Pilkington Group Ltd.

4.6 "Vita" Glass advertisement. Source: *The Architectural Review*, May 1934. Permissions courtesy Pilkington Group Ltd.

than healthy life being a statistically derived or socially determined, static ideal, Gauvain portrayed the healthy life as fundamentally dynamic, in which the body had an active, changing relationship with its environment; the healthy body was norm-seeking, rather than merely normal.[58]

Gauvain's position challenged the idea of statistical, fixed norms with the notion that norms were provisional responses to a dynamic world. Humans were norm-seeking and flexible, rather than normal and determined. This was something that American physiologist Walter Cannon called *homeostasis* in his 1932 text, *The Wisdom of the Body*. Cannon drew on the work of the French physiologist Claude Bernard who had coined the term *milieu intérieur* to refer the body's stable, internal environment maintained by a set of regulating mechanisms, and on the work of a number of others who had since been investigating disparate regulating systems in the body. Cannon conceptually linked the regulator systems and proposed a relationship between the nervous system and unstable, highly reactive material in the body. Together, this system actively retrieved and responded to environmental stimuli to maintain the body in a constant, steady state. Thus, it was precisely the instability of the body that enabled it to maintain stable conditions in the face of a changing environment.[59] German neurologist Kurt Goldstein echoed this position. For Goldstein, normality was neither predefined and statistical, nor an ideal condition, but ordered and responsive behavior, which enabled the organism to inhabit a state of balance with respect to the surrounding world.[60] Similarly, for the French medical doctor and philosopher Georges Canguilhem, because the environment was inherently variable due to the dynamics of growth, development, interaction, and death, life was a process of continual self-regulation and self-preservation to negotiate this environment. Health was a buffer for the organism, which provided for its present and future security by maintaining the necessary flexibility to adapt to change.[61] Illness, on the other hand, was a failure to adapt and thus a byproduct of stasis and stability. Adhering to fixed, statistically derived norms was antithetical to life itself in that it denied life of the necessary mutations, novelty, and creativity to cope with change. Rather than adhering to a rigid definition of normal rates and responses, the healthy organism was always creating and innovating—seeking new patterns and new states of overall stability in the face of a changing environment.

For Canguilhem, the outward manifestation of this *homeostatic* body was no less than the physically fit image of the athlete that was popularized in the interwar years.[62] Bodybuilder Eugen Sandow founded the Health and Strength League in 1906 to advocate muscle building for preventing disease and physical deterioration, and for building national productivity and strength.[63] Through its promotion of physical culture, it gained influence and by the end of the 1920s, the League had over one hundred thousand members, and over three hundred physical culture clubs were operating in Britain. The 1920s and 1930s witnessed the rise of a myriad of staged athletic events. On one hand, there was the rise of mass-participant exercise gatherings—or calisthenics—in Germany, Italy, and the Soviet Union, at which people gathered for choreographed exercise routines in a collective display of fitness. On the other, spectator events, such as the Olympics, resurrected in 1896, and the World Cup, beginning in 1930, demonstrated a fit and active lifestyle to an international audience.[64] In the rising militarism of the 1930s, the Health and Strength League was at its most influential, shaping Neville Chamberlain's National Fitness Campaigns of 1931 and 1937, which sought to improve the physical fitness of the nation.[65]

The photographs of children presented the vigorous, lively body as no less than an outward manifestation of the polyvalent and self-regulatory behavior of *homeostasis*. The outstretched children appeared inherently flexible and innovative, as they responded to the dynamic environmental conditions, as embodied in patterns of light and shade which suggest the presence of the sun. "Vita" Glass, through association with the children, was portrayed as enabling a life-supporting atmosphere. "Vita" Glass assumed a normative function, aiding the body in adjusting to and finding provisional points of stability in a changing world.[66] Although "Vita" Glass was itself a product of scientific management, manipulating material and manufacturing processes for optimum ultraviolet transmission, its portrayals depict it also as part of a normative practice by providing an armature for a creative and innovative healthy life. It was part of a designed and managed environment that provided the body with a means of reducing bodily suffering, mitigating threats and disasters, and supporting it in seeking stability in a dynamic environment. At a time when Claude Bernard's concept of the *milieu intérieur* was segueing into Walter Cannon's *homeostasis*, "Vita" Glass simultaneously alluded to the flexibility of self-regulatory systems, as it also embodied the idea that the healthy body was an active one.

Although eventually undone by further developments of the bacteriology and chemistry it embodied, notably sulfa drugs and antibiotics, "Vita" Glass marked a spectacular moment where materials science, medical theory, and the built environment intersected to create a tale of two bodies.

NOTES

1 John Duffy, *The Sanitarians: A History of American Public Health* (Urbana: University of Illinois Press, 1990), 67–68.

2 Erwin Heinz Ackerknecht, *Therapeutics from the Primitives to the Twentieth Century (with an appendix: History of Dietetics)* (New York: Hafner Press, 1973), 128–130.

3 On the work of Louis Pasteur in this respect, see, for instance, René J. Dubos, *Pasteur and Modern Science* (Garden City, NY: Masterworks Program, 1960). On Robert Koch's contributions, see Thomas D. Brock, *Robert Koch, a Life in Medicine and Bacteriology*, Scientific Revolutionaries series (Madison, WI: Science Tech Publishers; and Berlin and New York: Springer-Verlag, 1988).

4 On the sunlight cure, see Paul De Kruif, *Men Against Death* (New York: Harcourt, Brace, 1933).

5 Auguste Rollier and George de Swietochowski, *Heliotherapy with Special Consideration of Surgical Tuberculosis*, 2nd edn, Oxford Medical Publications series (London and New York: H. Milford, 1927).

6 Simon Carter, *Rise and Shine: Sunlight, Technology, and Health*, English edn (New York: Berg, 2007), 73.

7 Ina Zweiniger-Bargielowska, "Raising a Nation of 'Good Animals': The New Health Society and Health Education Campaigns in Interwar Britain," *Social History of Medicine* 20, no. 1 (2007).

8 Carter, *Rise and Shine*, 68.

9 Zweiniger-Bargielowska, "Raising a Nation of 'Good Animals,'" 77.

10 On the Crystal Palace, see, for instance, Michael Wigginton, *Glass in Architecture* (London: Phaidon, 1996).

11 Paul Scheerbart, Bruno Taut, and Dennis Sharp, *Glass Architecture* (New York: Praeger, 1972).

12 Arthur Korn, *Glas im Bau und als Gebrauchsgegenstand* (Berlin-Charlottenburg: E. Pollak, 1929); Raymond Herbert McGrath, A.C. Frost, and H.E. Beckett, *Glass in Architecture and Decoration* (London: Architectural Press, 1937).

13 Charles R. Kurkjian and William R. Prindle, "Perspectives on the History of Glass Composition," *Journal of the American Ceramic Society* 81, no. 4 (1998): 800.

14 Ibid., 801–803.

15 On Finsen's findings, see K.I. Moller et al., "How Finsen's Light Cured Lupus Vulgaris," *Photodermatology, Photoimmunology and Photomedicine* 21, no. 3 (2005).

16 See, for example, A.J. Pleasonton, *The Influence of The Blue Ray of The Sunlight and of the Blue Color of the Sky; In Developing Animal and Vegetable Life; In Arresting Disease and in Restoring Health in Acute and Chronic Disorders to Human and Domestic Animals* (Philadelphia, PA: Claxton, Remsen & Haffelfinger, 1877).

17 Moller et al., "How Finsen's Light Cured Lupus Vulgaris," 120.

18 Frederick Urbach, "The Historical Aspects of Sunscreens," *Journal of Photochemistry and Photobiology B: Biology* 64, no. 2–3 (2001): 100–101.

19 De Kruif, *Men Against Death*. See also Angela Newing, *Light, Visible and Invisible, and Its Medical Applications* (London: Imperial College Press, 1999), 95–96.

20 William Crookes, "The Preparation of Eye-Preserving Glass for Spectacles," *Philosophical Transactions of the Royal Society of London. Series A, Containing Papers of a Mathematical or Physical Character* 214 (1914). Crookes's (1832–1919) work is also referenced in a 1927 Pilkington Bros. document. See J. Dickinson, "Pilkington Brothers Ltd. Vita Glass. Instruction to Counsel," (St. Helens: Pilkington Brothers Ltd., 1927).

21 On Lamplough, see T.C. Barker, *The Glassmakers; Pilkington; the Rise of an International Company, 1826–1976* (London: Weidenfeld & Nicolson, 1977), 301–302.

On Hill, see Claude Gordon Douglas, "Leonard Erskine Hill. 1866–1952," *Obituary Notices of Fellows of the Royal Society* 8, no. 22 (1953). On the architectural history of the London Zoo, see Peter Guillery and Royal Commission on Historical Monuments (England), *The Buildings of London Zoo* (London: Royal Commission on the Historical Monuments of England, 1993), 8–10, 14–18.

22 Dickinson, "Pilkington Brothers Ltd. Vita Glass. Instruction to Counsel."

23 Matthew Luckiesh, *The Meaning and Magic of Windows* (Toledo, OH: Libby-Owens-Ford Glass Co., 1945), 3.

24 Ibid., 1.

25 On Luckiesh's ideal of artificial light "challenging the sun," see Matthew Luckiesh, *Applications of Germicidal, Erythemal and Infrared Energy* (New York: D. Van Nostrand, 1946), 1–28.

26 Ibid., 114–117.

27 Ibid., 1. On Luckiesh's interests in the therapeutic value of light, see Matthew Luckiesh and August John Pacini, *Light and Health; a Discussion of Light and Other Radiations in Relationship to Life and to Health* (Baltimore, MD: Williams & Wilkins, 1926); Matthew Luckiesh, *Artificial Sunlight, Combining Radiation for Health with Light for Vision* (New York: D. Van Nostrand, 1930).

28 Luckiesh, *Applications of Germicidal, Erythemal and Infrared Energy*, 23–28.

29 R. Arsenault, "The End of the Long Hot Summer: The Air Conditioner and Southern Culture," *Journal of Southern History* (1984): 600–602.

30 On the attributes of artificial weather, see Gail Cooper, "Custom Design, Engineering Guarantees, and Unpatentable Data: The Air Conditioning Industry, 1902–1935," *Technology and Culture* 35, no. 3 (1994): 520–521.

31 On the standard definition and properties of air quality, see Gail Cooper, *Air-Conditioning America; Engineers and the Controlled Environment, 1900–1960*, Johns Hopkins Studies in the History of Technology series (Baltimore, MD: Johns Hopkins University Press, 1998), 59.

32 Ibid., 86.

33 Arsenault, "The End of the Long Hot Summer," 608–611.

34 On artificial climate, see Cooper, "Custom Design, Engineering Guarantees, and Unpatentable Data," 521–522.

35 Luckiesh, *The Meaning and Magic of Windows*, 3.

36 On magic and weather control, see Marcel Mauss, *A General Theory of Magic*, Routledge Classics series (London: Routledge, 2001), 23–25.

37 P.V.W. Gell, Esq., "Interview with Messrs Pilkington Brothers, Euston Hotel, London, 17th February 1928," (London, 1928).

38 On the research into and nature of the campaign, see F.C. Pritchard & Partners Ltd, "Memorandum on Proposed Plan for Marketing 'Vita' Glass for Messrs. Chance Bros & Co."

39 On the mechanization of the home, see S. Giedion, *Mechanization Takes Command: A Contribution to Anonymous History* (New York: Oxford University Press, 1948). On the ways in which mechanization influenced the reorganization of the home, see Ruth Schwartz Cowan, *More Work for Mother: The Ironies of Household Technology from the Open Hearth to the Microwave* (New York: Basic, 1983).

40 On the history of National Efficiency, see Geoffrey Russell Searle, *The Quest for National Efficiency: A Study in British Politics and Political Thought, 1899–1914* (Oakland, CA: University of California Press, 1971).

41 "'Vita' Glass in Schools," undated internal report, Pilkington corporate archive.

42 Ibid.

43 Ibid., 16.

44 "'Vita' Glass for Birds and Animals," undated internal report, Pilkington corporate archive, 6–7.

45 On medical diagnostics, see Roy Porter, *The Greatest Benefit to Mankind: A Medical History of Humanity*, 1st American edn (New York: Norton, 1998), 293.

46 On Durkheim's role in the development of statistics and concepts of normality, see Richard Stivers, *Technology as Magic: The Triumph of the Irrational* (New York: Continuum, 1999), 95–98.

47 Ibid., 90–91.

48 On the "average man," see Porter, *The Greatest Benefit to Mankind*, 406.

49 On the contested meanings of "normal," see Stivers, *Technology as Magic*, 97–98.

50 Ibid., 79–82.

51 On the proliferation of statistics and the creation of norms, see ibid., 79–100.

52 Frederick Winslow Taylor, *The Principles of Scientific Management* (Mineola, NY: Dover, 1998).

53 Thorstein Veblen, *The Engineers and the Price System* (Kitchener, ON: Batoche Books, Édition Électronique, 2001).

54 On technocracy, see David E. Nye, *Electrifying America: Social Meanings of a New Technology, 1880–1940* (Cambridge, MA: MIT Press, 1990), 343–345; Frederick Lewis Allen, *Since Yesterday: The Nineteen-Thirties in America, September 3, 1929–September 3, 1939* (New York and London: Harper & Brothers, 1940), 89–92.

55 On Technocracy, Inc., see Howard Scott, "A Statement of the Social Objectives of Technocracy," *Technocracy Information Brief*, no. 66 (1933). On the development of PEP, see E.S. Turner, *The Shocking History of Advertising*, rev. edn (Harmondsworth: Penguin, 1965), 193.

56 On the disproportionality between action and benefit in magic, see Mauss, *A General Theory of Magic*, 41.

57 F.C. Pritchard & Partners Ltd, "'Vita' Glass Proposed Advertising Policy" (London, 1928).

58 Henry Gauvain, "Light Treatment in Surgical Tuberculosis," *The Lancet* 209, no. 5406 (1927).

59 Walter B. Cannon, *The Wisdom of the Body*, 1st edn (New York: Norton, 1932).

60 On normal life, see Kurt Goldstein, *The Organism: A Holistic Approach to Biology Derived from Pathological Data in Man* (New York: Zone, 1995), 327. On individual norms and balance, see ibid., 333–335.

61 On health and disease within the context of the dynamic environment, see Georges Canguilhem, *The Normal and the Pathological*, trans. Carolyn R. Fawcett and Robert S. Cohen, 1st pbk. edn (New York: Zone, 2007), 197–200. On the functional role of health, see ibid., 164–169.

62 Ibid., 201.

63 On the Health and Strength League, see Ina Zweiniger-Bargielowska, "Building a British Superman: Physical Culture in Interwar Britain," *Journal of Contemporary History* 41, no. 4 (2006).

64 On mass-participant athletic events, see Christopher Wilk, "The Healthy Body Culture," in *Modernism: Designing a New World: 1914–1939* (London: V&A Publications, 2006), 265. On the resurrection of the Olympics in 1896 and its extension to the participation of women in the early twentieth century, see ibid., 284.

65 See Carter, *Rise and Shine*, 67.

66 On the relationship between the mechanical and the biological, see Georges Canguilhem, "Machine and Organism," in Jonathan Crary and Sanford Kwinter, eds., *Zone 6: Incorporations* (New York: Urzone, 1992), 55–64.

5

Isolation, Privacy, Control and Privilege: Psychiatric Architecture and the Single Room

Leslie Topp

The single room, or cell—that is, the room designed for one person alone inside it—was at one time the fundamental unit of psychiatric architecture. In the earliest purpose-built asylums of the seventeenth and eighteenth centuries, multiplied and arranged repetitively off a corridor, cells stood for both the collection of the mentally ill under one roof, and for their separation one from another in an ordered array of isolated individuals.[1] By the late nineteenth century, though, the single room was the exception, rather than the rule, in newly built asylums. Its physical presence was diminished, but despite that—or indeed because of it—it loomed large in discussions of asylum design. Most asylums built around 1900 in Western countries included a small number of single rooms in the sections of the institution for pauper patients (that is, for patients who could not afford their own maintenance and became wards of the state); these were meant for the temporary isolation and observation of patients in a highly disturbed state. Most asylums also had designated wards for paying patients; here, only those paying the highest rate (first-class patients) were entitled to single rooms. These single rooms were meant to guarantee privacy, with all the protection of sensibility and of individual identity that that brought with it.

This chapter examines the dichotomous meanings of the single room in psychiatry and the various uses to which it was put. The Steinhof psychiatric hospital complex, built 1903–07 on the outskirts of Vienna, serves here not so much as a case study but rather as a jumping-off point for the exploration of the various contexts and positions that fed into the single room's ambiguous status. Steinhof had both types of single rooms, and there were extended discussions about them and their spatial configuration in the documents emerging from the process of planning the institution. The first part of this analysis, using Steinhof as a starting point, looks back into the history of asylum design, focusing on the provision and role of single rooms for pauper patients. The second part moves from a vertical, roughly chronological account of debates within psychiatry to a more horizontal enquiry. Asylums may have been imagined as worlds unto themselves, but they were connected in important ways to the proliferating spatial types and contexts of the modern built environment. From this point of view, the complex handling of the single room at Steinhof can be understood not only with reference to the history of asylums but also with reference to the panoply of living spaces—and the discourses surrounding those spaces—in turn-of-the-century Europe, and specifically Vienna. In dwellings and in pseudo-domestic spaces (such as hotels and sanatoria) for the middle and upper classes there was an increasing emphasis on individual solitude and privacy, even within the home and the family unit.

THE STEINHOF PSYCHIATRIC HOSPITAL, VIENNA

Steinhof was a very large state asylum designed on the villa system.[2] Patients were housed in pavilions, or villas, and types of patients were grouped together, classified according to a combination of gender, class (or, more precisely, ability to pay), chronicity, and behavior. Individual patient pavilions were designated, for example, for "Noisy acute men third-class" or "Quiet women first-class"; separate pavilions for recent admissions, patients sent by the criminal courts, and those with infectious diseases were also provided. The complex was divided into a larger section for pauper patients and a smaller section for paying patients (called the sanatorium); each of these sections was in turn divided into sections for male and female patients, separated by a central axis of common service buildings (Figure 5.1).

The internal arrangement of spaces occupied by patients in the pavilions of the pauper section of the institution was markedly different from that in the paying

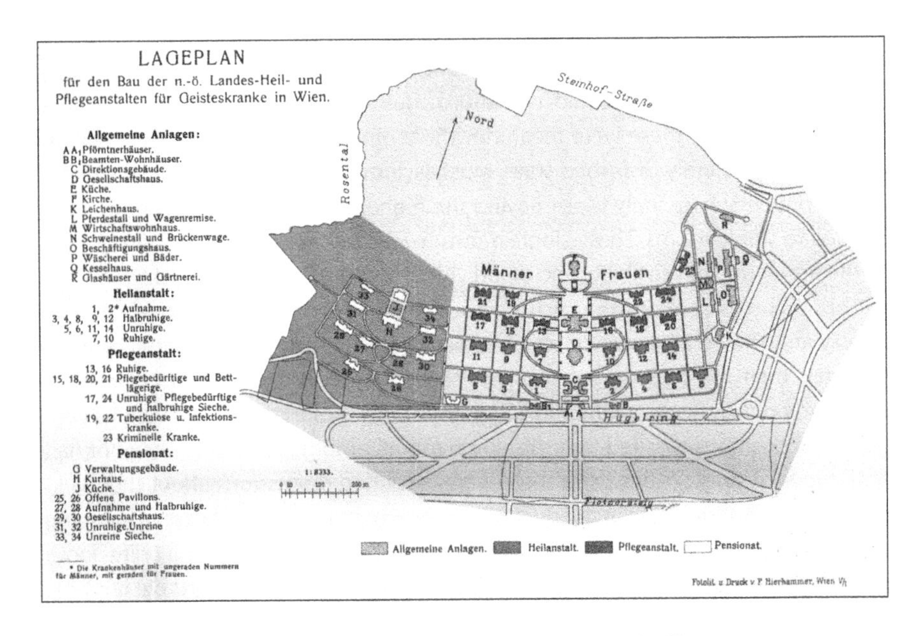

5.1 Lower Austrian Crown Land Asylum "am Steinhof," Vienna, Otto Wagner and Franz Berger, 1903–07, site plan. Source: *Bericht des Landesausschusses des Erzherzogtums Österreich u.d. Enns über seine Amtwirksamkeit*, vol. 6a, 1903–04, n.p., Nieder-Österreichische Landesbibliothek.

section. In the pauper section, patients slept in large dormitories, with nine to fourteen patients to a room, and most of them spent the large part of their waking hours either in bed, in adjoining dayrooms, in the common buildings, or outside. The floor plans for almost all categories of pauper patient pavilions shared a similar basic configuration: a series of large dormitories and dayrooms arranged along the long south side of the building, opening onto each other and onto a corridor, which in some cases also doubled as a dayroom.[3] Many of the pavilions also had short wings projecting from either end of their north sides, containing a number of much smaller rooms, each with a single door and a single window. These are labelled either "single room" (Einzel-Zimmer) or "single cell" (Einzel-Zelle) on the floor plans (Figure 5.2).

Any sense that it was naturally to be expected that any psychiatric hospital would need to have a certain number of small spaces for the individual isolation of patients (even when most slept in dormitories) is dispelled by Steinhof's own building brief, published in 1902. In a preamble on the configuration of patient pavilions, the authors staked out a position in an ongoing, and heated, debate:

> *Certain psychiatrists, basing their claims on one-sided and inadequate evidence from the actual observation of patients, argue that in future we will be able to completely abolish the isolation of mental patients and therefore be able to build asylums without cells. In claiming this, all they are proving is that first, they lack experience with large patient numbers and second, that a trite slogan is worth more to them than the careful consideration of the range of facilities that are needed in a well-designed asylum. Among these, the single room plays an essential, irreplaceable role.*[4]

While the current predominance of *Bettbehandlung* (treatment of patients in shared wards, as in a general hospital) had meant that it was often possible to *avoid* the use of isolation, the authors were convinced that it would never be possible to eliminate it entirely: "We will continue to have to isolate, no matter what the reasons are and

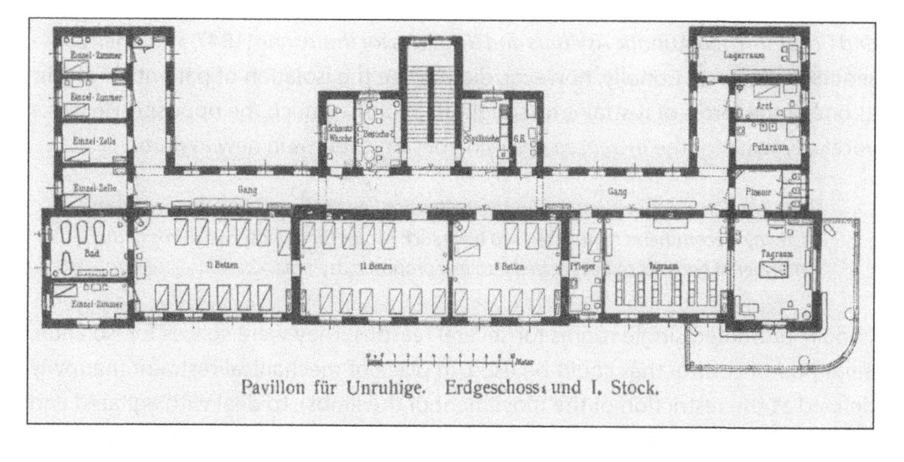

Pavillon für Unruhige. Erdgeschoss und I. Stock.

5.2 Steinhof, Pavilion for noisy pauper patients, plan of ground and first floors. Source: Heinrich Schlöss, ed., *Die Irrenpflege in Österreich in Wort und Bild* (Halle: Carl Marhold, 1912), 181.

how we choose to describe it. Therefore we need [in laying out a new asylum] to plan for an adequate number of single rooms."[5]

CONTROL, PRIVACY AND THE PAUPER PATIENT: SINGLE ROOMS AND CELLS

The debate referred to in Steinhof's building brief between those who sought the abolition of cells from asylums and those who insisted on the continuing need for them had its roots in Britain, in the mid-nineteenth-century movement to abolish mechanical restraint (chains, straitjackets, etc.) from psychiatric institutions. The discussion was complicated, and cannot be reduced to a battle between advocates of increased patient freedom, on the one hand, and those who wanted to maintain strict control, on the other. What emerges from the series of texts discussed below is the ambiguity of the single room as a place of privacy which is also a site of isolation, and shifting attitudes to the appropriate connection between patients' class origins and the spaces provided for them in a public institution. The room itself and its purpose was a shifting thing too: sometimes the discussion is about where patients should sleep at night (together in dormitories or alone in single bedrooms); sometimes it is instead, or also, about a secure place in which the patient should be confined for limited periods to protect him/herself and others, or to return to a calm state of mind; occasionally it is about the room as protection for the patient's individuality, a haven for quiet contemplation. The lines between these types of single rooms (single room as bedroom, as secure cell, as retreat) are sometimes definite, and sometimes blurred.

The early Victorian asylum director John Conolly was the foremost British advocate of strict non-restraint principles in asylum management. In the early 1840s, at the Middlesex County asylum at Hanwell, he instituted a complete abolition of methods of restraint that hindered the free movement of patients' limbs (so-called "mechanical restraint"), and disseminated his approach in his book *The Construction and Government of Lunatic Asylums and Hospitals for the Insane* (1847, with many subsequent editions).[6] Conolly, however, did not see the isolation of patients in rooms as one of the forms of restraint he sought to abolish—much the opposite. He was a vocal advocate for the *increased* provision of single rooms in new asylums:

> *In all asylums the proportion of single bedrooms appears to me to be too small; and I always recommend to architects to have such rooms for at least two thirds of the number of patients to be received into any proposed asylum.*[7]

Conolly promoted single rooms for several reasons. They were spaces for isolation, a method of control that could be used, in place of mechanical restraint (narrowly defined as the restriction of the movement of the limbs), to deal with agitated and dangerous patients. Such patients were always a minority, however, and would not justify the provision of single rooms for two thirds or more of the patient population. Most patients, whatever their condition, would be happier, he believed, sleeping in their own bedroom rather than in a dormitory:

> *as for the clean, and orderly, and tranquil, and convalescent patients, no complaint is so constantly on their lips as that which arises from their not having a single room, and, consequently, not having a single moment to themselves, or any place where they can be quiet, or, in their frequently uttered words, where they can even say their prayers without interruption.*[8]

It is worth emphasizing what an original and contentious idea it was to propose that pauper patients should have their own rooms, not for reasons of control or security, but rather for the protection of their own time, space and individuality against the onslaught of communal life in the asylum. Conolly envisioned those rooms as carefully furnished, and indeed as themselves an essential tool in helping the patient adapt to his or her new life in the institution: "A clean and cheerful sleeping-room, clean bedding, and a little coir matting on the stone floor, are appreciated by the patient, and help to reconcile him to the house." He continued: "We possess, indeed, in county asylums, this advantage, that our simplest accommodations and our scrupulous cleanliness constitute comforts rather above those enjoyed by the greater number of our poor patients in their sane state."[9] As will be discussed at length below, the single bedroom was a distinctly middle-class phenomenon; here the asylum's cell is converted into a "comfort," a feature protective of the individual's sensibilities and need for privacy to which the poor are given access for the first time upon institutionalization.

During the time in which Conolly was active at Hanwell, the British government regulation and inspection body known as the Metropolitan Commissioners in Lunacy was issuing regular reports.[10] The Commissioners were an influential voice for the reduction to a minimum of the numbers of single rooms included in new asylum buildings.[11] They also sought to reduce the range of associations and uses the single room could have: for the Commissioners, single rooms in the asylum could only be "cells" (a word which had, in that time of active prison reform, distinctly carceral associations). The Commissioners were closely attentive to class, as was Conolly, but for them class and its association with living spaces was something static rather than something capable of change and amelioration.

In their report of 1844, the Commissioners concerned themselves with how high levels of expenditure on public asylums might be reduced without compromising the quality of those institutions, and suggested that, for instance, "no unnecessary cost should be incurred for architectural decoration; especially as [County] Asylums are erected for persons who, when in health, are accustomed to dwell in cottages."[12] Likewise, many more beds could be provided at a lower cost if the proportion of single rooms was reduced to a minimum, and this could also be justified with reference to the inmates' usual living conditions—which it was not the role of the asylum to improve. Dormitories, according to the report's authors, "better accord with the pauper's previous habits than sleeping alone in a solitary cell with a single window."[13]

In an article in *The Asylum Journal of Mental Science* thirteen years later, the editor J.C. Bucknill indicated that the debate over whether dormitories or single rooms should predominate in asylums was ongoing, and would resemble the battle between the "Little Endians" and the "Big Endians" in Swift's *Gulliver's Travels*, if the issue in question were not so serious.[14] He himself argued that a certain number of what he called "single sleeping rooms" would always be necessary in an asylum, and that four types of patients would need recourse to them. Three of these were patient types for whom the room was a necessary security measure (that is, a cell): recent admissions, chronic patients with habits "obnoxious to persons occupying the same sleeping rooms, or dangerous to themselves" and chronic patients "suffering from temporary excitement or illness."[15] The single room served a different purpose for the fourth category, which consisted of "patients whose education or habits would render the use of a dormitory a painful infliction upon their delicacy or self-esteem."[16] Bucknill cited for support the passage from Conolly's book quoted above, in which he had, as we have seen, embraced the idea that all patients could benefit from single rooms, including the ones who wanted them solely for privacy (even if they were not necessary for security).[17] However, he turned Conolly's ameliorative impulse—his conviction that even the poor deserved a privacy in the asylum that they lacked in the outside world—on its head (without acknowledging that he was doing so). Poor patients were used to living day and night without privacy, and did not value it; therefore patients of a higher class needed protection from them (and indeed having to cohabit with them at night could worsen their mental state).

> *Anyone who has run a county asylum will know, from painful experience, how hard is the lot of many men bred in luxury and affluence, of many women nurtured in gentleness and delicacy, whom the decrees of a hard fate have compelled to associate in the wards of a lunatic asylum, with the rude sons and daughters of toil. To associate with them by day is often a severe trial, modified, however, by the orderly arrangements of an institution which, to a great extent, repress and prevent the boisterous rudeness and vulgarity common in the lower classes. But to associate with them at night, in a large dormitory, is a far greater trial, and one which cannot be softened. To sleep in a dormitory at all, for the first time in one's life perhaps, would be a most painful shock to persons of delicate feeling, to dress and undress in the presence of others, to have no moment for privacy, for the exercises of devotion, would drive many a sane woman out of her senses, and many an insane woman frantic.*[18]

Bucknill's emphasis on the desirability of spatial segregation by class was not unusual—it was a consistent trend in asylum design throughout the nineteenth century. But the indication that there would inevitably be mixing (presumably because there would always be a certain number of patients who, while well educated, could not afford—because of "the decrees of hard fate"—the rates for private institutions, or for the first-class sections of public ones) is interesting. Conolly suggested that the solution was to provide accommodation for patients of all classes which would approximate the levels of privacy, and protection of individual dignity, usually enjoyed by the middle and upper classes. For Bucknill, dormitories were entirely appropriate for the great (unwashed) majority; single rooms could serve to lock away those among them whose mental state made them unwelcome or unsafe companions, but they could also be havens of solitude for the minority of poor but well-bred patients, where they could lock themselves away, at least metaphorically.

The symbiotic relationship between non-restraint and seclusion kept the single room at the forefront of debates in asylum planning. In this context, the emphasis was always on control and the unruly patient, and the single room lost its multifariousness—it was distinctly cell. Conolly himself was open about the ways in which single rooms could be measures of control. He specified that the doors of all single patient bedrooms, while left open during the day, should be locked at night.[19] As has been mentioned, his principled objection to mechanical restraint did not rule out the confinement of patients in a locked room: "the safety of attendants, and of the patients themselves, required that those in charge of the wards should have authority to place violent or unruly patients in their bedrooms for a time, locking the door."[20] The doors of single rooms were therefore equipped with peep holes, or "inspection plates," so that the confined patient could be observed without the room being entered:

> *By occasionally looking through the inspection-plate, the attendant is enabled to ascertain the effect of the seclusion; and the medical officers, to whom every seclusion is, or ought to be, immediately reported, are enabled to judge of the propriety of continuing or putting an end to it.*[21]

Conolly also saw a role for the padded cell (or "padded room," as he called it), used for violent patients, those "disposed to strike their heads against the wall," or epileptic patients, as an alternative to chaining such patients to their beds.[22]

We have seen how the Commissioners in their 1844 report paid close attention to the cost of public asylums, and rejected the large-scale provision of single rooms as both wasteful and inappropriate for poor patients. They set forth another reason for opposing the single room, stemming from a concern with patient liberty. They pointed to what they saw as a contradiction in the non-restraint movement as promoted by Conolly and others:

> *Those who profess the entire disuse of restraint employ manual force and seclusion as parts of their method of management, maintaining that such measures are consistent with a system of non-restraint. It is said by these persons that when any of the limbs (as the legs or the hands of a patient) are confined by the strait-jacket, the belt, or by straps or gloves, he is under restraint. But in cases where he is held by the hands of attendants, or when he is for any excitement or violence forced by manual strength into a small chamber or cell, and left there, it is said that restraint is not employed, and the method adopted in these cases, is called "the non-restraint system." In those cases where the patient is overpowered by the number of keepers . . . it is said that there is no mechanical restraint. Here restraint of some form or other is manifest; and even in those cases where the patient is forced into a cell by manual strength, and prevented from leaving it until his fit of excitement shall have passed, it is difficult to understand how this also can be reconciled with the profession of abstaining from all restraint whatsoever, so as to be correctly termed "Non-restraint." It seems to us that these measures are only particular modes of restraint, the relative advantages of which must depend altogether on the results.*[23]

The practice of "seclusion" in the institution at the heart of the non-restraint movement, Hanwell, and its impact on the atmosphere in the ward, is vividly illustrated by a first-hand account in the same report:

> *The system of non-restraint at Hanwell has been carried on by mild and kind treatment, by an increase in the numbers of attendants, and by adopting seclusion or solitary confinement, sometimes in darkened cells, in lieu of mechanical restraint. At*

> *our visit to this Asylum in 1843, there was no patient under mechanical restraint; but we saw a violent female lunatic, who had been endeavoring to bite other persons as well as herself, seized by four or five of the nurses, and after a violent and protracted struggle, forced with great difficulty into and fastened in, one of the cells. During this scene, there was much confusion in the ward, and the great efforts of the patient to liberate herself, and (after her seclusion) the violence with which she struck the door of the cell, and threw herself against it, must have greatly exhausted her.*[24]

The authors see the non-restraint movement as giving rise to a marked *increase* in this particular kind of (non-mechanical) restraint, and they adopt the term "solitary confinement" from prison reform terminology to describe it:

> *Seclusion or solitary confinement is now getting into general use in the treatment of the insane, and great numbers of the superintendents of public, and of the proprietors of private Asylums throughout the country are fitting up and bringing into use solitary cells, and padded rooms for violent and unmanageable Lunatics.*[25]

By the late nineteenth and early twentieth centuries, with dormitories predominating, the issue of single rooms was still the subject of vigorous debate, though the issue of privacy for pauper patients had receded. It was the function of the room as a secure cell that came to the fore, as the single room became less multifarious and multifunctional.

In Germany and Austria we see this debate being taken up, with a somewhat different emphasis, but with similar attention to terminology and suspicions of hypocrisy. The role of cells/single rooms, the extent of their provision in new asylums, their nomenclature and their positioning within the ward were all matters of extended discussion in the literature. Adolf Funk, author of the section of the multi-volume *Handbuch der Architektur* devoted to psychiatric hospitals (published in Germany in 1893), sees the issue of "wards for the raving," and specifically the provision of cells within them, as the point on which there is the most divergent range of opinion among asylum directors. Movements in Britain and France which challenged the necessity of providing any isolation cells at all, he wrote, had had their impact in Germany, but there was a very wide spectrum of views.[26] He provided a table showing the relationship between the numbers of cells and the numbers of patients at sixteen different hospitals in Germany. At Oldenburg, for instance, 22 percent of patient beds were in cells while at the asylum at Alt Scherbitz, near Leipzig, the number was only 2.8 percent.[27]

That Alt Scherbitz should have the lowest proportion of cells is unsurprising; established in 1876, it was publicized as a model for so-called "free," or "open door" treatment. Albrecht Paetz, the director of Alt Scherbitz, in his 1893 treatise promoting the new free asylum, presented a complex theory of the single room in psychiatry: the "cell" had to disappear, but the "single room" would remain, devoid of all cell-like configurations and appurtenances. Paetz used a vivid example to argue that forced isolation in a cell in fact created the behavior it was meant to control:

> *The paranoid patient . . . sees himself (due to his lack of understanding his illness) as unjustly confined and punished and may express vigorously what he sees as*

> *justified indignation. If such a patient is isolated due to his excitability and reduced self-control, he reacts in an abnormally angry manner and gives voice with even greater volume to his indignation. He soon moves from grumbling to pounding on the doors and windows and, when he doesn't achieve his liberation that way, moves on to ripping sheets, smearing the walls with excrement and destroying the room, degenerating into a true frenzy.*[28]

This kind of frenzy in patients was, in the great majority of cases, according to Paetz, a *product* of repeated and/or prolonged isolation in a cell, rather than its cause.[29]

But Paetz argued that there remained a need for rooms in which patients could be isolated temporarily, whether to calm them down, or to protect other patients from them.[30] These rooms, however, "should never be identified with, or have the character of prison cells, indeed should not be labelled with the repulsive word 'cell.'"[31] Paetz referred to them as "isolation rooms" (*Isolierzimmer*), while others, as the authors of the Steinhof building brief pointed out, preferred the even more neutral "single room" (*Einzelzimmer*).[32] Not just the nomenclature, but the physical environment represented by the single room needed to be changed, as did its location in and connection to the other parts of the building. The door must not have a peephole, the window must have a view, unimpeded by bars, and there should not be a toilet within the room. The room should be located, not alongside other such rooms off a corridor in a distant pavilion or wing, but directly adjacent to a common dayroom, and observable from it. The door, whenever possible, should be kept open (Figure 5.3).[33]

As common dormitories were introduced for the great majority of pauper patients, the tendency in asylum design had been to build dedicated "raving wards," consisting of multiple secure rooms/cells arranged along a corridor, in a section of the institution itself physically isolated from the other wards.[34] (The instance related by the British Commissioners in Lunacy of the patient isolated at Conolly's asylum at

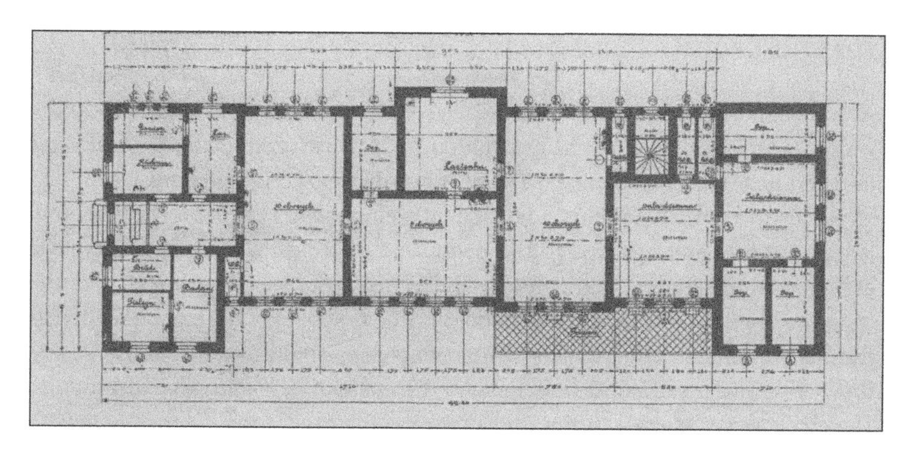

5.3 Galician Crown Land Asylum at Kobierzyn, near Krakow, begun 1910, Władysław Klimczak, architect. Pavilion for noisy pauper patients, ground-floor plan. Source: Eugen Hofmokl, ed., *Heilanstalten in Österreich* (Vienna: Hölder, 1913), 290. The small rooms labeled "Sep." are the isolation rooms, following Paetz's principle of integration of isolation rooms and interconnection with dormitories and dayrooms.

Hanwell, whose screams and poundings could be heard by patients using the adjacent corridor, points both to the impetus behind locating isolation cells at a remove from the rest of the institution, and to its result—the compounded isolation of the patient.) Paetz believed that raving wards encouraged the misuse of isolation, and should where possible be eliminated.[35] Others, however, adopted a more moderate, or pragmatic, position, and such a position informed the layout of Steinhof's pavilions. Josef Starlinger, an Austrian psychiatrist who held a series of positions in Lower Austrian asylums in the years during which Steinhof was being planned, agreed that cells (he did not flinch from using the term, and we see it used in Steinhof's floor plans) should be distributed among patient pavilions rather than being centralized in one structure. But he objected to the idea, promoted by Paetz, that they should open directly onto other patient spaces. Instead, they should be gathered in mini-tracts of cells in wings projecting off of the main pavilions, thus protecting the peace and quiet of the wards and making "surveillance and control easier."[36]

Looking back at Steinhof's third-class, or pauper section (see Figure 5.2), we can see now how its designers responded to the range of positions that were possible when approaching the role of the single room. The careful distinctions made in the labelling of rooms between "Einzelzelle" and "Einzelzimmer" pointed to some tolerance of shifting meaning and status. But the basic spatial configuration emphasized what were fairly stark distinctions. Significant provision was made for the isolation of certain, disturbed pauper patients in secure rooms, grouped together at a spatial distance from the rest of the ward. The dominance of the dormitory as the main, default accommodation, meant that the privacy of pauper patients, and their own desire for solitude, was not accommodated spatially. There was a strong either/or distinction made: single rooms could not do both.

DESIRABLE ISOLATION AND THE PAYING PATIENT: THE SINGLE ROOM AS COMMODITY

As has been mentioned, single rooms played a fundamentally different role in the wards at Steinhof which were designated for patients paying the highest rates (referred to as first-class patients). Pauper patients were considered passive objects of psychiatric care; the discussion of spatial arrangements for them was therefore largely internal, and oriented to the needs and priorities of those managing the asylum. Paying patients, on the other hand, were consumers. The marketing of the institution deployed associative terminology (the branding of the paying section as the "Sanatorium," and the pavilions within it as "villas," for instance); it also, crucially, drew on spatial associations from beyond the realm of psychiatry and institutions. The associations relevant to the single room at the turn of the century were with bourgeois domestic and quasi-domestic spaces.

These associations were signaled in the section of Steinhof's building brief devoted to the Sanatorium:

> *The educated public demands thorough individualization and lays great importance on the greatest possible isolation. In almost every case of a new*

> *admission, the patient's relatives ask anxiously how many patients he or she will have to share a room with. Large wards and large common dormitories should therefore best be avoided in planning a new paying section and the first-class rooms should have entrances as separate as possible from each other.*[37]

"Isolation" takes on a completely new meaning here; it secures privacy and is a sign of privilege, rather than being a mode of imposed, security-driven, restraint. How would such isolation be best achieved for the greatest number? Through corridors with repeated single rooms ranged along them, each with their own entrance from the corridor only (i.e., not interconnected). This is a very old spatial convention in asylums, dating back to Robert Hooke's building for Bethlem (1674–76), and it survived in the form of the tracts of cells in the raving wards referred to above. But the authors of the building brief preferred, naturally, non-institutional associations. They referred to the design of pavilions according to a "hotel model," which they contrast with the "surveillance model,""the former with corridors, the latter without."[38] The hotel model, they argued, maintained "the greatest possible separation, especially on the first class floors, and represents, after the family home, the most familiar form of dwelling."[39] The floor plan of one of the Sanatorium villas (Figure 5.4), intended to house several first-class patients, is on a strict corridor system. In the advertising prospectus and poster for the Sanatorium, disseminated after Steinhof was completed, a watercolor rendering of a first-class patient's single room was included (Figure 5.5). In layout, decoration, and furnishing, it resembles a single room in a comfortable modern hotel.

The emphasis on the single room as a highly desirable commodity—indeed a marker of cultivation—comes not only out of the desire on the part of middle- and upper-class patients ("the educated public") for separation from the mass of mentally ill fellow-inmates. We have seen how in Britain already at mid-century

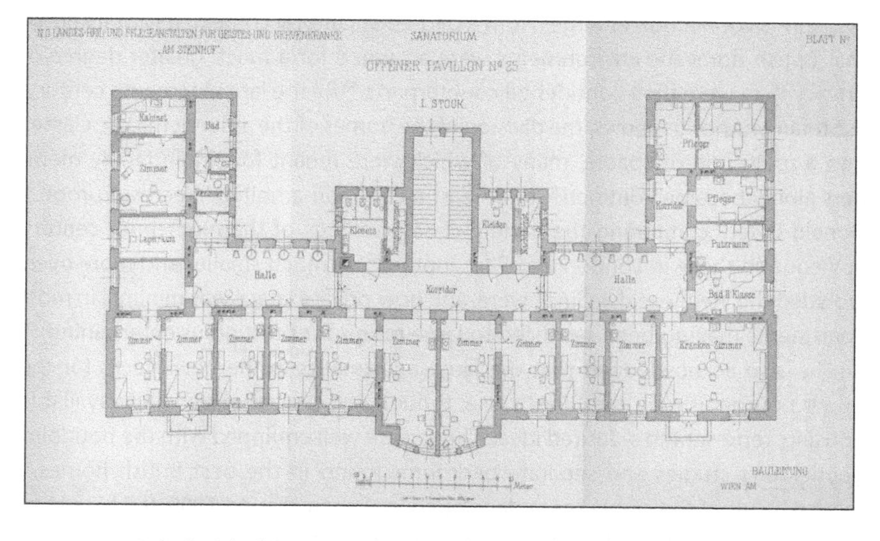

5.4 Steinhof, Open pavilion for first-class patients, first-floor plan.
Source: *N.-Ö. Landes- Heil- und Pflegeanstalten für Geistes- und Nervenkranken "Am Steinhof" in Wien*, n.p., Niederösterreichische Landesbibliothek, St. Pölten.

5.5 Erwin Pendl, Illustration of first-class single room, Steinhof. Source: *The Provincial Sanatorium of Steinhof in Vienna (Austria) XIII* (Vienna: Province of Lower Austria, no date, 1907–08?), 30, Niederösterreichische Landesbibliothek, St. Pölten.

there was a close association made in the commentary on asylum arrangements between cultivated sensibilities, affluence, and the ability to close the door and be alone. This connection emerges from a particular cultural context; it is well known that British domestic environments were arranged for a much greater degree of privacy than were their continental counterparts.[40] By the late nineteenth century, as Stefan Muthesius shows, the division of the homes of the affluent middle classes into a multitude of spaces, many of which were meant for single family members alone, became common—or at least a common ambition—across Europe.[41] Donald Olsen, comparing the middle-class dwellings of the nineteenth century in Vienna to those in London and Paris, noted how much smaller and more overcrowded the Viennese dwellings were, and how private space was minimal in most apartments (having been sacrificed to large rooms for prestigious entertaining).[42] But he also acknowledged that the large apartments in the new blocks for the upper bourgeoisie on the Ringstrasse, though not typical of generally available housing, represented a desired ideal. These were well equipped with the boudoirs, gentlemen's studies and separate bedrooms found in the best British homes.[43] Indeed a cult of the single room developed in Vienna around 1900, fed by a literary and artistic culture of interiority, as well as by shifting performance of gender, with men and women both using single rooms (studies, boudoirs) as frames for self-presentation.[44]

The first-class rooms at Steinhof were not, of course, studies or boudoirs; they were bedrooms. The room in the bourgeois dwelling that most closely approximated the single first-class room in the asylum was not the study, the boudoir, or the marital bedroom, but the bedroom for the adolescent child. Karl Weissbach, in his 1902 volume providing guidance for architects designing homes for the affluent, wrote of the need for children who had grown too old for the common nursery to have bedrooms of their own. Since these rooms would be at once bedroom and sitting room for their occupants, their furnishing should include seating and a work table, and the beds, to prevent them from dominating the tone of the room, should be screened off during the day by curtains.[45] To have one's own bedroom, carefully decorated and useable in the day, allowed a degree of privacy within the household for the older, but still dependent child.[46] To have such a room was a sign of privilege too, of course; children of less well-off or less up-to-date families would continue sharing rooms throughout their adolescence. For the affluent and educated psychiatric patient, subject to the rules of the institution, prescribed a daily regime of exercise and social activity, and taking meals in large dining rooms with fellow patients, the single room served a similar role. In the first-class bedrooms at Steinhof, the beds may not have had curtains, but the room was carefully decorated and equipped with a dressing table, and seating (see Figure 5.5). It provided a pleasant cocoon for evening and morning rituals, and sleep; it also stood for the *possibility* of privacy, even if most of life went on outside of it.

The hotel room was another reference point. As has been mentioned, the building brief for Steinhof's Sanatorium called for the first-class rooms to have "entrances as separate as possible from each other," extending the realm of privacy from the room itself to a zone around its entrance way (and distinguishing the first-class room from the isolation cell, the door of which, with its peephole, doubled as a frame for the surveillance of the occupant—see Figure 5.6). The way to achieve maximum separation, according to the building brief, was to base the floor plan on the "hotel type," the hotel being a familiar environment for the class of people who might be first-class patients. The "hotel type" meant rooms ranged along straight corridors (rather than, for example, ranged around a common room or atrium); comparing the floor plan of the first-class villa (Figure 5.4) with late nineteenth-century hotel floor plans, consisting of repeated small rooms along corridors, shows what they meant.[47]

Mary Guyatt, in her study of interiors in psychiatric hospitals in Britain around 1900, argued that the asylum and the hotel shared a common hybrid status. They were

> *private in that they were open to only to a selected minority, but public in that they housed large, unrelated and transitory populations. To meet these needs, both asylums and hotels required some small private rooms and some much larger reception rooms, the ratio varying according to the type of institution.*[48]

A writer about hotel design in the 1920s referred to the hotel room as "the unit or cell around which the entire building was oriented";[49] it is in part the repetition of small, individually accessible units in hotels that the Steinhof planners sought to emulate. The name "Sanatorium" given to the paying section of the institution

5.6 Steinhof, Cell door from a pavilion in the pauper section, with peep hole. Source: Wellcome Trust.

points to the importance of a closely related building type; that is, the quasi-medical establishments that pervaded the Central European countryside, originating in the tradition of the spa, and treating a range of ailments, including nervous ailments. These private institutions were housed in buildings with strong similarities to hotels, except that while hotels tended to have a combination of single and double rooms, catering to couples travelling together, sanatoria catered to individuals, and provided exclusively single-room accommodation.[50] Sanatoria, like grand hotels, were highly social places, which at the same time exposed the individual to a transitory public of unfamiliar fellow residents.[51] The sanatorium shared with the asylum the expectation that the patient would submit him- or herself to the control of the doctor and the surveillance of staff. In this context, the room was not simply a place to sleep, but a shell into which the individual could retreat from the company of other patients and from medical oversight and control.

Likewise, the first-class single rooms at Steinhof represented sites of retreat from the institutional. For a price, a patient could secure a place of occasional solitude, away from the masses of other patients. It was a space in which the patient, for a time, could exit the realm of the medical and enter that of the domestic, or quasi-domestic. The isolation cell, on the other hand, far from being an escape from medical control, was an extreme manifestation of it; rather than seeking it out for a moment's silence, patients were forcibly confined there, and were often vociferous in their protestations against this restriction on their liberty. What these spaces shared, besides their status as single rooms for one person alone, was a position outside of the therapeutic rationale of the institution. Therapy at Steinhof—as at all institutions in this period—was social. For pauper patients, this meant bed treatment in dormitories; occupational therapy in the fields, farm, kitchen, and laundry; fresh air in the pavilion gardens; parties and performances in the theater; and worship in the church. For paying patients, there were strolls in the grounds, conversation in the salon, games, painting, and common meals. For these patients, the single room was a place of respite from the social demands of such therapy. Pauper patients ended up in single rooms (or cells) when their behavior made coexistence with others apparently impossible, and the space alone thus also represented a space apart from the therapeutic. The idea that solitude in a single room could itself be therapeutic—and specifically mentally healing—disappeared from view with the loss of Conolly's vision of an asylum in which the social and private existed in balance. Here, patients whose poverty had denied them time alone when at home, had found it in a clean and comfortable little slice of middle-class existence—the asylum bedroom. Those same patients, though, if they lost control of themselves when beyond the walls of their own room, might find themselves, like a transgressing child, back in their room with the door firmly locked.

NOTES

1 For the cell and corridor in the earliest purpose-built asylums, and an account of the early meanings of "cell," see Christine Stevenson, *Medicine and Magnificence: British Hospital and Asylum Architecture, 1660-1815* (New Haven, CT: Yale University Press, 2000), 53–55. Thanks to Christine Stevenson for many helpful conversations about single rooms.

2 For an account of the villa system and of Steinhof's design, see Leslie Topp, "Otto Wagner and the Steinhof Psychiatric Hospital: Architecture as Misunderstanding," *The Art Bulletin* 87, no. 1 (March 1, 2005): 130–156, doi:10.2307/25067159.

3 The exceptions were the pavilions for quiet patients, which on the first and second stories had dormitories on the north and south sides, opening onto a common hall, and dayrooms on the ground floor; and the pavilion for violent patients (who had been committed by the courts). The floor plans of all the pavilions were published in a commemorative volume: *N.-Ö. Landes- Heil- und Pflegeanstalten für Geistes- und Nervenkranken "Am Steinhof" in Wien* (1907?).

4 Bericht des niederösterreichischen Landesausschusses über den Landtagsbeschluss vom 9. Juli 1901, betreffend die Abtretung der Landes-Irrenanstaltsrealität im IX. Wiener

Gemeindebezirke zum Zwecke des Neubaus von medizinischen Unterrichtskliniken (Beilage XLVI)," *Stenographische Protokolle des niederösterreichischen Landtages* VIII Wahlperiode, 1901–02 (1902). "Wenn gewisser Psychiater, auf ein einseitiges und dürftiges Beobachtungsmateriale gestützt, die Behauptung aufstellen, man werde in Hinkunft auf eine Isolirung der Geisteskranken vollständig verzichten und die Irrenanstalten demgemäß zellenlos bauen können, so beweisen sie damit nur, dass ihnen die Erfahrungen in einer großen Irrenanstalt mit hohen Aufnahmsziffern mangeln und dass ihnen ein wohlfeiles Schlagwort höher gilt, als die Rücksichtnahme auf eine Summe von Einrichtungen, welche in einer gut angelegten Irrenanstalt nothwendig sind und unter welchen die Einzelzimmer eine wesentliche, in dem gesammten Heilapparate durch nichts zu ersetzende Rolle spielen."

5 Ibid. "Man wird daher auch künftighin in gegebenen Fällen zu isolieren gezwungen sein, einerlei, aus welchen Gründen und wie man diese Isolierungen bezeichnen will. Demgemäß muss auch für eine genügende Anzahl von Einzelzimmern vorgesorgt werden." The passage continues: "In the planned *Heilanstalt* [the acute section of the asylum] the requirement for single rooms is calculated at a ratio of 1:10, meaning there will need to be 80, of which at least 30 will need to be designed as secure rooms." "Bei der projectirten Heilanstalt wird sich der Bedarf an Einzelzimmern wie 1:10, somit auf 80 stellen, von welchen mindestens 30 als feste Zimmer einzurichten wären."

6 John Conolly, *The Construction and Government of Lunatic Asylums and Hospitals for the Insane* (1st edn 1847), reprinted with an introduction by Richard Hunter and Ida Macalpine, Psychiatric Monograph Series 6 (London: Dawsons, 1968). For a detailed account of Conolly's activities in the wider context of British politics and reform movements, and for full references to the literature on Conolly, see Akihito Suzuki, "The Politics and Ideology of Non-Restraint: The Case of the Hanwell Asylum," *Medical History* 39 (1995): 1–17.

7 Conolly, *The Construction and Government of Lunatic Asylums*, 24.

8 Ibid., 25.

9 Ibid., 20–21.

10 Kathleen Jones, *A History of the Mental Health Services* (London: Routledge & Kegan Paul, 1972), 101–149.

11 See J.C. Bucknill, "Asylum Architecture and Arrangements," *Asylum Journal of Mental Science* 3 (1857): 286.

12 *Report of the Metropolitan Commissioners in Lunacy to the Lord Chancellor* (London: Bradbury & Evans, 1844), 12.

13 Ibid., 13.

14 Bucknill, "Asylum Architecture and Arrangements," 286. For Bucknill and the Asylum Journal, see Chris Philo, "'Enough to Drive One Mad': The Organization of Space in Nineteenth-Century Lunatic Asylums," in Jennifer Wolch and Michael Dear, eds., *The Power of Geography: How Territory Shapes Social Life* (Boston, MA: Unwin Hyman, 1989), 258–89.

15 Bucknill, "Asylum Architecture and Arrangements," 291.

16 Ibid., 293.

17 Ibid., 294–295.

18 Ibid., 293.

19 Conolly, *The Construction and Government of Lunatic Asylums*, 20, 22.

20 Ibid., 26.

21 Ibid., 26–7.

22 Ibid., 28.

23 *Report of the Metropolitan Commissioners in Lunacy*, 137–138.

24 Ibid., 141.

25 Ibid., 146.

26 Adolf Funk, " Irrenanstalten," in *Verschiedene Heil- und Pflege-Anstalten*, Teil 4, Bd 5, Heft 2, *Handbuch der Architektur* (Darmstadt: Bergsträsser, 1891), 10.

27 Ibid., 10–11.

28 Albrecht Paetz, *Die Kolonisirung der Geisteskranken in Verbindung mit dem Offen-Thür-System, Ihre Historische Entwickelung und die Art Ihrer Ausführung auf Rittergut Alt-Scherbitz* (Berlin: Springer, 1893), 88.

29 Ibid., 89.

30 Ibid., 86.

31 Ibid., 89.

32 Ibid., 86. Luigi Canestrini, in his 1903 research trip account, reports on liberal institutions in which the few cells that exist are better known as "einzelne Zimmer" (he uses the German term in his Italian text). Luigi Canestrini, "Note Manicomiali, relazione presentata il 13 gennaio 1903 all Associazione Medica Triestina," *Bolletino dell'Associazione Medica Triestina* 6a (1902–03): 87.

33 Paetz, *Kolonisierung*, 86, 89–91. "So-called padded cells" also had no place in the modern asylum (91).

34 For an extended discussion of debates about single rooms and cells, the "raving ward" specifically and the role of the corridor more generally in Central European psychiatry, see Leslie Topp, *Freedom and the Cage: Modern Architecture and Psychiatry in Central Europe, 1890–1914* (University Park, PA: Penn State University Press, forthcoming), Chapter 6.

35 Paetz, *Kolonisierung*, 89.

36 Josef Starlinger, "Ein Beitrag zum Irrenanstaltsbau (Aus einem Reiseberichte)," *Psychiatrische Wochenschrift*, no. 13 (1901): 135–136.

37 "Bericht des niederösterreichischen Landesausschusses über den Landtagsbeschluss vom 9. Juli 1901," 44.

38 Ibid.

39 Ibid.

40 John Tosh, *A Man's Place : Masculinity and the Middle-Class Home in Victorian England* (New Haven, CT: Yale University Press, 2007), 17, 38, 60, 182.

41 Stefan Muthesius, *The Poetic Home : Designing the Nineteenth-Century Domestic Interior* (London: Thames & Hudson 2009). See also Karl Weissbach, *Wohngebäude*, Handbuch der Architektur, Teil 4, Bd 2, Heft 1 (Stuttgart: Bergsträsser, 1902).

42 Donald J. Olsen, *The City as a Work of Art : London, Paris, Vienna* (New Haven, CT: Yale University Press, 1986), 125–131.

43 For a study of single rooms and gender in housing for the affluent in Austrian and Germany, see Anne Katrin Rossberg, "Frauenzimmer: Die Tradition des Boudoirs im 20. Jahrhundert," PhD thesis, University of Vienna, 1994.

44 Tag Gronberg, "The Inner Man: Interiors and Masculinity in Early Twentieth-Century Vienna," *Oxford Art Journal* 24, no. 1 (2001): 67–88. Anne-Katrin Rossberg, "Ein 'Fideles' Gefängnis: Der Erker als Weiblich Definierter Raum," *Frauen in Der Literaturwissenschaft* 45 (1995): 8–10.

45 Weissbach, *Wohngebäude*,155.

46 See Rossberg, "Frauenzimmer," 59–69, for a discussion of the bedroom for the adolescent daughter.

47 Karl Wilhelm Just, *Hotels, Restaurants*, 3rd edn, *Handbuch der Architektur*, Teil IV, Bd 4, Heft 1 (Leipzig: J.M. Gebhardt, 1933), 9, Figures 1 and 2.

48 Mary Guyatt, "A Semblance of Home: Mental Asylum Interiors, 1890–1914," in Susie McKellar and Penny Sparke, eds., *Interior Design and Identity* (Manchester: Manchester University Press, 2004), 53.

49 Just, *Hotels*, 10.

50 For a study of sanatorium buildings in Central Europe, see Nicola J. Imrie, "The Architecture and Culture of Sanatoria for Nervous Ailments in the Austro-Hungarian Empire 1890–1914," PhD thesis, Birkbeck College, 2008. See especially Figure 1.17, showing the first-floor plan of the Priessnitz Sanatorium (architect Leopold Bauer, 1910), with single rooms off a double-loaded corridor. The second floor of Josef Hoffmann's building for the Purkersdorf Sanatorium (1904) contained single rooms along both sides of a central corridor. Gunter Breckner, *Sanatorium Purkersdorf* (New York and Vienna: Galerie Metropole, n.d.), 11, 27.

51 Imrie discusses the connections between the sanatorium and the grand hotel in "The Architecture and Culture of Sanatoria," 68–122.

PART 2

Healing Landscapes and the Body Out-of-Doors

6

Freeing Bodies and Prescribing Play in the Humanization of New York City: Richard Dattner's 1960s Playgrounds

Camille Shamble

In the post-World War II era, the perception of increasingly unsafe and deteriorating urban conditions led to a desire to improve cities for children, and an interest in urban children's spaces as catalysts for greater social, cultural, and economic renewal. Architect Richard Dattner's work with New York City playgrounds in the late 1960s highlights this investment in the potential power of childhood. Dattner was concerned with the loss of community and humanity caused by decades of urban renewal projects and patterns of suburbanization that had left New York City undervalued, vacant, and dangerous. His focus on children's health and playgrounds was an attempt to revitalize New York. Public life, community, and civility, were being threatened by the privatization of citizens' lives, the increasing segregation and polarization of classes, and the loss of precious public space claimed for the automobile. Dattner wrote, "The diminishment of the public sphere disturbs the balance needed for a healthy, civilized existence . . . ."[1] For Dattner, to "humanize the city" was to create spaces of play that would cultivate healthy, intelligent, and free public citizens. In short, Dattner was striving to create active urban communities with thriving civic engagement. As a tool for much-needed reconstruction and progress, playgrounds for children were assigned an important role in this urban renewal.

In considering Dattner's writings and representation of his imagined and constructed works, this chapter examines the relationship between his designs and theories and their implications for the children who would occupy the spaces in question. An investigation of Richard Dattner's work can also be a starting point for broader questions about the relationship between children and the postwar urban environment: How were children envisioned as part of urbanism? How did sociological, psychological, and medical theories about childhood influence urban design? How did forms of architectural representation reflect the attention given to the urban child? How were children's spaces used to improve the health of the child and the city?

In 1969, Dattner positioned himself as a theorist and designer when he wrote his book, *Design for Play*, which was partly a campaign for children's rights, partly a young architect's manifesto, and partly a psychological outline and ergonomic atlas. Dattner's book outlined the value of play, play's relationship to the learning process, and advice for successful play facilities. Dattner intended his playgrounds to be places of autonomy, agency, and unhindered invention, imagination, and creative expression. His intense interest in child psychology and physical and mental growth informed his choice of materials as well as the form, organization, and programming of the playgrounds. As Dattner waged a war on the barren asphalt projects that threatened the life of the city and children's potential, his work became exceptionally forceful and unyielding itself. Dattner's playgrounds were rigidly employed as regenerative elements of the city and park system and as a necessary generative influence on children's ideal health and character. As a result, Dattner's playgrounds provide insight into the relationship between postwar architecture and notions of childhood, illuminating concerns about children's health and well-being in an evolving urban environment—concerns that remain prevalent today. Indeed, in current debates about urbanism, practitioners and scholars such as Liane Lefaivre continue to assert that children's play has the potential to heal and activate a neighborhood. Lefaivre argues that urban playgrounds can serve as truly public and communal spaces, making urban environments more livable, with safer, stronger, more integrated communities.[2]

We can begin by considering the impact of Dattner's own coming of age and education on his contributions to New York City playgrounds. In a variety of ways, Dattner's childhood spawned his interest in both community and the visual realm. Before he was nine years old, Dattner had lived and attended schools in Poland, Italy, Cuba, Queens and Upstate New York. Not being able to speak the languages upon arrival in many of these places, he was especially sensitive to visual culture, and this sensitivity played out in his expressive and universal playground forms.[3] For instance, Dattner resented the "antiseptic" and "unfriendly" play structures that he experienced as a child in New York.[4] At the same time, Dattner also appreciated and wanted to capture the freedoms he experienced as an immigrant youth in America, enabled by extensive public transportation systems, organized public schools, and wide streets and public parks.[5] Later, as an architecture student, Dattner was inspired by his urban theory instructors. At the Massachusetts Institute of Technology, he studied under Lewis Mumford and Joseph Hudnut, and he would credit Mumford with foregrounding the link between architecture and culture that, for Dattner, demonstrated that "urban form was the manifestation of political structure and systems of belief."[6] But perhaps most relevant to Dattner's playground designs was his third year in college (1957–58), when he studied abroad at the London Architectural Association under Peter and Alison Smithson, but most closely under studio teacher James Gowan, then in partnership with James Stirling. Their work, and the massive reconstruction of London housing and schools, then underway, by the London County Council was an example of public investment in the social well-being of a city. In the 1950s, London, like many European cities, was still undergoing postwar reconstruction. Architects like the Smithsons, Gowan, and Stirling were interested in modern architecture as a purveyor of social justice and a source of renewed public life in the face of poverty, limited resources, and destruction. In this climate, Dattner came to believe that architecture could improve public life and could serve as a community catalyst in times of recovery.[7]

Although Dattner has been actively working in New York City for half of a century and has had a traceable influence on contemporary discourse surrounding children and play in urban environments, his work and writings have not received significant scholarly attention.[8] Susan Solomon, in her book *American Playgrounds: Revitalizing Community Space* (2005), wrote about Dattner's playgrounds as "abstract and non-dictatorial," arguing that his playground design encouraged users to "invent unstructured play situations."[9] While this might appear to be the case, as this chapter will discuss, Dattner carefully considered children's varied sizes in designing his abstract playground forms, consistently evaluated their usefulness given the developmental processes outlined by contemporary child psychologists, and used administrative play supervisors to maximize children's development and foster democracy and community. Michael Gotkin's essay "The Politics of Play" (1999) on the preservation history of Dattner's Central Park Adventure Playground discussed Dattner's design philosophy as it related to child psychology but avoided considering how more complicated, multi-layered concerns regarding children's health mapped onto underlying political strategies. A closer analysis of Dattner's playgrounds reveals intriguing ironies of freedom versus control embedded in postwar playground design.

Roy Kozlovsky's essay "Adventure Playgrounds and Postwar Reconstruction" (2008) underscored the political paradoxes embedded in the concept of the postwar playground, but in England, commenting that

> *on the one hand, modernity has conceptualized play as a biologically inherited drive that is spontaneous, pleasurable, and free . . . play as an attribute of the autonomous, individual self. On the other hand, modern societies began to rationalize and shape children's play from the outside to advance social, educational, and political goals.*[10]

In short, the playground was seen as a stabilizing and mitigating element that was entrusted with healing postwar society. This study looks at these political and social contradictions but examines them through an architectural lens as they were physically manifested in Dattner's New York City playgrounds and considers the dynamics of Dattner's work as responses to the following factors: the increasing fear of the urban environment as a safe and healthy place for children, the circulation of shared ideas between American and European postwar playgrounds, an increasing postwar focus on children's rights and child development, and a reorientation of children in the city.

THEORETICAL AND POLITICAL CONTEXT

Children's spaces such as playgrounds were intended to serve a larger purpose beyond the children themselves, activating greater urban change while also unifying city dwellers into communities. In 1959, the United Nations adopted the *Declaration of the Rights of the Child*, which stated in Principle 7, "The child shall have full opportunity for play and recreation, which should be directed to the same purposes as education; society and the public authorities shall endeavour to promote the enjoyment of this right."[11] This international declaration positioned play as a basic human right along with food, shelter, and medical care. "Authorities" were required to guarantee the child's enjoyment of play for the purpose of bettering society.

The spirit of Principle 7 reflected the development of adventure playgrounds. Traditional playground design persisted from the early 1900s through the first half of the twentieth century, with regimented play structures such as jungle-gyms, swings, slides, and see-saws made of steel or wood, permanently set in a concrete or asphalt field. Adventure playgrounds, in which children were given access to moveable parts, abstract compositions, and a variety of play opportunities (often directed by a play leader) developed in Europe starting in the 1930s. They began as "junk playgrounds" by Danish landscape architect C.T. Sorensen and were later popularized by English landscape architect Lady Allen of Hurtwood and Dutch designer Aldo van Eyck, Dattner's inspirations. Sorensen's junk playground allowed children to engage with objects often forbidden to them. The junk playground was a collection of everyday objects, an abstract compilation of everyday life and local landscapes, rather than a playground based on form or composition. Just one year before Dattner's book was published, Hurtwood published *Planning for Play* (1968), which advocated for adventure playgrounds as places where children could "develop their own ideas of play" by allowing them to engage with malleable and mobile materials in a "free and permissive atmosphere."[12] Hurtwood's advocacy for adventure playgrounds stemmed from her desire to decrease postwar anxiety through play therapy and, like Dattner, to mitigate juvenile delinquency and improve urban children's welfare.

Meanwhile, van Eyck wrote about how playgrounds functioned as design laboratories and miniature test cases for larger urban ideas; they were places to make constructive contributions to the city and to reinstate traditional values.[13] Likewise, when philosopher Henri Lefebvre wrote about cities undergoing processes of modernization, regularization, and technological advancement, which he worried were lessening traditional values such as community activism, historic preservation, and human engagement, he advocated for the integration of play into the fabric of the environment.[14] Clearly, Dattner was working in the midst of a passionate dialog when, with the child as his mascot, he set out to cultivate a more humane city.

In a way, these international developments were also prefigured by developments in child psychology dating back to pediatrician and psychoanalyst Dr. Benjamin Spock's 1946 book, *The Common Sense Book of Baby and Child Care*.[15] This book represented a marked shift towards child-centric thinking in which children became their own advocates and controllers of their own environments. Simultaneously, the discipline of developmental psychology was blossoming and eventually led to the founding of several child-centric health and education organizations. Erik Erikson, a German-American psychologist, outlined eight phases of development organized into binaries such as Trust vs. Mistrust and Autonomy vs. Shame & Doubt, theorizing that in order to develop, a child needed to understand both values and then arrive at a healthy middle-ground.[16] Swiss psychologist Jean Piaget suggested in *Origins of Intelligence in Children* (1952) that childhood could be separated into developmental stages, also that children play to imitate adult behavior and prepare for adulthood.[17] Such theories ultimately contributed to the establishment of the National Institute of Child Health and Human Development in

1963 and the Head Start Program in 1965, which argued that a happy and healthy childhood should be understood as a distinct and essential component of human development that could be properly facilitated by a supportive family, a safe environment that allowed play and experimentation, and access to health care, nutrition, and exercise. Ultimately, these same psychologists would also inspire Dattner's interest in developmental stages and the didactic power of play, leading him to argue that "[i]n the process of mastering familiar situations and learning to cope with new ones, [children's] intelligence and personality grow, as well as their bodies."[18] Indeed, as we will see later, Dattner's playgrounds physically manifested some of the specific concepts emphasized by thinkers such as Erikson, with similar dualities intentionally contrasted in his playscapes.

At the same time, however, the local political environment surrounding Dattner's work was equally influential. Dattner was working in the time of the infamous New York City Parks commissioner Robert Moses when his career began, and Moses was a controversial figure. On the one hand, he was known as a powerful and successful builder of public works, but his massive, imposing architectural installations and circulation systems also encouraged many to see him as insensitive and destructive—even antipathetic to democracy.[19] Change came in 1965, when John Lindsay ran for mayor on a platform that advocated for the child as part of a nationwide movement to rethink the nature of city parks and urban spaces in the wake of the mass exodus to suburbia. Lindsay won the election and appointed Thomas Hoving as Parks Commissioner, ushering in an era of leadership that was supportive of innovative, adventurous, and unique playgrounds and community activities. The latter contrasted starkly with Moses' standardized and fixed steel and asphalt playgrounds. Hoving also argued that the more people were present on a playground, the safer the space would be. The Parks and Recreation Department published new policies suggesting that architecture alone was not enough to guarantee a safe and productive space for play but that programmed activities needed to be implemented as well: "Park and recreation people must begin to take seriously their obligations to provide recreation experiences for people rather than recreation facilities."[20] Inventive activities such as kite flying, group games, and concerts were implemented to attract crowds. On Sundays, Central Park was closed to automobiles and bicycles filled the park. These were developments that would dovetail well with Dattner's own work, which was encouraged and supported by Hoving.

UNPACKING DATTNER'S PLAYSCAPES

With this architectural and theoretical grounding, Dattner completed his first Central Park playground, called the Adventure Playground, in 1967. The playground was located at the West 67th entrance to the park, serving a community that included a mix of upper-middle-class families and lower-income families, primarily recent immigrants in apartments and individuals living in single-room-occupancy housing. Dattner's intention was for the playground to ensure a shared public space that would bring together the many types of people in the city.[21]

The playground entrance was located near the street, which ensured its surveillance by the community and its integration into the fabric of the neighborhood. The playground's forms essentially created a large elongated oval with two entrance points. The play structures within the park followed the rounded shape, forming a continuous loop of ziggurats, tree houses, pools, poles, tunnels, and slides (Figure 6.1).

The forms were simple but monumental and primitive; they included mounds, pyramids, circular mazes, arcs, and channels. Dattner chose the circular form because it fostered "inclusion"—the child could select from a variety of different activities while still feeling like part of a larger group.[22] While there was no prescribed order of play, the circular arrangement suggested continuous directional movement. Dattner also divided the plan into two halves: one end was for physical activity, such as "running, jumping, sliding, climbing, tunneling, balancing," and the other end was for mental and motor development, such as building, painting, and playing with water.[23] He ensured physical and developmental activities were programmed into the inert structures, envisioning certain objects being used for certain games: "The tower and maze, which resemble a fortress, were designed to be used also for games of strategy . . . all kinds of cowboy-and-indian type battles as well as short-range snowball fights."[24] There was a continuous low wall just wide enough for children that circumscribed the playground. At one point along the wall (which was Dattner's intended start and finish), he placed a special section of heavy wooden timbers set on end and of varying heights as a way of creating one final obstacle, encouraging a sense of accomplishment at the completion of a task. Dattner's formal arrangement was almost entirely functional and was based on child engagement, play patterns, and the development processes.

On the whole, Dattner's *playscape*, as he called it, was a landscape of experiences designed with the goal of ultimate freedom, empowerment, and imagination. Dattner, inspired by Dutch cultural historian and theorist Johan Huizinga, believed

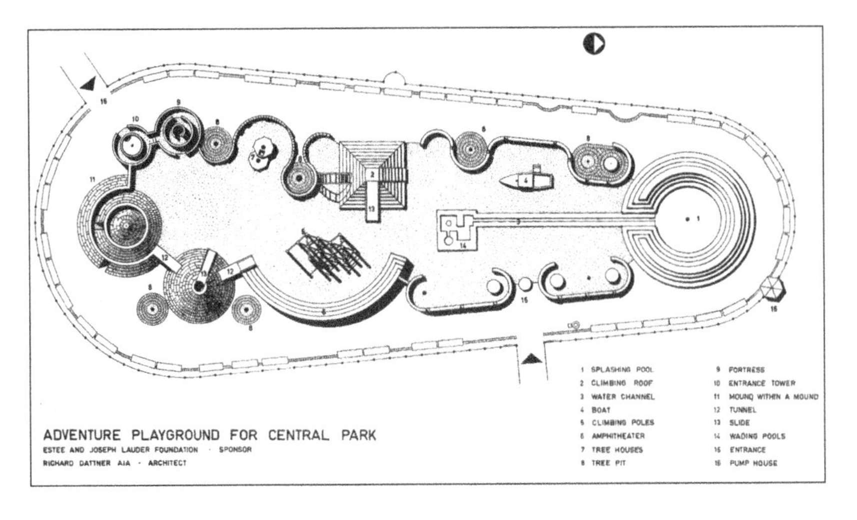

6.1 Plan of the Adventure Playground, Central Park, New York. Courtesy of Richard Dattner.

in the intersection of freedom, play, and imagination. In Huizinga's *Homo Ludens: A Study of the Play-Element in Culture* (1938), he posited that play was an expression of freedom, the essence of human nature, and a shaper of culture and civilization. Along these lines, Dattner wrote, "All work and no play not only makes Jack a dull boy but deprives him of that full expression of personal freedom which makes him uniquely human."[25] Dattner suggested that without play, the child's mind would not develop properly and, more importantly, the child would fail to realize his or her potential as a human being and as a citizen.

In addition to paralleling the discourse surrounding the postwar urban environment, this perspective reflects the aforementioned shift in the value of play. Nevertheless, despite Dattner's intentions, his playground's design elements were static and unrelenting: rigid, somber, and heavy in their materials and their monumental structures. Within this concrete armature, the children themselves became the moving parts. His playground forms were primitive and composed of elementary shapes—abstract representations of natural and manmade landscapes. He also created a simplified and scaled world that was devoid of artificial color—yet he did so because he associated abstract forms with the cultivation of children's imaginations. A playscape composed of basic forms—circles, rectangles, cylinders, mazes, walls, tables, and mounds—would encourage children to exercise their minds: "The child who plays with real sticks and leaves transforms them in his imagination into whatever he wants and creates another, more personal, reality not bounded by the real and commonplace."[26] As a result of Dattner's provocative views, there were no elephants, dolphins, or imitations in Dattner's playscapes. Though there was a boat in preliminary designs, it was not included in the built version.

While he worked to encourage freedom, Dattner also worked to cultivate what he called a "creative interaction between the individual and his environment," inspired by psychiatrist R.D. Laing.[27] The aim was to make sure not only that the playground allowed for a wide range of experiences but also that the child could control, reinterpret, and modify the environment. Control and variety were critical; in fact, Dattner dramatically likened children's environments that lacked these elements to dehumanized ones such as war camps. Dattner structured his playground with reference to Laing's theories of Experience, Control of Experience, Graduated Challenge, Choice, Exercise of Fantasy, Separation from Adults, and Expressive Play. He even specifically documented populating his playgrounds with moving parts, pieces that moved not just within a range of fixed and predictable motion (like a swing or see-saw) but parts that were totally flexible and mobile that a child could relocate, reinterpret, and reinvent in unpredictable improvisation.[28] Again, however, the reality was that his play forms were calculated, programmed, and fixed; the variety came from the diversity of forms and textures but primarily from toys and play pieces distributed by a play supervisor.

SAFETY AND AGE IN DATTNER'S PLAYGROUNDS

The play forms exhibited an urban character and employed urban materials. Dattner intended for the playgrounds to blend into the context of the urban park through a material palette of unfinished concrete, granite blocks, wood timbers and poles, sand, rope, and steel pipe, all of which would merge in color and texture with the site. Dattner's concerns about children's safety, however, led him to assert that a playground architect should exercise caution when dealing with natural materials and only use scrap lumber, for example, "with edges rounded."[29] In most of Dattner's images of children at the playground, the children, and even the adults, are pictured with bare feet. Through the usage of landscape materials not usually found in the ground plane of the urban context—sand and water—Dattner created a mediated and protected natural environment, like a groomed beach or a family backyard, and provided children with a rare opportunity to remove the protective layer of their shoes in an urban environment. And indeed, Dattner's park was prescribed and programmed to separate, stimulate, and safeguard, beginning at the entrance gate. The entrance gateway led to a maze with thick board-formed concrete walls in the shape of concentric circles that separated children from adults using scale; the size was purposely petite so that an adult would not comfortably fit. Likewise, adults were discouraged from the inner circle of the playground by several inconvenient access points, while they were invited to settle around the edges by benches and shade trees. Dattner gently called parents or adults in the playscape "trespassers" and lamented parents' need to follow their children to ensure their safety or to take their picture.[30] However, even if the adults were impeded from readily accessing the children, their protective presence was interwoven into the developmental structure of the playscape. For example, the playscape had a tunnel that ran underneath the volcano. The entrances to the tunnel were just large enough for adults to enter if it became necessary, although they were also just small enough that it was difficult for most adults to scrunch in, keeping them from following the child through.[31] Dattner wrote: "In this way children and parents are separated naturally";[32] yet the architectural arrangement intended to achieve this effect was in fact expressly programmed rather than spontaneously occurring.

At the same time, Dattner's playscape finely balanced safety and danger. Water ran through the center of the playground, with a concrete trough for a water channel culminating in a collection of shallow pools that ranged in depth from two to six inches. Dattner carefully determined the depth of the water, calculating that this range was enough water to encourage learning and coordination processes such as scooping up water in pails but was not deep enough to necessitate a lifeguard or to worry parents and cause interference.[33]

Today, one of the playground's most controversial play structures in terms of safety would have to be Dattner's climbing poles. They were a set of tall redwood posts connected by steel bars in a ladder formation. The steel rungs were spaced progressively wider as they got further off the ground, effectively encouraging children of all ages to climb, but limiting the distance that an individual child would climb based on the child's expected reach and level of maturity. In the event that the safety mechanism failed and a child clambered above his ability and fell, the child's fall would be cushioned with a base of thick sand around the poles. In fact, safety and limits were expected to be taught through minor falls and upsets, whereas a playground that protected children entirely from injury might give them a false impression of the world at large. Dattner wrote, "No playground can prevent a child from being hurt (and if it protected him from upset completely, it would convey the very misleading impression that he has nothing to fear from his environment)."[34] Finally, a knotted rope was suspended from one rung on the climbing poles. While Dattner encouraged children to climb the rope by making child-sized hand-holds with the knots, he discouraged the more unpredictable activity of freely swinging from the rope by rigidly securing the bottom of the rope to the ground.

As might be expected from the above description of Dattner's climbing poles, his play forms were based on ergonomics and the structure of a child's movement in space. In *Design for Play*, Dattner included a measurement chart called "Comparative Dimensions of Children" (Figure 6.2). The chart showed the height, weight, arm reach, and chair height for boys and girls every two years from age two to age fourteen, mapping a silhouette of a child's body against a grid of measured units. The measurements came from industrial designer Henry Dreyfuss's book *The Measure of Man: Human Factors in Design* (1960).[35] In Dattner's chart, the child was reduced to his/her abstract essential form—a calculable object reflected as larger, taller, and stronger in two-year increments until s/he reached the age that signaled the end of playground use and the start of adulthood. The simplified silhouettes depicted children at play, demonstrating their reach upward or outward as they caught a ball, jumped, walked with a balloon, or leaned against an object. In this way, Dattner distilled the child–environment interaction into a receptive technology loop in which the body and the exterior would interact and affect each other; he noted that "[i]n computer parlance, this would be described as a situation with constant feedback of information . . . ."[36] Dattner employed ergonomics as a precise technological interplay of idealized bodies mapped on a spatial grid. His playgrounds were calibrated to maximize the "feed-back" and projected growth of the child, and his playground forms became a three-dimensional representation of this charted interplay.

Even where safety might be less of a concern, Dattner's forms were regulated by age and activity based on these measurements. Each form was designed to engage certain functions at precise levels. There were two tree houses, octagonal wooden platforms suspended from trees, each with a simple wooden horizontal slat fence. The tree houses were designed for two different age groups: one for two- to four-year-olds

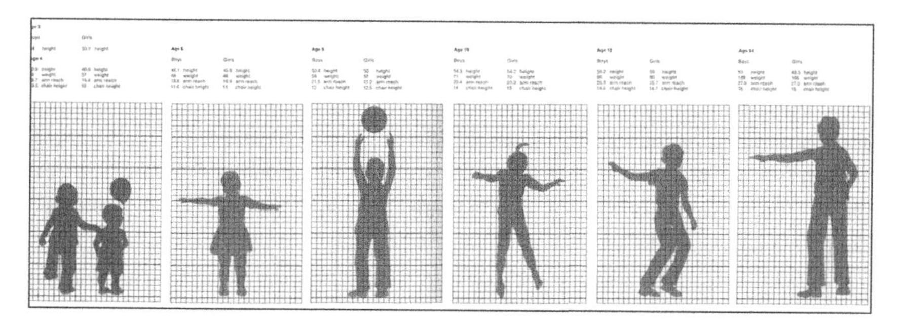

6.2 Measurement chart in *Design for Play*: comparative dimensions of children. Courtesy of Edward Marson.

6.3 The volcano at the Adventure Playground. Courtesy of Richard Dattner.

and one for older children. Again, Dattner used the spacing of the ladder rungs to encourage the children to make this distinction during play. The volcano, a heavy pyramid faced with large rough bricks and mortar with accessible flat concrete peak, was also tiered by age with several options for climbing up or down—a ramp, a ladder, or climbing rocks—depending on ability (Figure 6.3). The pyramid structure, a solid ziggurat constructed of dark wooden boards, was also designed for children to ascend. Then, from the comfort of a viewing platform, they could select their method of descent: should I slide down the big, bumpy side or just take the stairs instead?

PLAY AND THE "WORLD OF ADULTS"

Dattner, like the psychologists from whom he took inspiration, believed that development should unfold naturally. However, theories of development that labeled individual stages and used these labels as measurement tools created a certain pressure on children to grow and change. Dattner's play objects exhibit some of this irony, as Dattner called their progressive sequence "graduated challenge" and planned for them to provide opportunities for continuous improvement and growth.[37] Dattner also wrote that play, unlike work, could not be "classified, measured, counted, or sold."[38] Nevertheless, his play forms functioned as mechanisms for quantifying and measuring not only child development but also social progress. In fact, Dattner's book argued that controlling children's play was "one way in which a society transmits its values and prepares children to participate in the adult world."[39] Dattner also cited physiologist Ivan Pavlov as an influence, highlighting his interest in repeated instigation, conditioned response, and concerted education. In short, Dattner's highly calculated play spaces were intended to help children speedily acquire valuable characteristics and skills.

Dattner's concern about maximizing these benefits was visible in the way the playgrounds were designed to include the use of a play supervisor. The play supervisor's role, ironically, was to teach children how to play autonomously. The 1955 Conference of Play Leaders had described the play leader or supervisor as "the humanizing element, the person who brings the whole thing to life."[40] The play supervisor was present six days a week. She or he gave instructions, led games, and handed out play materials such as art supplies, sand utensils, or construction objects. The play supervisor was also on site to administer first-aid and supplies. Dattner even designed a special office and storage unit for the play supervisor that was open only to adults and was located in the interior of the pyramid structure.

The play supervisor's sex was predetermined in the planning of the playground and reflected constructions of gender. A young female supervisor was to be hired for the mornings because the children were younger and were expected to thrive under a woman's care. A young male supervisor, however, was to be hired for the afternoons because men were seen as ideal for interactions with older children. Regardless of his or her gender, the play supervisor would exhibit the "good qualities of a parent without the parent's emotional stake in the children's performance."[41] Toward that end, the play supervisor would aid the children in achieving goals and would suggest activities that challenged them to develop new skills, but they would not experience typical parent–child relationship issues such as separation problems or irrational concerns about safety.[42] The architecture and the child were deemed insufficient; without a play supervisor, play was not expected to be as efficient, inspiring, or humane. The employment of the play supervisor, paired with the desire for child agency, highlights the paradoxes surrounding postwar play and playgrounds.

Beyond parents and play supervisors, other adults were also more tangentially involved in Dattner's playscapes, as Dattner sought community empowerment and the humanization of the city by engaging the public in the architectural process and the appropriation of urban space. In this way, Dattner followed in the footsteps of many postwar theorists who saw public participation in the design process and communal urban place-making as paramount. From Henri Lefebrve's *Critique of Everyday Life* (1947) to Shadrach Woods' *Urbanism is Everybody's Business* (1968), "everybody" was intended to be involved "everyday," while the accessible format of Christopher Alexander's architectural text *Pattern Language* (1977) encouraged the public to participate in the design process more specifically.[43] The public played a correspondingly large role in Dattner's adventure playground project, assisting with site selection and outlining the needs of specific user groups. This was particularly important in New York City, where Dattner saw community participation as a way of minimizing complaints and encouraging the community to help maintain playgrounds. Thus, Dattner held regular large community meetings and smaller meetings with specific user groups such as parents, children, neighbors, city officials, and maintenance staff, hoping to categorize and prioritize each specific group's requirements.[44] He simultaneously expressed special concern regarding the involvement of children in the design process, suggesting that children's needs and desires should be envisioned, interpreted, and manifested by adults: "The next best thing to a playground designed entirely by children is a playground designed by an adult but incorporating the possibility for children to create their own places within it."[45] For instance, Dattner made slide presentations at local public schools, talking to the children and encouraging their questions, although he did not conceptualize the children as actual designers shaping the playscape themselves. Dattner worried that the most influential group, the city administrators, were actually the least affected by the design of the play facility, while the children, the most affected, had the least input; he tried to balance city involvement with the apparent needs of the children based on interviews and observations.[46]

CHILDREN AND THE CITY IN TWO DIMENSIONS

Dattner's attention to children's movement and activity was so pervasive that it was evident in the way that he visually represented his playground designs and the

6.4 Dattner's design drawing of the Adventure Playground. Courtesy of Richard Dattner.

design process he employed. The postwar focus on the child and children's development affected how design ideas and intentions were rendered and presented. For instance, the use of children's tools, rendering techniques, and color palettes gave architectural drawings a simplistic, playful quality. Van Eyck, for example, used crayons and primary colors to render architectural drawings of his playgrounds. Meanwhile, Kevin Lynch's book *The Image of the City* (1960) included a child's illustration on the cover.[47] In short, through such imagery, the postwar child was given unprecedented attention and a special status.

Dattner's presentation models for the playground described here were made out of loosely molded clay with sticks inserted to represent trees. The loose shaping and bumpy texture of the clay in the model was realized in the final design through a variety of concrete finishes, relief textures, and rock aggregates; in the meantime, this element gave the model a childlike quality. In his illustrations, Dattner also employed a simple black pen technique reminiscent of that used in children's books (Figure 6.4). There was a looseness to the dots, hatches, and squiggles, and the children did not have clearly defined faces. Nevertheless, while Dattner's hand remained loose, charismatic, and playful like that of a child, he articulated the details of the scene in depth, meticulously representing a variety of ages, sizes, clothing, tools, vegetation, and play forms. The children represented in the illustrations were engaged in an array of activities at different levels and interacted with each other in various ways: sailing boats in the water, digging with a bucket and shovel, and climbing on structures.

If Dattner's play forms were inspired by children's omnipresent physical engagement with the city in which they lived, Dattner's book provides a window into that engagement by pairing his theories with black and white photographs of children playing in the cityscape. The photographs, most of which were taken by Dattner himself, represented a personal, grassroots interest in the child in the street (Figure 6.5). The photographs were usually taken at eye level, with simple framing, recalling documentary photography and an anthropological approach. Dattner recorded children sliding down stair rails; swinging on fire escapes; kicking, collecting, and stacking beer cans; climbing stoplights; dancing in the spray of open fire hydrants; and milling about the rubble in a building construction site. The photographs were playful and intimate as well as intensely curious, studying the movements of the children in their environment.

In turn, the photographs and the activities captured in them often became abstracted elements in Dattner's playscapes. For instance, Dattner designed a splashing pool at one end of the playground with a fountain that sprayed like a broken fire hydrant and channeled the water around the playground through a series of "gutters" (Figure 6.6). Dattner paid careful attention to the usage of the water channel by different age groups, noting that the five- to eight-year-olds would float

6.5 Dattner photograph from *Design for Play*: buildings provided possibilities for play. Courtesy of Richard Dattner.

6.6 The splashing pool and water channel (a redesigned version of the gutter) at the Adventure Playground. Courtesy of Richard Dattner.

things in the stream while the older children attempted to create dams with their bodies and found objects.[48]

TAKING PLAY TO THE STREETS

In Dattner's historical and professional context, some urban advocates argued against playgrounds that were detached from the city environment; many theorists, politicians, and planners supported the appropriation of the street instead. American urban theorist, Jane Jacobs, in her book, *The Death and Life of Great American Cities* (1961), devoted a chapter to railing against detached and enclosed playgrounds, arguing that children's play should inhabit the sidewalks, well integrated into everyday street life, enlivening the street, and protected by neighbors' watchful eyes.[49] Designers, planners, and many child advocates were looking for the accidental open space or the "antipark," as a 1972 Parks and Recreation brochure called it.[50] The street was the "most exciting space in the city," argued city planners.[51] Correspondingly, Dattner sought to integrate the playscape into the urban environment, which he manipulated to integrate urban structures with children's play. Thus, the urban environment became a way to entertain children, help them grow, and prevent socially destructive behaviors. Play was essential to the health of the child, but also to the health of the city. Building walls could become chalkboards, fire hydrants could become benches, and slides could be placed next to stairs at building entrances.

This approach was visible in the range of Dattner's work in the city, which included children's environments and playgrounds at water parks, museums, large housing complexes, hospitals and rehabilitation centers, community and daycare centers, and elementary schools. In Dattner's proposal for the Riverdale Neighborhood House Playground in New York City, the buildings themselves became part of the playground, reducing the distinction between urban structure and playscape through controlled integration. The building wall had a relief sculpture of an alphabet, a working clock, and a blackboard. Providing chalk was less expensive than removing spray paint, Dattner argued.[52] The walls of the building had child-sized alcoves, and a raised walkway between buildings was fitted with a sliding pole that landed in the playground.

Likewise, in his Play Nodes proposal, Dattner appropriated the street for play, creating designated zones along the sidewalks for recreational moments. The sidewalks were widened, and play began to take over excess space around intersections, fire hydrants, and loading zones. Patterns were embedded into and painted on the street and sidewalks to slow traffic, and games could be played in shapes cast in the ground. The texture of the street was especially important, as Dattner noted that children recognized patterns in paving more than adults because of the child's proximity to the ground. Concrete booths that had molded benches, shade trees, and sandboxes protected the area from the cars and allowed for rest, shade, and diversion. The play nodes were designed to be replicated throughout the city and were intended to adapt all urban elements: mailboxes became seating, garbage cans became stages, lampposts became basketball hoops, and manhole covers became the setting for a game of marbles. The fire hydrants and parking meters were shaped into concrete boxes and became seating areas and play tables. Dattner envisioned Play Nodes as a flash of urban anarchy, where the street could be chained off and the fire hydrants could be turned on to flood the space.[53]

CONCLUSION

Today, the 67th Street adventure playground still exists. The playscape has been renovated—railings have been added atop the pyramids, the height of the tower has been lowered, and rubber surfacing has been installed. When this chapter was written in early 2015, the playground was again under renovation by the Central Park Conservancy. Due to building codes, accessibility standards, and fear of litigation, the playground is continually redesigned so that it will be safer and more risk-averse. This development process underlines the built environment's role in protecting children.

Dattner, however, aimed for his Central Park adventure playground to be a "replica of the world."[54] He took care to recreate experiences of the city, though he made them contained and benign. Dattner's play-world was one of carefully orchestrated chaos and censored freedom. The playscapes were a manufactured and controlled world, one intended to enhance children's development through ultimate control of their experiences. Indeed, by just a few years later, in 1973, Dattner had clarified his design intentions, moving further away from a rhetoric of freedom and play and towards a didactic and civic purpose with an article in *The American School Board Journal* titled "Playgrounds Aren't for Playing; Playgrounds Are for Growing and *Learning*."[55]

In post-urban renewal New York City, Dattner saw playgrounds as a tool for the much-needed reconstruction and humanization of the city. Critical progress hinged on urban children's ability to play—and to play according to new developmental standards that facilitated dynamic and imaginative exploration and established stages of challenge and mastery. Dattner saw himself as an advocate for the underrepresented and fragile child in an urban world that was inadequately constructed for their physical and mental needs. He lamented, "It is as if children were supplied with shoes with absolute disregard for the size of their feet—the size of the shoes having been determined by persons who would never have to wear them . . .."[56] Dattner's concern for children's physical and mental development inspired the forms and programming of his playgrounds, which were intended to cultivate their physical growth, intellectual development, and civic involvement, in turn generating better future citizens and improving the urban environment. Dattner's fight for children's right to play ultimately reflects modern concerns about the protection and sanctity of childhood as well as the anxiety about children's health and well-being in an urban environment.

NOTES

1 Richard Dattner, *Civil Architecture: The New Public Infrastructure* (New York: McGraw-Hill, 1995), 1.

2 Liane Lefaivre and Döll, *Ground-Up City: Play as a Design Tool* (Rotterdam: 010 Publishers, 2007), 23–25.

3 Dattner, *Civil Architecture*, 3.

4 Ibid., 4.

5 Ibid.,7.

6 Ibid.

7 Ibid., 8.

8 See Susan G. Solomon, *American Playgrounds: Revitalizing Community Space* (Hanover, NH: University Press of New England, 2005); Michael Gotkin, "The Politics of Play: The Adventure Playground in Central Park," in Charles A. Birnbaum, ed., *Preserving Modern Landscape Architecture: Papers from the Wave Hill-National Park Service Conference* (Cambridge, MA: Spacemaker, 1999).

9 Solomon, *American Playgrounds*, 207.

10 Roy Kozlovsky, "Adventure Playgrounds and Postwar reconstruction," in Marta Gutman and Ning De Coninck-Smith, *Designing Modern Childhoods* (New Brunswick, NJ: Rutgers University Press, 2008), 171.

11 *Declaration of the Rights of the Child*, GA res. 1386 (XIV), 14 UN GAOR Supp. (No. 16) at 19, UN Doc. A/4354 (1959).

12 Lady Allen of Hurtwood, *Planning for Play* (Cambridge, MA: MIT Press, 1968), 55–56.

13 Aldo van Eyck, Vincent Ligtelijn, and Francis Strauven, *The Child, the City and the Artist: An Essay on Architecture: The In-Between Realm* (Amsterdam: SUN, 2008).

14 Henri Lefebvre, *Critique de la vie quotidienne I: Introduction* (Paris: Grasset, 1947).

15 Benjamin Spock, *The Common Sense Book of Baby and Child Care* (New York: Duell, Sloan & Pearce, 1946).

16 Erik H. Erikson, *Childhood and Society* (New York: Norton, 1963); Erik H. Erikson, *The Challenge of Youth* (Garden City, NY: Doubleday Anchor, 1965).

17 Jean Piaget, *Play, Dreams, and Imitation in Childhood* (New York: Norton, 1962).

18 Richard Dattner, *Design for Play* (New York: Van Nostrand Reinhold, 1969), 137.

19 See Robert A. Caro, *The Power Broker: Robert Moses and the Fall of New York* (New York: Knopf, 1974).

20 Galen Cranz, *The Politics of Park Design: A History of Urban Parks in America* (Cambridge, MA: MIT Press, 1982), 139–141; Donald G. Brauer, "Park Planning for the Future," *Parks and Recreation* 7 (November 1972): 14.

21 Dattner, *Design for Play*, 70.

22 Ibid., 76.

23 Ibid., 77.

24 Ibid., 79.

25 Ibid., 7.

26 Ibid., 14.

27 Ibid., 42.

28 Ibid., 42–45.

29 Ibid., 45.

30 Ibid., 89.

31 Ibid., 85.

32 Ibid., 78.

33 Ibid., 81.

34 Ibid., 87.

35 Ibid., 138–139; Henry Dreyfuss, *The Measure of Man: Human Factors in Design* (New York: Whitney Library of Design, 1960).

36 Dattner, *Design for Play*, 24.

37 Ibid., 47.

38 Ibid., 8.

39 Ibid., 18.

40 Kozlovsky, "Adventure Playgrounds," 186; National Playing Fields Association, "Play Leadership on Adventure Playgrounds," April 27, 1955, CB I/67, PRO.

41 Dattner, *Design for Play*, 74.

42 Ibid., 49–51.

43 Shadrach Woods and Joachim Pfeufer, *Urbanism Is Everybody's Business* (Milan: Hoepli, 1968); Christopher Alexander, Sara Ishikawa, and Murray Silverstein, *A Pattern Language: Towns, Buildings, Construction* (New York: Oxford University Press, 1977).

44 Dattner, *Design for Play*, 33.

45 Ibid., 65.

46 Ibid., 33–34.

47 Kevin Lynch, *The Image of the City* (Cambridge, MA: MIT Press, 1960).

48 Dattner, *Design for Play*, 81.

49 Jane Jacobs, *The Death and Life of Great American Cities* (New York: Vintage, 1961), 74–88.

50 Cranz, *The Politics of Park Design*, 147; Brauer, "Park Planning for the Future," 14.

51 Cranz, *The Politics of Park Design*, 144; "Recreation and Open Space Programs: Recommendations for Implementing the Recreation and Open-Space Element of the Comprehensive Plan of San Francisco," Department of City Planning, July 1973.

52 Dattner, *Design for Play*, 124–125.

53 Ibid., 125–127.

54 Ibid., 44.

55 Dattner's emphasis. Richard Dattner, "Playgrounds Aren't for Playing; Playgrounds Are for Growing and *Learning*," *The American School Board Journal* 160, no. 4 (April 1973): 30–31.

56 Dattner, *Design for Play*, 33.

7

Garden Walks: Physical Mobility and Social Identity at Dumbarton Oaks

Robin Veder

In 1934, the sociologist and anthropologist Marcel Mauss called attention to the "American" style of walking that Parisian girls copied from Hollywood movies. Mauss's point was that kinesthetic habits are learned within time, place, and culture; he called them "bodily techniques."[1] The timing of Mauss's analysis coincided with a history of more than forty years of accumulated study by European and American physicians, educators, and dancers in kinesthetic-awareness techniques for fundamental movements such as walking. That history of bodily techniques coexisted with a longer history of inquiry, by experimental psychologists, philosophers, and writers on art, into physiological aesthetics, which asserted that viewers respond to art and architecture primarily through muscular, vascular, and nervous systems.

Consequently, according to period understandings of physiological stimulation and response, spatial design could heal or proactively accommodate and strengthen the body in two ways. Most obviously, structured environments "afford" (in James J. Gibson's sense) different kinds of physical movement.[2] Additionally, according to the physiological aesthetics of the period, even through vision alone, the built environment stimulates minute neuromuscular movements, thereby regulating nervous energy. Such theories of bodily response were premised on concerns about the evolution and survival of the human body in the modernized environment. Even spaces that may not appear visually modern, like the Italianate/Arts and Crafts-style estate landscape I discuss in this chapter, were invested in these highly rationalized approaches to bodily management.

The "walks" of my title are double: aesthetically designed spaces for walking bodies, and historically specific kinesthetic conditions and techniques of bodies walking. This study puts landscape gardener Beatrix Farrand's design for steps, landings, and paths at the Dumbarton Oaks gardens (Figure 7.1) in Washington, DC, into the contexts of early twentieth-century practices of walking and notions of aesthetic muscular response. When landscape historians consider movement through designed landscapes, we usually focus on the semiotic viewing experience or the designer's plan for traffic flow. The body is either individualized or universalized. I propose that the body of the walker is itself a historically specific and contingent subject.

My larger goal is to provide a methodological demonstration of how the history of the body can be employed to denaturalize and historicize phenomenology, and thus enrich explanations of how other built environments contribute to "health."

Since 2000, the field of landscape studies has become increasingly interested in movement, and findings have identified the personal or (presumed) universal responses invoked by the space itself. In these studies, investigations of movement include physical elements that direct orientation, pace, and visual experience. They consider the semiotics of the culture that produced the designed space, and the likely emotional and intellectual responses to changing views of the environment, but rarely is the style, much less the sensation, of movement historicized.[3]

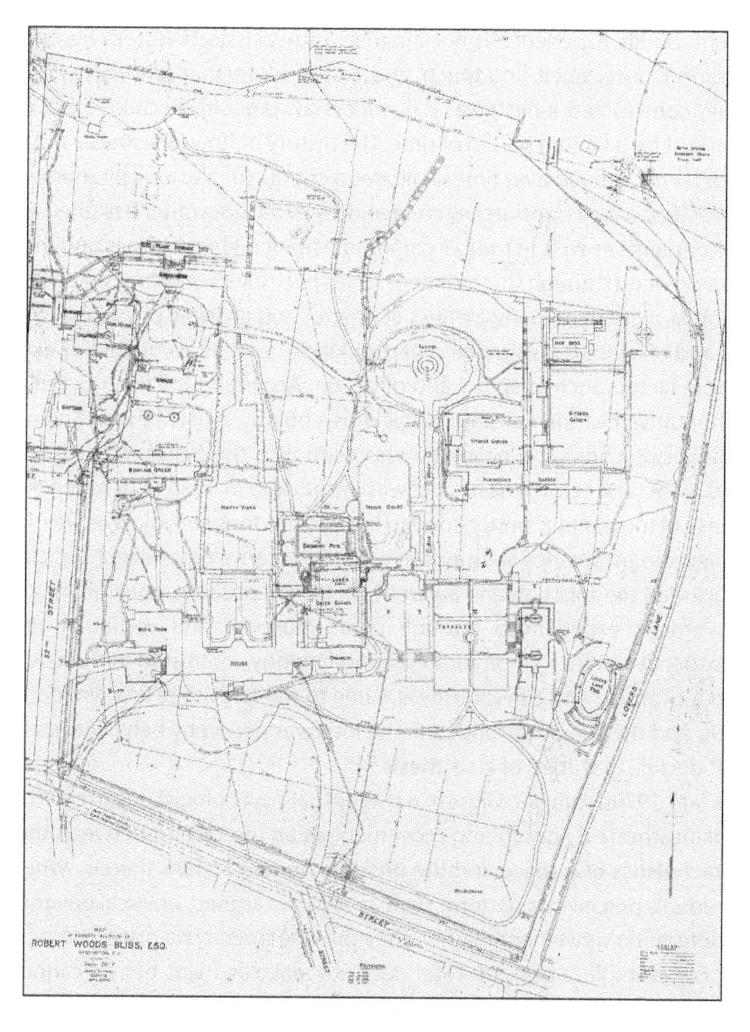

7.1 James Berrall, "Map of Property Belonging to Robert Woods Bliss, Esq.," April 14, 1930, rev. November 2, 1931 (cropped reverse polarity image of original blueprint 2012). Source: AR.AP. GG.SP.006, © Dumbarton Oaks Research Library and Collection, Archives, Washington, DC.

Even when the topic is explicitly movement, bodily experience tends to be "aggressively naturalized" in retrospect, a critique that historian Timothy O'Sullivan has made about the history of walking in ancient Rome.[4] Like gardens, body practices can naturalize identity positions and social relations. Just as garden designs may be identifiably from a certain culture, and practices of looking indicate a "period eye," body management and presentation techniques (such as costume, posture, and gesture) can be stylistically consistent and recognizable as a "period body."[5] Even so, because gardens and bodies are biologically organic, both are easily co-opted by ideologies that claim the authority of "natural" place and "natural" body, ignoring the implicit hierarchical relations in the conditions that shape experience as well as access.

My perspective aligns with the field of history of the senses, and so addresses the historical dimensions of bodily experience—specifically kinesthesia—the sense of movement. Bodily experience is not limited to the classical Western five senses of sight, hearing, taste, smell, and touch, and, furthermore, that sensory experience is historically constructed; kinesthesia is ripe for study precisely because it was incredibly important for a limited period of time. The history of how kinesthesia's value and meanings have changed over time facilitates a critique of ahistoric phenomenological approaches to landscape architecture and, by extension, other designed and natural environments as well. In today's common parlance, kinesthesia is understood to signal how motion through three-dimensional space alters one's physiological sense of position and orientation. Awareness of interior and invisible physiological action, tension, and relaxation is as much a part of kinesthesia as awareness of externally measurable factors such as speed and direction. According to Edwin G. Boring, the first authoritative historian of physiological psychology, a field of experimental and *non*-Freudian psychology, kinesthesia was central to the field's research between 1850 and 1920.[6] The term "kinesthetic" was introduced in 1880 to describe the muscular "sense of movement," understood to include tendons and joints as well. In 1906, English neurologist Charles Sherrington coined the term "proprioception," clarifying that it included the function and awareness of body position, equilibrium, tension, and movement, experienced through neuro-muscular and vestibular systems.[7] The introspective branch of physiological psychology, interested in the correlation between movement and consciousness, came to the fore in the first two decades of the 1900s, and then was out-funded in the interwar period by behaviorism, leading to a swift decline in studies of kinesthesia.[8]

In the late 1970s, James J. Gibson, a perceptual psychologist, resurrected discussions of kinesthesia by describing movement as an interaction between the physical characteristics of a space and the possible human actions therein. Whether or not individuals perceive or perform such actions, he argued, physical environments do not determine movement. Rather, they provide interactive opportunities: affordances.[9] For example, a body of water does not make us swim, but we cannot swim without a sufficient mass of enclosed water; the pool affords swimming. Cultural geographers quickly took up Gibson's concept of affordance, applying it to studies of highway and sidewalk culture. Following suit, landscape architects, theorists, and historians also paid attention to how landscapes afford action, and how visual and tactile clues communicate such affordances to users, leading to discussions of passive versus "dynamic" landscapes. Even so, in the last forty years, the visual experience of movement—the "view from the road"—has received more attention than the kinesthetic sensation and perception of movement—the proprioceptive feel of the road, which may include sensations like the passive tactile sense of gravel underfoot and the active muscular strain of resisting gravitational pull while driving a car around a corner.[10] Thus, Gibson's theory of affordances remains a needed tool for describing how landscape choreography works.

In current landscape design, "choreography" refers to the designer's program for how users will move through space."[11] As applied within landscape studies today, the term *choreography* can also be seen as a location's assembly of affordances. Affordances such as circulation paths, stairs, points of access, viewing platforms, paving materials, and open or enclosed spaces all participate in a garden's choreography by inviting, or in Gibson's term *affording*, particular directions, speeds, and types of bodily movement.

An analysis of how specific affordances at Dumbarton Oaks might have been perceived during the 1920s through the 1940s reveals a forgotten aesthetic discourse of bodily responses to landscape choreography. Dumbarton Oaks is a rare surviving example of early twentieth-century American country-estate landscape architecture. The Washington, DC, land and its nineteenth-century mansion were purchased in 1920 by Robert Woods Bliss and his wife Mildred Barnes Bliss (Figure 7.2). Her inherited wealth, traceable to her father's investments in pharmaceuticals, made their lives easy, and his career in foreign diplomacy made it peripatetic. They took up residency in 1933 and seven years later transferred the estate, grounds, and their art and rare book collections to Harvard University. Previous historians have thoroughly documented the Italianate and Arts and Crafts design elements that landscape gardener Beatrix Farrand and Mildred Bliss used to transform the Dumbarton Oaks farm into a formal garden.[12] In contrast, it is my contention that the history of the design, construction, and use of Dumbarton Oaks elucidates early twentieth-century bodily practices and physiological aesthetics. Conventional approaches to understanding movement through landscapes, namely choreography (the designer's intention) and performance (the user's reception), are supplemented here with the histories of bodily techniques and physiological aesthetics.

7.2 Mildred and Robert Woods Bliss in the Rose Garden at Dumbarton Oaks, c. 1938. Source: LA.GP.6.21, © Dumbarton Oaks Research Library and Collection, Rare Book Collection, Washington, DC.

Set upon a hill overlooking Georgetown, the Dumbarton Oaks topography presented some circulation challenges that Farrand framed as a kinesthetic problem. Bliss referred to the substantial slopes from the north and east sides of the house as "the lay of the incurable land."[13] To conquer (or cure) it, they cut, filled, and added stone walls, constructing four terraces between the house and the pond below.

This resulted in a series of staircases, not all of them equally navigable. It appears that while these stairs leading from the Orangery to the Rose Garden worked topographically and visually, Farrand deemed the kinesthetics of climbing or descending the steps to be unsatisfying. In the *Plant Book*, a combined design manifesto and maintenance plan she prepared between 1941 and 1944 for Harvard's ongoing stewardship of the estate, she commented on the importance of designing steps in short runs with easy riser–tread proportions, and of well-spaced landings in order to avoid "one wearisome continuous climb."[14] In the chapter "The Stairway East of the Orangery" she apologetically recites the terrain challenges that justified the "conspicuously narrow terraces and their accompanying flights of steps," and the "high walls" that separate the levels, as unavoidable design compromises between access and aesthetics.[15] Then, she gives the following direction:

> *It was also established as a general principle that, where possible, no flights of more than six steps should be built without a landing between the first and the next run of another six or eight steps. These landings have been made longer than three feet wherever possible, in order to give rest to the climber by a change and a pace between the series of rising runs. The runs have been constructed either of odd or even numbers. In other words, a flight of steps which starts out with an even-number of steps in its runs, is continued throughout with even-numbered steps. This makes the rhythm of climbing less wearisome than if added paces have to be made on each landing in order to start the new set of steps keeping the same rhythm of right or left foot used on the first step of the first flight.*[16]

The manuscript draft shows that Farrand edited the final sentence in order to emphasize the importance of rhythm and clarify the choreographic detail that users should ascend or descend each set of stairs with the same starting foot, effectively favoring the dominant leg.[17]

It is hard to say at what point in the 1920s Farrand decided on this formula, but it was certainly after building the first steep staircase from the Orangery to the Rose Garden and before 1931, by which time the majestic and gradual Box Walk was in place. After trying multiple variations, Farrand settled on a cadence that punctuates the Box Walk's long, stepped ramp with several runs of stairs, each of them four steps at a time.[18] As the hardscaping exists today, the original formal gardens contain few staircases that conform to Farrand's recommendations for consistently odd or even-numbered flights, and no more than eight risers between landings.

In setting out her rules for stairs, Farrand was attending to what she believed would be a manageable pattern of exertion and rest for the garden walker, and she was asserting choreographic control.[19] Her perspective puts great faith in the designer's ability to pace the walker, not unlike how a trainer paces a horse, by creating conditions that direct the length of the walker's stride and facilitate a pattern of initiating movement with the same foot. Despite designers' intentions, few humans conform to a predictable stride, and most of us walk differently when we are in a hurry or in conversation, tired, sight-seeing, injured, or fragile. The affordances—the physical characteristics of a space that determine the range of possible actions—are neither universal nor consistent for a single person. In the *Plant Book*, Farrand suggested that within a long ascent, a minimum distance of three feet (one meter) was necessary for each landing to give the stair-climber a rest. When combined with a consistently odd or even number of risers, these features (as quoted above) "mak[e] the rhythm of climbing less wearisome."[20] Stairs, like stepping stones, tend to be taken one at a time, thus establishing a standard length of tread that can also set walking rhythm. Most of the stairs at Dumbarton Oaks have 6-inch (15cm) risers and 15-inch (38cm) treads, with the exception of the Box Walk's more generously paced 20-inch (51cm) tread, but the landings are irregular and do not obviously conform to period standards of an average 24-inch (61cm) stride for smaller adults or a 30-inch (76cm) military stride.[21]

Farrand's interest in how hardscaping relates to stride length and kinesthetic comfort was not unusual. In the 1910s and 1920s, *Landscape Architecture*, the journal produced by the American Society of Landscape Architects, published a number of essays on the best proportions for stairs and stepped ramps. The writers agreed that most people preferred ramps over stairs and, in an early nod to disability accommodations, suggested that ramps should be employed unless there was a distinct disincentive such as "the necessities of the design or as a frank barrier to keep baby carriages from certain paths."[22] In 1915, Robert Wheelwright argued that most people prefer ramps over stairs, particularly if the length of each ramp is spaced to accommodate a comfortable number of strides.[23]

Frederick Law Olmsted Jr., co-director of the period's dominant landscape architecture firm, offered an alternate explanation for ramp-preference: ramps do not assume or enforce a uniform stride. He noted that step-climbers were more likely to accept imposed standards of stride length when stairs were obviously necessary because the grading was relatively steep. The milder the grade, the less tolerant pedestrians were likely to be. "On stairs of very gentle slope the inconvenience both to short-steppers and to long-steppers of making this accommodation becomes very irksome," Olmsted wrote, because "the interference with the individual's normal length of stride in walking becomes more noticeable."[24] In 1928, he elaborated on the individual physiological and psychological conditions that could alter stride, including "the build of the individuals, their vigor, their accidentally acquired habits, and their momentary impulses toward haste and effort or toward leisureliness and ease." Furthermore, if the choreography was uncomfortable, then visitors were likely to go off-path:

> *they will be tempted to turn aside from the steps and walk, or run, up or down the smooth earth bank alongside, if there be one, on which they are free to stride as long or as short as they choose. Many of them do so to the great annoyance of the maintenance men.*[25]

Such oppositional "readings" that walkers perform with their feet can reciprocally shape choreography by establishing desire lines worn into the lawn or requiring revised affordances. In such circumstances, pedestrians exerted the live performer's option to alter choreography, to respond to landscape design by refusing to follow direction.[26]

At Dumbarton Oaks, Farrand's formula for non-tiring stair rhythms applied to leisure paths only. In contrast to the tiered grading between the lower east terraces, the utility path for the same decline was treacherously steep

7.3 Stewart Brothers (photographers), Goat Trail, c. 1931–32. Source: LA.GP. 21.10, © Dumbarton Oaks Research Library and Collection, Rare Book Collection, Washington, DC.

and irregular (Figure 7.3). Known as the Goat Trail, it ran straight down from the north end of the Urn Terrace (Figure 7.1, area C) alongside the northern retaining wall to the Arbor Terrace (Figure 7.1, area E). Without it, gardeners would have to loop through the east terraces. With it, their shortcut was veiled from the leisure areas, as were other service paths.[27] The hidden stairs and paths concealed garden labor while revealing that the rules for kinesthetically sensitive—and fundamentally safe—design did not apply to work areas. While this is not surprising in the history of built environments, it is telling that the estate refused modern labor efficiency while embracing the new class-inflected bodily techniques of bourgeois leisure.

After Dumbarton Oaks opened to the public in 1941, the number of guests, their tendency to veer off paths, and the variable needs of their bodies necessitated physical alterations. In the beginning, tours were guided and by appointment only. When this overwhelmed the staff, Farrand prepared a guidebook for unsupervised public guests, suggesting specific routes. Nevertheless some wandered off-course, too often finding their way to the unauthorized Goat Trail.[28] Consequently, in 1946 Farrand collaborated with Bliss and director John Thacher on a plan to protect the garden and its guests. They agreed that the Goat Trail did not provide "safe and comfortable steps" and that such a path was necessary to facilitate access between the Rose Garden and the Herbaceous Border below the sloping orchard hill to the north.[29] With a quick sketch, Mildred Bliss scripted a new Goat Trail that would be "safe for elderly knees and careless ankles." Soon after, a new stepped path was installed, providing a slow curved descent with plenty of landings.[30]

As accessibility standards have changed, there have been other alterations to the Dumbarton Oaks landscape, each an accommodation to the variety of walking performances that visitors trace despite the design choreography. For instance, the sturdy cobblestones of the gardeners' Service Court, seen in a 1944 photograph of the second and third Superintendents of the gardens (James Bryce and Matthew Kearney), are impossible to navigate without flat shoes and a steady gait (Figure 7.4). At present, the resident scholars daily traverse about ten feet (three meters) of this rough surface, when they go from the new (2005) library across to the Refectory (formerly the Director's House) to have lunch; the route has been ground down to literally smooth their way. Meanwhile, a "desire line" adjacent to the top third of the old Goat Trail shows that the gardeners still cut through rather than take the long way around.[31]

These alterations are signs that our body cultures—our ideas about how bodies should look, work, move, and feel—have also changed over time.[32] Many factors contribute to group body cultures, and within that, to each individual's kinesthetic ability, memory, and receptivity; these include habits of diet, type and amount of physical activity, access to varied clothing and conveyances, strengths and disabilities, and previous experiences of built and natural environments. These contingencies of place, time, economics, and socially constructed identities contribute to historically specific physical postures, gestures, and modes of comportment. In addition to material factors, the early twentieth-century kinesthetic experience of walking through gardens is also subject to and a generator of social semiotics. Socially constructed subjectivities, whether determined by ideological institutional power or by reified representations of identity performance, are also part of the genealogy of the modern body. As mentioned above, in 1934 Marcel Mauss argued that "bodily techniques," the body-movement habits such as styles of swimming and walking, are learned and specific to time, place, and culture. This may happen unconsciously through imitation, through enforced discipline, or by cultivating self-awareness about how both basic and highly specialized movements feel and look.[33] Movement vocabularies become markers of social identity, a phenomenon more explicitly articulated in the early twentieth century than it is today.

7.4 Matthew Kearney, James Bryce, and unidentified man, March 1944. Source: AR.PH. Misc.268, © Dumbarton Oaks Research Library and Collection, Archives, Washington, DC.

Between the 1880s and 1940s, several transatlantic body cultures similarly focused on increasing awareness, ease, and efficiency of posture, breathing, and fundamental movements such as walking, bending, sitting, and lifting. Such self-conscious attention to posture and movement was central to the early twentieth-century project of cultivating kinesthetic awareness. In some educational, industrial, and military situations, the bodily techniques were purely disciplinary, and were employed only temporarily, in order to teach and train bodies into new habits. Once the muscles were re-educated, the job was done. For others, continued kinesthetic awareness facilitated the thrill of deducing class by analyzing others' posture or, alternatively, the possibility of manipulating one's persona with a variety of movement styles. Social identification was communicated not only in what one wore but in how one's body moved with consciously cultivated or subconsciously imitated bodily techniques. Like the more obvious examples of knowing how to play golf or tennis, the ability to walk with the carriage, rhythm, and breathing patterns favored by a sociological group contributed to identity construction. Sociologist Pierre Bourdieu connected the structuring environment for class distinction, the "habitus," to specific physical behaviors and motor patterns, the "hexis."[34] When Dumbarton Oaks opened to the public, it offered access to upwardly mobile bourgeois aspirants, such as the readers that physical-culture authors addressed, those who would have enjoyed the tourist's fantasy of vicarious ownership and class identification. But would they have had the bodily techniques to inhabit the space as did the Blisses?

Dumbarton Oaks's stair design accommodated the pace of leisure and impeded efficient gardening. Nevertheless, climbing stairs tested muscular habits, specifically the ability to propel forward and up while maintaining the illusion of effortlessness. In 1931, Bess Mensendieck, an instructor in posture and functional mechanics, criticized the "many people [who] delude themselves with the idea that they are walking, when in reality they are shuffling, stamping, dawdling, waddling, or hobbling."[35] A consistent stride, either the youthful "springy" step or the "dignified Rhythm" of the "legato" step were preferable, both for appearance and health. She called this manner of coordination "Physiological Rhythm."[36] The first stage in developing this walking style was increased sensory awareness.

Mildred Bliss, her private guests, and some members of her staff participated in these techniques. Bliss had her own physical trainer and masseuse, Emery Siposs, a Hungarian who followed them back from Europe in 1933 and continued to treat her, her husband, and their guests until his death in 1948.[37] Sir Shane Leslie visited Dumbarton Oaks in the early 1930s and was put through his paces:

> *I did not moon or meander while staying with the Blisses, for their Austrian instructor put me through physical exercises and before I knew where I was Mrs. Bliss . . . had picked me up and thrown me with the sheer strength of her little shoulders.*[38]

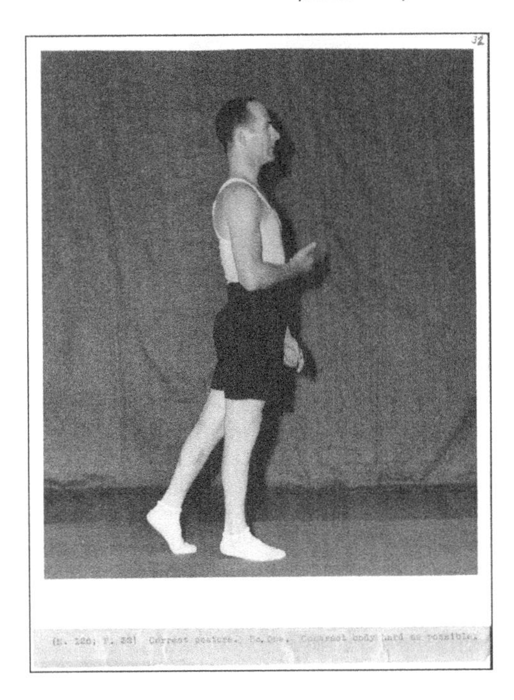

7.5 Karl Obert (photographer). Emery Siposs demonstrating "Correct Posture," 1934–48. Source: Photograph on typescript, from "Siposs: List Exercises" manuscript, Papers of Robert Woods Bliss and Mildred Barnes Bliss, Harvard University Archives.

A few years later, one of the staff reported that the Siposs technique facilitated walking on water. During the cold January of 1941, "the swimming pool froze . . . so that one could run across it, very quickly, very lightly, holding oneself very tall in approved Siposs posture 'tummy in, buttocks well contracted,' the diaphragm muscles carrying one's weight proudly."[39]

Siposs himself demonstrated how this might look in a series of instructional photographs prepared for the Blisses (Figure 7.5). In one, the trainer instructs them to "contract body [as] hard as possible" in order to achieve "correct posture"; in another, he shows the "posture step" that was performed by raising oneself "up on toes, stretch[ing] arms upward together, [and] walking for ten minutes in this position each day, [if] possible."[40] The photographs were taken by estate-photographer Karl Obert in Santa Barbara, where the Blisses stayed for extended periods at her mother's Casa Dorinda estate and then at the Hotel Miramar after the property was sold in 1942. In the summer of 1941, Siposs was on site administering hydrotherapy to Robert Bliss, who was recovering from gallbladder surgery. Soon, Bliss's doctors also tried the treatment, leading Mildred Bliss to speculate, "perhaps in the future Santa Barbara may develop into the leading hydrotherapeutical center of America."[41] Indeed, five years later, Siposs had become "the indispensable man at this fabulously rich seaside resort where folks come from far and near to take his treatments," reported syndicated columnist Alice Hughes. "He wrestles, pummels and exercises them way beyond his 122 pounds' worth and he gets results . . . I asked one of his patients what Siposs did for him and he said, 'He gives me bounce.'"[42] Access to such treatments was a mark of socioeconomic privilege; the resulting "bounce" and poise were embodied (and thus portable) markers of class. These were the bodies for whom Farrand designed the walks of Dumbarton Oaks.

During the period when Farrand was concerned with the "rhythm" of Dumbarton Oaks's stairs and landings, kinesthetic awareness of physiological rhythm was also the subject of extensive scientific and aesthetic investigation. In the 1910s through the 1930s, landscape writing and landscape architecture instruction were among the areas of artistic production that built upon the "physiological aesthetics" theories that grew out of German experimental physiological psychology and aesthetic philosophy.[43] Scientists at Johns Hopkins, Harvard, Cornell, Princeton, Yale, and other American university psychology laboratories tested and expanded these theories from the 1890s through the 1920s. They evaluated bodily response to aesthetic stimuli by gathering data based primarily on the subject's reported kinesthetic sense of muscular tension, alignment, balance, speed and direction of movement, and affiliated metrics such as the rate of heartbeat, respiration, and walking stride. Physiological aesthetics offers another context that explains why Farrand reiterated the term "rhythm" when arguing that the stairs at Dumbarton Oaks should be numbered and spaced so a pedestrian could begin each new climb consistently with his or her dominant leg.

Walking had a special place in the discourse of physiological aesthetics, wherein the activity facilitated perception of rhythm, time, and three-dimensional space. Wilhelm Wundt, who first combined physiology and psychology into the science underlying physiological aesthetics, wrote in 1874,

> *Consciousness is rhythmically disposed, because the whole organism is rhythmically disposed. The movements of the heart, of breathing, of walking, take place rhythmically. [. . .] Above all, the movements of walking form a very clear and recognisable background to our consciousness.*[44]

This English translation appeared in Christian Ruckmich's 1913 article on "The Role of Kinaesthesis in the Perception of Rhythm," as did Carl Stumpf's similar observation, made in 1883: "It looks, indeed, as if our sense of rhythm and time was essentially developed in connection with the movements of locomotion."[45] In 1895, Edward Wheeler Scripture, director of Yale's psychological laboratory, explained: "you have been executing rhythmic actions ever since you began to walk. By rhythmic action we understand an act repeated at intervals which the doer believes to be regular."[46] Ruckmich's survey of transatlantic scholarship found that "by far the greater number of investigators and systematic writers on the subject of rhythm emphasise the primary importance of kinaesthesis and of motor response in rhythmical perceptions."[47]

Early twentieth-century landscape architects drew upon such ideas when constructing spaces for human movement, considering how to harmonize spatial rhythms with those of the inhabiting bodies. These theories of kinesthetic rhythm explain Farrand's choreographic designs for rhythmic stair-climbing, and it is possible to situate the landscape gardener's likely exposure to them during a formative moment in her career. In late spring and early summer of 1903, she was recovering from appendicitis at the home of her aunt Edith Wharton while the latter was writing *Italian Villas and Their Gardens*. Wharton's understanding of and access to Italian gardens depended on the insights and contacts of her friend, the English writer Vernon Lee, to whom she dedicated the text.[48] Lee's articulation of kinesthetic responses to landscape provides the starting point of an arc that puts Farrand's ideas about walking rhythm and step design firmly within the physiological aesthetics that characterized American mainstream landscape architecture design theory of the 1910s through the 1930s.

In her 1897 essay, "The Lie of the Land," Vernon Lee set out a theory of landscape experience premised on muscular memories of walking. In paintings, she asserted, color and light are pleasant reminders of how a landscape changes over time, but only the "lie of the land"—its topography—awakens the pedestrian's kinesthetic memory.

> *We praise color, but we actually* live *in the indescribable thing which I must call the* lie of the land *. . . [It] means walking or climbing, shelter or bleakness; it means the corner where we dread a boring neighbor, the bend round which we have watched some one depart, the stretch of road which seemed to lead us away out of captivity.*

We live in line, she argued, because repeatedly walking any path deposits and reinforces muscular memories that can be awakened by similar affordances elsewhere. In contrast to nineteenth-century associationism, Lee's "lie of the land" stimulated memories that were kinesthetic and purely personal, *not* historical, literary, romantic, or spiritual.[49]

This was in the mid-1890s, and while Lee was writing this and other evocative essays on landscape perception, she was also at work on a theoretical tract about physiological aesthetics. The 1897 study she co-authored with Kit Anstruther-Thomson, called "Beauty and Ugliness," builds upon William James's theory of embodied emotion (also known as the James-Lange theory). James posited that one recognizes one's own emotions because of somatically generated sensations such as a clenched fist or watering eyes; such physical feelings *are* the basis of emotion. Explicitly building on James, Lee and Anstruther-Thomson argued that we know when we are experiencing beauty or ugliness through the same kind of kinesthetic clues, in this case initiated by the "perception of Form."[50] Consequently, in their opinion, a viewer's somatic awareness of walking and breathing rhythms facilitated perceptive aesthetic responses to art objects and designed and natural environments.

In "Beauty and Ugliness," Lee's partner Anstruther-Thomson wrote that one can sense a kinesthetic response to a painted landscape, but aesthetic perception is activated fully only when one is in motion in a three-dimensional landscape because "our visual memory of things is gained during our moments of movement." Visible patterns such as paving stones and brick set the pace of movement across surfaces and through space; they "have a power akin to that of march music, for they compel our organism to a regular rhythmical mode of being."[51] These ideas about the aesthetic benefits of kinesthetic sensations might seem idiosyncratic today, but they fit perfectly into their own period's emerging theories of rhythmic physiological aesthetics.

Lee was preparing and publishing several new essays on physiological aesthetics in the same period when Wharton researched, wrote, and published *Italian Villas and Their Gardens*.[52] Living near Florence, Lee suspended work between February and April 1903, instead escorting Wharton on her research tour of Italian gardens.[53]

If Wharton talked with Farrand about Lee's ideas, most likely she would have done so in 1903, because when Wharton returned home at the end of April, notes in hand and ready to finish the manuscript, her niece Farrand was on-site for a two-month convalescence.[54] Ultimately, the resonance between Lee's theory of aesthetic response and Farrand's steps at Dumbarton Oaks indicates how physiological aesthetics worked as a historically specific way of kinesthetically experiencing landscapes, one that landscape architects employed elsewhere and that other visitors may have brought with them into the garden.

The Harvard Graduate School of Design, which granted the first degree in landscape architecture in 1901, actually taught physiological aesthetics in its curriculum. Henry Vincent Hubbard was one of the program's first professors, and in 1917, he and librarian Theodora Kimball co-authored *An Introduction to the Study of Landscape Design*; this became the standard foundational text in the field in the period under discussion.[55] Hubbard and Kimball cautioned that although kinesthetic memory might seem like an insufficient explanation for the aesthetic pleasure of good design:

> *we should remember that the emotions associated with repetition, sequence, and balance [in landscape design] are associated also with and automatically expressed by repeated, sequential, or balanced muscular motions and positions of the whole body, and these in turn intensify the emotion that suggested them. The delicately balanced nervous and muscular machinery of the body is thus in a way a reverberator for the increasing of the effect of these experiences.*[56]

Walking, breathing, and swinging one's arms are the precise "repeated, sequential [and] balanced muscular motions" referenced here. Hubbard and Kimball claimed that muscles accustomed to such rhythmic motions are more ready to reverberate in response to the physical environment. Furthermore, like Lee, they asserted that muscular sensation is the primary form of experiencing aesthetic pleasure, and they recognized its origins in physiological aesthetics.[57] Flights of steps punctuated by landings correspond to the definition of rhythm that Hubbard and Kimball quoted from design theorist Denman Ross, who was himself part of Harvard's physiological aesthetics community. Ross, as quoted in *Landscape Design*, wrote, "When any line or sequence is broken repeatedly and at equal intervals, we get alternations which give us the feeling of Rhythm. Rhythm means not only a continuation merely but a continuation with regularly recurring breaks or accents."[58]

In 1935, landscape architect Marjorie Sewell Cautley made the equation between physiological aesthetics and stair design explicit. She illustrated her description of rhythm in garden design by contrasting "tiresome repetition in an unbroken flight of steps," and "restful rhythm in terraced steps" (Figure 7.6). (The first resembles the steep Rose Garden steps; the second approximates the cadence of the Box Walk.) Cautley explained, "to relieve the monotony of repetition, units may be arranged in groups of harmonious lines, forms, or colors. The repetition of these groups produces a certain rhythm." Then, to illustrate how accented repetition creates rhythm, Cautley used the following metaphor: "this is perhaps the most common way of creating harmony, being probably the oldest form of design. It seems almost instinctive, perhaps derived from the rhythms of breathing and walking."[59]

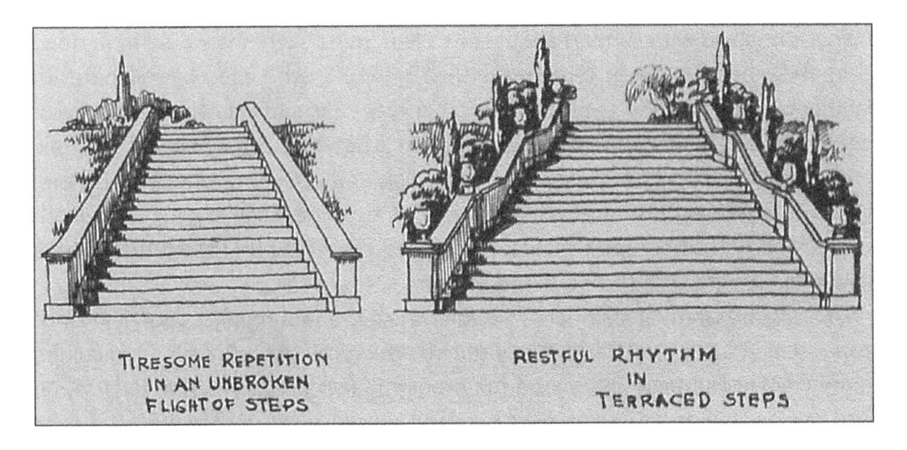

7.6 Stair rhythms. Source: Marjorie Sewell Cautley, *Garden Design: The Principles of Abstract Design as Applied to Landscape Composition* (New York: Dodd, Mead, 1935), 15.

When designing the staircases and ramps for Dumbarton Oaks, Beatrix Farrand's concern with the "rhythm of climbing" fit into the body-inflected aesthetics of her period. The kinesthetic sensation of walking was important to the design and experience of early twentieth-century American landscapes, but in terms that cannot be excavated by looking at the designer's drawings or by walking the extant grounds. Farrand's design for Dumbarton Oaks was informed by the historically specific theories of physiological aesthetics, and these theories functioned in complementary relationship with bodily techniques of kinesthetic self-awareness. The bodily techniques of this culture and period framed pedestrians' kinesthetic experiences, as did notions of muscular response taken from physiological aesthetics. The rhythm of walking at Dumbarton Oaks may be embedded in the landscape architecture, but the ways of walking, and the meaning of walking, reveal what it meant in the 1920s for the garden to have rhythm.

Landscape architecture was considered a site for training bodies in the habitual movement patterns that were markers of social identity. Primary sources suggest that landscape architects themselves, following theories of physiological aesthetics, believed that by affording movement patterns, designed spaces functioned as structuring environments for neuromuscular programming. Within this logic of environmental determinism, landscapes physiologically discipline and even transform the bodies of people who live in them, whether engaged in recreation or labor.

NOTES

This chapter is excerpted and revised from "Walking through Dumbarton Oaks: Early Twentieth-Century Bourgeois Bodily Techniques and Kinesthetic Experience of Landscape," originally published by the University of California Press in *Journal of the Society of Architectural Historians* 72, no. 1 (March, 2013): 5–27. This research would not have been possible without the support of the Dumbarton Oaks Research Library and Collection community, particularly John Beardsley, Sarah Burke Cahalan, James N. Carder, Allen Grieco,

Gail Griffin, David Haney, Walter Howell, Sheila Klos, Michael G. Lee, Linda Lott, and Alla Vronskaya. Additional thanks go to Grey Gundaker, Brandy Parris, Silvia Margarita Serrano, and Alan Wallach, and, for this version, to Sarah Schrank and Didem Ekici.

1 Marcel Mauss, "Techniques of the Body," 1935. Trans. Ben Brewster, *Economy and Society* 2, no. 1 (1973): 72, 70–88.

2 James J. Gibson, "The Theory of Affordances," in *The Ecological Approach to Visual Perception* (Boston, MA: Houghton Mifflin, 1979), 127–145.

3 John Dixon Hunt, "'Lordship of the Feet': Toward a Poetics of Movement in the Garden," 187–213; and Michel Conan, "Landscape Metaphors and Metamorphosis of Time," 287–317, both in Michel Conan, ed., *Landscape Design and the Experience of Motion*, Dumbarton Oaks Colloquium on the History of Landscape Architecture XXIV (Washington, DC: Dumbarton Oaks Research Library and Collection, 2003).

4 Timothy M. O'Sullivan, *Walking in Roman Culture* (New York: Cambridge University Press, 2011), 33.

5 I am indebted to art historian Sarah Burns for the term "period body," a modification of Michael Baxandall's "period eye."

6 Edward G. Boring, *Sensation and Perception in the History of Experimental Psychology* (New York: Appleton-Century-Crofts, 1942), 524–535.

7 Barry C. Stillman, "Making Sense of Proprioception: The Meaning of Proprioception, Kinaesthesia and Related Terms," *Physiotherapy* 88, no. 11 (November 2002): 667–676; Nicholas J. Wade, "The Search for a Sixth Sense: The Cases for Vestibular, Muscle, and Temperature Senses," *Journal of the History of the Neurosciences* 12, no. 2 (2003): 175–202.

8 Kurt Danziger, *Constructing the Subject: Historical Origins of Psychological Research* (Cambridge: Cambridge University Press, 1990).

9 Gibson, "Theory of Affordances."

10 Donald Appleyard, Kevin Lynch, and John R. Myer, *The View from the Road* (Cambridge, MA: MIT Press, 1964); Meto J. Vroom, *Lexicon of Garden and Landscape Architecture* (Basel: Birkhäuser Publishers for Architecture, 2006), 111–114, 239–241; Simon Bell, *Landscape: Pattern, Perception, and Process* (London: E. & F.N. Spon, 1999), 55–58.

11 This usage can be traced to Lawrence Halprin, "The Choreography of Gardens," *Impulse Dance Magazine* (1949): 34 (I am indebted to Alison Hirsch for sharing a copy of this rare article). For application of "choreography" and "affordance" to landscape by scholars from outside the field of landscape architecture, see Peter Merriman, "Architecture/ Dance: Choreographing and Inhabiting Spaces with Anna and Lawrence Halprin," *Cultural Geographies* 17, no. 4 (2010): 427–449.

12 Robin Karson, "Beatrix Farrand's Design for the Garden of Dumbarton Oaks," in James Carder, ed., *Home of the Humanities: The Collecting and Patronage of Mildred and Robert Woods Bliss* (Washington, DC: Dumbarton Oaks Research Library and Collection, 2010), 117–137; Diana Kostial McGuire, "Foreword," in Beatrix Farrand, *Beatrix Farrand's Plant Book for Dumbarton Oaks*, ed. Diana Kostial McGuire (Washington, DC: Dumbarton Oaks, Trustees for Harvard University, 1980), xi–xix (hereafter *Plant Book*); Georgina Masson, *Dumbarton Oaks: A Guide to the Gardens* (Washington, DC: Trustees for Harvard University, 1968). For more on Farrand's process, see: Diana Balmori, "Beatrix Farrand at Dumbarton Oaks: The Design Process of a Garden," in Diana Kostial McGuire and Lois Fern, eds., *Beatrix Jones Farrand (1872–1959): Fifty Years of Landscape Architecture*, Dumbarton Oaks Colloquium on the History of Landscape Architecture

VIII (Washington, DC: Dumbarton Oaks, Trustees for Harvard University, 1982), 97–123; Diana Balmori, Diane Kostial McGuire, and Eleanor M. McPeck, *Beatrix Farrand's American Landscapes: Her Gardens and Campuses* (Sagaponack, NY: Sagapress, 1985).

13 Mildred Bliss (hereafter MB) to Beatrix Farrand (hereafter BF), April 16, 1923, Dumbarton Oaks Research Library and Collection, Archives, Washington, DC (hereafter DO Archives).

14 Farrand, *Plant Book*, 47, 68. For other remarks on steps, see also 48, 53–55, 75–76, 90, 116.

15 Ibid., 53.

16 Ibid., 53–55.

17 Farrand, "Orangery" chapter in "Plant Book" manuscript, n.p., Dumbarton Oaks Research Library and Collection, Rare Book Collection, Washington, DC (hereafter DO RBC).

18 Farrand, "Box Walk leading north from Terrace 'B'" [plan and profile], April 16, 1923, drawing, LA.GD.K 3.02; Farrand, "Box Walk Steps" [plan and profile], March 1925, LA.GD.K 3.03b; Farrand, "Box Walk Steps" [plan and profile], March 1926, LA.GD.K 3.03a, DO RBC. As shown in the 1931 Berrall plan, there were six sets of steps; the seventh was added much later.

19 Farrand, *Plant Book*, 47, 51, 75–76, 99.

20 Ibid., 53–55.

21 Frederick Law Olmsted [Jr.], "Notes upon the Sizes of Steps," *Landscape Architecture* 1, no. 2 (January 1911): 85, 89.

22 Charles Downing Lay, "Garden Ramps," *Landscape Architecture* 11, no. 3 (April 1921): 124–125.

23 Robert Wheelwright, "Notes on Stepped Ramps," *Landscape Architecture* 5, no. 3 (April 1915): 134–135.

24 Olmsted, "Sizes of Steps," 86.

25 Frederick Law Olmsted [Jr], "Some Further Notes on Steps," *Landscape Architecture* 18, no. 2 (January 1928): 125–127.

26 Anthropology and cultural geography have an extensive literature exploring this approach, as does dance history. See Merriman, "Architecture/Dance," 428, 441–442n3–4; Susan Leigh Foster, *Choreographing Empathy: Kinesthesia in Performance* (New York: Routledge, 2011), 2–6.

27 Farrand, *Plant Book*, 111–112.

28 Dumbarton Oaks Memorandum, March 1, 1941, Administrative Records, 1941–49, DO Archives; Beatrix Farrand, "Dumbarton Oaks Gardens," manuscript for guide book, typescript, c. 1944, DO RBC.

29 BF to MB, "Suggestions discussed with Mr. Patterson, May 27–29, 1946; John Thacher to BF, February 16, 1946, DO RBC.

30 MB, "Notes by Mrs. Bliss," [on] BF to MB, May 27–29, 1946; MB to BF, July 26, 1946; BF to MB, October 1, 1946, DO RBC.

31 Full disclosure: I was one of those research fellows in 2011–12, and my partner has worked on the garden crew from 2009 to the present.

32 I have taken the term "body culture" from Karl Eric Toepfer, *Empire of Ecstasy: Nudity and Movement in German Body Culture, 1910–1935* (Berkeley, CA: University of California Press, 1997).

33 Mauss, "Techniques of the Body," 70–88.

34 Pierre Bourdieu, *The Logic of Practice*, trans. Richard Nice (Stanford, CA: Stanford University Press, 1990), 52–79.

35 Bess M. Mensendieck, *"It's Up to You"* (New York: Bess M. Mensendieck, 1931), 189. She may be referring to the hobble skirt that was popular from 1908 until the 1910s.

36 Mensendieck, *"It's Up to You"*, 187–190.

37 Robert Woods Bliss to Royall Tyler, March 7, 1934; Royall Tyler to MB, June 14, 1934; BF to MB, August 8, 1948, DO Archives.

38 Shane Leslie, *American Wonderland: Memories of Four Tours in the United States, 1911–1935* (London: Michael Joseph, 1936), 225.

39 "Gardens," *The Underworld Courier* 1, no. 1 (January 11, 1941): 3, DO Archives.

40 Karl Obert to Robert Bliss, February 28,1950; Emery Siposs, untitled typescript with photographs by Karl Obert, 32–33, Papers of Robert Woods Bliss and Mildred Barnes Bliss Papers, Harvard University Archives, HUGFP 76.

41 MB to BF, August 4, 1941, DO RBC.

42 Alice Hughes, "A Woman's New York," *Reading Eagle*, October 1, 1946, courtesy James Carder.

43 For other discussions of physiological aesthetics and aesthetic modernism, see Robert Michael Brain, *The Pulse of Modernism: Physiological Aesthetics in Fin-de-Siècle Europe* (Seattle, WA: University of Washington Press, 2015); Robin Veder, *The Living Line: Modern Art and the Economy of Energy* (Hanover, NH: Dartmouth College Press, 2015). For physiological aesthetics in the history of architectural theory, see Harry Francis Mallgrave and Eleftherios Ikonomou, eds., *Empathy, Form, and Space: Problems in German Aesthetics, 1873–1893* (Santa Monica, CA: Getty Center, 1994).

44 Wundt as quoted in Christian A. Ruckmich, "The Role of Kinaesthesis in the Perception of Rhythm," *American Journal of Psychology* 24, no. 3 (July 1913): 308.

45 Stumpf as quoted in Ruckmich, "Role of Kinaesthesis," 308.

46 Edward Wheeler Scripture, *Thinking, Feeling, Doing* (Meadville, PA: Flood & Vincent, 1897), 253.

47 Ruckmich, "Role of Kinaesthesis," 308–309.

48 Edith Wharton, *Italian Villas and Their Gardens* (New York: Century, 1905); Vivian Russell, *Edith Wharton's Italian Gardens* (Boston, MA: Bulfinch, 1997), 17; Shari Benstock, *No Gifts from Chance: A Biography of Edith Wharton* (London: Hamish Hamilton, 1994), 138; Diane Kostial McGuire, "Sermon on 'The Mount': Edith Wharton's Influence on Beatrix Jones Farrand," *Journal of the New England Garden History Society* 1, no. 1 (Fall 1991): 11–17; Edith Wharton, *A Backward Glance* (1934; New York: Simon & Schuster, 1998), 129–142; Penelope Vita-Finzi, "Italian Background: Edith Wharton's Debt to Vernon Lee," *Edith Wharton Review* 13, no. 1 (Fall 1996): 14–18.

49 Vernon Lee, "The Lie of the Land: Notes about Landscapes," in *Limbo and Other Essays* (London: Grant Richards, 1897), 47, 60–61.

50 Vernon Lee and Clementina Anstruther-Thomson, "Beauty and Ugliness" [1897] in Vernon Lee, *Beauty and Ugliness and Other Studies in Psychological Aesthetics* (London: John Lane, 1912), 157–161.

51 Ibid., 185, 180.

52 For a list of Vernon Lee's publications in 1903 and 1904, see Phyllis F. Mannocchi, "'Vernon Lee': A Reintroduction and Primary Bibliography," *English Literature in Transition, 1880–1920* 26, no. 4 (1983): 255–256.

53 Edith Wharton to Vernon Lee, April 7, 1903, reprinted in Hilda M. Fife, "Letters from Edith Wharton to Vernon Lee," *Colby Quarterly* 3, no. 9 (February 1953): 2; Lee, *Beauty and Ugliness*, 299. See also Suzanne W. Jones, "Edith Wharton's 'Secret Sensitiveness,' *The Decoration of Houses*, and Her Fiction," *Journal of Modern Literature* 21, no. 2 (Winter 1997–98): 180, 196; Suzanne W. Jones, "The '*Beyondness* of Things' in *The Bucccaneers*: Vernon Lee's Influence on Edith Wharton's Sense of Places," *Symbiosis* 8, no. 1 (April 2004): 7–30.

54 Farrand sailed for Europe on July 4, 1903. Benstock, *No Gifts from Chance*, 138; McGuire, "Sermon on 'The Mount,'" 11–17.

55 Ruth D. Happel, "A Survey of Courses in Landscape Appreciation," *Landscape Architecture* 23, no. 3 (April 1933): 182; Melanie Simo, *The Coalescing of Different Forces and Ideas: A History of Landscape Architecture at Harvard, 1900–1999* (Cambridge, MA: Harvard University Graduate School of Design, 2000), 16.

56 Henry Vincent Hubbard and Theodora Kimball, *An Introduction to the Study of Landscape Design* (New York: Macmillan, 1917), 97–98.

57 Ibid., 13–15.

58 Denman Waldo Ross, *On Drawing and Painting* (Boston, MA: Houghton Mifflin, 1912), 70, quoted in Hubbard and Kimball, *Landscape Design*, 95; Marie Frank, *Denman Ross and American Design Theory* (Hanover, NH: University Press of New England, 2011), 110–134.

59 Arthur Wesley Dow, *Composition*, 3rd edn (New York: Baker & Taylor, 1900), quoted in Marjorie Sewell Cautley, *Garden Design: The Principles of Abstract Design as Applied to Landscape Composition* (New York: Dodd, Mead, 1935), 15, ix.

8

Shaping Fascist Bodies: Children's Summer Camps in Fascist Italy

Stephanie Pilat

> *At Ostia, with unusual haste, was born by the brilliant fantasy of an artist, a true small peasant village from barns covered with straw roofs and free walls, to allow the little ones to live fortified by the sun, by the weather, and the great air of the sea.*[1]

The "peasant village," described above and constructed on the Mediterranean coast just outside Rome, was a *colonia* (plural *colonie*)—a summer camp designed to provide urban children with the opportunity to experience the natural landscape of the seashore. Basic rustic wood structures with thatch roofs on the beach provided relief from the intense sun for the campers at Ostia. *Colonie* like the one at Ostia were founded throughout Europe starting in the nineteenth century and were often funded by the Church or other charitable organizations. Anxiety over unhealthy living conditions in urban centers led proponents to build these recreational camps and open-air schools for children in natural regions, including mountainous areas, river valleys, and along the seashore. Starting in the late 1920s, the Fascist regime adopted the *colonia* building type and mission on behalf of the state, transforming it into one of the primary means of shaping the lives of Italian youth.

During the more than two decades of Mussolini's reign in Italy (1922–43), the Fascist regime sponsored and encouraged the construction of hundreds of *colonie*. Figure 8.1 illustrates, for example, that between 1929 and 1933 alone, the number of *colonie* in Italy grew from 571 to 2,022. By the late twentieth century there were roughly 3,800 *colonie* scattered along all Italy's coastlines and sprinkled throughout rural and occasionally even urban landscapes.[2] Fascists developed the *colonie* into a key mechanism through which they sought to influence the nation's youth. The number of *colonie* constructed, their spread across the country, and their architectural prominence illustrate the importance of youth and wellness in Fascist ideology. The regime sought to use *colonie* projects as a means to control and regulate the bodies of children, particularly those from urban areas and working-class families. This was part of a broad campaign to indoctrinate youth into Fascist ideology and to ensure that Italians would be physically prepared in the case of war. The imperial ambitions of the regime would require an army of healthy battle-ready

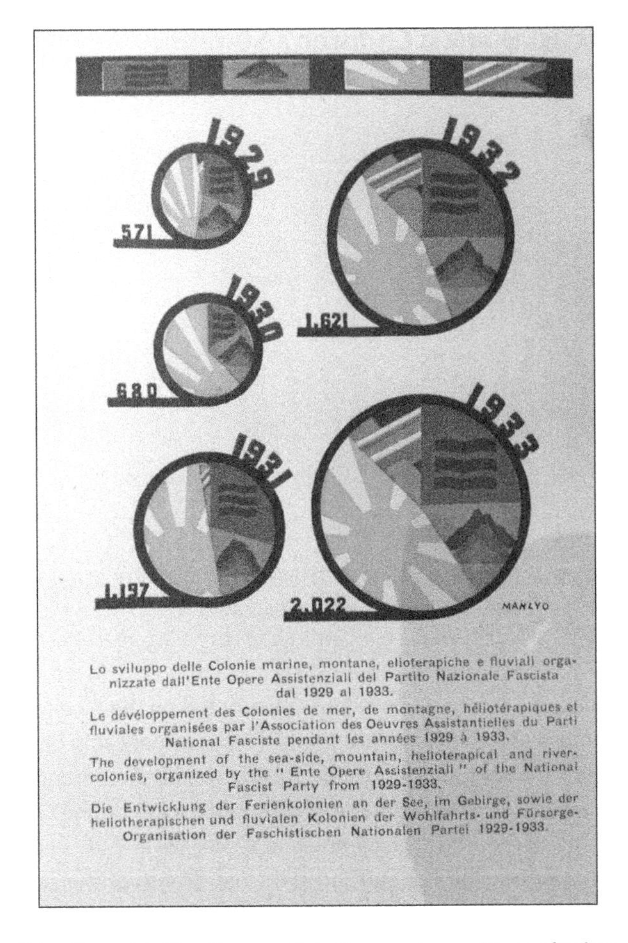

8.1 Chart detailing the growth in the number and type of Italian *colonie* from 1929 to 1933. Source: *La lotta contro la tubercolosi in Italia*, Wolfsonian-Florida International University Library Collection.

soldiers. As the *New York Times* reported in 1934, "In the very young, dictators see plastic raw material on whose mind it is comparatively easy to impress their aims and ideals and seek to make their systems of government permanent by raising generations of unquestioning loyalty."[3] The *Times* article noted that 3.5 million Italian children were enlisted in various Fascist youth groups in 1934.

Projects such as the *colonia* at Ostia also reflected a broader Fascist social agenda that sought to reconnect Italians with their rural heritage, landscapes, and traditions. In some cases, the anti-urban rhetoric of the Fascists led to initiatives to return Italians to agrarian ways of life. Under Fascism, for example, previously uninhabitable marshlands were drained and filled in and new villages for farmers were built in their place. The *colonie* thus served the regime's aim of reconnecting city dwellers with rural environments by providing Italian children with access to the natural landscape, if only for a few weeks a year. By the 1930s, however, the "peasant village" described at Ostia and the primitive fantasy it reflected was an exceptional form for *colonie* rather than the standard. The *colonie* constructed in the 1930s bore little resemblance to rural architecture; they were often stark modern buildings, devoid of ornamentation and usually made of glass, concrete, and stone. These *colonie* looked more like the contemporary factories of the city that the children were supposed to be escaping from, rather than the rustic villages to which they were supposed to be returning. If part of the program for the *colonie* was to return children to the land, and in a sense to take them back in time, then one must ask why so many projects embodied a modernist style rather than a more traditional one.

As the description of the *colonia* at Ostia suggests, the desire to expose children to sunlight and fresh air were important objectives for these projects. Although the program for the *colonie* developed out of a complex set of concerns and goals, by the 1930s one motivating factor superseded all others when it came to the architectural form of these projects: a concern for health in response to the spread of tuberculosis (TB) throughout Italy. In Italy, the mortality rate in 1925 for children aged five to ten was 37.9 per thousand, a tragic figure.[4] For much of the first half of the twentieth century, tuberculosis was believed to have spatial and environmental causes and remedies. Professionals in both medicine and architecture believed that sunlight and fresh air—sorely lacking in the cities of the time—could help prevent and treat tuberculosis.[5] The development of ideas about how to create a healthier environment affected buildings outside of the medical profession including housing and especially the *colonie*. In what follows, I review the history of spatial remedies for tuberculosis, and ideas about health in architectural discourse of the thirties in order to illustrate the understanding that architects had at the time regarding what types of spaces promoted good health. How these ideas about health and space became central to *colonie* design in the 1930s will be illustrated by an analysis of two *colonie* projects from the 1930s.

THE EMERGENCE OF THE *COLONIE* BUILDING TYPE

Pre-dating Fascism, *colonie* developed in France and Switzerland in the nineteenth century as summer camps and open-air schools designed to provide children—especially those from urban environments—with access to the wonders and health benefits of the natural world. The first *colonia* in Italy was founded in 1881 and more developed thereafter throughout the country with the same agenda. Early *colonie* were funded and developed by a number of different sources, including religious institutions, municipal governments, political organizations, and private individuals. While their mission varied with each sponsor, the common goal of such projects was to provide relief from the city for the children of the poor in order to improve their health and, at times, also their manners or morals. As one architect described the children who visited the *colonie*, "many of them come from slums, modest social housing or uneasy family experience and will feel disposed for the first time, in a calm and comfortable atmosphere."[6] By 1922 when the Fascists came to power, over 100,000 Italian children were spending time at *colonie* of various types each year.[7]

In the 1930s, the *colonie* became a centerpiece of the Fascist youth- and health-oriented agenda. Yet, as the *colonie* form evolved, tuberculosis, rather than political ideology, became the main driver of *colonie* designs. Not only is tuberculosis highly contagious, but as many as one in every three people carry the bacteria that causes the disease, although most never become ill.[8] Thus the threat of the spread of tuberculosis was very real and ever present for Italians at the time. As the Italian architect Lodovico Belgioioso recalled:

> *We should remember that tuberculosis was very common at the time—it was the bogey-man that our parents would frighten us with—and the* colonie *in industrial areas were built in part to give the children a chance of some fresh air and sunshine.*[9]

As Belgioioso recounts, the *colonie* were understood as a response to tuberculosis. Emerging scientific understandings of TB motivated justifications for *colonie* designs.

The decades between the 1882 discovery of the bacillus that causes tuberculosis and the discovery of a vaccine in 1944 were a time of experimentation with treatments for the disease.[10] Spatial remedies were among the leading treatments prescribed during this period for both the prevention and treatment of tuberculosis and the *colonie* emerged as one of the key weapons in the fight against the spread of TB among children. The medical community led the call for increasing the number of summer camps and advocated for prevention measures to be undertaken at the *colonie*. The medical journal *Lotta contro la tubercolosi* (The Fight Against Tuberculosis), for example, praised the Fascist youth organization the Opera Nazionale Bailila (ONB) for its mission to "protect the health of the next generation of Italians" and suggested that the best way for the ONB to help in the struggle against tuberculosis was through the construction and management of *colonie*, as well as by monitoring sanitary conditions in the schools.[11] With these prevention measures undertaken by the ONB, the journal promised, "tuberculosis would soon enough be no more than a memory."[12] Included in reports on the *colonie* in this journal were statistics suggesting a correlation between the decline of tuberculosis and the increase in the numbers of *colonie*.[13]

The Italian *colonie* of the 1930s were primarily focused on the prevention rather than the treatment of TB. The spatial remedies for prevention and treatment were, however, similar; in both cases, fresh air and sunlight were prescribed. Lifting sleeping quarters off the ground was also believed to be beneficial. The *colonie* increasingly took on formal characteristics similar to those of sanatoria or hospitals rather than the rustic or natural forms one might associate with summer camps. Materials used in the *colonie*, for example, reflected ideas of hygiene or cleanliness; easily washable materials and an absence of intricate detailing or ornament prevail in these projects. Most interestingly, two traits that could easily conflict with one another became defining architectural characteristics of the 1930s *colonie*: the separation of functions and bodies, and permeability or openness in order to ensure plentiful ventilation and natural light. Architects developed ingenuous ways to balance the desire for both separation and openness from the level of site design all the way down to the wall and fenestration details. A comparison between two Fascist era projects—the Torre Fiat in Marina di Massa designed by Vittorio Bonadè Bottino, and the AGIP *colonie* in Cesenatico designed by Giuseppe Vaccaro—illustrates how the regime's obsession with youth and health evolved from the rural fantasy at Ostia into more modernist and health-oriented forms and the role TB played in that development.

COLONIA AGIP AT CESENATICO, DESIGNED BY GIUSEPPE VACCARO

The *Colonia* "Sandro Mussolini," sponsored by the Italian Energy Corporation AGIP, is located on the Adriatic coast between Rimini and Ravenna. Designed by the Bolognese architect Giuseppe Vaccaro, the project was completed in 1938.[14] The *colonia* complex is comprised of four buildings distributed across the site: a dormitory and kitchen in the center; staff lodging to the south; a caretaker's and admissions building to the north; and an isolation pavilion on the far north side of the site (Figures 8.2 and 8.3). Together the buildings form an open courtyard connected by covered walkways, with the *piazzale della bandiera*, a ceremonial courtyard centered on the Italian flag, in the middle of the site. The buildings are spread so far apart, however, that the space formed by them is a vast one, an exploded courtyard. Rather than creating a sense of enclosure or protection, the area formed by the collection of buildings is weakly framed, space seeps out of the area throughout the site. On the seashore side, the unbounded sense of space is more pronounced still, first by

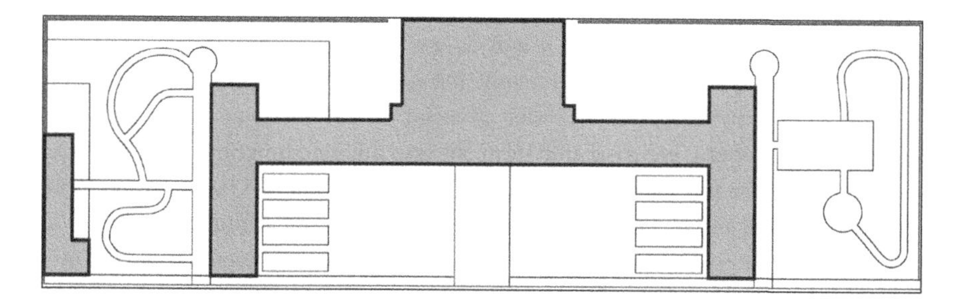

8.2 Site plan of *Colonia* AGIP in Cesenatico. Drawn by Aaron Pilat, 2015.

8.3 *Colonia* AGIP, Cesenatico. Photograph by author, 2004.

the ocean view and secondly by the form of the cafeteria pavilion, which protrudes out from the rest of the complex and is thereby open on three sides. The cafeteria pavilion is an object in space, almost entirely engulfed in the vast horizontal landscape of the seaside.

From the site plan a desire for spatial separation of functions is evident in the way the various programmatic requirements are allotted dedicated buildings spread across the site, rather than clustered together in a single mass. The site arrangement thus reflects the spatial manifestation of emerging beliefs about the prevention and treatment of TB, which suggested isolation—or at least separation—was key to preventing the spread of the disease. The dense, dark, polluted, and damp conditions in which much of the urban working class lived were believed to be responsible for the higher TB rates in urban areas. In contrast, treatments developed by doctors around the turn of the century emphasized removing patients from the city whenever possible and providing them with access to fresh air and sunlight. Coinciding with the discovery of the bacterium that causes TB in the late nineteenth century and the development of treatment was a more comprehensive understanding of germs and hygiene more broadly. Although quarantines had long been used as an effective tool against the spread of disease, it was only with the development of laboratory science that ideas about how to prevent the spread of germs, through hygiene, became commonly accepted. The idea of isolating patients was key in sanatoria design, as new patients were isolated from old, and building functions such as eating and sleeping were separated from one another. Trash and linen facilities had to be separated as well and in some cases patients were to be as far from one another as possible.[15] As the environmental principles associated with TB were translated into *colonie* designs the practice of *isolation* associated with sanatoria evolved into one of *separation*—separation of bodies, buildings, and functions in the *colonie*. At the architectural level, the principle of separation not only helped prevent the spread of disease; it could, at times, be adapted to help ensure plentiful access to natural light and ventilation. These emerging beliefs about germs and hygiene suggested that the best treatment and prevention facilities were those with the greatest degree of separation both from society and within the complexes themselves through a separation of functions. Architects, however, had to avoid taking this to the extreme of sequestration. They could not isolate functions or patients by creating the overly confined spaces negatively associated with urban environments at the time. Air and sunlight had to be able to flow through the *colonie* complexes. Thus one of the most important challenges architects of *colonie* had to consider was how to balance the desire for separation with the need for openness and connectivity so that air and sunlight could flow freely.

A successful balance between separation and openness is illustrated architecturally at Cesenatico in the design of the central structure on the site: the five-story linear block which houses the dormitories. The ground level of the building is almost entirely open, defined by a colonnade upon which the dormitory rests (Figure 8.4). The structure of the colonnade has been separated from the enclosure system, which is primarily glass. At times, the columns are pulled outside of the buildings, but at others, they are behind the glass and the floor cantilevers out above them. As a result of this system of enclosure and structure, it is difficult to distinguish where the exterior ends and the interior begins. Approaching the building from the road through the *piazzale della bandiera*, the line between inside and out is nearly indistinguishable. One would first step onto the paved outdoor area, then pass under the roof overhang, then through the structural system of columns and only lastly through the glass enclosure. In essence, the traditional system of enclosure has been pulled apart, with each portion, ground plane, roof plane, structure, and walls marking a separate point of transition in the journey from outside to inside. Consequently, the visitor's sense of interior and exterior space would be distorted, as exterior space flows over the ground, under the roof, between the structure and perceptually through the glass.

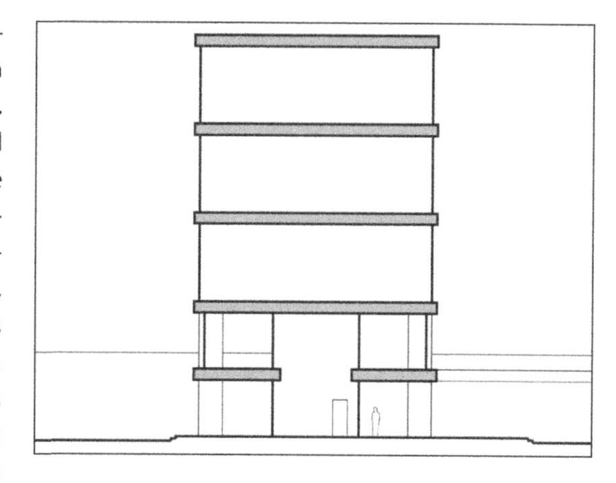

8.4 Diagram of *Colonia* AGIP entry sequence, Cesenatico. Drawn by Aaron Pilat, 2015.

The open quality of the ground plane contrasts with the clearly defined linear block of dormitories above and thus corresponds to yet another level of functional separation in the project: between daytime and nighttime activities.[16] The children's sleeping quarters have been entirely removed from the ground, whereas the daytime activities such as cooking, eating, gymnastics, and sunbathing all take place on the ground plane. Giuseppe Vaccaro explained the motivation for the spatial arrangement:

> *The services, the systems equipment, the dimensions and the distribution of the various parts are such as to guarantee the best possible hygienic and functional conditions based on the most recent criteria which dictates the evolution of this important field to the institutions of Fascism.*[17]

Vaccaro's mention of hygiene and recent design criteria indicate that concerns for the physical health of children housed at the *colonie* motivated design strategies. As the architect Mario Labó explained the importance of health concerns for *colonie* design, "On an architectural level, the objective of hygiene—the impeccable cleanliness of the rooms and their equipment—is but a premise, an implicit starting point."[18]

A closer examination of the details of the dormitory building further illustrates how these ideas about hygiene were translated architecturally. The long narrow form of the dormitory building was designed to gain as much exposure to fresh air and sunlight as possible. The glass skin system, for example, takes advantage of the building's form and allows for a great amount of sunlight and airflow within each of the shallow rooms (Figure 8.5). The skin system includes operable louvers and windows so as to enable adjustment of the amount of air and light flowing through the building. The concept of separation was carried into the details of the building as well. In the dormitories, for example, the exterior walls are again separated from the structure, which is located to the inside of the exterior wall. The interior partitions separating one dormitory from another illustrate a compromise between the desire for separation and the need for ventilation. The partition walls do not extend

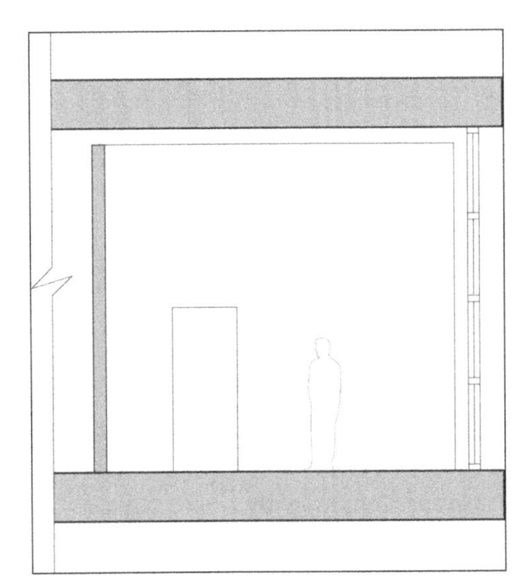

8.5 *Colonia* AGIP wall section diagrams. Drawn by Aaron Pilat, 2015.

all the way to the glass enclosure; they stop just short. This breach between the parts of the building allows air to flow through the building and prevents any one space from being completely enclosed. In a sense, the permeable separation of the rooms of the dormitory mimics the permeability of the massing arrangement in the site plan. This detail—reflecting the desire for separation of bodies and spaces combined with the need for airflow—was common in sanatoria of the time. As one sanatorium was described, for example: "They shared two-bedded cubicles clustered in pavilions built of uninsulated 'mack' slabs and concrete. Between the walls and ceiling there was a three-inch wide [8cm] unblockable gap."[19]

At Cesenatico, the desire to separate functions and bodies without ever fully enclosing them is evident from the level of the site plan and massing all the way down to the architectural details. Across the Italian peninsula on the Mediterranean coast we find another example of how beliefs about hygiene, tuberculosis, and spatial remedies were translated into a dramatic architectural form.

TORRE FIAT *COLONIA*, MARINA DI MASSA, DESIGNED BY VITTORIO BONADÈ BOTTINO

Located approximately 100 kilometers southeast of Genoa along the Mediterranean coast, the Torre Fiat *Colonia* is hard to miss. Situated among low-lying seaside hotels, restaurants, and resorts, the *colonia*'s cylindrical fifteen-story tower projects above the horizontal landscape of the region, making it visible from a distance (Figure 8.6). Perched atop a two-story linear base, the tower looks like a monolithic, squat, and fluted classical column.[20] The dramatic spaces formed by the tower inside are, however, anything but classical: the central atrium is enclosed by a spiraling ramp that rises up and connects the fifteen floors of the tower. Standing inside looking up is dizzying; the ribbon-like ramp revolves around and around, creating a pattern of alternating voids, floors, and railings (Figure 8.7). When completed in 1933, the tower contained 235 dormitory-style rooms housing up to 750 children. The elongated two-story building upon which the tower sits is formed of two projecting wings that parallel the line of the coast and house the public spaces of the facility. Vertical ribs alternate with windows and wrap the white exterior of the tower and the two-story building below, uniting the two forms in a singular exterior expression. A few smaller single-story buildings line the boundaries of the site and share the architectural language of the main building.

The Torre Fiat *Colonia* was designed by an architect from Turin, Vittorio Bonadè Bottino, to serve the children of Fiat workers. Bonadè Bottino had previously worked with architect Matte Trucco on the design of the legendary Fiat Lingotto factory, known for the spiraling organization of the assembly line that culminated in a rooftop racetrack. The dramatic ramps and spatial organization of the factory clearly served as a source of inspiration for Bonadè Bottino at Marina di Massa.[21] In the *colonia*, however, cars are not being moved and assembled; rather the bodies of the state's youngest citizens are on display. Newsreels promoting the Torre Fiat *Colonia* from the time, for example, show happy children in uniform parading down the long spiraling ramps illustrating the way in which the building serves as a stage for human action.[22]

8.6 Torre Fiat *Colonia*, view of tower. Photograph by Fontema, 2013, distributed under a Creative Commons License.

At first glance, the site plan and form of the Torre Fiat *Colonia* appear quite different from the *Colonia* AGIP in Cesenatico. The Torre Fiat *Colonia* is dominated by the centralized mass—the two-story block with the tower above—which reads like an object building surrounded by open space. Although there are some smaller pavilions along the boundaries of the site, the visual power of the cylindrical fifteen-story tower overshadows everything else and gives the sense of a greater whole. The sense of a massive building floating in space at Marina di Massa is in opposition to the sense of buildings enclosing space at Cesenatico. This is partly a reflection of the fact that, although the two projects have relatively equivalent sites in terms of size, the Marina di Massa *colonia* has eight times the amount of built space at Cesenatico.[23]

Despite the differences in site design and massing, however, we find the play between separation and openness from Cesenatico manifest in original ways in Marina di Massa. Bonadè Bottino aimed to separate functions while at the same time allowing air to flow and sunlight to penetrate the structures of the Torre Fiat *Colonia* just as Vaccaro had done in Cesenatico. The formal means of achieving these aims was, however, quite different in Marina di Massa. In the spiraling dormitory tower, the volume of the whole was largely united; air and light flowed freely throughout. The bed spaces were separated from the ramp by a half-wall and demarcated from the vast space of the atrium by relatively low ceilings (Figure 8.8). Within the dormitory rooms, distinct areas were further partitioned by low walls circumscribing smaller units of four beds. Thus we find in the Fiat tower a sense of balance between the volumetric unity of the whole and psychological division into smaller zones similar to that found in Cesenatico. Bonadè Bottino, however, achieved this balance between the desire for the free flow of air and the separation of spaces through the use of a dramatic form: the cylindrical tower and spiraling ramp. De Martino and Wall cited this project as among the most radical of *colonie* forms, noting: "The departure from all other projects lies in relating each bed space to the volume of the building, so that a continuous dormitory, rising in a spiral, determines both the external form and the internal volume.[24]

8.7 Interior of Torre Fiat. Photograph by Gregorovius, 2014, distributed under a Creative Commons License.

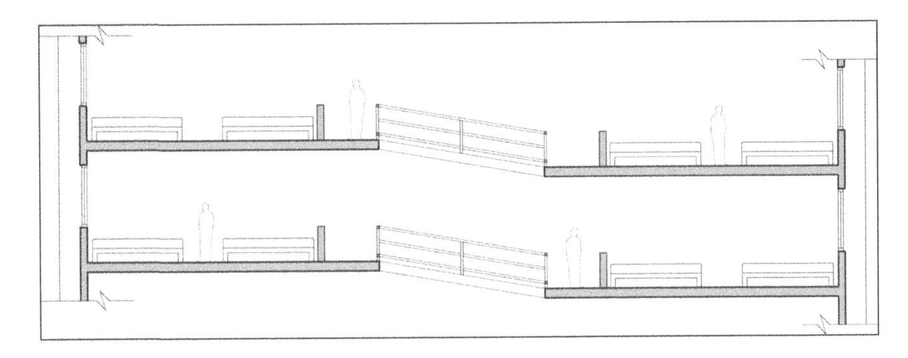

8.8 Section diagram of Torre Fiat. Drawn by Aaron Pilat, 2015.

CONCLUSIONS

The designs of 1930s Italian *colonie* illustrate how the fear of tuberculosis and ideas about prevention and treatment influenced architectural form and motivated innovative attempts to balance a desire for separation and openness. The modern aesthetic of these projects shows that although some Fascist rhetoric and policies suggested that the problems brought on by industrialization could be solved by returning Italians to the land and turning back the clock on modernity, such rhetoric did not always translate into practice. Medical professionals and architects embraced new approaches to design inspired by science and technology in order to address the health problems brought on by life in the industrial city; chief among these problems was tuberculosis. Italian children were to be saved from the grave ills of the city not simply by returning to the countryside and peasant lifestyle after all, but in the *colonie* through the provision of modern and hygienic environments. Thus, despite widespread anxiety about conditions of life in the industrial metropolis, there was no turning back; only through modern science and architecture would the very problems wrought by modernity be addressed.

NOTES

1 N. Ciampi, "Le Istituzioni all'Aperto e le Colonie Climatiche," *Capitolium* (1928): 303. All translations are by the author unless otherwise noted. "Ad Ostia poi, con fretta inusitata, nacque, per la geniale fantasia di un artista, un vero piccolo villaggio rustico da capannoni coperti da tetti di paglia e liberi dale pareti, si da permettere ai piccini di vivere, difesi dal sole e dale intemperie, alla grande aria marina."

2 Stefano de Martino and Alex Wall, eds., *Cities of Childhood: Italian Colonie of the 1930s* (London: Architectural Association, 1988), 3.

3 Arnaldo Cortesi, "Children Prepare for Rule in Italy," *New York Times*, April 8, 1934.

4 "Lo Sviluppo delle Costruzioni Sanatoriali in Italia," *Lotta contro la tubercolosi*, (March 1932): 350–351.

5 Ibid.

6 De Martino and Wall, *Cities of Childhood*, 78.

7 Giorgio Frisoni, Elizabetta Gavazza, Mariagrazia Orsolini, and Massimo Simini, "Origins and History of the Colonie," in *Cities of Childhood: Italian Colonie of the 1930s* (London: Architectural Association, 1988), 7.

8 Thomas M. Daniel, *Captain of Death: The Story of Tuberculosis* (New York: University of Rochester Press, 1997), 1.

9 De Martino and Wall, "Interview with Lodovico Belgioioso," in *Cities of Childhood*, 73.

10 For a history of tuberculosis, see F.B. Smith, *The Retreat of Tuberculosis 1850–1950* (London and New York: Croom Helm, 1988). For a history of tuberculosis in Italy around the turn of the century, see Tommaso Detti, "La questione della tubercolosi nell'Italia giolittiana," *Passato e presente* 2 (1982): 27–60.

11 "O.N.B. nei Confronti della Prevenzione e della Profilassi Infantile Contro La Tubercolosi," *Lotta contro la tubercolosi* (November 1932): 1227.

12 Ibid.

13 "Lo Sviluppo delle Costruzioni Sanatoriali in Italia," 350–351.

14 On *Colonia* AGIP, see *Giuseppe Vaccaro: Colonia Marina a Cesenatico* (Rome: Clear, 1994).

15 David L. Ellison, *Healing Tuberculosis in the Woods: Medicine and Science at the End of the Nineteenth Century* (Portsmouth, NH: Praeger, 1994),150.

16 Mario Labó and Attilio Podestà, "Colonie Marine—Montane—Elioterapiche," *Casabella* 167–168 (1942), trans. and repr. in *Cities of Childhood*, 80–81.

17 Giuseppe Vaccaro, "La Colonia 'Sandro Mussolini' dell'AGIP a Cesenatico," *Architettura* (January 1939), repr. in *Giuseppe Vaccaro: Colonia Marina a Cesenatico 1936–39*, (Rome: Clear, 1994): 71. "I servizi, la dotazione di impianti, le dimensioni e la distribuzione di vari organi sono tali de garantire le migliori possibli condizioni igieniche e di funzionamento in base ai criteri piu recenti dettati dall'evoluzione di questo importante settore delle istituzioni del Fascismo."

18 Labó and Podestà, "Colonie Marine," 78.

19 Smith, *The Retreat of Tuberculosis*, 109.

20 Michelangelo Pivetta, "La Colonna d'Eracle Torre FIAT a Marina di Massa di Vittorio Bonadè Bottino," *Firenze architettura* 1 (2011): 100–107.

21 De Martino and Wall, *Cities of Childhood*, 20.

22 "Colonie estive a Marina di Massa," *La settimana Incom*, accessed August 1, 2015, https://www.youtube.com/watch?v=La1sVDvhdx8.

23 The *Colonia* Fiat at Marina di Massa includes 35,000 square meters of built space on a 55,000 square meter site. The *Colonia* AGIP in Cesenatico includes just 4,000 square meters of built space on a site of 51,300 square meters. De Martino and Wall, *Cities of Childhood*, 21, 37.

24 De Martino and Wall, *Cities of Childhood*, 20.

9

Bodies at Work and Leisure: Therapeutic Landscapes of Early Nineteenth-Century New York State Insane Asylums

Jennifer L. Thomas

Industrialization and urbanization transformed New York State into an economic and cultural powerhouse that utilized abundant natural resources, highly navigable water systems, railroads, large immigrant populations, and market forces to create a complex state structure. As part of this structural development, between 1843 and 1890, New York also built seven state-run insane asylums at Utica, Ovid, Binghamton, Poughkeepsie, Middletown, Buffalo, and Ogdensburg. Most asylums required large amounts of land to treat hundreds of patients because farming, access to natural resources, and a largely rural setting were considered essential for treating the mentally unwell. Moral treatment, the Quaker-inspired psychiatric practice embraced at the time, combined spiritual guidance, behavior modifications, and physical labor to administer healing to patients and restore moral strength. Doctors and administrators believed that regimented daily routines could adjust mind, body, and spirit back to a reasoned state. A fundamental component of implementing moral treatment was asylum design. Within buildings and landscapes, the physical bodies of patients were organized by function, severity of illness, and gender. Class, ethnicity, and race also factored into the asylum patient equation, often in biased or opaque manners.

This study focuses on landscape-related design and treatment practices at the three earliest state-funded facilities in New York—the Bloomingdale Asylum in Manhattan (1821), the New York State Lunatic Asylum at Utica (1843), and the Willard Asylum for the Chronic Insane (1869) (Figure 9.1). These settings were spatialized responses to evolving therapeutic ideologies. In each facility, patient labor and recreation combined treatment ideologies with asylum function and maintenance, reinforcing socially normative behaviors, and spatially articulating larger societal and state concerns related to mental illness, class, gender, and race.

NEW YORK HOSPITAL'S BLOOMINGDALE ASYLUM

Prior to the construction of state asylums, mentally ill New Yorkers were cared for by families or housed in municipal or county asylums, poorhouses, and prisons. New York

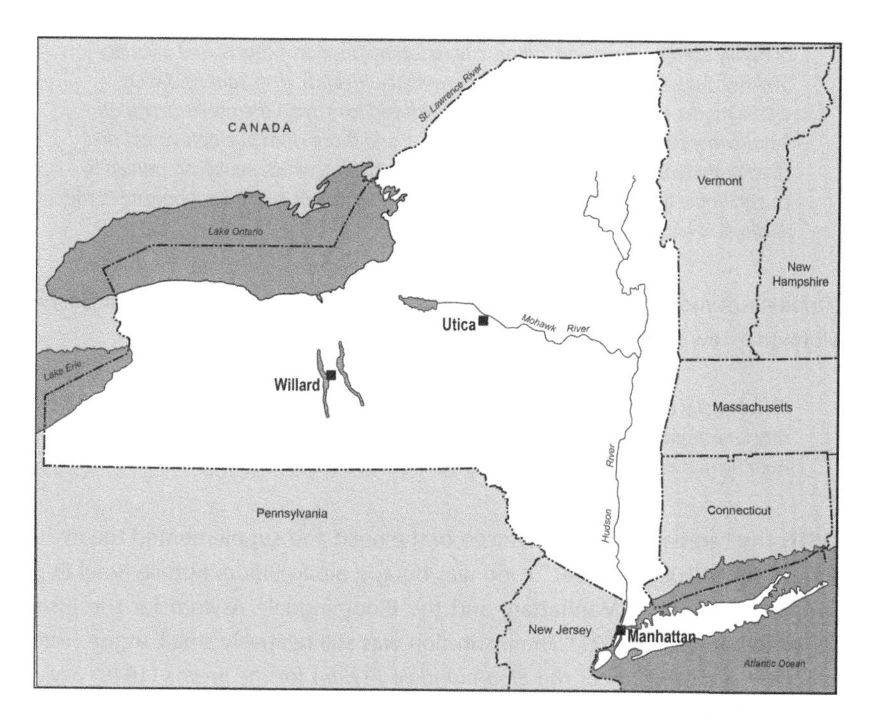

9.1 Map of New York State, showing asylum locations and basic spatial context. Drawn by the author.

State officials, doctors, and prominent citizens grappled with what should be done for the insane, especially those in poverty. In New York City, New York Hospital—an institution chartered during the late colonial era—began treating mental patients in a separate building as early as 1808—partially funded by the State Legislature.[1] In 1809, the Legislature passed a law

> *empowering overseers of the poor of any city or town . . . to contract with the governors of the New York Hospital for the maintenance and care of insane persons, and the cost of maintenance was paid by the city or town from which the patient came.*[2]

Thomas Eddy (1758–1827), a prominent Quaker, merchant, and penitentiary reformer, served on the New York Hospital Board of Governors during that time and focused particularly on the asylum.[3] In an essay, "Hints for Introducing an Improved Mode of Treating the Insane in the Asylum read before the Governors of the New York Hospital" (1815), Eddy implored fellow asylum committee members to embrace moral treatment methods practiced by Samuel Tuke (1784–1857) at the York Retreat in England, an institution founded by Samuel's grandfather, William Tuke (1732–1822) and father Henry Tuke (1755–1814).[4] Eschewing corporal punishment, chain restraints, and fear tactics, Eddy encouraged kindness towards patients, physical labor, amusement, religion, and appeals to their inner "rational being:"

> *every means ought to be taken to seduce the mind from unhappy and favourite musings; and particularly with melancholic patients; they should freely partake*

> *of bodily exercises, walking, riding, conversations, innocent sports, and a variety of other amusements; they should be gratified with birds, deer, rabbits, &c. Of all the modes by which maniacs may be induced to restrain themselves, regular employment is perhaps the most efficacious; and those kinds of employment are to be preferred, both on a moral and physical account, which are accompanied by considerable bodily action, most agreeable to the patient, and most opposite to the illusions of his disease.*[5]

To implement moral management, Eddy proposed locating the New York Hospital asylum on a new site,

> *[one] not less than ten acres . . . within a few miles of the city . . . [to accommodate] fifty lunatic patients; the ground to . . . serve for agreeable walks, gardens, &c for the exercise and amusement of the patients . . . at this Rural Retreat.*[6]

In 1816, the Legislature was convinced of the need and supplemented the asylum budget with $10,000 per year.[7] Land was bought along Bloomingdale Road in the rural part of northern Manhattan, and the Bloomingdale Asylum for the Insane opened to patients in 1821.[8] The institution was still relatively small; in the *History Description and Statistics of the Bloomingdale Asylum for the Insane* (1848) asylum physician Pliny Earle specified that the "average daily number of patients" in residence between 1821 and 1844 was 110.44.[9] Patients' socioeconomic condition was generalized. Male occupations are divided into what Earle called "imperfect" classifications, such as "merchants and traders," "professional men," and "outdoor" or "indoor employments."[10] Female occupations received only brief note, with thirteen listed and a qualifier that "of the 510 [patients] whose occupation is not stated, it is probable that most of them were from the non-laboring classes of society."[11] Places of birth for all patients are recorded, the vast majority being European or North American locales.[12]

9.2 Bloomingdale Asylum for the Insane, Manhattan. Source: Rev. J.F. Richmond, *New York and Its Institutions 1609–1872* (New York: E.B. Treat, 1872), 294. Collection of the author.

Earle quoted fellow asylum physician James Macdonald's laudatory description of the Bloomingdale grounds, noting the pleasing approach to the main building, with "various avenues gracefully winding through so large a lawn"; the aesthetic placement of trees, shrubs, and flowers; and the landscape's ability to "relieve the melancholy mind from its sad musings"[13] (Figure 9.2). Macdonald declared it "one of the most successful and useful instances of landscape gardening."[14] Earle also explained how the asylum implemented facets of moral treatment through "manual labor, various games and other amusements, a good library, and horses and carriage for riding," plus religious services on the Sabbath for both patients and staff.[15]

While these early descriptions portray the beginnings of a state care system being carried out in a bucolic setting, Bloomingdale proved insufficient to the needs and expectations of the region. A New York State census in 1825 listed 819 insane persons, 556 of whom were poor and "confined in jails, poor-houses or in private families."[16] In 1827, the state Legislature passed "An Act Concerning Lunatics" which prohibited housing the mentally ill in "any prison, gaol, or house of correction" or in any situation with a charged or convicted criminal.[17] That made the Bloomingdale Asylum and various poorhouses and almshouses the only option for those without family support. In 1830, Governor Enos T. Throop (1784–1874) appealed for an increase in care for poor, mentally ill citizens of New York: "By the census of 1825, there were three-hundred and forty-eight insane paupers at large, and suffering . . . all the privations attending penury and want. The condition of those under poorhouse regulations or confined in jails is, if possible, worse."[18]

A legislative committee was formed and investigations launched, resulting in a lengthy report (1831) that criticized much of New York Hospital's construction expenditures and management of Bloomingdale Asylum.[19] The committee was also asked to determine the need for additional "establishments for the insane," preferred sites for such places, potential layouts of buildings and grounds, and estimated construction costs.[20] Their report included a brief historical view of insanity, emphasized moral treatment methods, and advocated for the construction of public hospitals that could be inspected, regulated, and funded consistently and adequately by the state. Christian benevolence, public safety, and scientific medical advancement were invoked to persuade readers of the government's obligation to the pauper insane. Even though Bloomingdale Asylum, by law, could contract with any municipality or county in New York State to admit poor patients, the committee found that very few communities did, declaring "there exists no provision whatever in this State for the comfortable support and the proper treatment of the insane poor."[21]

The report also included a brief survey and discussion of existing asylums in the United States, including the Quaker "Friends Asylum for the Relief of Persons Deprived of their use of Reason" (Frankford, PA, just outside Philadelphia), the McLean Asylum (Charlestown, MA), the Connecticut Retreat for the Insane (near Hartford), and the Pennsylvania Hospital's admittance of mentally ill patients since its establishment in 1752.[22] European examples in France, Scotland, Ireland, the Netherlands, England, and others were noted, with special emphasis on English models. Calling Bethlem and St. Luke's in London "radically defective in their structure," the report lauded the asylum at Wakefield; built for 300 patients, its plan was based on advice in Samuel Tuke's *Practical Hints on the Constructions and Economy of Pauper Lunatic Asylums*.[23] A floor plan, with commentary on how Wakefield could be adapted, was included in the report.[24] The ideal asylum should "have the appearance of a cheerful country residence" with "all semblance to a place of confinement . . . avoided"; patients should be separated by gender and spatially organized within the building "according to the state of their minds . . . according to the degree, rather than the species or duration of the disease."[25] The landscape should have "purity of water, salubrity of air, and cheerful and attractive scenery," and an adjacent farm "of rich soil and easy of cultivation"; "to the building should be attached work-shops and spacious grounds for the employment of patients . . . moral treatment cannot be carried into effect without a proper arrangement of the building."[26] During the remainder of the nineteenth century, variations of those suggestions were adopted as each new state asylum was constructed.

THE STATE LUNATIC ASYLUM AT UTICA, 1843

Political momentum for building a public asylum continued to grow in the years after the 1831 report. In January of 1836, the Medical Society of Oneida County published a "memorial" for the State Legislature claiming there were "about 3,000 . . . insane persons" in the state, 2,000 of whom were poor and could not afford asylum care.[27] Two months later, "An act to authorize the establishment of the New York State Lunatic Asylum" passed in the Legislature.[28] Through trial and error, and political appeal, a 130-acre (48.6 hectare) site on the outskirts of Utica in Oneida County was purchased for $16,300. New York State paid $10,000, while the citizens of Utica paid the rest.[29] Three commissioners were selected to oversee construction: William Clarke of Utica, Francis Spinner of Herkimer, and controversial prison administrator Elam Lynds.[30] The commissioners visited other asylums to gather design ideas. Clarke, a local entrepreneur and former army captain, drafted the building plans himself.[31]

In his annual message of 1839, Governor William H. Seward (1801–72) declared:

> *the site of the lunatic asylum was well chosen. It is an elevated plain, susceptible of that ornamental cultivation which is wonderfully auxiliary in the treatment of the insane. The vicinity of the flourishing central city of Utica affords many facilities for its construction, and promises those moral and social aids which such a public charity requires.*[32]

Utica had become a significant transportation hub, connected to the Erie Canal (completed 1825), the Chenango Canal (1836), the Utica and Schenectady Railroad (1837), and the Utica and Syracuse Railroad (1839), which enabled its primary industry, cotton and woolen milling, to flourish. That same network also made Utica a sensible choice for the state's first insane asylum, given that patients could be transported to it from most locations throughout the state.

The original building scheme was meant to house 1,000 patients in four buildings, "each 550 feet [168 meters] long, to be located at right angles" to one another, connected by "verandahs of open latticework" at the corners[33] (Figure 9.3). All four foundations were laid but cost overrun forced the project to be scaled back; only the main building, with a four-story Doric portico and three-story patient wings in gray limestone, was initially completed.[34] A board of managers was chosen, and Dr. Amariah Brigham, the former superintendent at the Hartford Retreat, was named superintendent in 1842.[35] As the administration prepared for the asylum's opening, several infrastructural problems needed to be addressed, including an inadequate heating system, dampness in the basement, and an insufficient water supply. Even though the site was less than half a mile from the Erie Canal, no pipes had yet been laid to the canal.[36] A well of sixteen-foot (4.9 meters) diameter was dug to a depth of thirty-four feet (10 meters). Horsepower pumped water from that "to a cistern in the attic of the center building, from whence it was distributed to all parts of the house."[37] The first patients were admitted on January 16, 1843, while construction continued.

The entry façade faced northeast, towards the Erie Canal and the Mohawk River beyond. The "center main" part of the building (as it was called) housed offices, parlors, a chapel, and employee residences. Double-loaded corridors extended off the center main, giving access to patient rooms, water closets, storage, and dayrooms.

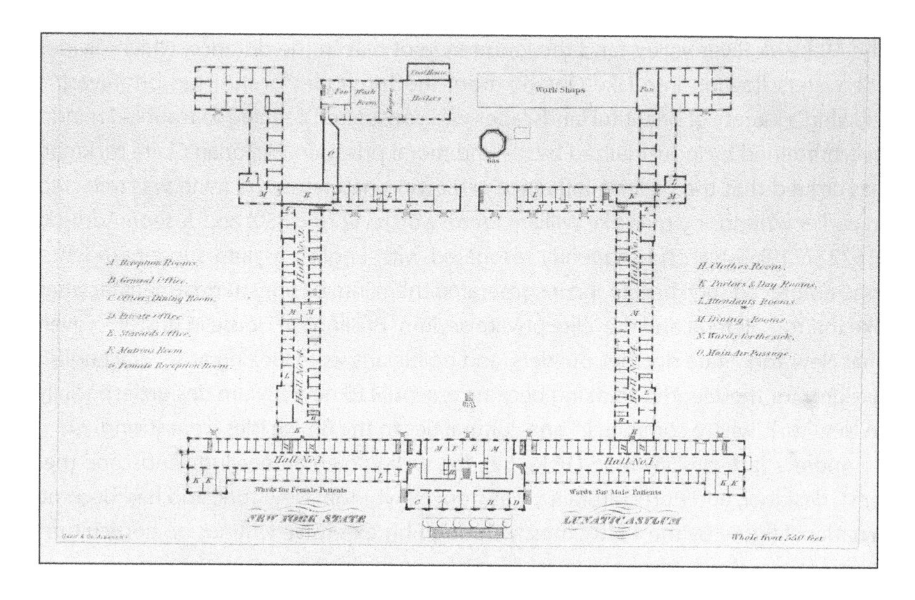

9.3 New York State Lunatic Asylum, Utica, floor plan. Source: *The Twenty-First Annual Report of the Managers of the State Lunatic Asylum for the Year 1863, Transmitted to the Legislature, February 3, 1864*. New York State Library, Albany.

Wards (and certain yards) were segregated by gender; each room, whether individual or dormitory style, had one window for light and views outside (Figure 9.4). From the grounds, one could see the city to the east, the Erie Canal to the northeast, as well as

9.4 New York State Lunatic Asylum, Utica. Source: Frontispiece, *The Twenty-First Annual Report of the Managers of the State Lunatic Asylum for the Year 1863, Transmitted to the Legislature, February 3, 1864*. New York State Library, Albany.

the Mohawk River valley, "and the long range of hills in the distance, which divides the waters flowing into lake Ontario, from the tributaries of the Hudson [River]."[38] Viewing a variety of beautiful landscapes was considered calming to troubled minds, overburdened by industrialized bustle and moral privation. Historian Claire Hickman has argued that the positive influence of viewing nature on the mind was reflected in earlier writings by men like William Wordsworth (1770–1850) and Joseph Addison (1672–1719), which subsequently resonated with English asylum superintendents, who embraced such beliefs and incorporated them into designs at treatment facilities like the York Retreat and the "elite private asylum" Brislington House in Bristol.[39] Given that New York State doctors, builders, and politicians were looking at several English asylums for models, this thinking became essential to new asylum design, especially in New York, where commercial and cultural ties to the British Isles were strong.

Andrew Jackson Downing (1815–52), the well-known antebellum landscape theorist, designer, and horticulturalist, was from Newburgh, New York, and had become a national figure by the 1840s, mostly through his extensive writings on horticulture, landscape, and architectural design. Thus it is not surprising—given the importance of landscape to antebellum moral treatment ideologies—that Downing was chosen to design the grounds of New York State's first insane asylum at Utica. Downing's father owned a nursery in Newburgh, and Andrew learned about plants in the family business. After Downing Sr. died, Downing and his brother Charles (1802–85) took over the nursery, but Downing was keenly interested in design and writing.[40] John Claudius Loudon (1783–1843), a Scottish botanist, landscape designer, and writer greatly influenced Downing's thinking. Downing obtained a copy of Loudon's *The Suburban Gardener, and Villa Companion [. . .] and the Laying Out, Planting, and General Management of the Garden and Grounds* (1838), which outlined ways to arrange domestic space for middle- and upper-class dwellings. Downing wrote his own book, *A Treatise on the Theory and Practice of Landscape Gardening, Adapted to North America* (1841), as well as several other related books.[41] Downing was also a contributing editor to *The Horticulturist and Journal of Rural Art and Rural Taste*.[42] As landscape historian Judith Major has pointed out, Downing's books were generally targeted towards the more well-to-do, whereas the magazine was geared for a broader audience in hopes of disseminating taste, refinement, and a uniquely American sense of place.

In the opening section of his *Treatise*, Downing praised both Joseph Addison and Alexander Pope (1646–1744) for instilling in the "British public a taste for the natural style."[43] He also stressed that English estate gardens were important to the history of design.[44] Popular English garden styles of the time embraced a pastoral aesthetic that opposed French geometric formalism. With sweeping, asymmetrical vistas and carefully designed, "natural" looking landscapes, this genre appealed to prevailing middle- and upper-class American taste. In an article for *The Horticulturist*, "A Chapter on School-Houses" (1848), Downing lamented the poor exterior conditions of many American rural schoolhouses shaping schoolboy minds.[45] He implored readers "to implant . . . in the schoolboy days, a love of trees; of flowers; of gardens; of the country; of home" so that the memories of those days could be a "blessed panacea, amid the dryness and dustiness of so many of the paths of life—politics—commerce—[and] the professions."[46] He decried unkempt schoolhouse exteriors, calling them "wild bedlams," evoking the infamous English Hospital of Bethlem, colloquially known as Bedlam.[47] By contrast, Downing emphasizes the positive influence of American rural beauty on the mind:

> *There is a strong illustration of our general acknowledgement of this influence of the beautiful . . . in this country . . . We allude to* our Rural Cemeteries, *and our Insane* Asylums. *It is somewhat curious, but not less true, that no country seats, no parks or pleasure-grounds, in America, are laid out with more care, adorned with more taste, filled with more lovely flowers, shrubs and trees, than some of our principal cemeteries and asylums. Is it not surprising that only when touched with sorrow, we, as a people, most seek the gentle and refining influence of nature? . . . Many a fine intellect, overtasked and wrecked in the too ardent pursuit of power or wealth, is fondly courted back to reason, and more quiet joys, by the dusky, cool walks of the asylum, where peace and rural beauty do not refuse to dwell.*[48]

Downing produced two plans for the Utica managers, both of which are presumed lost: "one curvilinear, and the other . . . axial with grand elms lining the driveway."[49] The managers chose the latter after contemplating both approaches drawn by Downing on "slips" of paper that could be superimposed on a general illustration of the grounds.[50] Downing emphasized his preference for the curvilinear plan, although, he added, "the straight avenue will have the most imposing and magnificent effect when the Elms are partially grown, say 18 years hence."[51]

Utica Superintendent Brigham "employed [patient] *labor* as a therapeutic agent," with farming, landscaping, and various trades including "carpenter, shoemaker, cabinet maker, tailor and blacksmith, and also a *whittling shop* [original emphasis], for those who needed occupation rather than systematic employment."[52] In 1849, Superintendent Brigham died; first assistant physician Dr. George Cook served as interim superintendent until Dr. Nathan D. Benedict accepted the post. During Benedict's brief tenure, completion of landscape projects became complicated after the premature death of Downing in 1852. At Utica, much of the asylum grounds were "swampy"; tile drainage was installed in various areas, including the land in front of the asylum.[53] In 1854, Dr. Benedict resigned and his first assistant physician, Dr. John P. Gray, became superintendent.[54] In the annual report that year, Dr. Gray detailed patient labor activities. Able-bodied male patients cultivated crops, tended livestock, and constructed and maintained grounds. Dr. Gray noted that

> *Our great resources of occupation . . . are the farm, garden, and lawn . . . we have had from 120 to 150 male patients engaged on the grounds . . . During the summer one-half [of] the front lawn was graded and laid out according to the plans furnished by Mr. A.J. Downing several years ago. The farm and garden have been more productive than in any previous year.*[55]

Earlier, Superintendent Brigham had established a print shop where the *American Journal of Insanity* and annual reports to the legislature were published, as well as the patient paper *The Opal*.[56] The managers boasted that some patients acquired a trade during their stay because of these opportunities.[57] Outdoor labor activities were the purview of men; women generally worked indoors, cleaning wards, sewing, doing laundry, and making "useful and ornamental articles." Some of these items were sold at annual fairs held on the grounds, with proceeds funding the purchase of books and the construction of a greenhouse.[58] Acceptable "amusements" for the patients included games such as "ninepins, checkers, chess, dominoes, backgammon, battledore, and cards . . .." Religious services were provided regularly in the chapel, and the better-behaved patients could attend and perform in theatrical productions.[59]

In *Theaters of Madness: Insane Asylums and Nineteenth-Century Culture*, Benjamin Reiss explored how notions of blackness permeated asylum culture at Utica during the 1840s through the 1860s.[60] According to Reiss, minstrelsy

> *originat[ed] as a series of song and dance routines traded by black and white workers along the piers and canals of New York in the early 1830s, it quickly developed into a kind of cross-racial musical street theater of the urban proletariat [which mocked the genteel sensibilities of] the moralizers of the upper class and the bourgeoisie.*[61]

By the 1840s, however "as it became commercialized, routinized, and stripped of some of its oppositional social content, the minstrel routine also emphasized racist caricature that masked the cross-racial, class-based alliance that had given birth to the form."[62] Most asylums had amusement halls where theatrical productions, musical events, and lectures were held for patients. Watching or performing in theatrical productions was considered therapeutic, at least for the less troublesome patients. At Utica during the 1840s and 1850s, a "troupe of blackface [patient] performers" was formed, which provided minstrel entertainment for patients, staff and select members of the public.[63]

Asylum annual reports recorded statistics on patients' place of birth and residence but race was not noted, perhaps because people of color rarely crossed state asylum thresholds as patients.[64] Those committed were mostly of European descent and many were recent Irish or German immigrants.[65] Gradual shifts in slavery and emancipation laws in New York State reflected the complex and unequal ways African-Americans were regarded by those in power. The 1799 Emancipation Law passed by the State Legislature was highly conditional, requiring children born to slave mothers between 1799 and 1821 be indentured servants for a period of 28 years for males and 25 years for females before they were freed.[66] By 1817, however, the Legislature revised the law and "voted to emancipate all New York slaves by July 4, 1827 . . . all slaves born before 1799 gained their freedom in 1827."[67] There was a legal caveat again, though: those born to slaves between 1799 and 1817 still had to complete their term of indentured servitude, even if it extended beyond the 1817 Emancipation Law deadline of 1827.[68] Changes in suffrage laws in 1821 extended voting rights to some black men, so long as they held at least $250 worth of property. White men could vote as long as they paid taxes or served in a militia, but they had no property requirement.

As laws changed and popular opinion fluctuated, debates raged about the potential influence African-Americans could or would bear on New York politics and culture. The same legislators and pundits arguing for or against emancipation and suffrage were also shaping laws regarding the insane poor. According to historian Leslie Harris, "working-class as well as many middle-class and elite whites believed that free black people were unable to overcome either their own inherent inferiority or the legacy of slavery and live as equals in a republican society."[69] Derogatory commentary and caricatures about black culture and bodies were plentiful and often evoked to sway political or popular opinion about a multitude of topics, including insanity. News coverage of the 1846 criminal trial of William Freeman, a black man, in Auburn, New York, for the murders of four members of the white Van Nest family, reflected contemporary anxiety about race, criminal insanity, safety, and the law.[70] Moreover,

> *New York [City]'s black population dropped precipitously between 1840 and the Civil War . . . The decrease in population was due partially to the massive influx of Irish immigrants, who competed with blacks for unskilled jobs. But it was also due to the increasing danger of kidnapping and southern enslavement that northern free blacks faced in the wake of the 1850 Fugitive Slave Law.*[71]

Many fled north to the Hudson Valley, to western parts of the state, or Canada. In light of this history, the fact that so few patients of color were admitted to state asylums in New York becomes more telling. Patients, visitors, and staff in official and popular asylum imagery were almost exclusively white, yet notions about class, ethnicity, and color significantly informed written or visual depictions of madness, alcoholism, and drug addiction as well as medical opinions about treatability.

An article called "Insanity and the Colored Race" by Dr. J.M. Buchanan, a physician at the East Mississippi Insane Asylum, is an example of racism thinly masked as psychiatric theory.[72] Buchanan described a nearly idyllic living situation for "negroes" under slavery and blamed the rise of insanity amongst blacks on the inability to adjust to newfound freedom. He argued that "the mind of the negro is not susceptible of as high a development as the white" but later added

> *the negro is with us to stay; he is an acknowledged factor in the body politic, a part and parcel of our Government, and as a citizen and tax-payer he is entitled to all the benefits accruing from our eleemosynary institutions.*[73]

Although black patients were entitled to treatment, Buchanan advocated segregation, noting "each State should build separate asylums for the colored insane."[74] The article ended with a statistical table, "Colored Insane in the United States; Census of 1880," which listed the total number of insane in each state, followed by the "number in asylum."[75] Editors at the *American Journal of Insanity* repeated some of Buchanan's findings in a summary in the October 1886 volume, noting that the article "contains some statistics worthy of attention, illustrating the great changes that have occurred in the diseases and the hygienic conditions of the negro race since the [federal] Act of Emancipation."[76]

WILLARD ASYLUM FOR THE CHRONIC INSANE, 1869

Debate about separating incurable chronic patients from the curable acute patients abounded in psychiatry during the 1850s and 1860s, although such discussions began before the Utica asylum opened in 1843. Social reformer Dorothea Dix toured county almshouses in New York State in order to assess their conditions and the treatment of poor, developmentally disabled, and mentally ill citizens. She presented her findings to the State Legislature in January 1844, strongly criticizing many of the almshouses for insufficient care. Citing an 1841 report from the Trustees of the State Lunatic Asylum verbatim, she noted, "the incurables should not be received or retained, to the exclusion of the curables; and of the latter class, recent cases should always be accommodated rather than old ones."[77] Dix also criticized the Utica and Bloomingdale asylums as being "insufficient ... for the reception of even the curable insane; large numbers of both classes are accumulated in the county almshouses, and in private dwellings."[78] The County Superintendents of the Poor held their annual convention in the city of Utica in 1855. The subsequent report to the Legislature recommended "the immediate erection of two State lunatic hospitals ... and so relinquish the undersigned the pain of longer continuing a system fraught with injustice and inhumanity."[79] In 1864, Dr. Sylvester D. Willard, then "secretary of the State Medical Society and Surgeon-General of the state," conducted a state survey of the insane.[80] There were "about 1400 insane persons confined to poorhouses" who were not receiving sufficient treatment and the State Asylum at Utica could only house 600 patients total.[81] Enough New York State legislators were convinced so the act for "the establishment of a State Asylum for the chronic insane, and for the better care of the insane poor" passed in 1865.[82] New York State Agricultural College (the future Cornell University), located on the eastern shore of Seneca Lake in Ovid, sold its property and extant buildings to the state, establishing a new Asylum for the Chronic Insane. Named "Willard," in honor of the doctor after his sudden death in 1865, the new asylum opened to patients in 1869 (Figure 9.5).

Unlike the institution at Utica, which admitted middle- and lower-class patients, Willard only served the poor and "no private patients [were] received."[83] Counties were responsible for the cost of residents they sent. While the New York State

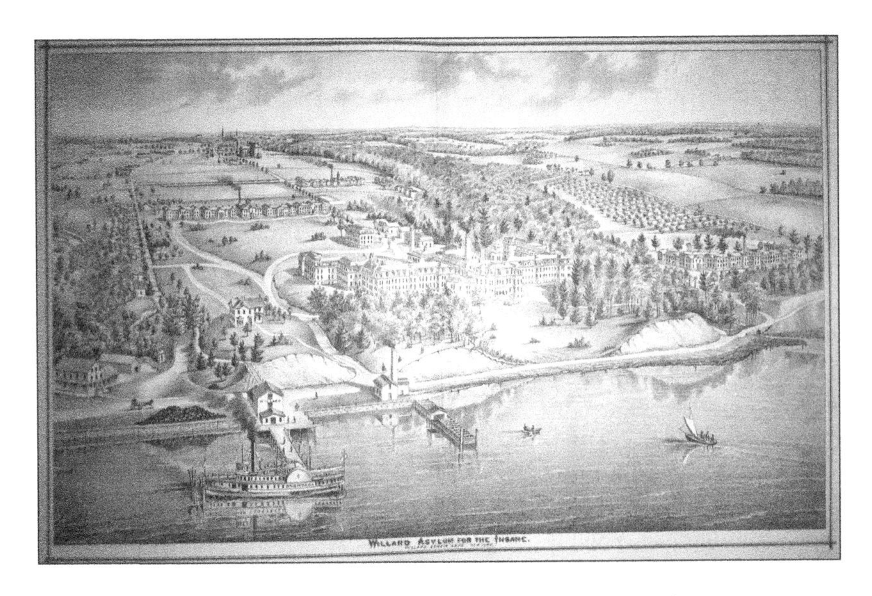

9.5 Willard Asylum for the Chronic Insane, not dated but before 1877, when a narrow-gauge railroad was built to deliver coal to various buildings on site. Artist: P.F. Goist (1841–1913). Source unknown. Collection of the author.

Lunatic Asylum was on the outskirts of Utica—making access to supplies, transportation, potential employees, and cultural networks easier—the Willard Asylum was more isolated and rural; it had to be more self-sufficient. Supplies, patients, and visitors often arrived by boat at Willard Landing, downhill from the main building on the lake's edge.[84] The Willard Hotel, a property leased to the asylum, housed visitors close to the landing but off the asylum grounds proper.[85]

According to a nineteenth-century State leaflet, Willard

> *has a capacity to accommodate 1,750 patients . . . The asylum grounds and farm contain 929 acres, of which about 600 acres are tilled . . . labor for the farm and grounds is chiefly supplied by patients . . . 800 [of them] are daily occupied on the farm, at domestic work or at trades.*[86]

An 1889 newspaper article in the *Watkins Express*, unsigned but written by someone at Cornell University, stated, "the farm [at Willard] is made to supply, as far as possible, the meats and vegetables used in the institution."[87] Crops included cabbage, wheat, corn, oats, and potatoes; beets were grown "for fodder purposes."[88] The dairy had approximately 120 cows, and a piggery of roughly 1,000 hogs supplied the asylum with meat, income from sales, and fertilizer for the farm.

Justifications for using patient labor varied. Some argued its therapeutic effects and moral impact, while others emphasized its economic benefits. Because Willard was a custodial asylum, many of the patients remained there for years, even decades. Legislators and pundits argued that asylum costs should be minimized, given Willard's size and patient demographic.[89] In an 1891 letter to the editor of the *Penn Yan Express* entitled "The Insane Must Work. Is Insanity a Crime?" author "S" argued that outdoor labor was preferable to indoor labor for the insane: "Instead of confining these unfortunates to factory rooms, they should be encouraged to spend all the time possible in the open air, under the blessed influence of God's sunlight."[90] "S" described Willard as "a hive of very busy industry—of much-varied and cheerfully performed labor—which annually saves the people many thousands of good, hard dollars." Cheerful patients or not, the financial benefit to taxpayers and hospital function were clear. "S" continued: "patients have . . . built nearly seven miles of railway, the Willard Branch of the Lehigh [Valley Railroad]" which delivered anthracite coal to portions of New York, Pennsylvania, and New Jersey. Patients also built

> *one mile of superb Telford road*[91] *within the grounds, with a solid cement walk beside it . . . they have also quarried the stone and [. . .] hauled sand for the foundations of new structures . . . last winter, those patients gathered and housed 1,400 tons of ice.*[92]

Outdoor recreational activities were also a part of asylum life for patients. Carriage and sleigh rides on the grounds were common, as were supervised walks.

By the late 1880s, state asylum superintendents were implementing annual "Field Days" at their facilities.[93] Both patients and employees, especially ward attendants, participated in the competitions. Events at the initial field days included running, hurdling, pole-vaulting, dashes, rope-climbing, and obstacle and potato races; cash prizes and subscriptions to various local papers were awarded for first, second, and third place. Prizes for "climbing the greased pole" were cash but for the most unusual event at Utica—"catching the greased pig"—the prize was the pig itself. Field days at state asylums may have been inspired by events such as county fairs and they certainly brought an air of levity to the grounds. Local townspeople attended and newspapers covered the events, often specifying by name employee and patient winners. By the first decade of the twentieth century, the now "state hospital" field days had become grand events. Military and other types of bands played, covered bleachers were installed, theatrical skits performed, and more elaborate games were played and prizes awarded. Displays of male athleticism included typical track events, while the women's events reflected milder versions of physically challenging endeavors, like a 50-yard dash instead of a 100-yard dash, and egg or potato races. Male attendants engaged in a tug of war; female attendants competed in a bed-making contest. Men won a variety of tobacco products, shoes, or shirts while women won items like slippers, stockings, handkerchiefs, handbags, hatpins, or gloves. These accouterments reinforced and reified preferred gender norms as well as preferred bodily and behavioral performance on the hospital grounds for patient and staff alike.

Bloomingdale, Utica, and Willard asylums encapsulate early ways in which New York State began to implement treatment and design philosophies for the moral management of some of its mentally ill citizens—especially the poor—during the nineteenth century. Landscape-related labor and leisure activities shaped patient minds, bodies and environments as a means of therapy on asylum sites but broader local, regional, and state concerns also impacted patient facilities. After Willard opened in 1869, new asylum construction grew precipitously during the remainder of the century, together with the state's population. The Hudson River State Asylum in Poughkeepsie opened in 1871; the Middletown Homeopathic Asylum in 1874; the Buffalo State Asylum in 1880; the New York State Inebriate Asylum in Binghamton was converted into an insane asylum for chronic patients in 1881; and the St. Lawrence State Asylum in Ogdensburg opened in 1890. Treatment and design methods evolved and conflated on these subsequent sites. Dr. Thomas Kirkbride's influential *On the Construction, Organization and General Arrangements of Hospitals for the Insane* (1854) was translated into built form, especially by architects Frederick Clarke Withers at Poughkeepsie and Henry Hobson Richardson at Buffalo; Frederick Law Olmsted and Calvert Vaux designed those landscapes. A more detailed landscape-based history of the nineteenth-century New York State asylum system will be discussed in forthcoming work.

NOTES

1 William L. Russell, M.D., "Bloomingdale Hospital," in *The Institutional Care of the Insane in the United States and Canada: Volume III*, ed. Henry M. Hurd et al. (Baltimore, MD: Johns Hopkins University Press, 1916), 133–135. See also Pliny Earle, *History Description and Statistics of the Bloomingdale Asylum for the Insane* (New York: Egbert, Hovey & King, 1848), 9; and *Charter of the Society of the New York Hospital* (New York: Daniel Fanshaw, 1856), 16–17.

2 Robert M. Elliott, M.D., "The Care of the Insane in New York," in *The Institutional Care of the Insane in the United States and Canada: Volume III*, ed. Henry M. Hurd et al. (Baltimore, MD: Johns Hopkins University Press, 1916), 112.

3 Earle, *History Description and Statistics*, 1–2. For more on Eddy's involvement with New York State's penal system, see W. David Lewis, *From Newgate to Dannemora: The Rise of the Penitentiary in New York, 1796–1848* (Ithaca, NY: Cornell University Press), 2–5, 29–35; and Arthur A. Ekirch Jr., "Thomas Eddy and the Beginnings of Prison Reform in New York," *New York History* 24, no. 3 (July 1943): 376–391.

4 Thomas Eddy, *Hints for Introducing an Improved Mode of Treating the Insane in the Asylum: Read before the Governors of the New-York Hospital...* (New York: n.p., 1815), http://collections.nlm.nih.gov/catalog/nlm:nlmuid-2553007R-bk, accessed July 6, 2015. Earle mentions Eddy's ardent appeal in *History Description and Statistics*, 10. For a more complete history of the Retreat see Anne Digby, *Madness, Morality, and Medicine: A Study of the York Retreat, 1796–1914* (Cambridge: Cambridge University Press, 1985).

5 Eddy, *Hints*, 8–9.

6 Ibid., 16.

7 Russell, "Bloomingdale Hospital," 137; Earle, *History Description and Statistics*, 10.

8 Earle, *History Description and Statistics*, 10. Columbia University now occupies the majority of the former asylum site.

9 Ibid., 19. A more detailed account of patient admissions and discharges are found in tables on pages 15–19.

10 Ibid., 42–43, 71–75.

11 Ibid., 75.

12 Ibid., 41, 63. The table of insane patient statistics on page 63 does note exceptions to this generalization: six men and eight women are listed from the West Indies, one is from South America and one from Africa.

13 Pliny Earle, "Historical and Descriptive Account of the Bloomingdale Asylum for the Insane," *American Journal of Insanity* 2, no. 1 (July 1845): 10.

14 Ibid., 10.

15 Ibid., 9. For more details regarding Earle's perception of moral treatment at Bloomingdale, see "Section II: Moral Treatment" in *History Description and Statistics*, 26–38.

16 *Twenty-Fifth Annual Report of the Managers of the State Lunatic Asylum [at Utica], for the Year 1867, Transmitted to the Legislature March 10, 1868* (Albany: Van Benthuysen & Sons, 1868), 43. [Hereafter listed as *25th AR Utica (1867)*.] See also *Census of the State of New York, 1825*, New York State Government Documents, "Recapitulation: Or whole number of Deaf and Dumb Persons, and of Idiots and Lunatics, in the State of New York (App. Table Y)," page number not listed, http://www.nysl.nysed.gov/scandocs/nyscensus.htm, accessed June 25, 2015.

17 For a more complete quote from "An Act Concerning Lunatics," see Elliott, "The Care of the Insane in New York," 113.

18 *25th AR Utica (1867)*, 44.

19 *New York State Legislative Document No. 263 (10 March 1831)*, 5–11. [Hereafter listed as *NYS Leg. Doc. No. 263 (1831)*.] Members of the investigative committee were:

Assemblymen Alonzo C. Paige (Schenectady Co.), Eli Savage (Oneida Co.), and Peter Gansevoort (Albany Co.).

20 *NYS Leg. Doc. No. 263 (1831)*, 14.

21 Ibid., 29.

22 Ibid., 36.

23 Ibid., 32. See also Samuel Tuke, *Practical Hints on the Constructions and Economy of Pauper Lunatic Asylums; including Instructions to the Architects who offered plans for the Wakefield Asylum, and a sketch of the most approved design* (London: William Alexander, Darton and Co., et al., 1815), https://archive.org/details/39002011122984.med.yale.edu, accessed June 27, 2015.

24 *NYS Leg. Doc. No. 263 (1831)*, 78. Two additional floor plans were included: an unnamed French asylum and the Glasgow Asylum for Maniacs.

25 Ibid., 38.

26 Ibid., 37, 39.

27 *25th AR Utica (1867)*, 50. Their count of the insane included "idiots," the term used then to describe the developmentally disabled.

28 Ibid., 52.

29 Ibid. For a more detailed history of events surrounding the 1836 act, see "The Economics of Compassion," in Ellen Dwyer, *Homes for the Mad: Life inside Two Nineteenth-Century Asylums* (New Brunswick, NJ: Rutgers University Press, 1987), 30–34.

30 Dwyer, *Homes for the Mad*, 35. Lynds was *twice* the warden at both Auburn and Sing-Sing Prisons; he also oversaw the initial construction of Sing-Sing in 1828. For more detail, see Lewis, *From Newgate to Dannemora*, 86–101, 136–138, 147–149, and 206–218. His second tenure as Auburn Prison warden began in 1838 (207).

31 *25th AR Utica (1867)*, 53.

32 Ibid.

33 Ibid. See also Carla Yanni, *The Architecture of Madness: Insane Asylums in the United States* (Minneapolis: University of Minnesota Press, 2007), 42.

34 *25th AR Utica (1867)*, 55; Yanni, *The Architecture of Madness*, 42.

35 *25th AR Utica (1867)*, 61. See also "Memoir of Dr. Amariah Brigham," *American Journal of Insanity* 14, no. 1 (July 1857): 18.

36 *25th AR Utica (1867)*, 57

37 Ibid., 57; Yanni, *The Architecture of Madness*, 43.

38 *25th AR Utica (1867)*, 54.

39 Clare Hickman, "Cheerful Prospects and Tranquil Restoration: The Visual Experience of Landscape as Part of the Therapeutic Regime of the British Asylum, 1800–1860," *History of Psychiatry* 20, no. 4 (2009): 425–441.

40 For an in-depth analysis of Downing's writing, see Judith Major, *To Live in the New World: A.J. Downing and American Landscape Gardening* (Cambridge, MA: MIT Press, 1997). Other significant books about Downing include *Prophet with Honor: The Career of Andrew Jackson Downing, 1815–1852*, eds. George B. Tatum and Elisabeth Blair

MacDougall (Washington, DC: Dumbarton Oaks, 1989); and David Schuyler, *Apostle of Taste: Andrew Jackson Downing, 1815–1852* (Baltimore, MD: Johns Hopkins University Press, 1996).

41 Andrew Jackson Downing, *Treatise on the Theory and Practice of Landscape Gardening, Adapted to North America* (New York and London: Wiley & Putnam, 1841).

42 Many of Downing's influential essays were first published here, including "On the Moral Influence of Good Houses," *The Horticulturist* 2, no. 8 (February 1848): 345–347.

43 Major, *To Live in the New World*, 41.

44 Downing mentions two main schools of English landscape gardening, "the Picturesque school, at the head of which were [Uvedale] Price [1747–1829] and [Richard Payne] Knight [1750–1824], and the more formal school, whose champions were [Lancelot "Capability"] Brown [1716–83] and [Humphry] Repton [1752–1818]. . . ." Downing, *Treatise*, 30.

45 Andrew Jackson Downing, "A Chapter on School-Houses," *The Horticulturist* 2, no. 9 (March 1848): 393–396. Girls are never mentioned.

46 Ibid., 396.

47 Ibid., 395.

48 Ibid., 396. See also Schuyler, *Apostle of Taste*, 78–89.

49 Yanni, *The Architecture of Madness*, 43. In footnotes #70 and #71, Yanni cites both Schuyler *Apostle of Taste*, 78–80; and Tatum and MacDougall, *Prophet with Honor*, 69–70.

50 Tatum and MacDougall, *Prophet with Honor*, 70; Schuyler, *Apostle of Taste*, 79. See also Kenneth Hawkins, "The Therapeutic Landscape: Nature, Architecture, and Mind in Nineteenth-Century America," PhD diss., University of Rochester, 1991, 127–128.

51 Tatum and MacDougall, *Prophet with Honor*, 70; Hawkins, "The Therapeutic Landscape," 128.

52 *25th AR Utica (1867)*, 62.

53 Ibid., 64.

54 For a more details about the progression of Utica superintendents, see Dwyer, *Homes for the Mad*, 55–71.

55 *Twelfth Annual Report of the Managers of the State Lunatic Asylum, Utica, January 16, 1855 [Senate No. 14]*, 37. See also Hawkins, "The Therapeutic Landscape," 132–133.

56 For a more about *The Opal*, see Maryrose Eannace, "Lunatic Literature: New York State's 'The Opal', 1850–1860," PhD diss., State University of New York at Albany, 2001. Male and female patients contributed to the paper. See also Benjamin Reiss, *Theaters of Madness: Insane Asylums and Nineteenth-Century Culture* (Chicago, IL: University of Chicago Press, 2008), 23–50.

57 *25th AR Utica (1867)*, 62.

58 Ibid., 62–63. See also "Second Annual Fair at the N.Y. State Lunatic Asylum," *American Journal of Insanity* 1, no. 4 (April 1845): 347–352; and Janet Miron, "In View of the Knowledge to be Acquired: Public Visits to New York's Asylums in the Nineteenth Century," in *Permeable Walls: Historical Perspectives on Hospital and Asylum Visiting*, eds. Graham Mooney and Jonathan Reinarz (Amsterdam and New York: Editions Rodopi, 2009), 249.

59 *25th AR Utica (1867)*, 63.

60 Reiss, *Theaters of Madness*, Chapter 2, "Saneface Minstrelsy: Blacking up the Asylum," 51–78.

61 Ibid., 51.

62 Ibid.

63 Ibid., 52.

64 Dwyer, *Homes for the Mad*, 106. "Neither of New York's first two state asylums received many nonwhite patients, although Willard had slightly more (2.2 percent in contrast to Utica's 0.8 percent). Like the old, blacks and American Indians were largely excluded from costly state-level asylum care."

65 See, for example, *Annual Report of the Managers of the State Lunatic Asylum, Utica, January 25, 1845*, 23; and *Eighteenth Annual Report of the Superintendent of the New York Lunatic Asylum [. . .] November 30th, 1860*, 43. New York State as patient "place of nativity" was the highest number; Ireland was usually second and Germany third, reflecting mid-century immigration patterns of the time.

66 Leslie M. Harris, *In the Shadow of Slavery: African Americans in New York City, 1626–1863* (Chicago, IL: University of Chicago Press, 2003), 70.

67 Ibid., 94.

68 Ibid.

69 Ibid., 96.

70 See Andrew W. Arpey, *The William Freeman Murder Trial: Insanity, Politics, and Race* (Syracuse, NY: Syracuse University Press, 2003).

71 Harris, *In the Shadow of Slavery*, 7.

72 J.M. Buchanan, "Insanity in the Colored Race," *New York Journal of Medicine* 44 (July 1886): 67–70.

73 Ibid., 69.

74 Buchanan, "Insanity in the Colored Race," 69. See also Yanni, *The Architecture of Madness*, 64, 69–71.

75 Buchanan, "Insanity in the Colored Race," 70.

76 "Insanity and the Colored Race," *American Journal of Insanity* 43 (October 1886): 278.

77 Dorothea Dix, *Memorial to [. . .] The Legislature of the State of New York*, Assembly No. 21 (January 21, 1844), 53.

78 Ibid., 4.

79 *Report and Memorial of the County Superintendents of the Poor of this State on Lunacy and its relation to Pauperism, and for relief of Insane Poor*, Senate No. 17 (January 23, 1856), 16. See also Elliott, "The Care of the Insane in New York," 115–116.

80 Elliott, "The Care of the Insane in New York," 118.

81 Ibid.

82 Willard leaflet, n.d., but Dr. P.M. Wise is listed as superintendent (his tenure began in 1884). See *Scrapbooks, 1875–1901 Willard State Hospital (N.Y.)* (Col. #B1461), New York State Archives, Albany. [Hereafter listed as NYSA, Albany.]

83 Ibid.

84 There are numerous 1870s and 1880s shipping receipts (aka "way bills") for various goods in the *Historical Background and Research Files, 1869–1987,Willard Psychiatric Center (N.Y.)* (Col. #B1440-96), NYSA, Albany. Newspapers also describe arriving at Willard by boat; for example, see "Trip to Willard Hospital" in the *Waterloo Observer*, June 11, 1890. See also *Scrapbooks, 1875–1901*, NYSA, Albany.

85 Documentation of hotel lease terms with the asylum, especially during the 1890s, can be found in the *Historical Background and Research Files, 1869–1987, Willard Psychiatric Center (N.Y.)* (Col. #B1440-96), NYSA, Albany.

86 Willard leaflet, n.d.

87 "Farming on the Shores of Seneca," *Watkins Express*, November 21, 1889. See also *Scrapbooks, 1875–1901*, NYSA, Albany.

88 "Farming on the Shores of Seneca."

89 See Dwyer, *Homes for the Mad*, Chapter 2, "The Economics of Compassion," especially the section "The Limits of Benevolence," 52–54.

90 S, "The Insane Must Work. Is Insanity a Crime?" *Penn Yan Express*, July 29, 1891; *Scrapbooks, 1875–1901*, NYSA, Albany.

91 Paragraph 4 of the *Penn Yan Express* article. Superintendent Wise strongly favored Telford Road construction and defended the labor-intensive practice. See: P.M. Wise, "Here is Sense: Superintendent Wise of Willard on Making Country Roads," *Rochester Morning Herald*, November 4, 1889, page unknown; *Scrapbooks, 1875–1901*, NYSA, Albany.

92 S, "The Insane Must Work. Is Insanity a Crime?"

93 Details about annual field days are derived from scrapbooks in the *Historical Files, 1849–1996, Mohawk Valley Psychiatric Center* (Col. #B1582-01) and the Willard *Scrapbooks, 1875–1901*, NYSA, Albany.

PART 3

Public Health and Modern Medical Institutions

10

Designing the Medical Museum[1]

Annmarie Adams

McGill University's medical museum was once the hub of a complex network of international medical museums. Such museums typically resided at universities with medical schools, serving as unique reference collections of anatomical and/or pathological specimens for teaching and research.[2] The core of most collections was a set of wet specimens, which were human body parts preserved in jars of fluid. The wet specimens came from autopsies and were accompanied by brief, textual information on the patients and his or her condition. Skeletal specimens, models, and medical instruments were also commonly found in medical museums. The basic intention of the medical museum was to provide students with opportunities to see typical and diseased body parts for study purposes. These specimens, separated from the hustle and bustle of the hospital and isolated from the rest of the patient's body, were carefully suspended in a jar-like container of transparent fluid and often positioned in a purpose-built architectural setting. This architecture allowed observation from many different angles and distances and also enabled the meaningful grouping of specimens.

Not surprisingly, some of these collections have thrived and become popular tourist and leisure sites, carefully preserved by professional associations. The Hunterian Museum in London, for example, is housed at the Royal College of Surgeons and attracts 50,000 visitors a year. A particularly popular medical museum in North America is the Mütter Museum, at the College of Physicians of Philadelphia, which receives 130,000 visitors a year.

Like many less popular medical museums, McGill's collection occupied various premises, prospered intensely for a time, but then almost completely disappeared in the mid-twentieth century. It has only recently been "rediscovered" as a museum, perhaps bolstered by its inclusion on CNN's list of "weirdest medical museums," published in 2013.[3] Historian Jonathan Reinarz notes the scant scholarly attention that medical museums have attracted, as opposed to the large areas they occupied in medical schools.[4] As anthropologist Elizabeth Hallam writes:

> *Deliberate destruction, calculated dismantling, dispersal and re-arrangement, consignment to storage, and unplanned disintegration, especially since the mid-twentieth*

> *century, have all played their part in the disappearance of these often massive collections along with the buildings and rooms that have housed them.*[5]

Hallam talks in particular about the "making and breaking" of medical museums in Scotland, a fate shared by the medical museums in North America.

This study explores the dynamic architectural history of McGill University's medical museum as a window onto the medical museum as an architectural typology.

An architectural perspective means we focus here on Hallam's "buildings and rooms," rather than on the collections per se. What does architecture tell us about the changing role of display in medical education? What roles did architects (and artists) play in the prominent positions given to specimens, artifacts, models and images in the medical curriculum? I contend that architecture is a key visual source in the history of medicine, revealing significant histories illegible in traditional written sources. While much has been written about the McGill museum from the perspective of its famous curator, Maude Abbott, there is no architectural history or material culture analysis of the institution.[6]

How did the medical museum evolve as a typology? The default model for twentieth-century medical museums appears to be a rectangular two-story gallery with a narrow mezzanine, what I will call for now the doughnut-in-a-box. This familiar form, for example, was used for the Hunterian museum before the bombing in 1941 as well as for many famous natural history museums.[7] Its continuing appeal for medical museums likely stems from the much longer tradition of displaying collections of all kinds in "cabinets of curiosity" or *wunderkammer*, spaces which ranged from large pieces of furniture to large institutions. Even contemporary museums set up on a *wunderkammer* model, like historic examples, invite viewers to make connections between objects that come from disparate sources, convey a potential for being both encyclopedic and infinitely expandable, and provide both close-up and distant views of objects. In the face of huge technological changes, in fact, the multi-story room with floor-to-ceiling shelves, narrow galleries, and abundant illumination remains the architectural standard in this regard. The 2005 renovations to the Hunterian are on this same model, described on the designers' website as an atrium: "The 3,000 glass jars containing Hunter's original anatomical preparations are housed in a dynamic central atrium of all-glass cases rising through the full height of the two-story space. Entrance portals at the four sides allow free visitor circulation."[8] Certainly the atrium and doughnut-in-a-box are related. The latter, however, always includes narrow galleries or mezzanines, features not necessarily present in an atrium.

As mentioned above, the protagonist of the McGill case study is cardiologist Maude Abbott, curator of the medical museum during its golden age, from 1898 to 1923.[9] Abbott was responsible for developing a large part of the collection and for establishing McGill as an important node in the complex network of medical museums. She was particularly influential as the long-serving editor of the *Bulletin of the International Association of Medical Museums*, which ran from 1907 to 1938 and linked professionals around the world who were shaping and maintaining medical museums.[10] As such, Abbott was much sought after as an advisor to other institutions.[11]

OLD MEDICAL

McGill University was founded in 1821 and its medical school, founded in 1829, is the oldest in Canada.[12] As the university campus changed, so did its buildings dedicated to medical education, in footprint, context, and location. In particular, the relation of the medical museum to the city's hospitals was especially important. Two of the city's general hospitals, the Royal Victoria Hospital and Montreal General Hospital, were never formally part of the campus, but the medical school and museum benefited greatly from its close proximity to the hospitals, their physicians, their patients, and their body parts once deceased. In each venue, the museum was the beneficiary of specimens from the hospitals, completing the all-important loop of knowledge that linked doctors, patients, students, and specimens and contributing to medical knowledge by privileging visibility as a way of learning.[13] Architecture was a tool that privileged this visibility.

The medical school's first purpose-built site, erected 43 years after its founding, is known today as "Old Medical."[14] It was designed by the prolific Montreal architects Hopkins & Wily in 1872, with significant interior additions by Andrew Taylor in 1885, 1893, 1894, 1897, and a final exterior addition in 1901, which dwarfed the original building.[15] A photograph (likely taken between 1901 and 1905, shows the five-bay, classical[16] greystone building in the foreground—perhaps fashioned after a Palladian villa—with Taylor's 1901 extension directly behind (Figure 10.1). The broader and taller extension and use of lighter stone preserved the integrity of the 1872 building, maintaining the legibility of the shallow, hipped roof and three of the four Old Medical's symmetrical elevations. The cornice lines of the addition correspond beautifully to the horizontal features of the earlier building; Taylor even made an effort to make two stories of the addition appear as a single level, presumably to harmonize with the existing context.

10.1 Aerial photograph, c. 1900, of Old Medical, McGill University, Montreal, showing additions. The Royal Victoria Hospital can be seen in the background. Source: View-3619, Notman Photographic Archives, McCord Museum.

Taylor's additions to Old Medical may be his most eccentric contributions to the McGill campus, especially the four-story classical block topped with rather strange spherical domes and lanterns. The Scottish-born architect spent two decades in Montreal—from 1883 to 1904—coinciding with a major construction and population boom.[17] With his work primarily funded by tobacco baron Sir William Macdonald, Taylor transformed McGill from "a medical school attached to an arts college into a full-scale university" with his monumental Engineering, Physics, and Chemistry buildings.[18] Indeed, Taylor's Scottish-inspired formula for free-standing, greystone pavilions with steep copper roofs established the general architectural character of the university.

Andrew Taylor's first addition to the medical building in 1885 was fairly modest, funded by a $50,000 gift by philanthropist Donald Smith, better known as Lord Strathcona. This building had very few windows as the addition filled the need for two large, theater-style lecture halls. A subsequent gift from Strathcona endowed chairs of hygiene and pathology, for which a separate wing was built in 1893.[19] Eventually, a $60,000 gift from J.H.R. Molson funded the major 1894 addition that dwarfed the original pavilion, joined the pathology wing to the other buildings, and featured a large lecture room, chemistry lab, and dissection rooms. In 1901, Taylor's final addition replaced his first, modest extension.

For our purposes Taylor's renovations in 1897 are most significant as the interiors of the original Hopkins & Wiley building included a new pathological museum and bone room. Taylor's plan of the medical building shows the museum spaces in the two square rooms (Figure 10.2). Although the rooms already existed, Taylor's design was a great improvement to the museum as he increased the display areas, connected the galleries to the main staircase, and added electrical lighting for the display cases.[20]

Very few photographs exist of the medical museum in Old Medical. An image from about 1898, however, shows Taylor's doughnut-in-a-box design: a rectangular space whose walls were lined with open shelves (Figure 10.3). He positioned five rows of shelves on the ground floor levels to hold wet specimens in jars; above this a narrow gallery provided viewers with close-up views of four more rows of shelves displaying specimens. Above this upper level, canted walls displayed illustrations, presumably carefully arranged to complement the specimens below. The architect's insistence on a wide skylight meant the museum was flooded with natural light. In the center of the room, seemingly wedged between slender iron columns, was a table with skeletal exhibitions; also visible in this photograph are a wooden filing

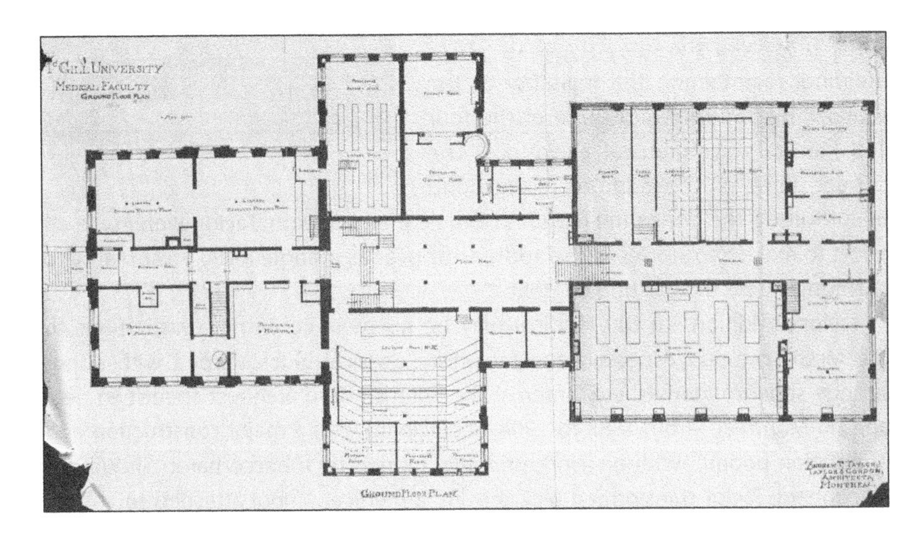

10.2 Ground-floor plan of Old Medical and additions, included in course calendars from the Medical Faculty. Source: McGill University, *Faculty of Medicine Annual Calendar: Sixty-Ninth Session, 1901–1902* (Montreal: Gazette Printing Co., 1901), between 36 and 37.

cabinet and a chair. The specimens displayed on the table and wall shelves prominently feature small, rectangular white labels that identified individual specimens.

Maude Abbott appears in our story in 1898, about the same time as the photograph. Despite the prejudice against women becoming physicians at that time, she had graduated from Bishop's University medical school in 1894 and then travelled to Europe. Returning to Montreal in 1897, Abbott was appointed assistant curator of McGill University's Medical Museum in 1898 working under the Chair of Pathology—whose duties included the care of the newly renovated museum—Professor John George Adami. Hailing from Cambridge, Adami was familiar with Britain's grand medical museums and understood the importance of building a quality collection.[21] By the time of Adami's arrival, the museum already had an impressive collection of pathological specimens, including those amassed by famous physician William Osler from 750 to 1,000 autopsies performed at the Montreal General Hospital between 1876 and 1884.[22] The museum's usefulness, however, was hindered due to a lack of organization. No one understood this better than Abbott, who evidently had no prescribed duties and was dissatisfied in her early days as assistant curator.[23] In a letter to Adami written less than a year after her appointment, Abbott expresses her malaise and hints at her aspirations to reorganize the material:

> *Jan. 4, 1899,*
>
> *[. . .] I am anxious to ask you about my work for the rest of the month. I find work in the laboratory somewhat difficult in your absence, with no position or definite work assigned to me. I would infinitely prefer to work there to anywhere else, even while you are away, but if there is no work for me there this winter could I not do something else till your return, while still keeping an eye on the ascitic fluids? [. . .]*
>
> *Dr. Johnston said that the museum needed cataloguing.*[24]

10.3 Museum in Old Medical. Source: *Illustrations of the Medical Faculty McGill University* (Montreal: M. Renouf, 1898), 27.

Abbott's persistence resulted in an eventual mandate to organize the collection of specimens for teaching purposes. Indeed her organizational scheme is one of her most significant contributions to the medical museum movement. Named for Dr. Wyatt Johnston, whom she mentions above, the organizational system Abbott adopted for the museum was infinitely expandable, like the Dewey Decimal system for libraries.[25] She described it in 1905 as "an anatomic classification with a pathologic subclassification" whereby the museum comprised ten sections according to ten systems of the body.[26] The number assigned to a particular specimen in the descriptive catalog, for example, means the number in front of the decimal was anatomy and that after the decimal was pathology; a third number in superscript, like a footnote reference, referred to the specimen. In the example she published: "Thus," as she explained, "if 11. represent the pericardium. and .34 fibrinous inflammation, 11.34 1 means the first specimen on the shelf of fibrinous inflammation of the pericardium."[27]

The spatial implications of such a system were that the particular specimen could be located on a particular shelf according to its classification, very much like the predictability of books on the shelves of a library. The museum itself was organized by ten numbered systems and then subdivided by organs. The main pathological classifications were also ten in number. "The organized museum is to general pathology what the autopsy room is to medicine, what dissection is to anatomy, what—to go further afield—traveling to see new countries is to the study of geography," she expounded in 1905.[28] A further function of the museum, in Abbott's mind, was the provision of illustrative material for classrooms across the faculty and hospital clinics. Remarkably, specimens could be borrowed for 48 hours, transported in special "strong baskets" for protection.[29]

A tragic fire in Old Medical accelerated the dynamic architectural history of McGill's medical buildings. Only nine years after Abbott first took her position, the blaze destroyed the adjacent anatomical museum and 2,000 pathological specimens, including the entire bone collection.[30] The extensive media coverage of the fire included useful assessments of the collection; a journalist in the *New York Times*, for example, declared it "one of the best on the continent."[31] The architectural press, on the other hand, looked at the tragedy as an opportunity for more commissions and philanthropy.[32] In retrospect, the material saved likely became even more precious because of its heroic past: about 1,000 specimens were secured, including a famous three-chambered heart known as the Holmes heart. This remarkable organ was obtained from an 1822 autopsy by Andrew Holmes, one of the school's four founders, and is still treasured by McGill today.[33] The fire ironically also led to the subsequent growth of the museum collection, with donations arriving from Washington, Berlin, London, Edinburgh, and Glasgow.[34]

The 1907 fire also took on epic proportions in accounts of Abbott's life and career. In a 2009 fictionalized account of Abbott's life, *The Heart Specialist*, novelist Claire Holden Rothman describes the scene after the fire when Abbott first spotted the burnt-out building from a distance, drawing on a famous literary analogy: "I felt like Jane Eyre returning to Thornfield Manor after the madwoman had torched it."[35] Ironically it was the destruction of the Old Medical building, along with Abbott's presence as curator, that would bring international prominence to McGill's medical museum in the decades to come.

STRATHCONA BUILDING

With the Faculty of Medicine left homeless, a new building was constructed, the Strathcona Medical Building. Named for benefactor Donald Smith, the new medical building opened its doors as the faculty's second, purpose-built home in 1911.[36] Launched as an architectural competition, the site for the Strathcona was strategically placed across from the ever-expanding, 15-year-old Royal Victoria Hospital, designed by British hospital specialist and architect Henry Saxon Snell and opened in 1893. Montreal architects Brown & Vallance designed the winning entry of the competition (Figure 10.4).[37] Seven other architectural firms were invited to participate in the competition, submitting plans, elevations, sections, and perspectives for the new building on the busy corner of Pine Avenue and University Street, the northeast corner of the campus.

10.4 Photograph of the Strathcona Building, McGill University, Montreal, designed by Brown and Vallance, 1911. Source: *Construction* 5, no 4 (March 1912): 46.

Although the brief has not survived, we know about it from a summary article in the *Canadian Architect and Builder*. It identified no cost limitations, only a list of programmatic elements and a schedule of floor areas.[38] As such, the submissions were remarkably diverse, representing the architects' own interpretations of the complex site and program adjacencies necessary for medical education at the time.

Figure 10.5 shows a plan of the new medical building, an E-plan with three wings projecting to the north. Brown & Vallance's (David R. Brown and Hugh Vallance) winning scheme gave the museum utmost importance in the central wing of the E, locating galleries on each of the three floors, with ample lighting provided by grand windows on all sides and connected to one another through a top-lit central, octagonal atrium. In the plan, the atrium-based museum took the shape of a cross and addressed busy Pine Avenue and the Royal Victoria Hospital, paying architectural homage to the hospital. The atrium was topped by "a flat, leaded-glass dome, with an outer one of prism glass."[39] Specimens were laid out in especially designed cases imported from New York.

Did Abbott's reign as curator have a hand in this museum-centric design? A journalist writing in the *Canadian Architect and Builder* in 1907 describes the building almost entirely through the relationships of adjacent spaces to the museum:

> *In the centre is the museum, top-lighted, and having two galleries. On each floor the outer corridors of this museum form the communication with the pieces in front and rear of the centre block [. . .] In this way good corridors of communication all around the museum are secured on each floor. The main stairways of the building being in direct proximity to the museum, the museum itself [is] not cumbered by special stairs of its own. [. . .] In the rear of the centre block is the principal assembly hall, with its platform against the rear wall of the museum.*[40]

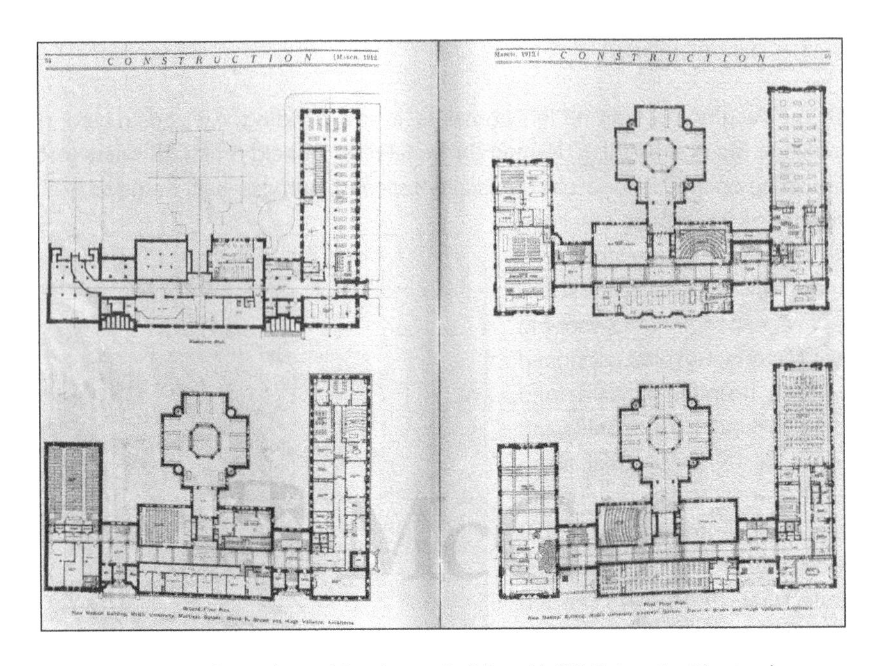

10.5 Four floor plans of Strathcona Building, McGill University, Montreal, designed by Brown and Vallance. Source: *Construction* 5, no. 4 (March 1912): 54–55.

To this journalist, all other spaces were subservient to the location of the museum.

With this central location of the museum, the E-planned arrangement provided important links between it and other crucial aspects of medical education, especially those dealing with real body parts. The Department of Anatomy, for example, occupied the east wing of the building, the longest arm of the E-plan. A basement mortuary accommodated up to eighty bodies; next to this, a preparation room led directly to the museum. Embedded in and inaccessible from an L-shaped locker room for students, the mortuary and preparation room faced the museum directly.

In this same east wing on the top floor, a grand dissection room (88 × 40 feet/26.8 × 12.2 meters), capable of holding 200 students, is evidence of the significance given at this time to the dissection of dead bodies. Indeed the sheer grandeur of the room meant that students could easily "see the work of his fellow dissectors and to note the common variations in structure that may be expected in any subject," a spatial counterpoint to the specimens on view at the nearby museum whereby all traces of context were purposefully removed.[41] Between the grand dissection room and the carefully choreographed museum were two other important tools in medical education: the library and the lecture room. I contend that these four room types: dissection room, museum, library, and lecture room comprised the essential spatial components of medical education outside the hospital prior to World War I.

Material evidence of Abbott's significant place in the museum is the space dedicated to her work as curator. This was likely in the 43 × 30 foot (13.3 × 9.1 meters) tripartite room on the ground floor just east of the museum. Functioning as a workroom, prep room and museum storage, it was here that Abbott likely classified and prepared specimens for display in her museum. According to the building's strict symmetry, the room has the identical footprint and location to the lecture room on the first floor and the anatomical theater on the second floor of the Strathcona Building. The three rooms are stacked vertically, illustrating how the museum curatorship and teaching had equal functional weights in the medical curriculum at this time.

In general, and like its predecessor the Old Medical, the Strathcona Building provides vital material evidence of the class and gender connotations of the profession at this time. Its material finishes and ample dimensions, that is, connoted wealth and pointed to associated building typologies such as men's business clubs, expensive hotels, and aristocratic mansions. The corridors and stairs of the new medical facility, for example, were an expansive 12 feet (3.7 meters) wide. "Nowhere does the building seem cramped," reported Philip J. Turner in his review for *Construction* in March 1912. Interiors featured granite, marble, dulled Carrara terracotta, and oak paneling. Most startling to our twenty-first-century sensibilities, perhaps, is the inclusion of a smoking room. Heraldic shields "on which are inscribed the names of celebrated men of medicine" line the corridors. Both the smoking room and the heraldic decoration were common in private men's clubs of the period.[42]

An additional and interesting feature of the Strathcona Building was its pair of off-center entrances facing south, inviting students to enter directly from the campus. The inclusion of two doors (rather than one) and particularly the greater importance given to the east door (it has a longer stairway than the west door due to the slope of the site towards University Street and a more significant interior stair corresponding) meant the building was frequently seen at an obtuse angle. This made it difficult, or at least unlikely, for viewers to take in the entire building in one glance, further emphasizing its domestic character by focusing on architectural pieces, rather than the whole. In addition, a particularly meaningful use of these east stairs (and those on University Street) was as the setting for graduating class photographs. Entrance stairs in North American medical buildings were typically used in this way. While the terraced levels of the stairs meant everyone's faces could be clearly seen by the photographer, the Asclepius symbol on the end of the railings clearly marked the group's affiliation with the profession of medicine. Earlier class photos often included skeletons as a way of expressing the group identity.[43]

In contrast, the unsuccessful design submission by architects Edward and William Maxwell, a firm responsible for many of the mansions in the city's famed Square Mile district, featured an E-shaped plan with a massive theater at its center (Figure 10.6). This entry placed the main entrance on Pine Avenue, facing away from the university campus. In fact, the winning scheme of Brown & Vallance is the only one that "quite emphatically selects the University grounds as its principal relationship."[44] The Maxwell brothers' scheme allots the museum the entire west wing, with a notable recurrence of the doughnut-in-a-box typology. Did Brown and Vallance's scheme win because it placed the museum at the building's heart?

McGill medical students flocked to the museum in great numbers: according to Abbott's autobiography

> *the entire final year had enrolled itself in groups which came [in] weekly in rotation, so that I met every student once weekly in serial demonstrations which covered all the material that was worth studying by the end of the session.*[45]

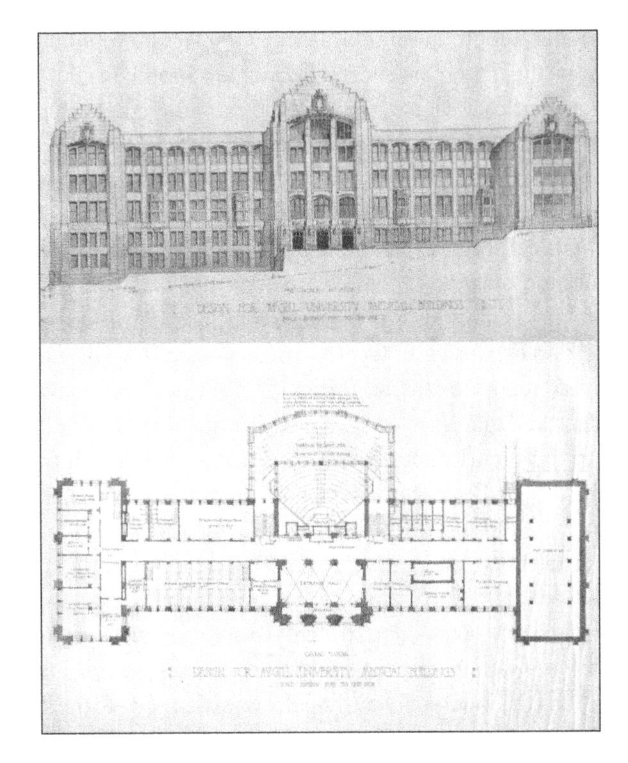

10.6 Elevation and plan of Edward and William Maxwell's competition submission for the Strathcona Building, McGill University, Montreal. Source: CAC 2, John Bland Canadian Architecture Collection, McGill University.

A photograph from a recently discovered private collection of images, taken by medical student James Lockhart between 1918 and 1921, reveals the intimate relationship the atrium afforded between student and specimen (Figure 10.7). In the

10.7 Photograph showing student in the medical museum in the Strathcona Building, McGill University, Montreal. Source: Lockhart Collection, Osler Library, McGill University.

photograph, the student is seated at a desk against the wall, reading a very large book. Matching his formal architectural surroundings (and in stark contrast to today's students), he wears a jacket and tie. He turns and glances towards the photographer, whose lens captures the sweep of the nearby skeletal collections displayed in free-standing glass cabinets. Note that Abbott believed the firsthand experience of the museum developed the student's "intellect, discrimination, agreement and retentiveness." According to her, ten minutes in the museum equaled a week's reading, echoing the well-known aphorism that a picture is worth a thousand words.[46]

PATHOLOGY INSTITUTE

Abbott's influence as a curator waned when the collection moved from the Strathcona Medical to the new, purpose-built Pathology Institute in 1923. The Pathology Institute is located diagonally across from the existing Strathcona building, on the northeast corner of the intersection of University Street and Pine Avenue (Figure 10.8). The story goes that Abbott's former technician, Ernest Lionel Judah, moved with the collection to Percy Nobbs's splendid Pathology Institute, while Abbott stayed in the Strathcona Building as the curator of a decidedly inferior collection that came to be called the Central Medical Museum.[47] Pathologist Horst Oertel,

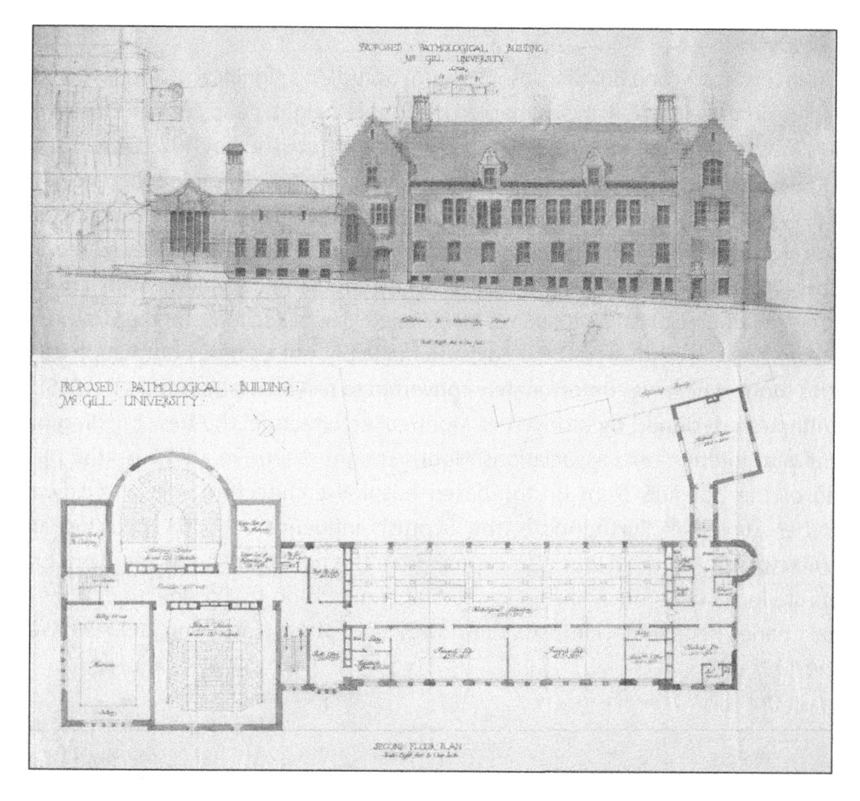

10.8 West elevation and second-floor plan of the Pathology Institute, McGill University, Montreal, designed by Percy Nobbs. Source: CAC 1, John Bland Canadian Architecture Collection, McGill University.

who served as Chair of Pathology from 1918 to 1938, was demonstrably unsupportive of Abbott.[48]

Fortunately, we have Oertel's detailed explanation of the new building, which offers a wonderful window on pathology at this moment. Oertel saw the building of the institute as an opportunity to combine pathology as an academic discipline and as part of a hospital. He described its overall emphasis as "pathological morphology," which meant an emphasis on the autopsy. This double-headed view on pathology was clearly reflected in the building's corner site, with equal access to the Royal Victoria Hospital and to McGill University. A particularly interesting feature of Nobbs's Pathology Institute is its cunning use of scale, perhaps as a response to this challenge to pathology to suit both the hospital and the university. Its façade along University Street, facing the hospital, is grand and unrelenting; while the elevation along Pine Avenue, facing a number of middle-class houses, is modest and nearly domestic. Perhaps with this dual character in mind, Oertel praised the architect's ability to combine "laboratory efficiency with effective appearance" and especially liked the abundance of natural light provided by Nobbs's large windows.[49]

Nobbs's plan for the Pathological Institute also satisfies the requirements for pathological morphology, especially in its reception of bodies and splendid provision for autopsies. The morgue, chapel, and undertakers' rooms occupied the ground floor; the next level was devoted to teaching, with a powerful trio of double-height spaces clustered at the north end: a lecture theater, autopsy theater, and the medical museum.

As in the Strathcona Building, the museum occupied a significant place within the building: in the elevation, it was marked by double-height, nearly ecclesiastical windows. Was this form of the medical museum firmly established by 1923? A perusal of images from other medical museums of the time shows a remarkable coherence with Nobbs's interiors. Like Nightingale wards, hospital kitchens, nurses' residences, and surgical arrangements, the interior design of medical museums looks nearly identical across time and space, which was almost always a rectangular volume with a simple narrow mezzanine or catwalk, such as in the failed Maxwell scheme for the Strathcona Building, and the renovated Old Medical. Remarkably, not a single photograph exists of this room, which was unfortunately converted to research laboratories in 1965.

Although designed by a doyen of Montreal architecture, the new building had significant international associations. Nobbs sought extensive advice on the planning of the building from Boston-based hospital architecture specialist Edward Fletcher Stevens.[50] Furthermore, the Scottish influence in both medicine and architecture in Montreal was also expressed in the new building as the Pathology Institute looks very much like an iconic building with no real connection to medicine: Charles Rennie Mackintosh's Glasgow School of Art (East Wing 1897–99; West Wing 1907–09).

***

What does architecture tell us about the medical museum? The design of these museum spaces for an evolving collection over time shows the criticality of artifacts and visual culture in twentieth-century medical education. Note the predominance of the doughnut-in-a-box typology, which maximized the display options in a room and also sometimes allowed the specimens to be viewed from a wide range of angles. We note, too, the place of the museum as the hub of an international network of correspondents and sources of specimens. Did the changing climate and significance of medical museums bring an abrupt shift in the architecture devoted to this institution? In this case, the museum has an inextricable connection to the life of Maude Abbott and, fortunately for us as architectural historians, the ways future generations will understand her work.

NOTES

1 Special thanks to McGill University architecture students Newsha Ghaeli, Leina Godin, Adriana Mogosanu, and Don Toromanoff for outstanding research assistance towards this study. Also to Duncan Cowie, Emily Lockhart, Gordon Burr, Richard Fraser, Mary Hunter, Chris Lyons, Joan O'Malley, David Theodore, and Carla Yanni for inspiration and access to material.

2 On other Canadian medical museums, see "Medical and Related Museums, Historic Sites, and Exhibits in Ontario: An Annotated Guide and Review," *Canadian Bulletin of Medical History* 8 (1991): 103–104.

3 www.cnn.com/2013/05/16/travel/world-medical-museums/.

4 Jonathan Reinarz, "The Age of Museum Medicine: The Rise and Fall of the Medical Museum at Birmingham's School of Medicine," *Social History of Medicine* 18, no. 3 (2005): 419.

5 Samuel J.M.M. Alberti and Elizabeth Hallam, *Medical Museums: Past, Present, Future* (London: Royal College of Surgeons of England, 2013), 44.

6 The sole study of the architecture of medical schools is Katherine L. Carroll, "Modernizing the American Medical School, 1893–1940: Architecture, Pedagogy, Professionalization, and Philanthropy," PhD dissertation, Boston University, 2009.

7 See Jessie Dobson, "The Architectural History of the Hunterian Museum," *Annals of the Royal College of Surgeons* 29 (1961): 113–126. On natural history museum architecture, see Carla Yanni, *Nature's Museums: Victorian Science and the Architecture of Display* (Princeton, NJ: Princeton Architectural Press, 2005).

8 http://www.julianbicknell.co.uk/view–hunterianmuseum_royalcollegeofsurgeons_london.php.

9 The scholarly literature on Abbott is huge and growing. The best accounts include Barbara Brookes, "An Illness in the Family: Dr. Maude Abbott and Her Sister, Alice Abbott," *Canadian Bulletin of Medical History* 28, no. 1 (2011): 171–190; Stanley B. Frost, "The Abbotts of McGill," *McGill Journal of Education* 13, no 3 (Fall 1978): 253–279; Richard Fraser, "*Hic est locus ubi mors gaudet succurrere vitae*: Maude Abbott and the Malformed Heart," in *Women and the Material Culture of Death*, eds. Maureen Daly Goggin and Bath Fowkes Tobin (London: Ashgate, 2013), 331–344; Erin Hunter McLeary, "Science in a Bottle: The Medical Museum in North America, 1860–1940," PhD dissertation, University of Pennsylvania, 2001. As biographies, see H.E. MacDermot, *Maude Abbott: A Memoir* (Toronto: Macmillan, 1941); and Douglas Waugh, *Maudie of McGill: Dr. Maude Abbott and the Foundations of Heart Surgery* (Toronto: Hannah Institute and Dundurn, 1991).

10 Waugh, *Maudie*, 67–75.

11 An example is the correspondence between Abbott and The New York Academy of Medicine in the early 1930s. Her responses to other institutions are very detailed descriptions of the museum's organization. See two-page letter from Maude Abbott to Archibald Malloch, April 18, 1934, McGill University Archives, as an illustration.

12 Joseph Hanaway and Richard Cruess, *McGill Medicine, Volume 1: The First Half Century 1829–1885* (Montreal: McGill-Queen's University Press, 1996), 17.

13 Fraser, "*Hic est locus*," 332.

14 The best architectural description of Old Medical is in "The New Building of the Medical Faculty of McGill University," *Canada Medical and Surgical Journal, Montreal* (June 1885): 693–696.

15 Susan W. Wagg, *The Architecture of Andrew Thomas Taylor Montreal's Square Mile and Beyond* (Montreal: McGill-Queen's University Press, 2013), 130–132.

16 Ibid., 110.

17 Ibid., 5.

18 Cited in ibid., 111; from the entry for William C. Macdonald in the Dictionary of Canadian Biography, www.biographi.ca/en/bio/macdonald_william_christopher_14E.html.

19 Wagg, *Taylor*, 131–132.

20 Ibid., 132.

21 Marie Adami and Humphry Davy Rolleston, *J. George Adami: A Memoir* (London: Constable, 1930), 151.

22 Abbott says "no less than 750 autopsies" in Maude E. Abbott, "The Osler Pathological Collection in the Medical Historical Museum of McGill University," *Journal of Technical Methods and Bulletin of the International Association of Medical Museums* 14 (March 1935): 21. The actual number of autopsies performed by Osler at the MGH is disputed by researchers. For details, see Hanaway and Cruess, *McGill Medicine, Volume 1*, 207–208.

23 MacDermot, *Abbott*, 65.

24 Ibid., 65–66.

25 Maude E. Abbott, "The Museum in Medical Teaching," *Journal of the American Medical Association* 44, no. 12 (1905): 935, 937.

26 Ibid., 937.

27 Ibid., 937.

28 Ibid., 936.

29 Ibid., 937.

30 "McGill's Medical Building Burned Early This Morning," *The Montreal Daily Star*, April 16, 1907: 10; "Medical Building of M'Gill in Danger," *The Globe*, April 16, 1907: 1; "M'Gill's Loss Irreparable," *The Globe*, April 17, 1907: 1–2; "Another Disastrous Fire at McGill Does Immense Damage to Medical Buildings—Museum and Library Gone," *The Montreal Daily Star*, April 16, 1907: 1; "Was the Fire at M'Gill Incendiary?" *The Montreal Daily Star*, April 16, 1907: 6; "Incendiary Cause Being Investigated," *The Montreal Daily Star*, April 17, 1907: 6. See also "The Fires," pages 43–44 in *Old McGill* (1909) (the yearbook published annually by the Junior Year of the University), which includes the story of the Macdonald Engineering Building fire as well, eleven days earlier. On the number of

specimens lost and saved, see "Curator's Report of Donations Received in the Museums of the Medical Faculty of McGill University, April 16, 1907 to July 1, 1910," Osler Library.

31 "McGill Fire Investigation," *New York Times*, April 17, 1907: 4.

32 "Montreal Notes," *Canadian Architect and Builder* (May 1907): 78. With regards to philanthropy, the Faculty of Medicine appealed to its graduates at least twice. See a list of subscribers from 1909 found in fonds, MB1070, container C6, file 0000-0684.01 45, McGill University Archives.

33 "Curator's Report of Donations." On the Holmes heart, see Anthony R.C. Dobell and Richard Van Praagh, "The Holmes Heart: Historic Associations and Pathologic Anatomy," *American Heart Journal* 132, no. 2 part 1 (August 1996): 437–445. The original publication was A.F. Holmes, "Case of Malformation of the Heart," *Trans Medico-Chir Society*, Edinburgh (1824): 252–254. Abbott republished the case in 1901.

34 See "Dean Roddick's Address," Convocation Medical Faculty, McGill University, fonds MG 1070, container C6, file 0000-0684.01 45, McGill University Archives.

35 Claire Rothman, *The Heart Specialist: A Novel* (Toronto: Cormorant, 2009), 222.

36 On the opening, see "Lord Grey Opens New Building," *Montreal Gazette*, June 6, 1911: 2.

37 Eight participating firms included Finley & Spence; E. & W.S. Maxwell; Ross & Macfarlane; Robert Findlay, Marchand & Haskell; Saxe & Archibald; and Hogle & Davis. For information on the competition, see "McGill Medical Building Competition," *Canadian Architect and Builder* 20, no. 8 (1907): 143–144.

38 "McGill Medical Building Competition," 143.

39 Philip J. Turner, "The Medical Building, McGill University," *Construction* 5, no. 4 (March 1912): 51.

40 "McGill Medical Building Competition," 143–144.

41 One of the best descriptions is S.E. Whitnall, "McGill University Department of Anatomy," in *Methods and Problems of Medical Education* (New York: Rockefeller, 1926), 4–9.

42 Turner, "The Medical Building, McGill University," 56. On men's clubs, see Annmarie Adams, "The Place of Manliness: Architecture, Domesticity, and Men's Clubs," in *Masculine Histories in the Making: Emerging Themes in Canada*, eds. Peter Gossage and Robert Rutherdale, under review.

43 John Harley Warner and James Edmonson, *Dissection: Photographs of a Rite of Passage in American Medicine, 1880–1930* (New York: Blast, 2009).

44 "McGill Medical Building Competition," 143.

45 This is an excerpt from the hand-written autobiography of Maude Abbott in the McGill University Archives, 23.

46 Abbott, "The Museum in Medical Teaching," 936.

47 Fraser, "*Hic est locus*," 342.

48 Waugh, *Maudie*, 65–66. See Abbott's letter to General Birkett, October 4, 1919, McGill University Archives, proposing the museum as an independent unit (from Pathology). On the conflict, see McLeary, "Science in a Bottle," 231–240.

49 Horst Oertel, "Pathological Institute of McGill University," *Methods and Problems of Medical Education*, third series (New York: Rockefeller, 1936), 8.

50 Letters to and from Stevens are in the collection of the former Royal Victoria Hospital, dated April 10, 1922 onwards.

11

The Decline of the Hospital as a Healing Machine

David Theodore

This chapter explores how the modern hospital came to be seen and planned as a *non*-healing environment during the twentieth century. The key turning point, I argue, arrived just after the Second World War, when governments in Britain and North America began to fund hospital construction with the goal of making hospitals the centerpieces of their healthcare systems. This decline maps a change in medicine cogently summarized by sociologist Norman Jewson as the "disappearance of the sick-man."[1] In modern medicine, the symptoms and feelings of being sick expressed by the patient became less important than medical testing, diagnosis, and treatment of his or her body parts. In the hospital patients lost authority over the narrative of their illness as well as their organic bodies, which became subject to medical inspection by both medical students and doctors. In parallel, architects began to promote the idea that the hospital environment need not explicitly contribute to healing the sick body, but must instead supply flexible support to the constantly progressing routines of biomedical practice. A host of "emerging and expanding activities," summarized a 1972 editorial in *Progressive Architecture*, "require multipurpose, flexible spaces geared to advances in communications, audiovisual systems, and diagnosis."[2]

My argument is comparative. Since I claim that the concept of the hospital as a healing machine declined, at one point the concept must have been ascendant. The decline is thus caught up in a series of shifts familiar in the history of medicine: a change in the emphasis of medical practice from care to cure; evolving requirements for medical training and education; changes in funding for medical care and hospital construction; and the split of hospital-based medical intervention from community-based public health prevention. The goal of healing bodies was only ever but one factor in the modern hospital's mission, which included medical education, medical research, technology development, and philanthropy. The change in hospital architecture was counterintuitive but logical: designers simply transformed hospitals to best support medical practices. Yet these are convoluted historical changes: disjunctive in the sense that there is no consistent development, and diachronous in the sense that similar changes happened in different places (geographical and social) at different times. In order to frame this transformation as a tableau of before and after, I will discuss related medical institutions whose buildings likewise lost their therapeutic mission; namely, tuberculosis sanatoriums (superseded by antibiotics) and mental asylums (whose usefulness diminished with the rise of psychiatry and neurobiology). But I will begin by considering what it means for a hospital to be a healing machine.

LA MACHINE À GUÉRIR

At first glance, the hospital might seem a privileged site to investigate the intersections of health, body, and architecture. In moments of ill health we become suddenly attentive to our embodiment.[3] Sickness can make us intensely aware of our near sensate environment: temperature, color, humidity, corporeal comfort, and sound. At the same time, as patients in the hospital, we also become attentive to abstract concepts about our bodies. Modern hospital practice deals with many kinds of illness, each of which assumes a biomedical body conceived as a system of parts: the tissues and organs involved in disease, the bones and muscles of surgical intervention, the chemical body of preventive care.[4] In the hospital, we directly confront this abstract body: blood is tested, X-rays taken, organs removed.

This concern for the patient's body marks the hospital as a healing machine. Michel Foucault popularized the term (*la machine à guérir*) in his studies of the hospital in late eighteenth-century France.[5] The healing machine is a normative concept about the ideal hospital: it should be a place not just where a sick patient *might* get better, but the instrument or machine that would cause a cure. The desire for cure motivates clear programmatic objectives for modern hospital design: the architect's task, it would seem, is to shape an environment that serves as a therapeutic environment for both the biomedical and the experienced body.[6] This notion is constant in the history of the modern hospital whenever patient ward design is considered. A typical instance is the experimental ward at Larkfield Hospital in Greenock, Scotland, developed around 1950 by the Nuffield Provincial Hospitals Trust. Images of the ward under construction and in models show architects searching to shape windows and openings, select materials, and lay out beds and furnishings so that patients might enjoy the therapeutic benefits of daylight without the discomfort of glare from sunlight (Figure 11.1).[7]

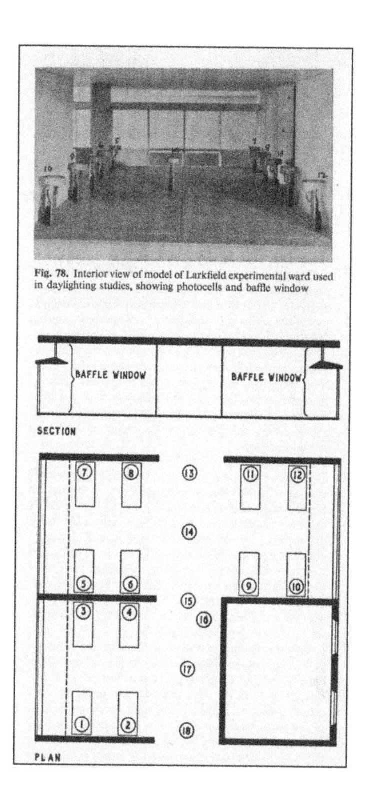

11.1 Model, plan and section of Larkfield Hospital experimental ward, Greenock, Scotland. Source: Nuffield Provincial Hospitals Trust, *Studies in the Functions and Design of Hospitals* (London: Oxford University Press, 1955), courtesy Nuffield Trust.

Yet hospitals connect health and architecture through other kinds of bodies, too. Most importantly, hospitals also register social bodies. Throughout the history of modern hospitals, cities have made place for special buildings based on race, religion, gender, socioeconomic status, and age: there are hospitals for women, children, blacks, Jews, Catholics, the elderly, and the poor. Hospitals are also segregated according to biomedical categories: heart and lung hospitals, or psychiatric hospitals, or hospitals for special diseases such as cancer centers, or for certain stages of disease, including convalescent homes, chronic care facilities, and the new palliative care facilities. In a healthcare system, a network of distinct hospitals attends to different bodies, stabilizing and producing social categories.[8] Producing good health for social groups implies that the machine works simultaneously at the level of the individual patient in a patient room, and at the scale of social groups: healthy populations. The buildings reproduce the biomedical body at the level of the social.

It matters little, for these social types of bodies, whether the hospital is a healing machine. It is still possible, however, to consider the healing machine as a hospital whose architectural organization supports the administration of both a patient and a city: the human body and the body politic. What matters is the way the hospital takes up its place in the city.[9] Consider two schematic section drawings of proposed hospitals from around 1965. The first, from a 1964 project for the Venice Hospital by Le Corbusier and Jullian de la Fuente, limns an intimate necessity between the human body and healthcare architecture (Figure 11.2).[10] It is a section cut through a hospital ward. A patient lies horizontally on a bed. There are no windows in the room. Natural light filters into the room from overhead, not quite affording the patient a view of the sky. The image manifests a deep concern for molding architectural form to receive the sick body. Entitled "Drive-In Hospital," the second image suggests a

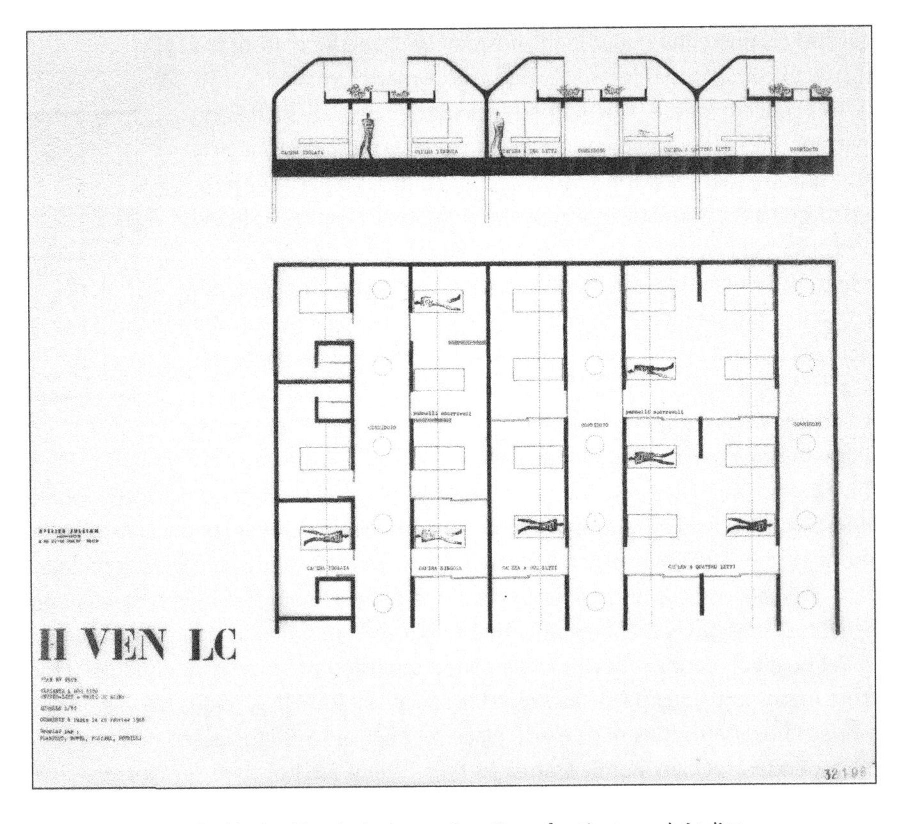

11.2 Venice Hospital, plan and section of patient ward, Atelier Jullian, architects, 1966. © FLC/SODRAC, 2015, Fondation Le Corbusier.

tight intertwining of the automobile and healthcare architecture (Figure 11.3). This is the University of Cologne Medical Center, designed by Heinle, Wischer & Partner.[11] Patients are not portrayed. The section shows no especial concern for daylight. Instead there is a sampling of hospital workers at work making beds or wheeling carts in corridors. Four or five cartoonish vehicles circle around the base of a twenty-story-tall tower. Here we seem to have a simple opposition between two kinds of hospitals: one, humanist, attuned to the body; one, mechanistic, attuned to technology. Yet this is only seeming. On the one hand the Venice Hospital design was famously patterned on the organization of streets and squares of the city, making for hospital life that "approximates urban life."[12] On the other hand, the drive-in hospital was publicized as an exemplary attainment of patient-centered hospital design.[13]

This link between the city, the hospital, and the individual is crucial. Foucault's main objective was to show how hospitals and medicine moved from considerations about healthy individuals to became part of governmental strategies for the rational management of healthy populations. Foucault and his colleagues

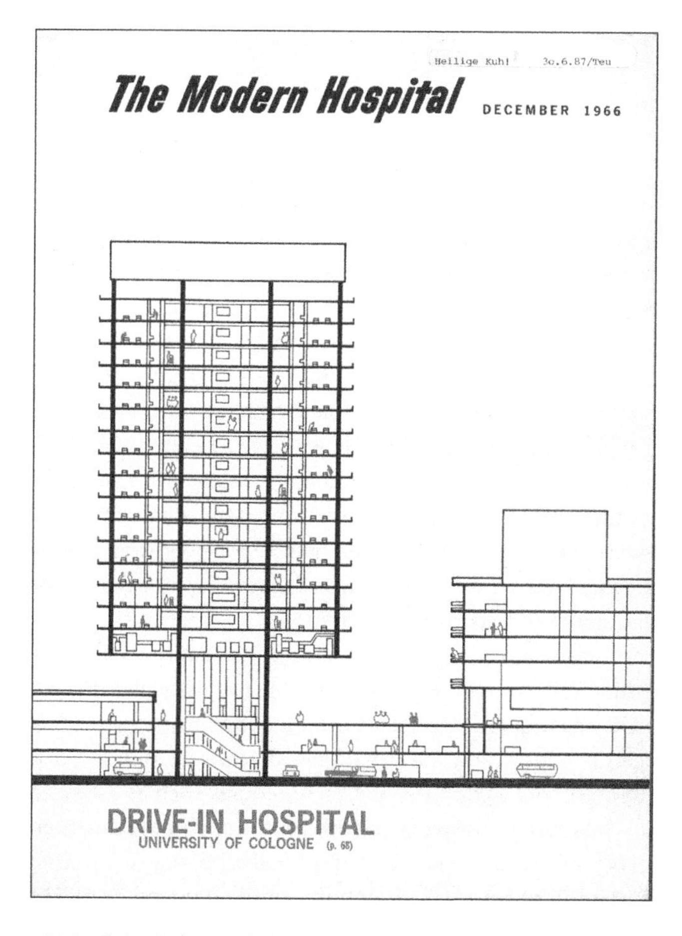

11.3 Drive-in hospital, designed by Heinle, Wischer und Partner, Freie Architekte. Source: Cover illustration, *Modern Hospital* 107, no. 6 (December 1966).

argued that new medical practices and new ideas about architecture gave birth to "the clinic," inaugurating a modern era in which hospital life is central to medical practice.[14] But this engagement with the city came at the same time as two new spatial relations inside medicine that happened inside the hospital. First, the healing machine named a new concern with the spatial arrangement inside hospitals based on the spatial location of a patient's individual body.[15] Second, hospital practices focused on a new spatialization of the body itself. This is the emergence of the dead body as the most important medical site. The natural history of disease (its life and death) gave way to a concern with the location of disease in the body's tissue. Since this location was most visible in the inert, dead body, medicine's interest (its "gaze" in Foucault's terms) shifted away from the living patient.[16] The advantages and disadvantages of Foucault's hospital studies, for instance, correlate almost exactly with the persuasiveness of his accounts of the links between the individual body and the city.[17] The point is that the hospital may still be in some sense a machine that links health and the body, but not because it offers an environment that cures disease.

THE HISTORY OF THE HEALING MACHINE

Foucault's influential account of hospital history places the dramatic emergence of the modern hospital at the end of the eighteenth century. Hospital historians, however, rarely adopt his periodization, for two important reasons germane here. One is that humoralism, the medical theory of disease that has dominated the West since the Greeks, was not displaced by scientific theories of disease until the end of the nineteenth century.[18] Until the mid-nineteenth century, medicine and health in the West followed the teachings inherited from Galen and the Hippocratic corpus. Under this humoral framework, both body and architecture were always addressed when doctors made prescriptions about how to live a healthy life. Indeed, even the title of the most well-known text in this tradition, the late fifth-century BCE text *Airs, Waters, Places* sets out a fundamental relationship between health and place.[19] The advent of new conceptions of disease and health, however, gradually led to a disavowal of the connections between health and place, displacing the notion that the hospital environment should be therapeutic.[20]

The second reason to question Foucault's periodization is something known as the "invention" of the modern hospital.[21] Social historians of medicine have established a key change in hospital life brought about by a series of factors in the nineteenth century, including the rise of anesthesia and aseptic surgery, trained nurses, the germ theory of disease, and technologies such as X-Ray and business accounting.[22] This modern hospital, invented at the end of the nineteenth century, and not, as Foucault would have it, at the beginning, was a success.[23] The new institution and its architecture were popular and in demand. In 1873, there were about 175 old-style hospitals in the United States; forty-five years later, in 1909 there were over 4,000 new ones.[24] Thus the modern hospital was not simply the old one multiplied, but a new institution closely caught up in urbanization.

We are now in a position to see how the idea of the hospital as a healing machine declined. We have in place a set of ideas about the hospital environment and about the environment that the hospital is in. We know that the hospital was entangled with social transformations such as urbanization, technological development, and the rise of science and business associated with modernism. The last part of this study will explore the ideal environment of the postwar hospital.

THE SANATORIUM AND THE MENTAL ASYLUM

The overall decline of the healing machine is most clearly visible in the rise and fall of two special kinds of hospital, the tuberculosis sanatorium and the mental asylum. Let us turn to sanatoriums first. In the mid-nineteenth century, doctors speculated that tuberculosis could be cured if patients undertook a regime of fresh air, sunlight, and good nutrition.[25] Doctors advocated isolating patients in sanatoriums: these were hospitals, located in rural and often mountainous regions, whose architecture was designed to provide homelike domestic comfort for patients while, at the same time, maximizing their contact with fresh air and sunlight. While the sanatorium was not the only place where tuberculosis affected the built environment—tuberculosis educators, for example, suggested modifying private homes to include sun porches and outdoor sleeping alcoves—in all cases the building itself circumscribed the therapeutic regime.[26] That is, a sanatorium was a healing machine; simply living in the building constituted treatment.

Scholars have documented strong connections between tuberculosis sanatoriums and the modern movement in architecture. Architects, too, were concerned with bringing fresh air and sunlight into a wide variety of modernist building projects; long-standing associations between sunlight and social amelioration entered into architectural thinking.[27] By World War II, a sort of symbiosis between the glass and sunlight of modern architecture and the glass and sunlight of sanatoriums was well established.[28] Nevertheless, the association was short-lived. The building-as-therapy was challenged by other therapeutic regimes, namely surgical interventions into the chest cavity of the human body: first pneumothorax, in which patients received periodic treatment to artificially collapse a lung, and then later surgical intervention to remove or resect the lung itself.[29] Finally, both surgical and architectural therapies were superannuated by chemical therapy.[30] The effectiveness and widespread availability of new drugs around 1950 made sanatoriums obsolete.[31] Medical advances trumped architectural modernism.

A second example is the mental asylum. Historians attribute the rise of asylums to multifarious factors, but one is architectural.[32] In the eighteenth century, the idea gained acceptance that particular environments, in this case, made from a combination of building and garden, were therapeutic.[33] The design of the building was part of the care regime; doctors believed patients improved through contact with nature, and that correctly organized buildings could control (augment or diminish) that contact.[34] In order to be medically efficacious, that is, good asylum architecture went beyond merely providing the symbols of benevolence, charity, frugality or other social qualities. It also provided precise means of engaging natural processes: daylight, ventilation and fresh air, and gardens.[35]

If, however, architectural modernism was key to the development of sanatoriums, it was less so in asylums. The basic plan type was not developed by architects, but rather by doctors and asylum managers. In the United States an asylum superintendent named Thomas Story Kirkbride created an influential template for asylum architecture based on the idea of controlled nature as essential to healing the disturbed mind.[36] At the same time, there is a parallel with sanatoriums in that the decline of this architectural-medico model for mental illness came with the ascendance of biological models of mental pathology. By the turn of the century, the rise of neuroanatomy, neurosurgery, and neurobiology began to make the asylum's therapeutic environment superfluous. The hospital, instead of being therapeutic, was portrayed as oppressive and harmful.[37] Finally, as with sanatoriums, the arrival of effective chemical treatments for certain mental disorders created a persuasive rationale for the movement to decommission buildings constructed in the asylum tradition.[38]

With the rise of biomedicine, tuberculosis sanatoriums and mental asylums lost their purpose. Sanatoriums were decommissioned and converted, and mental asylums deliberately depopulated through the de-institutionalization of care. In both cases, the specific architectural environment was no longer part of the therapy.[39]

AFTER 1945

This decoupling of architecture from therapy also happened to general hospitals. Modern biomedicine did not call for any particular therapeutic environment. In other words, if Foucault could argue that the *machine à guérir* of Revolutionary France re-placed disease into the patient and the patient in the hospital, the post-1945 factory was deliberately indifferent to patients. Or at least tried to be. The hospital's development, for instance, was marked early on by the idea that convalescence was a home-based activity; the sick who were merely getting well—in need of care rather than cure—had no place in the hospital.[40]

Nevertheless, unlike asylums and sanatoriums, after 1945 hospitals were not abandoned but instead went through a second period of robust reform and expansion. By the mid-twentieth century, hospital planners acknowledged three conditions: the move in medicine from acute to chronic care; the efficacy and ubiquity of machine-based medicine; and increased state funding for hospital construction. In response to these challenges, architects began thinking again of the hospital as a factory: workers, architecture and product (patient) could be optimized through research.[41] Each of these challenges involved a shift in the relationship between architecture and the body; each shift in turn revealed a new set of bodies, not all of which were posited in architectural experience. And by 1970, the key challenges for hospital design were to make buildings that were "anti-monumental, non-dramatic, irregular, expansible and cheap, satisfying ephemeral present requirements yet recognizing the uncertainty of the future."[42]

The first change, from acute to chronic care, is a complex shift that has not yet been deeply explored by historians.[43] The basic idea is that for the first half of the twentieth century, medical practices focused on dramatic intervention into the natural history of a disease or health problem: surgery is the guiding practice.[44] Then around World War II, a series of chemicals became available that changed therapeutic outcomes. Most famously, antibiotics meant that bacterial infections could be treated first by a series of injections and then by pills. The unhealthy human body became a site for disease at the bacterial level both as a conception of disease but now also of therapy. If in the nineteenth century cell-based disease was only visible in dead bodies (pathology), in the mid-twentieth century it was also *made visible* in the response of sick bodies to chemical treatment.

Such changes had a direct effect on healthcare architecture. I have already discussed the influence on tuberculosis sanatoriums, which quickly fell into disuse or were converted to other uses. But the efficacy of antibiotics also put pressure on hospitals. Surgery and childbirth were now much safer endeavors. Social practice confirmed the hospital rather than the home as the place where children are born.[45] Antibiotics also meant that the hospital began to move inpatients to outpatient clinics. That is, the experience of a sick person in the hospital was no longer centered on overnight tenure in the hospital ward, but moved to the efficient operation of day clinics. Overall, the dramatic effectiveness of antibiotics dwarfed any therapeutic effects observably due to the hospital architecture.

The second shift involved the rise of machine-based (or technology-based) medicine. The story of technology and the hospital is not one of linear change.[46] But there were two more or less direct sequential events. First, note that technologies introduced during the early part of the century were not immediately taken up as routine parts of medical practice. Novel products such as X-ray produced reliable, interpretable, and quotidian images of the body, making the body amenable to basic surgery, nuclear medicine, and diagnosis for certain diseases such as pneumonia and tuberculosis. Having tuberculosis in the body, for instance, now meant being able to see it on X-rays and detect the bacillus in the blood.[47]But almost all of this medical technology could be placed in the existing hospital setting. Indeed, the persistence of familiar settings helped the new technology become a familiar part of hospital equipment.[48]

Second, there was a host of new machines in the hospital that had little to do with therapy, but nevertheless preoccupied architects and planners. Foremost is perhaps the elevator. A series of studies in postwar Europe raised the problem of vertical transport in the hospital system.[49] It was at once essential to the skyscraper hospital plan, and yet an obvious bottleneck in the overall movement of goods, workers, and patients in the hospital. One approach, championed and marketed by Washington DC-based consultant Gordon A. Friesen, involved organizing the entire hospital around the needs of automated machinery. Friesen called this a patient-centered approach: the machines, he argued, would free up the nurse's time so that she could be as attentive as possible to the needs of the patient.[50] But this meant that the entire hospital needed to be planned according to the location of vertical transports (for food and supplies). In Britain, in particular, where Friesen's ideas found strong support, architects argued that this solution caused as many planning problems as it solved. Conceptually, however, the change was made. From now on the patient was imagined as static in the room, and the bodies of concern were the workers' bodies—especially the nurses, whose every footstep became a matter of architectural calculation.[51]

Moreover, the machines continued to multiply. In 1969 Donald Longmore published a popular book entitled *Machines in Medicine*.[52] A cardiac surgeon, in 1968 Longmore had been part of the first British heart transplant team. He listed over 140 machines now crucial to hospital medicine—and his list left out the computers he discussed in chapter six. Longmore was explicit that hospital care dealt mostly with the "crude," "gross statistical level" of the organic, or whole-body level, whereas the future of medicine was increasingly dependent on understanding and manipulating the intracellular level.[53] Computers, of course, had only been part of hospitals (and medicine) a scant decade, although in 1972, the announcement of computer-based imaging techniques would change that.[54] But none of this machinery needed architecture in the same way that the sick body needs it. The building was simply the box within which the machines operated.

The major shift was the third one: a change in the way hospital design and construction was funded. The shift here is understandable in Foucauldian terms, for in the new dispensation, government policies addressed individual bodies as part of populations. While that sounds abstract, the funding was concrete. Two exemplary programs, widely debated but not controversial, were the Hill-Burton Act (Hospital Survey and Construction Act; 1946) in the US and the National Health Service Hospital Plan (1962) in England.[55] There was widespread agreement that the hospital was no longer a special institution necessary for the isolation and care of specific populations (the mentally ill, the tubercular, the sick poor). Instead, it was now a central facility whose accessibility governments needed to ensure.[56] Ensuring accessibility especially meant building new hospitals in rural areas. And unlike the boom around 1900, there was a large stock of existing urban hospitals, so much funding went for their renovation, demolition, or replacement. These funding schemes were a success. "The golden years of the Hill-Burton program have made us fat and lazy," declared one US hospital architect in 1972.[57] The availability of money for construction raised the question: what kinds of hospitals should be built?

THE HOSPITAL AS MACHINE

"At present the similarities between hospital designs all over the world are more striking than the dissimilarities," wrote British planner, educator, and hospital specialist Richard Llewelyn-Davies in 1966.[58] He was summing up the "last ten or fifteen years" of hospital planning with an eye to the next twenty years. The challenge, Llewelyn-Davies wrote, was to find "a pattern of architectural design which will permit growth [and change] to take place freely."[59] The architectural plan instead needed to be perfectly flexible and amenable to operations. Some of these devices were new modifications of older ideas—clear-span floor plans, movable partitions, standardized user spaces, and modularized service spaces.[60] But some were new. In this section, I will briefly discuss three.

11.4 Northwick Park Hospital, London, under construction, 1969. The two-level "main street" is visible linking the pavilions. Source: London North West Healthcare NHS Trust.

The first concept is the idea that the overall hospital should be planned to grow and change over time in the same way as a village or small town. Around 1965, architects Llewelyn-Davies Weeks, who were involved in city planning, notably the new town of Milton Keynes, used this concept to plan Northwick Park Hospital in London. In effect, they used an updated pavilion plan, but made in a way that allows for different parts to grow at different speeds and according to different needs.[61] In addition, they argued that since there is no overall composition, the appearance of the building would not be ruined by additions or demolitions.[62] In short, planning the hospital as a village had medical and architectural benefits.

A second move, related to village planning, was the incorporation of a main street. At Northwick Park Hospital, the street was on two levels, one for services and supplies and one for walking (Figure 11.4). Because the main circulation path was autonomous, individual pavilions and services could be added to (or taken away from) the main street without interfering with the functioning of the overall hospital. In other words, it formed a working version of the plug-in architecture that other British architects were experimenting with on paper, allowing hospital extensions to be flexibly planned. This system allowed for innovations in project management, too. Individual buildings could be designed and funded autonomously. This was crucial when architects had to design a hospital not knowing what the final program would be, and not knowing when or even if certain departments would be financed.[63]

A third device was the utilization of interstitial space, which provided internal flexibility of planning arrangements. By putting services in the space between the ceiling and the floor, detailed planning of services and departments could be postponed. At Woodhull Medical and Mental Health Center in Brooklyn, the interstitial spaces contained waste disposal systems, HVAC, transformer rooms, and even self-propelled electric cars programmed to deliver supplies (designed by Kallmann & McKinnell, Russo & Sonder; Figure 11.5).[64] The device also allowed fast-track project management: construction could be well advanced before any detailed interior planning was done. The internal arrangements were only worked out during construction—or even afterwards.

Taken together, a hospital with village planning, a main-street circulation core, and interstitial service floors had almost no guiding principal grounded in close attention to the sick body. Health could now be delivered as a systematic effect of the operation of the whole hospital, and not as a therapeutic effect of the architecture on the individual patient. The hospital was no longer a healing machine but simply a machine.

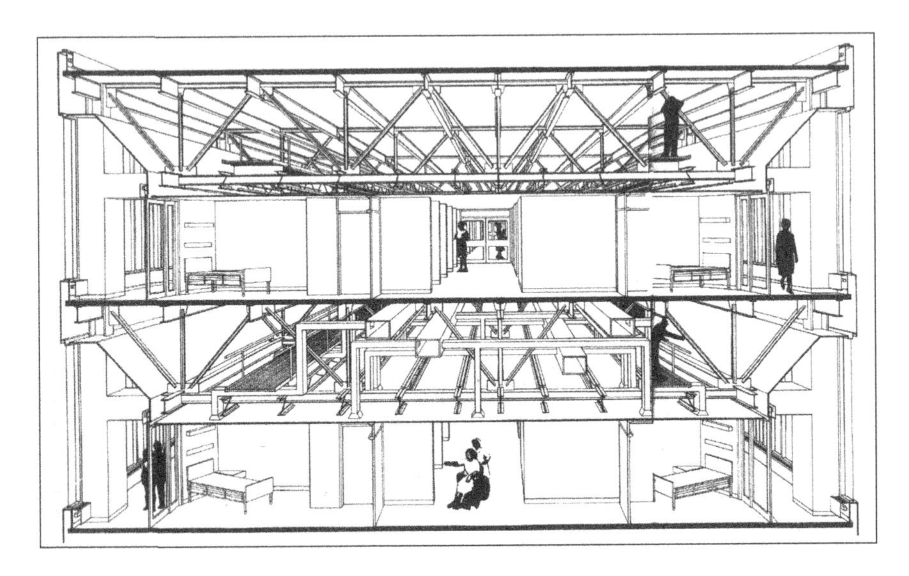

11.5 Sectional perspective of the interstitial space, Woodhull Medical and Mental Health Center, Brooklyn, Kallmann & McKinnell, Russo & Sonder. Courtesy KMW Architecture.

EPILOGUE

In the architectural history of the modern hospital, the normative ideal that the hospital should be a machine for healing tightly adapted to the patients' bodies remains firmly entrenched. The decline of the hospital as healing machine immediately created a reaction, a call for what was lost, a reanimation of hospital as healing machine. The most influential group of concepts about how to design hospitals today is evidence-based design. This movement, named in parallel to the evidence-based medicine movement, tries to evaluate design proposals and existing hospitals based on best evidence gathered from scientific studies. Researchers and hospital architects call for hospital design to focus on healing, to search for ways that architecture can be beneficial for both healthy bodies (the workers) and sick bodies (the patients).[65]

Implicit in evidence-based design is the notion that it is simply important—somehow better—to resurrect the ordering of health, body, and architecture envisioned in early modernism with the healing machine. We might ask, however, just how much the call for therapeutic environments is actually a call for efficacious hospital architecture. Clearly, some features of healing design are merely rhetorical. A recent prizewinning project in California, for instance, called for the inclusion of a farmers' market. And we know that some of the ills of hospital environments are better addressed through staff training rather than design. Hospital-acquired infection, for instance, is a real problem that needs to be ameliorated—but the role of architecture is clearly secondary here to the cultural practices of hospital work.

The story of the decline of the hospital as a healing machine, then, has some lessons for historians. We must consider that hospitals are about medicine more than they are about health; that there are ways to make hospitals that do not start with the patient's body, but rather with the relation of the hospital to the city; that health has to do with daily life and not those infrequent moments when we are sick and hospitalized; and that might we consider the possibility of an architectural history that begins to separate medicine and health rather than conflating them in the notion of the healthy body. That is, can we differentiate the history of therapeutic architecture, in which the body is healed, from the history of architecture that reflects social anxiety about the healthy body?

NOTES

1 Norman Jewson, "The Disappearance of the Sick-Man from Medical Cosmology, 1770–1870," *Sociology* 10 (1976): 225–244.

2 H. Robert Douglass, "Health Care: The Fastest Growing Industry," *Progressive Architecture* 53 (July 1972): 52–53, 90–92, 90.

3 Drew Leder, *The Absent Body* (Chicago: University of Chicago Press, 1990).

4 On theorizing the diseased body, see the influential essay by Charles E. Rosenberg, "Framing Disease: Illness, Society and History," in *Framing Disease: Studies in Cultural History*, eds. Charles E. Rosenberg and Janet Lynne (New Brunswick, NJ, Rutgers University Press, 1992), xiii–xxv; on surgery, see Thomas Schlich, "The Technological Fix and the Modern Body: Surgery as a Paradigmatic Case," in *The Cultural History of the Human Body*, eds. Linda Kalof and William Bynum, vol. 6 "1920–present," ed. Ivan Crozier (London: Berg, 2010), 71–92; on the pharmaceutical body, see Jeremy Greene, *Prescribing by Numbers: Drugs and the Definition of Disease* (Baltimore, MD: Johns Hopkins University Press, 2009).

5 Michel Foucault, Blandine Barret Kriegel, Anne Thalamy, François Beguin, and Bruno Fortier, *Les machines à guérir: aux origins de l'hôpital moderne; dossiers et documents* (Paris: L'institut de l'environnement, 1976). Revised version Michel Foucault, Blandine Barret Kriegel, Anne Thalamy, François Beguin, Bruno Fortier, *Les machines à guérir: aux origins de l'hôpital modern* (Brussels: Pierre Mardaga, 1979). The chapter by François Béguin recounts the origin of the term "*la machine à guérir*" in the reports of surgeon Jacques-René Tenon.

6 Note that in nineteenth-century French thought, the ideal architecture environment is supposed to affect the physiological body directly; see Martin Bressani and Marc Grignon, "The Bibliothèque Sainte-Geneviève and 'Healing Architecture,'" in *Henri Labrouste: Structure Brought to Light*, ed. Corinne Bélier, Barry Bergdoll, and Marc Le Coeur (New York: Museum of Modern Art, 2012), 95–122.

7 R.G. Hopkinson, "Lighting: Daylighting a Hospital Ward, *The Architects' Journal* 115 (February 21, 1952): 255–259. The team also studied sound, color, and artificial lighting. The complete set of studies undertaken at the ward is presented in Nuffield Provincial Hospitals Trust, *Studies in the Functions and Design of Hospitals* (London: Oxford University Press, 1955), 91–132.

8 Guenter B. Risse, in *Mending Bodies, Saving Souls: A History of Hospitals* (New York: Oxford University Press, 1999), argues that "The generic hospital is an abstraction. In reality, there are only particular hospitals, each with its own name, patrons and mission, buildings, staff, and patients" (4). Yet in modern life, the abstract social categories are made meaningful through the architecture of particular hospitals; see Annmarie Adams, *Medicine by Design: The Architect and the Modern Hospital, 1893–1943* (Minneapolis: University of Minnesota Press, 2007).

9 On the analogical and metaphorical parallels between modern hospital planning and urban planning, see Jonathan Hughes, "Hospital-City," *Architectural History* 40 (1997): 266–288. Hughes concentrates on the cases of overlap in postwar Britain, i.e. situations where professional firms were simultaneously carrying out hospital and urban design projects.

10 On the design of the hospital, see Hashim Sarkis, Pablo Allard, and Timothy Hyde, eds., *Case: Le Corbusier's Venice Hospital and the Mat Building Revival* (New York: Prestel Verlag, 2001); and Guillermo Jullian de la Fuente, "The Venice Hospital Project of Le Corbusier," *Architecture at Rice*, April 23, 1968.

11 On the design and construction of this hospital, see "Zentralklinikum der Med. Fakultät, Universität Köln," Sonderdruck aus *Bauen + Wohnen* (July 1974): 200–209.

12 See Peter G. Rowe, *Design Thinking* (Cambridge, MA: MIT Press, 1987), 28–30. Rowe observes: "The [Venice] hospital is viewed less as an instrument for the efficient technical practice and institutional delivery of medicine than as a part of the city, where patients and visitors alike can partake in something that, as closely as possible under the circumstances, approximates urban life" (30).

13 See "University Medical Center, Cologne, Germany," *Concepts* 7, no. 1 (1973): 14. Le Corbusier's proposition betrays a lingering nostalgia for earlier hospital types.

14 Michel Foucault, *Birth of the Clinic*, trans. A.M. Sheridan (New York: Pantheon, [1963] 1973). Foucault's clearest explication of his ideas about hospital architecture is in "The Incorporation of the Hospital into Modern Technology," trans. Edgar Knowlton Jr., William J. King, and Stuart Elden, in *Space, Knowledge and Power: Foucault and Geography*, eds. Jeremy W. Crampton and Stuart Elden (London: Ashgate, 2007), 141–151.

15 Hospital historians argue that the main impetus for the attention to ward design came later in the nineteenth century. In Britain, for instance, I.K. Brunel's prefabricated military hospital at Renkioi was a turning point, partly because it influenced Florence Nightingale, herself an influential advocate for reformed hospital design. On the early history of ward design, see Cor Wagenaar, ed., *The Architecture of Hospitals* (Rotterdam: NAi, 2006); Adams, *Medicine by Design*; and Philip Steadman, *Building Types and Built Forms* (Leicester: Matador, 2014); and for the postwar, Stephen Verderber and David J. Fine, *Healthcare Architecture in an Era of Radical Transformation* (New Haven, CT: Yale University Press, 2000).

16 See the evaluation in Edward S. Casey, "The Place of Space in *The Birth of the Clinic*," *Journal of Medicine and Philosophy* 12 (1987): 351–356.

17 For the importance of Foucault's hospital history for architectural theory, see Sven-Olov Wallenstein, *Biopolitics and the Emergence of Modern Architecture* (New York: Princeton Architectural Press, 2009). For the postwar era, see also Łukasz Stanek, "Biopolitics of Scale: Architecture, Urbanism, the Welfare State and After," in Sven-Olov Wallenstein and Jakob Nilsson, eds., *Foucault, Biopolitcs and Governmentality* (Stockholm: Södertörn University, 2013), 105–122.

18 Vivian Nutton, "Humoralism," in *The Companion Encyclopedia of the History of Medicine*, vol. 1, eds. William F. Bynum and Roy Porter (London: Routledge, 1993), 281–291.

19 The standard translation is in G.E.R. Lloyd, ed., *Hippocratic Writings* (Harmondsworth: Pelican, 1978), 145–169. For a discussion of the text as a *mentalité*, see Andrew Wear, "Place, Health, and Disease: The *Airs, Waters, Places* Tradition in Early Modern England and North America," *Journal of Medieval and Early Modern Studies* 38, no. 3 (2008): 433–465.

20 The change was differentiated geographically, too. See John Harley Warner, *The Therapeutic Perspective: Medical Practice, Knowledge, and Identity in America, 1820–1885* (Princeton, NJ: Princeton University Press, 1997). For a case study of one medical discipline, see George Weisz, "Spas, Mineral Waters, and Hydrological Science in Twentieth-Century France," *Isis* 92 (2001): 451–483.

21 The term comes from Morris J. Vogel, *The Invention of the Modern Hospital: Boston, 1870 –1930* (Chicago: University of Chicago Press, 1980). The benchmark account is Charles Rosenberg, *The Care of Strangers: The Rise of America's Hospital System* (New York: Basic, 1987). See also Morris J. Vogel, "The Transformation of the American Hospital, 1850–1920," in *Health Care in America*, eds. Susan Reverby and David Rosner (Philadelphia, PA: Temple University Press, 1979), 105–116.

22 The role of technology in the making of the modern hospital is particularly illuminating; see Stanley J. Reiser, *Medicine and the Reign of Technology* (Cambridge: Cambridge University Press, 1978).

23 Allan M. Brandt and David C. Sloane, "Of Beds and Benches: Building the Modern American Hospital," in *The Architecture of Science*, eds. Peter Galison and Emily Thompson (Cambridge, MA: MIT Press, 2000), 281–308.

24 Rosenberg, *Care of Strangers*, 5.

25 The benchmark social history of tuberculosis is Linda Bryder, *Below the Magic Mountain* (Oxford: Clarendon Press, 1988); see also the essays in Flurin Condrau and Michael Worboys, eds., *Tuberculosis Then and Now: Perspectives on the History of an Infectious Disease* (Montreal and Kingston, London: McGill-Queen's/Associated Medical Services Studies in the History of Medicine, Health and Society, 2010).

26 See, for example, Thomas Spees Carrington, *Fresh Air and How to Use It* (New York: National Association for the Study and Prevention of Tuberculosis, 1912).

27 Bressani and Grignon, "Healing Architecture," 122.

28 See Beatriz Colomina, "X-Ray Architecture: The Tuberculosis Effect," *Harvard Design Magazine* 40 (2015): 70–91; and Margaret Campbell, "What Tuberculosis Did for Modernism: The Influence of a Curative Environment on Modernist Design and Architecture," *Medical History* 49 (2005): 463–488.

29 On the bodily and architectural spaces of tuberculosis, see Annmarie Adams and Kevin Schwartzman, "Pneumothorax Then and Now," *Space and Culture* 8, no. 4 (2005): 435–448.

30 The so-called triple threat of chemotherapy treatment consisted of streptomycin (1946), para-aminosalicylic acid (1949), and isoniazid (1952).

31 Annmarie Adams, Kevin Schwartzman, and David Theodore, "Collapse and Expand: Architecture and Tuberculosis Therapy in Montreal, 1909, 1933, 1954," *Technology and Culture* 49, no. 4 (2008): 908–942.

32 On the institutional history of the asylum, see the seminal studies by Michel Foucault, *Madness and Civilization: A History of Madness in the Age of Reason*, trans. Richard Howard (New York: Random House, [1961] 1965); Andrew Scull, *Museums of Madness* (London: Allen Lane, 1979); and David Rothman, *The Discovery of the Asylum* (Boston, MA: Little, Brown, 1971).

33 Carla Yanni, *The Architecture of Madness: Insane Asylums in the United States* (Minneapolis: University of Minnesota Press, 2007).

34 Ibid., 7.

35 See Christine Stevenson, *Medicine and Magnificence: British Hospital and Asylum Architecture, 1660–1815* (New Haven, CT: Yale University Press, 2000); and "Madness and the Picturesque in the Kingdom of Denmark," in *The Anatomy of Madness: Essays in the History of Psychiatry*, vol. 3, eds. William F. Bynum, Roy Porter, and Michael Shepherd (London: Routledge, 1998), 13–47.

36 See Thomas Story Kirkbride, *On the Construction, Organization, and General Arrangements of Hospitals for the Insane* (Philadelphia, PA: Lindsay & Blakiston, 1854). See also Nancy Tomes, *The Art of Asylum-Keeping: Thomas Story Kirkbride and the Origins of American Psychiatry* (Philadelphia, PA: University of Pennsylvania Press, 1984).

37 See Thomas Szasz, *The Manufacture of Madness: A Comparative Study of the Inquisition and the Mental Health Movement* (New York: Harper & Row, 1970); and Erving Goffman, *Asylums: Essays on the Social Situation of Mental Patients and Other Inmates* (New York: Doubleday, 1961). For the architecture of madness, see Leslie Elizabeth Topp, James E. Moran, and Jonathan Andrew, eds., *Madness, Architecture and the Built Environment* (New York: Routledge, 2007).

38 See Roy Porter and David Wright, eds., *The Confinement of the Insane: International Perspectives, 1800–1965* (Cambridge: Cambridge University Press, 2003).

39 Note that, unlike the case of the tuberculosis sanatorium, however, there was a backlash in psychiatric design, as clinicians looked to environmental psychology to help with therapy. See Joy Knoblauch, "Going Soft: Architecture and the Human Sciences in Search of New Institutional Forms (1963–1974)," PhD diss., Princeton University, 2012; and Erika Dyck, "Spaced Out in Saskatchewan: Modernism, Anti-Psychiatry and Deinstitutionalization, 1950–1968," *Bulletin for the History of Medicine* 84, no. 4 (2010): 640–666.

40 Sally Sheard, "Getting Better, Faster: Convalescence and Length of Stay in British and US Hospitals," in *Daily Life in Hospital: Theory and Practice from the Medieval to the Modern*, eds. Laurinda Abreu and Sally Sheard (Oxford: Peter Lang, 2013), 299–329.

41 Richard Llewelyn Davies, "The Case for Research in Modern Architecture," *Royal Canadian Architectural Institute of Canada Journal* 33 (October 1956): 400–402.

42 John Weeks, "*AD* Briefing: Hospitals," *AD* (July 1973): 436–463, at 460.

43 See George Weisz, *Chronic Disease in the Twentieth Century: A History* (Baltimore, MD: Johns Hopkins University Press, 2014); and Allan M. Brandt, "A Reader's Guide to 200 Years of the *New England Journal of Medicine*," *New England Journal of Medicine* 366 (2012): 1–7. For a criticism of the concept of the epidemiologic transition, see George Weisz and Jesse Olsyzynko-Gryn, "The Theory of Epidemiologic Transition: The Origins of a Citation Classic," *Journal of the History of Medicine and Allied Sciences* 65, no. 3 (2009): 287–326.

44 For surgery and architecture, see Schlich, "Technological Fix and the Modern Body"; and Annmarie Adams and Thomas Schlich, "Design for Control: Surgery, Science, and Space at the Royal Victoria Hospital, Montreal, 1893–1956." *Medical History* 50 (2006): 303–324.

45 The extent of this shift from home to institution is best demonstrated by childbirth. My statistics are from Canada. In 1926, fewer than 1 out of 5 births took place in a hospital. By 1960 it was virtually 100 percent (94.6); see Wendy Mitchinson, *Giving Birth in Canada, 1900–1950* (Toronto: University of Toronto Press, 2002), 173–175.

46 Allison Kirk-Montgomery and Shelly McKellar, *Medicine and Technology in Canada, 1900–1950* (Ottawa: Canada Science and Technology Museum, 2008); Julie Anderson and Carsten Timmermann, eds., *Devices and Designs: Medical Technologies in Historical Perspective* (Basingstoke: Palgrave Macmillan, 2006).

47 See Joel D. Howell, *Technology in the Hospital: Transforming Patient Care in the Early Twentieth Century* (Baltimore, MD: Johns Hopkins University Press, 1995); and Keith Wailoo, *Drawing Blood: Technology and Disease Identity in Twentieth-Century America* (Baltimore, MD: Johns Hopkins University Press, 1997). On digital imaging technologies, see Kelly A. Joyce, *Magnetic Appeal: MRI and the Myth of Transparency* (Ithaca, NY: Cornell University Press, 2008); and Regula Valérie Burri, "Sociotechnical Anatomy: Technology, Space, and Body in the MRI Unit," in *Biomedicine as Culture: Instrumental Practices, Technoscientific Knowledge, and New Modes of Life*, eds. Regula Valérie Burri and Joseph Dumit (New York: Routledge, 2007), 109–121.

48 David Theodore, *Reforming the Hospital: Architecture, Medicine, and Computation, 1960–75*, forthcoming.

49 For a polemical summary, see Sheila Clibbon and Marvin L. Sachs, "Like-Spaces versus Bailiwick Approaches to the Design of Health Care Facilities," *Health Services Research* 5, no. 3 (1970): 172–186.

50 Friesen was a prolific proselytizer. See, for example, Gordon A. Friesen, "The Gospel According to Friesen," *British Hospital Journal and Social Services Review* (November 25, 1966).

51 David Theodore, "'The Fattest Possible Nurse': Architecture, Computers, and Post-War Nursing," in *Daily Life in Hospital: Theory and Practice from the Medieval to the Modern*, eds. Laurinda Abreu and Sally Sheard (Oxford: Peter Lang, 2013), 273–298.

52 Donald Longmore, *Machines in Medicine: The Medical Practice of the Future* (London: Aldus, 1969).

53 Ibid., 5.

54 Charles Süsskind, "The Invention of Computed Tomography," *The History of Technology* 6 (1981): 39–80.

55 On the US, see Joy Knoblauch, "The Work of Diagrams: From Factory to Hospital in Postwar America," *Manifest* 1 (2013): 155–163. On Britain, see Jonathan Hughes, "The 'Matchbox on a Muffin': The Design of Hospitals in the Early NHS Medical History," *Medical History* 44 (2000): 21–56.

56 This agreement was made into transnational policy as well; see, for example, the manual produced for the World Health Organization: Richard Llewelyn-Davies and H.M.C. Macaulay, *Hospital Planning and Administration* (Geneva: World Health Organization, 1966).

57 Douglass, "Health Care: The Fastest Growing Industry," 90.

58 Richard Llewelyn-Davies, "Similarities and Differences in Hospital Design: International Trends," *American Journal of Public Health* 56, no. 10 (1966): 1675–83, at 1675.

59 Ibid., 1678.

60 For an overview and evaluation of these techniques, see Weeks, "*AD* Briefing: Hospitals."

61 Jonathan Hughes, "The Indeterminate Building," in *Non-Plan: Essays on Freedom Participation and Change in Modern Architecture and Urbanism*, eds. Simon Sadler and Jonathan Hughes (New York: Architectural Press, 2000), 90–103.

62 Weeks designed the envelope using computer-oriented parametric design; see David Theodore, "The Forgotten Birth of Parametric Design," *Harvard Design Magazine* 40 (2015): 118–22.

63 John Weeks, "Indeterminate Design," *Transactions of the Bartlett Society* 2 (1963–64): 83–106, at 93.

64 Woodhull was planned around 1970, but did not open until 1977; see "Minimal Shell," *Progressive Architecture* 53 (July 1972): 54–63. The apotheosis of interstitial space was perhaps McMaster University Health Sciences Centre, designed by Craig, Zeidler and Strong, which opened in 1972 in Hamilton near Toronto, Canada. Reyner Banham called it the "ultimate medical megastructure," *Megastructure: Urban Futures of the Recent Past* (London: Thames & Hudson, 1976), 139.

65 See, for example, D. Kirk Hamilton, *Design for Critical Care: Evidence-Based Approach* (Amsterdam: Elsevier/Architectural Press, 2010); and Esther M. Sternberg, *Healing Spaces: The Science of Place and Well-Being* (Cambridge, MA: Belknap Press of Harvard University Press, 2009).

12

Passive and Active: Public Space at the McMaster Health Sciences Centre, 1972

Thomas Strickland

If one just happens to be standing in the massive courtyard at the center of the McMaster Health Sciences Centre (McMaster) surrounded on all sides by concrete and glass, at two in the morning, they will experience the slightest shudder, the lights will dim, the ubiquitous hum of the mechanical system will diminish, and, for a few seconds, an anxious quiet will overcome the vast core of the Brutalist hospital. Then, like an engine turning over, the mechanical noise will return, the lights will come up and the moment of solitude is lost into the workings of the great *machine à guérir*.[1]

Sitting squarely on the south/east corner of McMaster University's verdant lawn and tree-covered campus, the hospital is a striking building indeed. Next to its neighbor, the City Beautiful-inspired suburb of Westdale, the hospital's squat concrete elevations and glittering vertical glass and steel towers are a poignant architectural contrast to the peaked roofs, homey dormer windows and jaunty color palette of the adjacent community conceived in the 1920s.

Articulated by slightly protruding precast-concrete strips, rolled into the building at bottom and top, the hospital's windows peer out of massive concrete boxes, some hovering above and some sitting on the campus's landscape (Figure 12.1). Chunky concrete forms and horizontal runs of windows commingle with fifty-five steel and glass towers that divide the elevations at regular intervals. Clad in glass from top to bottom, the vertical column elements display to the passersby the inner mechanical workings of the of the medical building—its plumbing. Exposing the structure and mechanical system in this way celebrates an innovation known as the "servo-system." Simply put, the system was intended to function like an electrical socket. Hospital components could be unplugged from the servo-system, moved, and plugged in at another location. Equally, future additions could be plugged into the existing system. This innovation, it was imagined, would allow the building to literally reshape itself alongside medical developments and innovation. The "McMaster Experiment," as it was known, embodied the incredible faith placed in scientific discovery and the hope that the medical needs of Canadians could be met through a mix of groundbreaking technologies and architectural solutions.

12.1 Photograph of the south facade of the McMaster Health Sciences Centre designed by Craig, Zeidler and Strong Architects, 1972.
Courtesy of Zeidler Partnership Architects, *Healing the Hospital, McMaster Health Sciences Centre: Its Conception and Evolution*, 132–133.

Built between 1968 and 1972 and designed by the firm of Craig, Zeidler and Strong Architects, it is the technological prowess of the building that has received the most attention by architectural historians and writers.[2] But, at the time of its construction, the building was more than an auspicious medical machine, it was also supposed to be fun. Along with high-tech architectural decisions, open-air courtyards, playrooms, a spectacularly carpeted lobby, and splashes of pop culture iconography were incorporated into the new facility's public areas. It is these spectacular interiors that will come under the microscope, so to speak, in my analysis of what was touted at the time as no less than a revolution in hospital design.[3]

The interior, public spaces of McMaster should be understood in the context of the growth of biomedicine and the implementation of national health insurance in Canada in 1966. Thus, the building's form was in part driven by the need for hospital spaces that would accommodate an estimated threefold increase in patient numbers as well as spatialize the interdisciplinarity of biomedical activities. Incorporating spaces previously unimagined in hospital design—inviting spaces for the public—McMaster anticipates the mall-like qualities of the atrium hospital. And, in so doing, it appeared to make a dramatic break with the spatial hierarchies and hygienic austerity of previous hospital models. Was the development of public space at McMaster, then, an early form of commercial space? Not exactly. Something else was at stake. What did it mean to integrate public spaces in a realm that has traditionally gained power from its separation from the world beyond?[4]

MEDICINE, DESIGN, AND DISCIPLINE

Hospitals' interior spaces provide us with particular insights into how medical practices are organized, animated, and communicated through the built environment. Both historians of medicine and architecture have examined the clusters of rooms, corridors, windows, and furniture that constitute a healthcare environment to explore the quality of medical experience and efficacy of clinical practices. Annmarie Adams, Cynthia Hammond, and Lindsay Prior, for example, have analyzed hospital interiors to reveal how class, gender, age, race, and colonial relations have informed medical practices and hospital design.[5]

Jen Pylypa reminds us:

> *Medicine has objectified our bodies, bringing them under the surveillance of the medical system as objects to be manipulated and controlled. Thus, at the level of ideology, medicine constructs a discourse that defines which bodies, activities, and behaviors are normal.*[6]

A factor of concern, then, for most analyses of hospital interiors is medical surveillance as a mechanism in the medical institution's regulation and disciplining of bodies.[7] The open Nightingale wards of the pavilion hospital type are a clear example of the intensity around patient observation. Influential from the middle of the nineteenth century to the interwar period, open wards were designated rooms for the hospitalization and treatment of the poor, or those who could not afford to pay for healthcare. Within the programmatic organization of the charitable institution gender normative division was strictly adhered to—male and female patients being located in separate wards. This spatial distinction was regulated by design. The station for attending nurses was located at the end of the long narrow ward rooms offering an unobstructed view to all the patients at one time. To access the ward, one was required to pass by the station and attendant through a narrow corridor. Here, a collaboration between nurse and architecture instituted the capacity for medicine to observe and control who entered the ward (to check whether entrants conformed to the gender designation of the ward, for example) as well as oversee all patient activities and physical functions at once.

The open ward is a manifest example of how the built environment is cogent with the habituation of bodies to institutional disciplining and surveillance, what Micheal Foucault has coined "biopower." "According to Foucault," explains Pylypa, "political order is maintained through the production of 'docile bodies'—passive, subjugated, and productive individuals. Through its many institutions—schools, hospitals, prisons, the family—the state brings all aspects of life under its controlling gaze."[8] Foucault explained that over the course of the eighteenth and nineteenth centuries, Western societies witnessed a decrease in physical coercion, or domination of one group over another by threat of physical force, and an increase in self-discipline. This modern conception of power, he asserted, is dispersed throughout society, embedded in institutions and social relations, operating on and through our very bodies. Biopower derives its force from its ability to operate within forms of knowledge production and the desire for knowledge, experiences, and things. In rudimentary terms, individuals and groups assimilate information about cultural norms and practices and act on the desire to match norms. Rather than acting out of fear of physical punishment, this subjugation to power is via the exercise of self-discipline. Importantly, then, biopower is constituted through individuals and groups actively making choices in accordance with their understanding of a given message and/or desire.[9] While the nurse/architecture combination formed the disciplinary techniques on the nineteenth-century hospital ward, individuals, at the time, acquired awareness of symptoms that signaled illness via pamphlets and public lectures disseminated by public health officials. This acquisition of knowledge created a desire to seek medical attention in a hospital.[10]

Although I have presented a distilled version of events, the point to take forward is that the nineteenth century saw a spatial expansion of medicine into everyday life. Chris Philio, who provides a useful spatial reading of *Birth of a Clinic*, posits that the spread of medical practices and institutions across a diversity of sites over the course of the nineteenth century was consistent with what "Foucault described as the 'great dream of dehospitalization of disease and poverty.'" Yet, at the same time, the hospital remained. Reinvented however; its prime purpose was less focused on "directly curing sick people," and was thus more an exclusive site particular to medical learning, research and teaching.[11] Building from what Foucault termed *tertiary spatialization* of medicine, Philio describes the emergence of the nineteenth-century medical landscape as a dual structure. On the one hand, medicine sought a continuous supervision of social space, while on the other creating increasingly antisocial—exclusive—medical spaces.[12] This emergence of a specialist medical gaze focusing on extraordinary cases, as Philio puts it, was concentrated on poor patients who were looked upon more "as sources of data" then unwell individuals hoping to ease an illness.[13] On this development in particular, Foucault offers a poignant critique:

> *To look in order to know, to show in order to teach, is not this a tacit form of violence, all the more abusive for its silence, upon a sick body that demands to be comforted not displayed?*[14]

To optimize the body's capabilities, and thereby its usefulness to the reinvented hospital system, required a complex combination of actors: humans, institutions, and buildings. The open ward of the pavilion hospital typology was a salient example of the disciplinary techniques that, as Pylypa explains, "organize[d] time, space, and daily practices" to create bodies that are habituated to external regulation.[15] Hospital architecture and, in particular, the design of interiors is a crucial factor in the formation of sites that prepare individuals to be patients—passive, and thereby productive bodies—for medical research and teaching.

As one agent in the work of bodily discipline, the built environment has the capacity to communicate subtle messages; harness desires, imply direction, create barriers, and afford or limit views. Kim Dovey explains, "The built environment frames everyday life by offering certain spaces for programmed action, while closing other possibilities."[16] Embedded with information, learned over time and through use, buildings and urban design suggest behaviors. Dovey posits that if we suspect non-conformity to spatial forms will be met by force, we adjust our behavior accordingly.[17] In his book, *Framing Places: Mediating Power in Built Form*, Dovey provides some useful examples, or "frames," for the ways in which disciplinary power operates in the built environment. For the context of this paper, I have condensed his in-depth analysis and explanations here, providing three "frames" that will be valuable to my analysis of McMaster. "Seduction" appeals to a subject's interests and desires. It is a form of what Dovey describes as "power over," and appeals to one's self-identity. Based in the urge to social and cultural conformity, seduction is connected to how one conceives of oneself in relation to others in a given context, a given place. "Authority" is integrated and embedded in societies' institutional structures—state, corporation, family, etc. This is a very pervasive and stable form of power, which rests on a foundation of legitimacy.[18] "We recognize authority as legitimate because it is seen to serve a larger interest; in the case of the state, this is the public interest."[19] Architecture and urban design often integrate symbols and ritual spaces for making authority visible, monuments being a key example. As Dovey explains, "the nation-state is invisible and its authority would evaporate without the imagery of legitimacy."[20] Authority is particularly significant to the realm of healthcare; clinical practice in particular is replete with symbols of authority; the stethoscope, for example, legitimizes the authority of the medical practitioner in the workings of the heart.[21] Finally, "coercion." This form of "power over" can be understood as the threat of force, or the fear of physical harm if one does not comply with prearranged or implied terms of behavior. But coercion can also operate in more subtle ways in the built environment. Exaggerated scale of buildings or monuments, for example, can belittle a subject. Another form of coercion in the built environment is manipulation; wherein the intentions of a group or individual are hidden, thereby making resistance difficult. A subject can be "framed" in a context that appears to offer freedom of choice—a shopping mall, for example.[22]

While it is helpful to make distinctions amongst the different ways built environments survey and control, most buildings and urban places are a combination of seduction, authority, and coercion.[23] In this sense Dovey tells us that "while spatial coercion may be clear in intentional terms, in practice there is no clear line between necessary and problematic forms of spatial order."[24] Exploring the exercise of power in the built environment is a slippery project, it is ever changing. The ability to imagine, construct, and inhabit a house, make a room of one's own, or appropriate a space in the city, for example, are all valuable exercises in empowerment. Equally, physical and symbolic boundaries and learned behaviors can be powerful sites of resistant to repressive spatial regimes. "Humans do not live, by words alone," notes Henri Lefebvre, "all 'subjects' are situated in a space in which they must either recognize themselves or lose themselves, a space which they may both enjoy and modify."[25] Of the various socio-spatial formations and potentialities through which to explore the exercise of power, the hospital is conceivably second only to the prison in its overt use of design to strip subjects of identity and choice. The contribution of this paper, then, is to explore the concrete example of the McMaster Health Science Center to reveal how rooms, corridors, the arrangement of views within hospitals, and even color choices contribute to the creation of docile bodies, and to examine how, in one of the most important hospital designs of the twentieth century, the architectural work of subjugation operates differently in accordance with patient classification.

BETWEEN A TOWER AND A MALL

McMaster is an important development in both Canada and the world, falling in the interstice between two significant hospital typologies: the tower hospital (1920s to the 1950s) and the atrium hospital (1980s to the present). Each has its associations with broad categories within architectural history; the atrium hospital is linked to postmodernism, visible in the witty references to classical architecture,[26] whereas the tower hospital with its smooth surfaces and horizontal ribbons of windows along the elevation reveals the influence of International-Style Modernism on hospital design.[27]

12.2 Photograph of the entrance hall at the Montreal General Hospital designed by McDougall, Smith and Fleming Architects, c. 1955. Photo by Rapid Grip and Batten. Source: "The Montreal General Hospital," *The RAIC Journal* 32, no. 9 (1955): 317. Courtesy of Royal Architectural Institute of Canada.

The tower hospital focused on efficiencies and organized hospital activities and movements around a central elevator core. This vertical circulation system was an important way to control patient movement and define separate zones of activity. In-patient wards were generally located in the tower, while administration, technical activities, and out-patient services were located in the lower levels of the building. According to Jonathon Hughes, the landmark Lever House office building, located in Midtown Manhattan and designed by the architectural firm Skidmore Owens and Merrill (1952), is the prototypical example for this hospital scheme. This formal, and to some extent functional, link is demonstrative of hospital architects' involvement with the symbols, spatial aims, and practical expressions of modernity.[28]

Once inside a tower hospital, visitors found themselves in a hygienic, marble-clad, cathedral-like lobby. A good example of the tower hospital in Canada is the Montreal General Hospital (MGH) designed by McDougall, Smith and Fleming Architects and opened in 1955 (Figure 12.2). Here, as was common for this hospital typology, the hospital's crest fronted an internal balcony, which looked down upon the patients. Visitors were also confronted with a reception desk that controlled access to the elevators and the hospital beyond. The lobby's spatial and material qualities suggest that there was little, if any, place for patients and visitors. Instead, the space was filled with symbols of institutional power and medical authority. I have included an image of the MGH to provide a concrete example of the tower typology, and a visual that will help to make clear the remarkable changes from the lobby space of this type to the public spaces of McMaster.

Antecedent to the discussion of McMaster, a short description of its successor, the atrium hospital, is in order. Associated with what David Sloane and Beverlie Conant Sloane term "Mall Medicine," the entrance areas of this late twentieth-century hospital typology are filled with tables, seating, plants, and fast-food outlets.[29] Its lobbies are brightly colored and surrounded on all sides by signs of activity, in the lobby of atrium hospital the presence of people is emphasized over the trappings of medical authority. In fact, in most examples of this typology there are few signs of the hospital anywhere, at least not in the lobby. There are, however, signs of another kind of space—the mall. Sloane and Conant Sloane point out that by the 1960s hospitals had come to represent bureaucratic authority and appeared as giant impersonal monoliths that were more invested in science than people and thereby isolated from the community.[30] In the 1980s, in response to an increasingly negative attitude toward the healthcare institution, hospital administrators and architects sought to offer comfort in the face of illness by creating internal public spaces designed to evoke the ubiquitous shopping mall.[31] I use the term "public space" to describe such mall-like settings in hospitals, as that is how they are referred to in the literature, but it is also the tension between notions of public and commercial space that insists upon analysis.

Before moving onto McMaster's interiors, I will introduce a final yet significant development occurring within the realm of the medical institution, a development that would directly influence the formation of McMaster. Prior to the 1950s, scientific research and hospital medicine developed along two parallel yet complementary streams. Scientists worked in laboratories on biological discoveries, for example, while doctors worked in hospitals on healing patients. Since World War II, a primary development in the hospital has been to effect, as Allan Brandt and David Sloane note, a smooth transition between leading-edge research and the patient.[32] Peter Keating and Alberto Cambrosio have described this model of healthcare activities as translational research, a two-way transfer between the laboratory and the bedside. This is an approach to research and therapy that focuses on a one-to-one relationship with the patient, where a patient's blood sample for example, taken at the bedside, is tested at an in-hospital diagnostic laboratory and from these tests an outcome is determined that is then used in patient therapy. Translational research was convergent with the successful application of biological science to medicine, or the merger of biology and medicine into the activity known as biomedicine. Biomedicine, simply put, means bringing laboratory research (the hard sciences, in particular the biological sciences) and clinical practice (hospital medicine) together on the same problem—ultimately to put these practices together in the same building.[33] The need to put these aspects together motivated the search to find a different way to organize medical space. This, in principal, is the turn from the hospital to the health sciences center.

DESIGNING FOR PASSIVE AND ACTIVE PATIENTS

McMaster's conception as an institution was driven by Dr. Harry Thode. University President from 1961 to 1972, Thode's skill as a scientist and his capacity to organize complex research projects were honed during his work with the Canadian arm of the Manhattan Project (the organization that created the atomic bomb). This experience and unwavering dedication to scientific advance was manifest in McMaster University's acquisition of a nuclear reactor in 1959, the first on a Canadian university campus, and later it was Thode's vision that would see the creation of a novel approach to medical education, research and treatment, Canada's first health sciences center. Thode's belief, like many of his contemporaries and predecessors, doctors and architects, was that avant-garde design and architecture was the linchpin for medical ingenuity and the architecture of McMaster was a spatial experiment in new modes of organization.[34] It was the first purpose-built medical facility in the world to attempt through design to organize biological research, medical education, and clinical practice into a collective identity—in short, to spatialize medical interdisciplinarity. The specifics of how the interdisciplinary relationship between the biological sciences and clinical medicine evolved spatially is a complex ongoing debate that exceeds this text. What can be broadly stated is that between the late 1960s and the early 1970s, professionals in medicine and science—like those in city planning, architecture, and the visual arts—challenged vertically organized hierarchies, seeking instead new modes and forms for the exchange of ideas, information, and representation. Knowledge creation, it was thought, happens along a horizontal datum.[35]

At the bottom of Figure 12.3 is a section through McMaster running from the campus entrance on the left of the drawing to the public entrance on the right. What is first evident in this drawing is how long and flat the building is and how the structural, or servo-system, is clearly celebrated by the careful rendering of the trusses. Another notable feature of the design we can see in this drawing is that there are no distinct in-patient towers. Instead, the in-patient wards are integrated into this great platform. Research laboratories are situated directly north, or to the left, of the in-patient wards on the same floor. This spatial proximity offers relatively direct communication between patients and researchers. Here the close proximity of a patient to their component body parts (blood samples, for example) in the laboratory, when compared to the spatial scheme where a patient tower was located atop of a diagnostic platform (tower hospital), points to the intensification of the specialist medical gaze; the emphasis on patient as research material. I will return to this point in a moment.

The extent to which the patient had become cogent with the structure of medical research and education in the health science center is further emphasized when considering the location of the facilities teaching areas. Not visible in this section are four short elevator cores, which provide vertical circulation between patient floors and the floor below where the lecture theatre, the student and physicians' library, classrooms, surgical suites, and radiology department were located. On the plan drawing above, it is possible to see the four elevator cores located at the corners of an uneven square of varied dashed lines. Connecting the floors via elevator meant that transferring post-surgery patients back to their room was along a short, reasonably direct route. While the elevator was for moving supine bodies, a telling detail on the section drawing emphasizes a different mode of circulation: walking. On the bottom right corner of this drawing is a scale which, while measuring the building in linear feet, also measures it in accordance with the amount of time it takes to walk

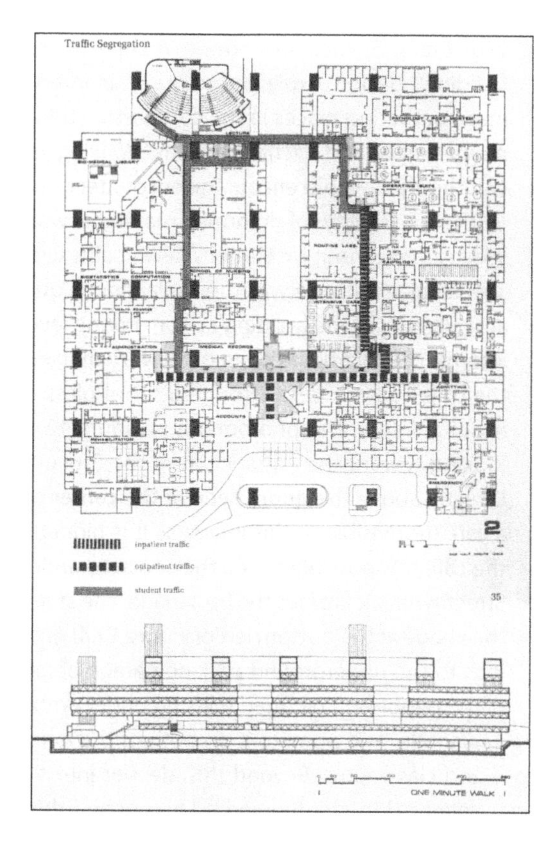

12.3 (Top) Plan drawing showing segregation of in-patient, out-patient, and student traffic at the McMaster Health Sciences Centre designed by Craig, Zeidler and Strong Architects, 1972. (Bottom) Drawing of a typical east/west section through the McMaster Health Sciences Centre designed by Craig, Zeidler and Strong Architects, 1972. Both images Courtesy of Zeidler Partnership Architects, *Healing the Hospital, McMaster Health Sciences Centre: Its Conception and Evolution*, 35 and 33 respectively.

the building. At McMaster, space was measured through the walking body in time—the mobile, ambulatory body.

This fact points to an integral component of the design: the Ring Street. The Ring Street was a critical pathway, which served to link all of the hospital's various medical, educational, and research activities. In the plan drawing at the top of Figure 12.3, the Ring Street is delineated by the previously noted uneven square. The circulatory combination of elevator and ring street was intended to foster exchange among disciplines. On this concept, William Spaulding, a doctor who was a key liaison between the university planning committee and the architects, explained: "Interdisciplinary activity called for close working relationships between surgeons, radiologists, clinicians, and basic scientists, locat[ing] many disciplines on each huge floor, permit[s] formal and informal contacts to take place easily.[36] Interdisciplinary exchange, as Spaulding noted, depended, in part, on the informal meeting, and the Ring Street was designed to afford just such an encounter. As Don Vetere, who was an intern

12.4 Photograph of the Esplanade at the McMaster Health Sciences Centre designed by Craig, Zeidler and Strong Architects, 1972. Courtesy of Zeidler Partnership Architects, *Healing the Hospital, McMaster Health Sciences Centre: Its Conception and Evolution*, 45.

with Craig, Zeidler and Strong Architects at the time of the building's design, explained to me in an interview, "We tried to make gathering places in the corridors . . . because that's where people meet and exchange ideas." Walking the Ring Street, it was thought, would encourage encounters.

The possibility of informal meetings was occasioned by spaces throughout McMaster's new health sciences center. One spectacular instance was the Esplanade (Figure 12.4). Situated at the center of the building on the ground level, one end of this internal courtyard was open to the verdant campus lawns, while the other gave access through a set of glass doors to the vast hospital lobby. The photograph in Figure 12.4 has been taken looking toward the entrance from the Esplanade to the lobby. Directly above the doors, seen at the center of this image, was a café (not visible in this image as it is hidden by trees). Above the café it is possible to see the concrete underside of the Ring Street where it crosses the Esplanade. The steel railing (entering the image at the bottom left of Figure 12.4) guarded large openings to the underground parking garage below. All around the plaza, people are pictured relaxing under umbrellas.

Surrounding the Esplanade, and open to it on both of the long sides, were staff and student lounges and classrooms. Beyond this, deeper into the building, were teaching laboratories, followed by the biomedical library and the animal quarters. Linking these medical and teaching activities to a space for relaxation suggests the importance of informal exchange in the design of the facility and the institutional program. What the Esplanade signals above all, however, is the introduction of public space—or space linked to but not specifically intended for medical activities—into the hospital. The Ring Street, while intended to inspire informality, was definitely a medical space. The Esplanade, on the other hand, was directed to the use of medical students, but also other university students, doctors, patients, and visitors. It tended more towards leisure than work or medicine.

As the definitive, vital core of McMaster, the Esplanade was imagined as an active, *urban* space. From the extensive, 24,000-square-foot (2,230-square-meter) rectangular plaza, the courtyard space rose up past the windows of laboratories, doctors' offices, meeting rooms, neo-natal care, and finally the out-patient units before it opened directly to the sky. The Ring Street crossed through this massive volume, at the second, third, and fourth levels, giving views onto the Esplanade below, and deeper, through openings in the plaza, to the parking underground. Combined with the cafés, trees, umbrellas, and people at the plaza level, the whole space created an ocular and spatial phantasm of the urban. The street/plaza, idealized as the ultimate generator of social exchange, was manifested here inside a hospital.

The idea of the internal urban plaza or street had appeared in the designs of Canadian architects by the middle of the 1960s. John Andrews' Brutalist concrete Scarborough College building for the University of Toronto, which received international acclaim, was organized around wide, street-like hallways that intersected at an internal plaza called "The Meeting Place."[37] Before the Andrews Building, as it is now known, the internal street had already begun to receive significant attention in the architectural press by the mid-1950s through the work of architects such as Team 10 and Aldo and Minnie van Eyck. These internal streets, as historian Hashim Sarkis explains, were a reaction against the rationalist planning of the functionalist city and its segregated activities. Marked by a rough-and-ready quality, they were "playable" places for action, to be worked on and in, not to be held precious or revered. With the internal street, architects sought to merge the urban and building to create, according to Sarkis, "setting for daily life."[38]

Perhaps the most exceptional example of the integration of the urban street into hospital design was Hermann Field's proposal for the Tufts-New England Medical Center. The Director of the institution's Planning Office presented a paper at the Ontario Hospital Services Commission's Programming and Planning Conference, during which the architect wondered if it was possible to "find the middle ground between hugeness and humanizing needs."[39] Continuing on this paradoxical line of reasoning, he pronounced that in the institutional and physical realms of healthcare, "maximum utilization suggests a massive concentration of facilities, hardware, and specialists for most efficient processing. Increasingly however, the urbanized human being is looking for identity, a sense of place, of compatible scale, of psychological support in sickness."[40] Presented during his talk, and later in the November 1967 issue of *Canadian Hospital*, the architect's design for a hospital in downtown Boston imagined open-air courtyards, public recreational facilities, and no less then an actual city street running right through the middle of the building's bulky horizontal frame. "The hospital," he stressed, "should open out to the neighborhood and become a focal point of activity of mutual benefit to the healthy and the sick." The Tufts-New England Medical Center was not built as proposed by Field, but in his discussion and design proposal there is an echo of Foucault's notion of the *tertiary spatialization* of medicine.[41] Simply, this is the expansion of medicine into everyday life, while at the same time the hospital is reinvented as a site for increasingly anti-social research activities.

Collateral to the growth of biomedicine, the twentieth century would see the focus of the medical gaze shift. Historian David Armstrong explains that "the medical gaze, which for over a century analyzed the microscopic detail of the individual body, began to move to the undifferentiated space between bodies and there proceeded to form a new political anatomy."[42] More broadly stated, clinical science began to compare sick individuals to other patients and the healthy population, measuring the difference between them. This would see arguments for the practice of clinical science to be collective in its outlook, rather than focusing on the individual.[43] What this meant for the normal population, the "healthy" so to speak, is that they would be increasingly visible to a more general, non-specialized medical gaze. In Canada, evidence of this diffuse medical gaze appeared in documents produced by the Royal Commission on Health Services (RCHS, 1964) as an expressed desire for a broadening of available research material. Simply put, the RCHS proposed that more and differentiated bodies were needed for research purposes.[44] Preceding the implementation of national health insurance by two years, it is argued that the RCHS helped to convince doctors, previously resistant to Medicare, to shift their opinion about the taxpayer-funded model.[45] Importantly, this fundamental broadening of medical research and treatment occurred simultaneously to the growth of more specialized practices and diagnostic techniques.[46] What I am homing in on here is the possibility of observing at McMaster an example of how the dual structure of the medical landscape, described by Philio, has been organized by design. "It would be fascinating," wonders Philio, "to consider the extent to which this double social and medical geography described by Foucault still pervades late-twentieth century Western Society. I would suggest that in all sorts of ways it does."[47]

Returning to McMaster, we recall that the Esplanade alluded to an ideal of urban rhythm. "The cafeterias and the staff lounges border the Esplanade," explained the building's architect Eberhard Zeidler, "and have been drawn into this focal area to create a meeting space full of life."[48] The Ring Street, like the Esplanade, was equally designed to engage with an active, mobile body. This is an important point because the design of building also signaled a clear distinction between spaces for active subjects and spaces for passive bodies. The interior spaces of the McMaster manifested two categories of patient: active and passive, ambulatory and non-ambulatory, or, as they were commonly termed, out-patient and in-patient. This distinction was widely and publicly acknowledged by doctors, the Ontario Government, and the architects involved in the design of McMaster. Describing the three main types of activities that factored into the organization of the design, Vetere explained, "The place was all about three things, research, in-patients, and out-patients."[49] The building's interior, its furnishing and fittings, reveals profound differences between the in-patient and out-patient areas regarding the hospital's approach to generosity of space, freedom of movement, and visual experience.

Looking to Figure 12.5, in-patients' rooms, observing strict hygienic practices, were stark and simple with few furnishings beyond the bed. A wide pane of glass created a separation between patient rooms and nursing stations, but at the same time ensured visual contact between patient and nursing staff at all times. Vetere told me that this intense surveillance was extremely controversial—but the expected critical condition

12.5 Photograph of an in-patient ward looking from the nursing station to the patient rooms, at the McMaster Health Sciences Centre designed by Craig, Zeidler and Strong Architects, 1972. Courtesy of Zeidler Partnership Architects, *Healing the Hospital, McMaster Health Sciences Centre: Its Conception and Evolution*, 65.

of the patient was argued as justification for the design.[50] Here the position of the patient as incapacitated by illness, and thus without the capacity to support themselves, situates the individual completely at the behest of the hospital; its doctors, nursing staff, researchers, and students. The visibility of the patient serves to control and protect patients at once, marking the special condition of the in-patient as passive.

The practice of subjugating patients to the medical authority of the hospital at McMaster is also reflected in the ways that the hospital organized physical movement to and from the in-patient wards. Returning to Figure 12.3, a legend at the bottom left of the drawing indicates how different types of traffic were meant to be separated. While the Ring Street was designed for exchange, it was also designed to segregate in-patients from out-patients. In this way the building's traffic flow was planned to distinguish between patient classes. Describing this arrangement in the facility's design, Zeidler explains: "In-patient traffic should not conflict with out-patient, a separate corridor leads directly from the in-patient to all services, and separate in-patient elevators are provided to maintain this segregation."[51] Separating in-patients and out-patients was doubtless to prevent the movement of illness between the patient types and sustain the hygienic requirements of in-patient spaces. At the same time, the separation further marks the in-patient's body as docile, in this case compliant and vulnerable in the face of contamination from the outside world.

The drawing in Figure 12.6 is a fragment of a larger floor plan of the building. It shows a pediatrics cluster, or "clinical investigation unit" as they were called, on level 3. Similar

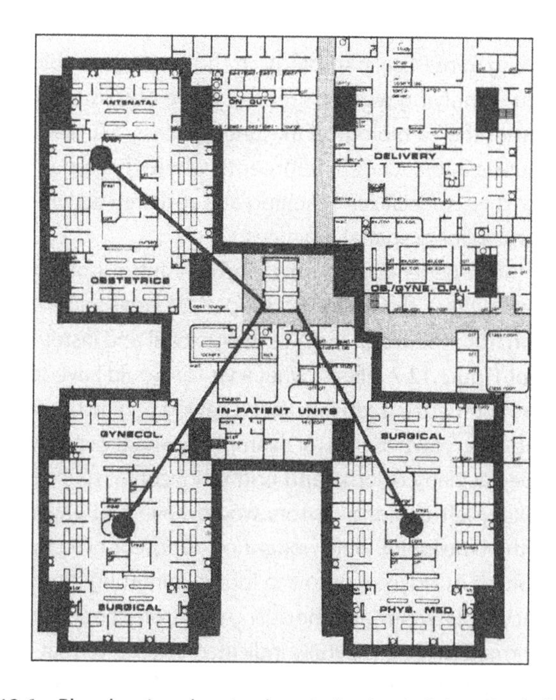

12.6 Plan drawing showing hospital unit administrative hub. The thick black lines indicating the spaces that constitute a unit were drawn by the architects, Craig, Zeidler and Strong Architects, as part of the original drawing. Courtesy of Zeidler Partnership Architects, *Healing the Hospital, McMaster Health Sciences Centre: Its Conception and Evolution*, 55.

clusters were arranged at each of the building's south corners on levels 2, 3, and 4. There are two primary forms of control designed into the clusters. First, as previously noted, direct observation on the wards was created through the relationship between the nurses' station, the glass wall, and the patient room. The second is control of movement to and from the ward. Examining this plan, we can see that there are three patient wards in the cluster. In each ward, patient rooms are located around the outside edges and the nurses' station and offices are at the center. At the center of the cluster of wards (where the lines on the drawing converge) is the elevator core. Directly below the elevator in this image is the administrative hub.

In this arrangement, there is only one way to access the ward: through the narrow passage leading left, away from the bottom of the elevator core and passing through to the entrance toward the obstetrics ward. Each cluster is a small territory, almost an annex to the building, emphasizing in-patients' isolation from the general hospital population. As in the nineteenth-century pavilion hospital, no one can access the ward without passing the nursing staff. While the rest of the facility was planned to be open, to inspire exchange, seize the possibilities of the unexpected, this revolutionary potential stopped where sickness began. Perhaps this is best emphasized by the fact that the Ring Street stops well short of the entrance to the wards. What is possible to see in this arrangement is that the medical program, the spatial and disciplinary technology of the ward, has not changed in over a hundred years of hospital design. What this suggests is that a much older hospital was secreted away inside a brand new form. In these clusters, a patient's illness, their pathology, supersedes their individual identity. On closer look, we see that wards are designated according to medical pathology, in this case the problematic pathologization of childbirth—implying women's reproductive bodies are a product of medical knowledge rather than a biological (natural) process.[52] Tucked away in this new hospital were exclusive anti-social environments, where the in-patient was the focus of increasingly intrusive, specialized teaching and research activities, fortified by an intensification of disciplinary spatial practices.

If the design of the in-patient clusters focused on control, isolation, and exclusivity to produce a passive subject, the design of out-patient areas eschewed notions of privacy and separation from the world outside the hospital and instead implied that visitors were in control. Figure 12.7 reflects what a visitor would have seen when arriving through McMaster's southern (street) entrance. Leaving behind the dark, underground parking or stepping off a crowded bus, for example, hospital visitors would have found themselves in a spectacularly colorful and bright horizontal space that spread out in all directions. Looking left or right, visitors would have had an unobstructed view along the full length of the lobby, which extended hundreds of feet in either direction. All major public functions opened onto the lobby: admitting area, concessions, and shops, the pharmacy, a playroom, and more. Forward from the entrance and slightly to the left was an information kiosk playfully indicated in large-format letters.

In his book *Healing the Hospital, McMaster Health Sciences Centre: Its Conception and Evolution* (1974), Zeidler refers to numerous studies on the psychological effect of hospital interiors and draws much from the historians Kevin Lynch and E.T. Hall to introduce the ways architecture encourages or discourages specific responses

12.7 Photograph of the concourse (lobby) at the McMaster Health Sciences Centre designed by Craig, Zeidler and Strong Architects, 1972. Courtesy of Zeidler Partnership Architects, *Healing the Hospital, McMaster Health Sciences Centre: Its Conception and Evolution*, 47.

from its users.[53] "Orientation (disclosure of visual aim) and visual diversion must be combined," explained the architect; "if you plan a large complex, these emotional requirements must be combined."[54] It is clear the architect was interested in the role design could play in conveying messages and spatial intentions befitting a medicinal environment. What is of particular note is that Zeidler believed emotions could be manifested through carefully designed visual experiences, which could encourage or discourage certain behaviors.

With this in mind, I return to the analysis of the lobby. The lobby was designed and organized to send the message that healthcare services were easy to find and thereby accessible. It was a place in which the visitor was offered the illusion of power by suggesting, through design, freedom of choice, or at least the appearance of choice. "From the centre of the foyer," exclaimed the architect, "the total organization of the complex can be comprehended visually."[55] To propose complete comprehension of an architectural space is to imply one is provided with enough knowledge of the environs to choose one's own pathway through it. A particularly powerful component of this message was the relationship between the lobby and the Esplanade (Figure 12.7). From the hospital entrance, strong linear elements on the floor and ceiling drew the visitor's gaze across the lobby to the bright, sunlight atrium directly opposite. On the other side of the lobby, a generous stairway invited visitors to join others in the Esplanade below, not in an area of sickness but in one of active urban life. The arrangement of the Esplanade, stairs and lobby suggests a new subject position for the out-patient. For an instant, at the top of the stairs, the visitor had visual and physical access to a multiplicity of spaces, and thus was occupying a position usually reserved for insiders.

The text on the information kiosk and the lobby's spectacular colors were part of a vast system of graphics deployed throughout the public spaces for decorative and didactic purposes. At important intersections, for example, life-size murals of teenagers "hanging out" were used to add color to the walls, but also to distinguish between the out-patient and in-patient areas. Zeidler described McMaster's design as "a total environment" whose wayfinding system would turn "outsiders," as he called them, into "insiders" capable of navigatng the complex maze of the building.[56] To appeal to visitors' knowledge of urban spaces, the building's designers mobilized a palette of popular-culture colors and aesthetics, and signs of urbane leisure throughout McMaster's public spaces; that is to say, out-patient spaces, where sending a message of access, or at least the illusion of access, was paramount. The multiple perspectives, as well as the visual and spatial invitations into the depth of the hospital, broke with the tradition of hospital lobbies as austere celebrations of institutional benefactors and inverted the containment and severity of McMaster's predecessor: the tower hospital. The tradition of limiting movement and surrounding visitors with symbols and signs of medical authority—the trappings of an exclusive and privileged domain—were cast off in McMaster's public spaces.

Yet this was a pseudo-public space as it claimed the expressions of the urban space without the difficulties. There was no poverty and no crime, for example, but, significantly, there was no sickness, or at least the building was designed to foil the presence of illness. Not everyone had equal access to the position of privilege at the top of the stairs. For wheelchair users, the top of the stairs was as far as the design allowed them to go. To take advantage of the urbane experience on the Esplanade, they would have to find the elevator at the very far end of the lobby—past the accounting and medical records departments. Once on the correct level, they would have to then find their way through the cafeteria to the Esplanade. This subtle exclusion from McMaster's public spaces is a cogent example of how "regimes of 'normalization,' potentially disruptive to the designed effect," as Dovey explains, "are recognized and evicted."[57] In a hospital, ignoring the everyday fact of wheelchair mobility, while privileging "normatively" abled bodies, seems an act of refusal and, by default, an eviction.

Yet there was more at stake in the design of public space at McMaster then keeping illness out. While the in-patient areas perpetuated the role of the patient as passive, the public, or out-patient, spaces promoted active patients. In McMaster's public spaces, control was not so much manifest through surveillance, but rather the design appealed to patients' desire for a new, more positive healthcare experience. Utilizing a series of visual cues, wayfinding devices, and directional and spatial options, the public spaces set the stage for visitors to direct their own way through the healthcare experience. Visitors were offered the illusion of being an insider, yet the experience was limited, or managed, by a carefully structured and designed environment. By alluding to a world beyond the walls of the institution, to stimulating sights, action, and movement, the Esplanade harnessed urban ambience, generating a curious double social and medical geography. In these terms, the Esplanade and the lobby proposed a coupling of the illusion of fluid urban encounters with the controls of interior design, a landscape that was both social and medical at once. By adapting the hospital to social and cultural desires, McMaster's public spaces can be understood as maintaining medical authority through subtle coercion; ultimately the production of subjugated and productive individuals. Unlike the in-patient wards, however, the public spaces required the user to actively participate, to act on and through the hospital as though it was public space—the world beyond the hospital.

CONCLUSION

In this examination of public spaces at McMaster, I have explored how the design played a role in signaling which areas of the new facility were designated for the in-patient, or passive patient, and those for the out-patient, or active patient. While the notion of active patient should be, in practice, a contradiction of purpose, it has been possible to see how the built environment was harnessed to mollify the disagreement. The built environment, then, can be a useful tool for understanding the complex workings of medical practices and intentions that would not otherwise be obvious.

What I propose in this reading of McMaster is that the formation of the health sciences center saw an intensification of design related to the work of producing docile bodies. I have suggested that this was part of an increasing integration of laboratory and clinic work and that the specialized work of this interdisciplinarity required increasingly tractable bodies. However, there are other possible factors for this significant investment in disciplinary design, which I have not explored but would provide value insights. For example, did the form of the ward clusters mean nursing staff had less distance to travel on regular rounds? And, if so, were fewer staff required per patient, or more? Was it equally a labor-related development? At the same time, my exploration of McMaster's public spaces reveals how the building design was complicit in fostering the active patient. In this way, I propose, McMaster, in terms of its medical and design intentions, foreshadowed the current consumerist patient.[58] Importantly, the agency implied by the design of the public spaces, wherein the design appealed to the desire for the hospital to be other than what it is and where the outsider was seemingly provided with insider knowledge, was a form of manipulation.

McMaster was one twentieth-century example of what Philio has deemed the dual structure of the medical landscape, a site of increasingly anti-social and isolated medical activities while at the same time creating new ways for social space and medical surveillance to interact—a medical and social geography at once. The public spaces of McMaster were planned to be the antithesis to the exclusivity and authority of medicine. Yet the design of the lobby and Esplanade reveal that, despite this change, the medical institution maintained its authority, but on new terms and by new means of spatial engagement. By no means was it planned that the "active" out-patient or visitor to McMaster be given access to the inner workings of the hospital—the forbidden depths of medical knowledge. Passage through to the inner sanctum was afforded only to the ostensibly "passive" in-patient, whose identity and body were subjected to nineteenth-century institutional authority. McMaster's informality stopped where sickness began.

NOTES

1 Michel Foucault, *Power: The Essential Works of Michel Foucault, 1954–1984, Volume 3*, ed. James Faubion (New York: New Press, 2000), 103–104. *Machines* à *guérir*, or curing machines, is a term used by Foucault to describe a combination of trends associated with the development of the modern hospital in France during the eighteenth and nineteenth centuries which form not just a private or public medicine, but a whole "curing machine" in which security, population, and information are intertwined. "The hospital," explained Foucault, "must function as a 'curing machine.' First, in a negative way: all the factors that make the hospital dangerous for its occupants must be suppressed . . . Second, in a positive way, the space of the hospital must be organized according to a concerted therapeutic strategy, through the uninterrupted presence and hierarchical prerogatives of doctors, through systems of observation, notation, and record-taking. These make it possible to . . . globalize the data that bear on the long-term life of a whole population."

2 Reyner Banham, *Megastructures: Urban Futures of the Recent Past* (London: Thames & Hudson, 1976), 59.

3 Eberhard Zeidler, *Healing the Hospital, McMaster Health Sciences Centre: Its Conception and Evolution* (Toronto: Zeidler Partnership, 1974), 58.

4 Annmarie Adams and Thomas Schilch, "Design for Control: Surgery, Science, and Space at the Royal Victoria Hospital, Montreal, 1893–1956," *Medical History* 50 (2006): 303–324.

5 Annmarie Adams, *Medicine by Design: The Architect and the Modern Hospital, 1893–1943* (Minneapolis: University of Minnesota Press, 2008). See also: Grace Goldin and John D. Thompson, *The Hospital: A Social and Architectural History* (New Haven, CT: Yale University Press, 1975); Cynthia I. Hammond, "Reforming Architecture, Defending Empire: Florence Nightingale and the Pavilion Hospital," *Studies in the Social Sciences: (Un)healthy Interiors: Contestations at the Intersection of Public Health and Private Space* 37 (2005): 1–24; Lindsay Prior, "The Architecture of the Hospital: A Study of Spatial Organization and Medical Knowledge," *The Journal of British Sociology* 39 (1988): 86–111.

6 Jen Pylypa, "Power and Bodily Practice: Applying the Work of Foucault to an Anthropology of the Body," *Arizona Anthropologist* (1998): 30.

7 Hammond, "Reforming Architecture." See also: Thomas A Markus, *Buildings and Power: Freedom and Control in the Origin of Modern Building Types* (New York: Routledge, 1993); David Charles Sloane, "Scientific Paragon to Hospital Mall: The Evolving Design of the Hospital, 1885–1994," *Journal of Architectural Education* 48 (1994): 82–98.

8 Pylypa, "Power and Bodily Practice," 22.

9 Ibid., 21.

10 Tina Young Choi, "Writing the Victorian City: Discourses of Risk, Connection, and Inevitability," *Victorian Studies* 43 (2001): 561–589.

11 Chris Philio, "The Birth of the Clinic: An Unknown Work of Medical Geography," *Area* 32 (2001): 17.

12 David Armstrong, *Political Anatomy of the Body: Medical Knowledge in Britain in the Twentieth Century* (Cambridge: Cambridge University Press, 1983), 48. See also: Philio, "The Birth of the Clinic," 17.

13 Philio, "The Birth of the Clinic," 17.

14 Foucault, *The Birth of the Clinic* (New York: Routledge, 2003), 84.

15 Pylypa, "Power and Bodily Practice," 23. See also Philio, "The Birth of the Clinic," 16.

16 Kim Dovey, *Framing Places: Mediating Power In Built Form* (New York: Routledge, 1999), 11.

17 Ibid., 12. It is important to note that Dovey is careful to note in his text that the "we" he is referring to is limited to the response one has to the threat of force. Beyond this, messages embedded in the built environment are, by and large, very much situated knowledge and conditional on experience of culture, class, gender, race, and nationality, for example. For a more in-depth explanation see Dovey, *Framing Places,* 9–28.

18 Ibid. See also Hannah Arendt, "Communicative Power," in *Power,* ed. S. Lukes (Oxford: Blackwell, 1986), 65. The use of term "frame" is deployed in the context of this text to provide kind of device that permits a relatively concise link between Dovey's description of types of power and my analysis of McMaster's public spaces. The term "frames" is borrowed from the title of Dovey's book, *Framing Places: Mediating Power In Built Form.*

19 Ibid.

20 Ibid., 11.

21 Marc R. Cohen, and Audrey Shafer, "Images and Healers: A Visual History of Scientific Medicine," in *Cultural Studies: Medicine and Media*, ed. Lester D. Friedman (Durham, NC: Duke University Press, 2004), 199–214.

22 Dovey, *Framing Places*, 11.

23 Ibib., 12.

24 Ibid., 11.

25 Henri Lefebvre, *The Production of Space*, trans. Donald Nicholson-Smith (Oxford: Blackwell, 1991), 21.

26 Annmarie Adams et al., "Kids in The Atrium: Comparing Architectural Intentions and Children's Experiences in a Pediatric Hospital Lobby," *Social Science and Medicine* 70 (2010): 656.

27 Jonathan Hughes, "The 'Matchbox on a Muffin': The Design of Hospitals in the Early NHS," *Medical History* 44 (2000): 28–29.

28 Ibid., 53–55.

29 David Charles Sloane and Beverlie Conant Sloane, *Medicine Moves to the Mall* (Baltimore, MD: Johns Hopkins University Press, 2003).

30 Ibid., 88–89; Zeidler, *Healing the Hospital*, 29, 63. Eberhard Zeidler, the architect of McMaster also expresses the largely negative attitude toward the hospital experience as a reason for re-thinking the hospital's interior design. See also Allan M. Brandt and David C. Sloane, "Of Beds and Benches: Building the Modern American Hospital," in *The Architecture of Science*, eds. Peter Galison and Emily Thompson (Cambridge, MA: MIT Press, 1999), 294.

31 See also Adams et al., "Kids in The Atrium," 658.

32 Brandt and Sloane, "Of Beds and Benches," 282–285.

33 Peter Keating and Alberto Cambrosio, *Biomedical Platforms: Realigning the Normal and the Pathological in the Late Twentieth-Century Medicine* (Cambridge, MA: MIT Press, 2003), 36; Hughes, "Matchbox on a Muffin," 28.

34 Associated Hospitals of Alberta, Submission, 18. See also Dr. Harry G. Thode, Confidential letter to George Gilmour, March 14, 1956, McMaster University Libraries, Office of the President, Dr. H.G. Thode Fonds, William Ready Division of Archives and Research Collections; David Coburn, "Canadian Medicine: Dominance or Proletarianization?" *The Millbank Quarterly* 66 (1988): "The Changing Character of the Medical Profession," S102; William B. Spaulding, *Revitalizing Medical Education: McMaster Medical School, The Early Years 1965–1974*, in collaboration with Janet Cochran (Philadelphia, PA: B.C. Decker, 1991), 129.

35 Hashim Sarkis, "Introduction," in *Le Corbusier's Venice Hospital and the Mat Building Revival*, ed. Hashim Sarkis (Munich: Prestel Verlag, 2001), 14–16. See also: Keating and Cambrosio, *Biomedical Platforms*; Peter Galison and Caroline A. Jones, "Factory, Laboratory, Studio: Dispersing Sites of Production," in *The Architecture of Science*, eds. Peter Galison and Emily Thompson (Cambridge, MA: MIT Press, 1999).

36 Spaulding, *Revitalizing Medical Education*, 79.

37 Banham, *Megastructures*, 59.

38 Sarkis, "Introduction," 14–16.

39 Hermann H. Field, "Complex Health Facilities Design: Exercising Town Planning Techniques," *Canadian Hospital* (November 1967): 41.

40 Ibid., 42.

41 Foucault, *The Birth of the Clinic*, 63.

42 Armstrong, *Political Anatomy of the Body*, 6.

43 Ibid., 44.

44 Hall Commission for the Government of Canada, *Royal Commission on Health Services: 1964, Volume 1* (Ottawa: Government of Canada, June 19, 1964). Referring to the patient number and variety, it is stated in the Royal Commission on Health Services that a leading objective connected to the creation of integrated teaching, research, and patient care facilities is to increase the "clinical material" available. Philio, "The Birth of the Clinic," 16.

45 Georgina Feldberg and Robert Vipond, "Cracks in the Foundation: The Origins and Development of the Canadian and American Health Care Systems," in *Staying Alive: Critical Perspectives on Health, Illness, and Health Care*, ed. Toba Bryant et al. (Toronto: Canadian Scholars' Press, 2006), 221–239.

46 "Correspondence. 'Quality Control of Medical Practice,'" *Canadian Medical Association Journal* 97 (October 21, 1967): 815. See also Alberta Association of Hospitals, Submission to the Royal Commission on Health Services, University of Alberta Archives, Faculty of Medicine, Buildings and Facilities, 1940–1979, February, 1962.

47 Philio, "The Birth of the Clinic," 17.

48 Zeidler, *Healing the Hospital*, 71.

49 Don Vetere, partner in Zeidler Partnership Architects, interview with author, July 23, 2009.

50 Ibid.

51 Zeidler, *Healing the Hospital*, 36.

52 Pylypa, "Power and Bodily Practice," 30.

53 Zeidler, *Healing the Hospital*, 67–70.

54 Ibid., 68.

55 Ibid., 45.

56 Ibid., 64.

57 Dovey, *Framing Places*, 133.

58 Adams et al., "Kids in The Atrium," 661.

Index

Printed and bound by CPI Group (UK) Ltd, Croydon, CR0 4YY
01/12/2024
01797771-0018